DEC 24 2019
P9-AFJ-035

CBEST® PREP

4th Edition

The Staff of The Princeton Review

PrincetonReview.com

WITHDRAWN

Penguin
Random
House

The Princeton Review
110 East 42nd St, 7th Floor
New York, NY 10017
Email: editorialsupport@review.com

Copyright © 2019 by TPR Education IP Holdings, LLC.
All rights reserved.

Published in the United States by Penguin Random House, LLC, New York, and in Canada by Random House of Canada, division of Penguin Random House Ltd., Toronto.

Terms of Service: The Princeton Review Online Companion Tools ("Student Tools") for retail books are available for only the two most recent editions of that book. Student Tools may be activated only once per eligible book purchased for a total of 24 months of access. Activation of Student Tools more than once per book is in direct violation of these Terms of Service and may result in discontinuation of access to Student Tools Services.

California Basic Education Skills Test and CBEST are registered trademarks of the Commission on Teacher Credentialing and Pearson Education, Inc., or its affiliate, which are not affiliated with The Princeton Review.

Printed in the United States of America.

ISBN: 978-0-525-56882-7
ISSN: 2687-8720

Editor: Meave Shelton
Production Editors: Wendy Rosen and Sara Kuperstein
Production Artist: Jason Ullmeyer
Content Contributors: Heidi Torres and Christine Lindwall

Printed in the United States of America.

10 9 8 7 6 5 4 3 2 1

4th Edition

Editorial
Rob Franek, Editor-in-Chief
David Soto, Director of Content Development
Stephen Koch, Student Survey Manager
Deborah Weber, Director of Production
Gabriel Berlin, Production Design Manager
Selena Coppock, Managing Editor
Aaron Riccio, Senior Editor
Meave Shelton, Senior Editor
Chris Chimera, Editor
Eleanor Green, Editor
Orion McBean, Editor
Brian Saladino, Editor
Patricia Murphy, Editorial Assistant

Penguin Random House Publishing Team
Tom Russell, VP, Publisher
Rebecca Holland, Publishing Director
Amanda Yee, Associate Managing Editor
Ellen Reed, Production Manager
Suzanne Lee, Designer

Acknowledgments

The Princeton Review would like to thank Rick Sliter and Sionnain Marcoux for their valuable contributions to previous editions of this book, and to Heidi Torres and Christine Lindwall for their outstanding work on the 4th edition.

As always, our gratitude goes out to the production team for their careful attention to every page: Jason Ullmeyer, Wendy Rosen, and Sara Kuperstein.

Contents

Get More (Free) Content at PrincetonReview.com/prep

As easy as 1·2·3

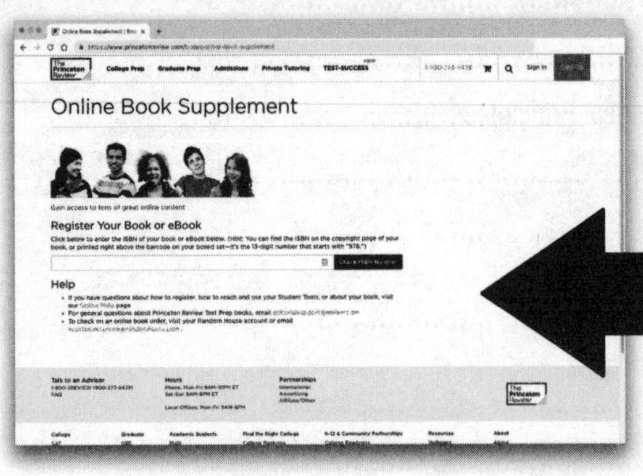

1 Go to PrincetonReview.com/prep and enter the following ISBN for your book:
9780525568827

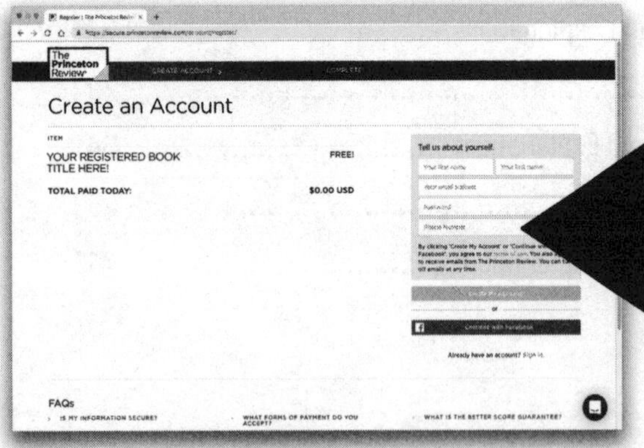

2 Answer a few simple questions to set up an exclusive Princeton Review account. *(If you already have one, you can just log in.)*

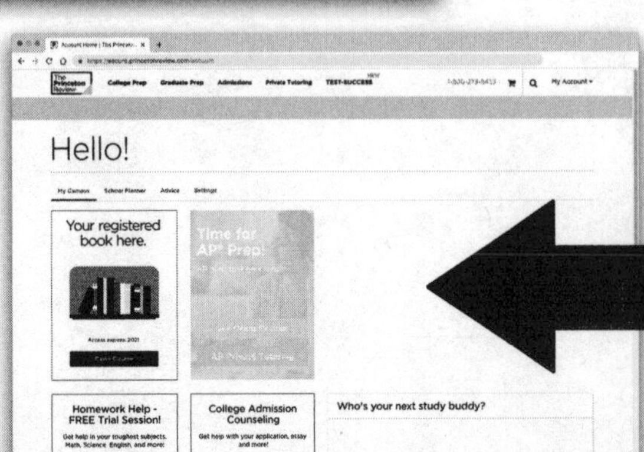

3 Enjoy access to your **FREE** content!

Once you've registered, you can...

- Get our take on any recent or pending updates to the CBEST.
- Access your 4th CBEST practice test (there are 3 right here in your book and 1 online)
- Download detailed answers and explanations to help you identify areas of strength and weakness and tailor your test preparation accordingly
- Check to see if there have been any corrections or updates to this edition

Need to report a potential **content** issue?

Contact **EditorialSupport@review.com** and include:

- full title of the book
- ISBN
- page number

Need to report a **technical** issue?

Contact **TPRStudentTech@review.com** and provide:

- your full name
- email address used to register the book
- full book title and ISBN
- Operating system (Mac/PC) and browser (Firefox, Safari, etc.)

Look For These Icons Throughout The Book

PROVEN TECHNIQUES

APPLIED STRATEGIES

OTHER REFERENCES

ONLINE PRACTICE TESTS

Part I
Orientation

Chapter 1
Introduction

WHAT IS THE CBEST?

The California Basic Educational Skills Test, or CBEST, is a four-hour exam divided into three different sections—a multiple-choice Reading Section, a multiple-choice Mathematics Section, and a Writing Section, which contains two essays. Currently, the CBEST is offered in two formats: the computer-based test and the paper-based test. The specific breakdown of the test is as follows:

Reading Section

According to the authors of the CBEST, the Reading Section "assesses basic skills and concepts that are important in performing the job of an educator." While this may sound intimidating, the reading questions are presented in a straightforward multiple-choice format. The Reading Section is presented first and contains 50 multiple-choice questions. The questions are broken down into two main categories:

1.	Critical Analysis and Evaluation	40%
2.	Comprehension and Research Skills	60%

All reading questions will be based on information presented in written passages, tables, and graphs. Passages range from 100 to 200 words in length. Often more than one multiple-choice question will be based on the same passage.

No outside knowledge will be required to answer these multiple-choice questions. All correct answers can be found by interpreting the information presented in the passage, table, or graph.

Mathematics Section

The Mathematics Section contains 50 multiple-choice questions. These questions cover three major skill areas:

1.	Estimation, Measurement, and Statistical Principles	30%
2.	Computation and Problem Solving	35%
3.	Numerical and Graphic Relationships	35%

What level of math is covered? To survive the CBEST Mathematics Section, you'll need to brush up on the basics—arithmetic, measurements, introductory algebra, and introductory geometry. Note that there is, sadly, no calculator permitted on the exam. Don't worry; there will be no calculus, advanced statistics, or trigonometry on the CBEST.

Writing Section

This section will include two writing topics that assess your ability to write effectively. You will be asked to write one essay from each of the following areas:

1. Analysis of a Situation or Statement
2. A Personal Experience

Readers who use a specific set of criteria to evaluate each essay will score your essays. (We'll explain this in more detail in Part IV.)

WHERE DOES THE CBEST COME FROM?

The CBEST is written by National Evaluation Systems, Inc. Unlike other companies that write a multitude of standardized exams, NES focuses primarily on this one exam. The CBEST was created, in the words of the authors, "to meet requirements of laws relating to credentialing and employment."

WHO NEEDS TO TAKE THE CBEST?

The CBEST is only used in California and Oregon. In California, you may need to take the CBEST when applying for the issuance or renewal of an Emergency Permit, seeking employment in California, applying for admission to a CTC-accredited teacher preparation program, or applying for admission to a CTC-accredited services credential program. In Oregon, the CBEST may be an option for teacher certification, depending upon your program.

There are ways in which teachers may be exempt from taking the CBEST. If you are uncertain as to whether you need the CBEST, read the CBEST registration bulletin, or contact either the California Commission on Teacher Credentialing or the Oregon Teacher Standards and Practices Commission.

WHEN IS THE CBEST ADMINISTERED?

The computer-based CBEST is offered year-round, by appointment at Pearson testing centers. Appointments are available Monday through Saturday, on a first-come, first-served basis. You should register for your exam well in advance, as seating is limited.

The paper-based CBEST is offered five times during the year. Currently, you can take the paper-based CBEST in the following months: July, September, December, February, and April. To register for the CBEST, visit the CBEST website at **www.ctcexams.nesinc.com**. Note that if you are taking the paper-based CBEST, the registration deadline will be approximately 1 month before the exam.

SHOULD I TAKE THE COMPUTER-BASED CBEST?

The decision to take the computer-based or paper-best CBEST is up to you. The structure and content of the exam will not vary between the two formats. You should choose the test format that is more comfortable or convenient for you. Note that only the computer-based exam is offered in Oregon.

The computer-based CBEST has an added fee. One benefit of the computer-based CBEST is that you will know your preliminary results (except for the Writing Section) immediately after finishing the exam. Official score reports are mailed in approximately two weeks.

If you take the paper-based CBEST, official score reports are mailed in approximately 3 weeks.

WHERE CAN I LOOK AT A CBEST EXAM?

We've included three full-length practice CBEST exams in the back of this book and a fourth exam online, complete with explanations and sample essays for each test. These tests have been designed to look exactly like the real thing, so you won't see anything you don't recognize on the day of the actual exam. In addition to our practice tests, the CTC website (**www.ctcexams.nesinc.com**) has a full-length practice CBEST, available in computer-based test format or printable PDF.

Get Your 4th Practice Exam!

Once you register your book online, you'll gain free access to Practice Test 4, as well as its answers and explanations, which you can download as PDFs. See pages vi–vii for step-by-step instructions.

HOW IS THE CBEST SCORED?

The scoring of the CBEST is somewhat complicated. We'll take the scoring of each section one at a time.

Reading Section

The Reading Section contains 50 multiple-choice questions. You will receive one raw score point for each correct answer. You will not lose any points for incorrect answers. This raw score of 0 to 50 is then converted into a scaled score, ranging from 20 to 80. To pass the Reading Section, you need a minimum scaled score of 41.

Mathematics Section

The Mathematics Section is scored in exactly the same way as the Reading Section. The Mathematics Section contains 50 multiple-choice questions. You will receive one raw score point for each correct answer. You will not lose any points for incorrect answers. This raw score of 0 to 50 is then converted into a scaled score, ranging from 20 to 80. To pass the Mathematics Section, you need a minimum scaled score of 41.

Writing Section

Two readers will evaluate each essay. These readers will assign each essay a value from 1 to 4 according to a specific set of criteria. Thus, a total of four readers will assign a score, yielding a Writing Section total that will range from a low of 4 to a high of 16. Again, this raw score will then be translated into a scaled score from 20 to 80. To pass the Writing Section, you need a minimum scaled score of 41.

ONE MORE WAY TO PASS!

If you have an overall total of 123 or higher, it is possible to pass the CBEST with a scaled score on one or two sections as low as 37. If you do not receive at least a 37, you will not pass that section, regardless of your combined CBEST score.

IS THERE ANY REASON TO TAKE THE CBEST AGAIN AFTER PASSING?

Not really. Whether you have a 123 or a 170, you pass. Credential programs will not use your overall score to determine entrance into any program (in fact, all that NES reports is that you have passed all three sections).

There is only one situation in which you may want to retake a section you have already passed. Let's say, for example, that you passed the Writing Section with a 42 and passed the Reading Section with a 42, but did not pass the Math Section (you got a 38). Your overall total is 122, one point shy of the 123 total needed to pass all sections. You could take the Math Section again, and hope to improve that total. Or, you could take the Reading or Writing Sections again. If you improve those scores, your overall total will exceed 123, and you will pass all sections of the CBEST, even with a math score of 38.

This situation is pretty rare. In general, once you pass the CBEST, you're done. Congratulations.

WHAT HAPPENS IF YOU DON'T PASS EVERY SECTION?

If you scored below 37 on one section, or between 38 and 40 on a section with an overall total under 123, you will need to retake only the sections you didn't pass the first time. When you retake the CBEST, you will be given all four hours to complete the sections you need to redo (even if you only need to take one section).

Apply the Strategy

Look for these throughout the book.

HOW THIS BOOK IS ORGANIZED

In the chapters that follow, you will get a step-by-step review of the fundamentals that are crucial to the CBEST. We will break down each of the three sections and provide both content review and strategies for the types of questions contained in each section. Finally, you'll have an opportunity to practice for the CBEST with the three full-length tests we've included at the end of this book (and the fourth exam on our website).

Because test-taking techniques and strategies that apply to all sections of the CBEST are so important, we've started the book with them. Chapter 2 contains the basic strategies for the CBEST. Be sure to apply these techniques to all parts of the exam.

YOUR STUDY PLAN

This book is intended to give you a fairly accelerated review for the CBEST. It's best to complete about one sub-section per day in order to adequately learn and absorb the material. Don't rush so much that you can't adequately take it all in, but likewise, don't go so long between sections that you forget everything you've learned!

Here is a suggested study schedule, which you can modify to fit your needs:

Week 1	Read and work through Part I: Orientation chapters
Week 2	Take Practice Test 1 in the book to identify your strongest and weakest sections. Carefully read through the answers and explanations.
Week 3	Read and work through Part II: Cracking the Reading Section chapters and complete the Reading Section Drills. Carefully read through the Reading Drill Answers and Explanations.
Week 4	Take Practice Test 2 in the book. Carefully read through the answers and explanations.
Week 5	Read and work through Part III: Cracking the Mathematics Section chapters and work all practice problems.
Week 6	Read and work through Part IV: Cracking the Writing Section.
Week 7	Take Practice Test 3 and the online Practice Test 4. Carefully read through the answers and explanations (also found online).
Week 8	Take the real CBEST

For additional practice, visit **www.ctcexams.nesinc.com** to take the official practice CBEST.

WHAT'S MISSING IN THIS BOOK

In this book, we will not review the following: vocabulary words, calculus, trigonometry, idiomatic phrases, antonyms, world history, derivatives, and linear programming. Why? Because none of these topics are covered on the CBEST.

It might sound obvious, but we are only going to prepare you for what you'll likely see on the CBEST exam. We're not going to waste your time by including a large, detailed generic review of math and English. Instead, we're going to help you focus specifically on what you need to know to pass the CBEST.

WHAT IS THE PRINCETON REVIEW?

The Princeton Review offers the nation's best in test preparation. We have offices in more than fifty cities across the country, and many outside the U.S. as well. The Princeton Review offers classroom and online courses, private and small group tutoring, and test preparation books, flashcards, and materials for myriad test types.

The Princeton Review's strategies and techniques are unique, and most of all, successful. We've written this book after carefully studying the CBEST, analyzing the patterns of the exam, and testing our techniques to make sure we're providing you with the most effective and efficient way to take this test.

And Finally . . .

We applaud your efforts to become a teacher. The CBEST should be a minor hurdle in your desire to teach. For most CBEST takers, it has been years since you have had to take a standardized exam. Don't get frustrated if you don't remember everything at once. It takes some time for these skills to come back. Stay focused, practice, and before you know it, you'll be giving tests, instead of taking them.

Chapter 2 Test-Taking Strategies

Before we get started, we need to set some ground rules for taking the CBEST. It is crucial that you use these strategies and techniques throughout the test. We'll refer to these throughout the book to make sure you are incorporating them into your practice. First, we will discuss how to take the test and how much time to spend on each question. Then, we will focus on the multiple-choice questions and how to take advantage of their structure.

TIME—YOU'RE IN CONTROL

In Chapter 1, we broke out the format and structure of the CBEST. You may have noticed that we left out the timing of each section. Good news! You have four hours to complete your work on the CBEST, and you may do so in any way you please. There are no time restrictions on any one section of the exam, so you will decide exactly how to map out your strategy for taking this test. Note that for the computer-based test, the four-hour period includes fifteen minutes to take a tutorial and complete a non-disclosure agreement.

How should you use these four hours? Well, since all test-takers have different strengths and weaknesses, there is no ideal strategy for all students. We recommend that you take Practice Test 1 with the following strategy:

You will determine how much time to spend on each section (there are no section time requirements on the CBEST).

1 hour, 10 minutes for the Reading Section
1 hour, 20 minutes for the Mathematics Section
1 hour, 20 minutes for the Writing Section

This strategy will give you a ten-minute cushion at the end of the test in case you get behind, want to check your work, or just want to take a few minutes relaxing between each section.

Of course, you may want to adjust our recommended timing to better fit your strengths and weaknesses. If you find that this timing is not ideal after taking Practice Test 1, add ten minutes to the section that gave you the most trouble (and subtract ten minutes from the section you finished with the most time remaining). Continue to adjust your timing after Practice Test 2, so on the actual test day you will have a timing strategy that works for you. If you plan to take the actual test by computer on exam day, remember that fifteen minutes will be spent taking the tutorial and completing the non-disclosure agreement. Plan your time accordingly.

If you are retaking the CBEST, you will still be given the entire four hours to work on the exam, even if you only need to complete one section. If you would like, spend as much time as necessary working on that one section. You *can* spend all four hours on the exam.

WHERE TO START?

You are in control of how much time you spend on each section, and you are also in control of the order in which you complete the sections. While you may complete the sections in any order you choose, we recommend that you start with the section you find the most difficult, and finish with the simplest. Leaving your least favorite section until the end of the test day will leave you tired, unfocused, and generally cranky at the end of the exam.

AN EMPTY SCANTRON SHEET IS NOT A GOOD SCANTRON SHEET

There is no guessing penalty on the CBEST! Your score is only determined by the number of questions that you answer correctly. You will not lose points for incorrect answers. Therefore, when you take the CBEST, there is one thing that you must do before you complete your test:

> You must answer every single question on the CBEST!

There are 50 questions in the Mathematics Section, and 50 questions in the Reading Section. Before you turn in or submit your test, make sure that you have selected an answer for all 100 questions on the CBEST.

So, now you know that you must select an answer on every question. Great. Now, let's talk about how to be an intelligent guesser.

PROCESS OF ELIMINATION (POE)

Try the following question:

> What is the capital of Malawi?

> **Unsure? Do you know even where Malawi is located? If not, don't panic. Geography and world capitals are not topics tested on the CBEST. If you had to answer this question without any answer choices, you'd probably be in trouble.**

Proven Technique
Use Process of Elimination (POE) to get rid of impossible answer choices.

Of course, on the CBEST, you will have some answer choices to choose from. Rather than close your eyes and select an answer choice at random, take a look at the answer choices—you might find some information that can help you. Try the following example:

1. What is the capital of Malawi?

   A. Paris

   B. Lilongwe

   C. New York

   D. London

   E. Moscow

Here's How to Crack It

Now do you know? Can you identify an answer choice that is not the correct answer? Sure! You can probably eliminate (A), (C), (D), and (E). While you probably didn't know that Lilongwe was the capital of Malawi, you could tell that (B) was the correct answer by eliminating incorrect answer choices. This procedure is called Process of Elimination, or POE for short.

Process of Elimination will help you become a more accurate guesser. Often it is easier to spot incorrect answer choices than the correct answer. If this happens to you, be sure to cross out any answer choice that you know is incorrect. Then, if you need to make a guess, select an answer from your remaining choices.

It is unlikely that POE will help you eliminate all incorrect answer choices as we did in the previous sample problem. However, every time you get rid of one answer choice, the odds of correctly answering that question increase significantly. Rather than a 20 percent chance of guessing a correct answer, you will often find yourself guessing with a 33 percent or 50 percent chance of getting a question correct.

Let's try one more example:

2. Store X recently had a sale promoting a 20 percent discount on all items. If Teresa bought a dress priced originally at $64, what did she pay for the dress during the sale?

   A. $12.80

   B. $32.00

   C. $51.20

   D. $76.20

   E. $128.00

Here's How to Crack It

Later in this book, we'll review exactly how to answer percent questions. For now, let's just think about the question. Teresa is buying a dress on sale. If the dress was originally $64, then the price she paid for it would be less than $64. Thus, you should be able to eliminate answer choices (D) and (E). You may have also noticed that answer choices (A) and (B) were much, much lower than the original price, and eliminated those too. (C) is the correct answer. At worst, if you needed to make a guess on this question, you would have a one in three chance. Again, using POE can help you get more points on the CBEST.

Process of Elimination is an important concept that we'll be referring to throughout this book, including in the explanations provided for the practice tests. There are some specific POE strategies for the reading and mathematics sections that will be presented in the chapters ahead. It is important that you practice using POE. Getting rid of incorrect answers is a powerful tool on the CBEST.

THE BEST ANSWER

CBEST questions are not about selecting the "right" answer, but the "best" answer. An answer choice that looks bad can actually be the credited response, as long as all the other choices are even worse. An answer choice that looks good can be wrong if another choice is even better.

CBEST questions, even ones that require you to "read between the lines," are NOT a matter of opinion. CBEST must have one single justifiable answer for each question; otherwise, they'd face a flood of lawsuits and challenged scores.

Your job is to find the best answer.

Best Answer and POE Go Hand in Hand

There are a variety of reasons why you may choose a particular answer to a particular question. If you had to justify your answer to a question, you might respond in any one of a few different ways, depending on the question and how you tackled it.

Different reasons to choose an answer can be summed up as follows:

- I think that this answer makes the most sense
- I eliminated the remaining answers
- I derived the answer on my own

While any one of those justifications may be valid, it's important that you take a careful, thoughtful approach to each question.

One way to feel more confident about your responses is to use not just one, but two different ways to justify an answer. Here are some example scenarios:

- You looked at the answer choices and determined that "A" seems to make the most sense. Great! Now, look at the remaining choices again, and think about the reasons that might allow you to eliminate some of them.
- You looked at the answer choices and you feel good about eliminating "A," "B," "C," and "D." Neat! It must be "E," then, right? Well, perhaps, but it's better to give choice "E" some careful consideration on its own.
- You completed a math problem on scratch paper, and derived an answer. The answer matches one of your choices. Super! Now, you might try a basic trick like estimation, and see if you still agree with your answer. You can catch silly mistakes this way!
- You looked at a reading question, and as you read it, you realized that you knew what the best answer should say. One of the choices matches your predicted answer. Lovely! Now, carefully consider each choice and make sure that you're choosing the best one.

Apply the Strategy

Try to approach each problem in a couple of different ways.

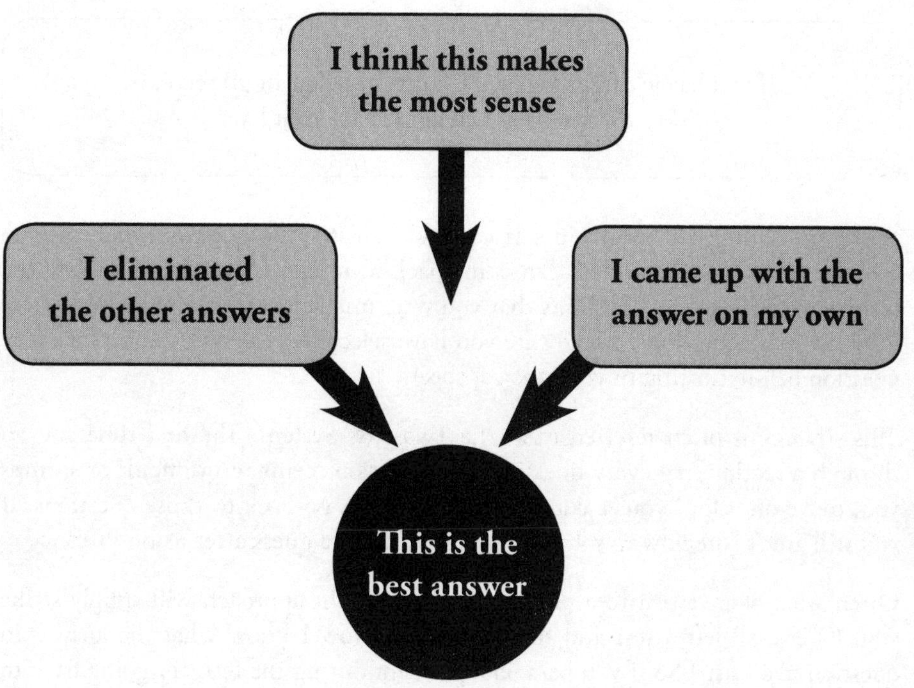

I'll Just Go From Question 1 to Question 50, Right?

There are some tests that contain an order of difficulty within each section. On these tests, the first question is generally very easy, and the questions become progressively more difficult. On the CBEST, however, there is no order of difficulty on the two multiple-choice sections of the exam. Questions will vary in difficulty throughout the Mathematics and Reading Sections in no particular order. So, doing the test straight through, from question 1 to question 50, may not always be your best strategy.

Uhhhh, I Know This One. Just One More Minute!!

Have you ever been given a question that stumped you, but were sure you could do? Have you ever said "Just one more minute. I know I can figure this out!" Well, we all have. Unfortunately, one more minute usually means five more minutes, and often, we don't end up with the right answer at all.

Do not let one question ruin your test day. If you are struggling on a particular question, leave it and move on.

Don't let one question ruin your day. No single question is that important. You've got 50 questions per section to tackle, and allowing just one of them to throw off your timing would really set you back. Here is a general rule for the reading and mathematics sections:

> If you haven't figured out the correct answer in 90 seconds, skip the question and come back to it later.

We're not telling you to give up. If you can't answer the question, make a note on your scratch paper, so you can come back to it later. After you complete the section, go back to the questions that you were unable to solve. Remember to use POE on these questions. Make sure you have selected an answer choice for every question before turning in your answer sheet.

Proven Technique

Use the Two-Pass System to maximize the time you have available.

This strategy is often referred to as the Two-Pass System. The first time you go through a section, try every question. If a question seems too difficult or stumps you, move on. Once you've completed the section, go back to those questions. If you still aren't sure how to solve the problem, make a guess after using POE.

Often when you return to a problem later, the right approach will simply strike you. (We've all left a test and said "Oh yeah! Now I know what the answer to question five was.") So if you pass on a problem during the test, try going back to it later, and giving it another try.

YOU ARE IN CONTROL

We know the CBEST can be an intimidating exam. We know the importance of passing this test. As with many such tests, we know that sometimes it feels as if the CBEST is totally out of your control.

By the end of this book, you'll be prepared to handle any question on the CBEST!

However, the opposite is true. You are in control. While you can't decide what kind of pencil you must bring to the exam, or where to sit during the test, you can decide how you take the CBEST. Let's review what we've discussed in this chapter. First, you can use the four-hour testing period in any way you see fit. Spend more time on your weakest sections. Second, you can take the sections in any order you choose. Want to start with mathematics? Great. Want to write an essay before doing the Reading Section? No problem. Third, you get to take advantage of the multiple-choice format of the Mathematics and Reading Sections. With no guessing penalty, and tools like Process of Elimination, you can add points to your score, without even knowing the correct answer.

Finally, you control the exact order of questions within each section. If question 12 is really stumping you, move on to question 13, and save question 12 for later.

So, you really are in control of the CBEST. And as you work through the next few sections, you'll gain more confidence in your knowledge of the material tested.

Part II Cracking the Reading Section

The Reading Section of the CBEST consists of 50 multiple-choice questions based on information presented in a variety of passages, tables, and graphs. Passage topics are drawn from a variety of sources, and are designed to simulate high school and college-level materials, student textbooks, teachers' guides, and written materials on psychology or student behavior. These passage topics will vary in difficulty, and are drawn from a number of different fields, such as social sciences, humanities, health, and consumer affairs.

You will be able to answer all reading questions without having any specialized knowledge about the subject matter (in fact, bringing in outside knowledge will often lead you to an incorrect answer). So, if the topic covers material that you are completely unfamiliar with, don't panic. All the information you need will be presented in the passage.

Passages will vary in length and difficulty. Some passages will be as short as one or two sentences. Other "short" passages will consist of about 100 words. The "long" passages you will see will consist of approximately 200 words. In general, longer passages will be accompanied by more multiple-choice questions. The number of questions based on each passage will vary greatly. Some passages will only have one question, while other passages could have up to five questions.

In this chapter, we will cover general strategies that you should apply to all questions presented in the Reading Section. Chapters 3 and 4 will provide you with specific strategies for handling the types of questions you might be asked. First, let's dissect the types of questions that may be asked on the CBEST Reading Section.

CRITICAL ANALYSIS AND EVALUATION QUESTIONS

Approximately 40 percent of the questions on the Reading Section will come from this skill area. Here are some of the things that a critical analysis question will ask you to do:

- Identify the author's tone, attitude, opinion, or viewpoint expressed in the passage.
- Find the techniques used by an author to make his or her point.
- Identify the assumptions an author makes to support his or her claim.
- Recognize the type of audience that the author is trying to address.
- Find examples, details, or facts that support an author's claim.
- Predict the outcome of an event based on the information presented in a written passage.
- Choose statements that will strengthen or weaken the claims made by the author in a reading selection.
- Distinguish between facts and opinions within a reading passage.
- Compare/contrast ideas or information presented in different sections of a reading selection.

Sample question: "With which of the following statements would the author most likely agree?"

- Identify inconsistencies or differences in points of view.
- Determine whether facts or ideas are relevant to an argument.
- Challenge the statements and opinions presented in the passage.

All of these types of questions will be discussed in detail in Chapter 3.

COMPREHENSION AND RESEARCH SKILLS

Approximately 60 percent of the questions on the Reading Section will come from this skill area. Here are some of the things that comprehension questions will ask you to do:

- Recognize the order of a passage (this may include outlining a passage, separating general ideas from specific ideas in a passage, and determining the sequence of events or steps in a reading selection).
- Identify the main idea of a passage.
- Summarize or paraphrase a reading selection.
- Identify the conclusion of a passage.
- Determine the meaning of underlined words in the context of the passage.
- Identify words and phrases that serve as transitions between ideas in a passage.
- Make an inference based on the information provided.
- Identify facts and details presented in a reading section.

Sample question: "What is the best conclusion to the passage above?"

In addition to these comprehension-based questions, you will need to solve questions that are based on information presented in table or graphic form. For these questions, you will be asked to:

- Locate the place in a book, chapter, article, or index where a specific kind of information can be found.
- Identify how a written passage is organized.
- Find conclusions that are supported by the information presented in a table or graph.
- Use the table of contents, section headings, index, and similar sections of a book to locate information.

Sample question: "How is the index below organized?"

Chapter 4 will cover possible question types involving comprehension and research skills.

READING INSTRUCTIONS

Before we begin with the general strategies you'll need in order to take the CBEST, let's take a look at the instructions presented by the test writers. Here are the directions that will appear at the start of each Reading Section:

> Each question in the Reading Section of the test is a multiple-choice question with five answer choices. Read each question carefully and choose the ONE best answer. Record each answer on the answer sheet provided.

Take the time to familiarize yourself with these directions, so you won't have to waste time reading them on the day you take the test.

The Treasure Hunt

If we told you that we had hidden $50,000 somewhere in your hometown and then handed you an envelope filled with clues, would you search every inch of your hometown before you opened the envelope and looked at the clues? Of course not! You'd look at the clues first and then decide on a plan of action. You'd use them to select some places where the treasure might be, and eliminate places where the treasure could not possibly be hidden. Well, the same is true with the Reading Section of the CBEST. Every reading passage contains some hidden treasure (points toward your overall CBEST score). Your job is to find that treasure. Where are the clues? Some of the clues are located in the passage; most are located in the questions and the answer choices. Our job over the next three chapters will be to help you identify these clues.

CRACKING THE READING SECTION

So what exactly do these instructions mean? While these instructions tell you what you need to do on the Reading Section, they certainly don't tell you how to do the section. The rest of this chapter will tell you what you need to know. Let's talk about the three elements of a Reading Section: the passage, the questions, and the answer choices.

The Passage

Believe it or not, the passage is the least important piece of the Reading Section. The questions will determine what parts of the passage you will need to use. If you actually tried to comprehend the reading passages on the CBEST—by carefully reading and analyzing every word until you understood all components of the passage—you'd find that you wouldn't have much time remaining for any of the other sections of the CBEST! Remember that your goal on the CBEST is to earn as many points as possible. We will show you how to accomplish this without having to read the entire passage for all question types. Some questions will only require that you use one or two sentences out of a 200-word passage. The types of questions you are asked will determine how much time you spend on the passage.

It is often unnecessary to read the entire passage before attempting to answer the questions.

The Questions

When attacking a reading passage, the first thing you should read is the question (or questions) that follows the passage. Each question type will give you clues as to the specific information you need to find within the passage. Some questions give you an obvious direction as to where you need to go within the passage:

- "Which of the following is the best meaning of the word solution as it is used in the passage?"
- "Which words should be inserted into the blanks on line 6 of the passage?"
- "According to the information presented in the passage, the inventor of volleyball created the sport in order to..."

All of these questions ask for specific information to be taken out of a passage. These questions provide you with a guide for finding the needed information. Where would you go to find the answer to the first sample question? First, you should locate the word "solution," and then read enough of the passage above and below the word to make sure you understand its context. Based on the question, you can reduce the amount of reading you need to do in order to find the correct answer.

We call the above types of questions "specific"—these questions focus only on a specific piece of information in the passage. We'll talk about specific questions in much more detail in the chapters ahead.

"Specific" questions ask you to find detailed information within a passage.

Other questions are not that specific. Instead, they will ask that you identify general information about the passage as a whole:

- "Which of the following would be the most appropriate title for this passage?"
- "Which of the following inferences may be drawn from the information presented in the passage?"
- "Which of the following best summarizes the main points of the passage?"

Do you think you'll need to know every detail about a passage in order to answer these questions? Absolutely not. You will need to have a general idea of what the passage states, how it is written, what techniques are used, etc. There are a number of techniques to solve the many different types of general questions, which we will discuss in the chapters ahead.

In summary, the types of questions you are given will determine the type of information you need to find within the passage. The questions are your treasure map—use them to help you narrow your search for the correct answer. We will show you how to distinguish question types from one another, and give you a specific list of things to find for each question type.

The Answer Choices

Have you ever read a question, then looked at the answer choices and thought that all of the answer choices could be correct? Many students feel that the most difficult part of the Reading Section is distinguishing among answer choices that sound the same. In the general introduction we emphasized the importance of Process of Elimination, or POE. On the Reading Section, POE plays a vital role in helping you narrow down the number of possible answer choices. Below we will talk about six things to look for that will help you eliminate answer choices:

1. Understanding the Author
2. Controversial Answer Choices
3. Strong Language
4. Scope
5. Common Sense
6. Stick to the Passage

UNDERSTANDING THE AUTHOR

An author will not be overly critical of professionals (teachers, administrators).

One key to doing well on questions of tone, attitude and style is understanding the CBEST authors' very predictable feelings about certain types of people. CBEST authors are deeply respectful of school administrators, educators, doctors, lawyers, scientists, etc. (essentially, anyone with a college degree). It is very unlikely that you will have a passage about an uncaring educator, a sloppy doctor, or a ruthless lawyer. This will help you to eliminate certain negative answer choices. Here is an example:

---

1. The author views the speech from the superintendent with:

   A. angered skepticism

   B. complete confusion

   C. resigned approval

   D. reluctant criticism

   E. sneering disrespect

Here's How to Crack It

Without even reading the passage, we know that the CBEST writers believe that a superintendent, like all educators, is a responsible professional. A superintendent ought to be admired. Therefore, you will not typically be presented with a passage that is negative toward someone that the CBEST authors like. If we look at the answer choices, we can see that (A), (B), and (E) are extremely negative. These answer choices leave no doubt that the author is against what the superintendent has to say. We can eliminate these three answer choices. This will be true of any professional. The author's attitude will usually be one of praise, admiration, approval, appreciation, or respect. It will never be one of disdain, apathy, puzzlement, confusion, disrespect, or cynicism.

On the rare occasion that a passage is somewhat critical of a group of professionals, the criticism will be mild at most. Choice (D) is an example of this ("reluctant criticism" isn't positive, but it certainly isn't aggressive).

Controversial Answer Choices

CBEST authors go to great lengths to avoid correct answers that would make anyone upset. (Most people are upset enough about having to take the CBEST!) The last thing the authors would want is to publish a test that gives students credit for selecting controversial or bizarre answers. On your test, you may encounter a reading passage about an ethnic group, an environmental issue, or a touchy political issue. You will want to be sure you eliminate all answer choices that seem negative toward one of these kinds of topics. Here is an example:

Avoid any answer types that may be controversial.

---

2. The author views the actions taken by the environmental group with:

   A. apathy

   B. naivete

   C. hopelessness

   D. admiration

   E. anger

Here's How to Crack It

The correct answer, (D), should be fairly obvious. CBEST authors will not include a passage where the writer has a negative view on environmental issues. The CBEST authors want to avoid any answers that say something negative or controversial. In the example above, the only possible answer is admiration. Apathy, naivete, hopelessness, and anger all convey a negative opinion of the environmental plan.

Strong Language

CBEST authors want to make sure that the correct answer to a question is not open to interpretation. Imagine the number of questions or complaints that would be fielded by the CBEST office if even a small percentage of test takers challenged some of the correct answer choices. In order to avoid this, CBEST authors will use correct answers that are almost impossible to argue against. Consider the following two answer choices:

A. Plant biology is absolutely the most vital component of the sixth-grade science curriculum.

B. Plant biology is an important part of the sixth-grade science curriculum.

Of these two answer choices, which one would be the easier to challenge? Statement (A) of course! Who is to say what the most important science topic is? How does one evaluate the importance of each topic to the overall curriculum? It's easy to think of a number of ways that one could challenge Statement (A). Statement (B), on the other hand, is much more vague and general, and is therefore very difficult to challenge.

In general, the more detailed and specific a statement is, the easier it is for someone to raise objections to it. The more vague and general a statement is, the harder it is for someone to challenge it. Because of these facts, we can learn a few things about correct answer choices:

Answer choices that say something *must be true* are usually incorrect.

Answer choices with *extreme language* are usually incorrect.

What is extreme language? We're not talking about R-rated movie language here, we're talking about words that are so categorical that they make it very easy to challenge an answer choice. Here are some examples of extreme words:

Must	Always	Impossible	Never	Cannot
All	Only	Totally	Every	Each

Be careful when you see these words in the answer choices. Ask yourself, "could someone make an objection to this statement?" If so, eliminate the answer choice. Let's take an example of another question, with some of the answer choices already eliminated.

Apply the Strategy
Use POE to eliminate answer choices with extreme language.

3. With which of the following statements would the author of the passage probably agree?

   A. There is no useful purpose in studying the works of Freud.

   B. A more complete understanding of recent theories may be achieved through the study of the works of Freud.

   C. <eliminated>

   D. <eliminated>

   E. It is impossible to gain more understanding of recent theories by studying authors of the past.

Here's How to Crack It

Do any of the statements involve extreme language? Answer choices (A) and (E) do. Choice (A) argues that there is no useful purpose to studying Freud. This statement is expressed in absolute terms. If someone were to find anything useful in Freud's works, the statement would be incorrect. The author of the passage would not make such a bold statement. Answer choice (E) is even more ridiculous. It goes far beyond what the text of the passage will support by making the sweeping statement that nothing can be learned in the present by studying the past. Not even once in a while? Obviously, there are some exceptions to this statement. Choice (B), however, is much more vague. Notice the use of the word "may." With the word "may," all we need is one example to prove this statement correct.

We talked about the need to avoid answer choices that use extreme language. Here are some words that are much more wishy-washy, and are therefore much more difficult to argue with:

May	Could Be True	Some	Most
Sometimes	Might	Probably	Suggests

Answer choices containing these words are often correct. When you spot these words, be sure to spend some time evaluating the statements in which they appear.

Scope

A CBEST passage, which is usually no more than about 200 words, will have to be narrow in focus.

The passages that you will be working with are not that long. Sure, some of them will be a few paragraphs, but at least you won't have to read a thesis! With the limited number of words, it becomes difficult for an author to accomplish a number of things within the passage. In other words: the focus, or scope, of the passage is very narrow. Imagine writing a fifty-page paper about the experiences you've had in education. What would it involve? What mechanisms would you use to support your paper? Would you use examples, anecdotes, and stories to enhance your claim? As you think about what would go into this paper, imagine if it had to be reduced to a twenty-page paper. What would you cut out? How would you narrow your focus? Again, what if you had to write a paper in just 200 words? You certainly wouldn't be able to address all the experiences you've had in education. At best, you would select one specific example, and use it to make a very specific point.

A dangerous answer choice on the CBEST is the one that tries to do too much. In other words, the answer choice is out of scope.

Here is an example:

4. The primary purpose of the passage is to:

   A. present an overview of the Great Depression.

   B. document the use of taxation as a means to control the economy.

   C. acknowledge all the social effects on Americans during the Great Depression.

   D. examine one way taxation helped to slow the effects of the Great Depression on the middle class.

   E. compare and contrast differing viewpoints of the Great Depression.

Here's How to Crack It

Try to eliminate answer choices that describe something that could not possibly be accomplished in a couple of paragraphs. Use this in combination with extreme language to help you eliminate answer choices. Choice (A) is probably too ambitious. The Great Depression was a complex time, involving many social, political, and economic factors. While the word "overview" is certainly less specific than, say, "complete account," it is still pretty impossible to do with the limited length of CBEST passages. Choice (B) is so vague that it seems to encompass a number of things. Taxation to control the economy—whose economy? During what time frame? This is a topic for several volumes of work, not a CBEST passage. Choice (C) uses extreme language, and is therefore out of scope. How could a 200-word passage describe *all* the social effects of the Great Depression? Choice (D) is perfect. It is possible to examine one way that taxation helped the middle class. As you can see, the scope of this answer choice is very narrow. That is exactly what we're looking for. Choice (E) is probably too lengthy. It would be quite a challenge to compare and contrast differing viewpoints. First, you'd have to identify the viewpoints, then compare them, and then contrast them. This is too much work for a CBEST passage. Using scope as a means to eliminate answer choices only takes a little common sense, which is our next technique.

Common Sense

Correct answers on the CBEST will never contradict an established fact. Therefore, common sense can enable you to eliminate answer choices that seem absurd or incorrect, without even reading the passage. Here is an example:

---

5. According to the passage, the first response of an individual to a shortage of atmospheric oxygen is:

A. a surge of activity in the bone marrow

B. an increase in respiratory intake

C. an increase in the number of respiratory passages

D. an increase in the growth rate of muscles

E. an increase in the blood cell count

Here's How to Crack It

You may be wondering why we're asking you to use common sense on a biology question. Well, even if you haven't had biology in years, take a look at the answer choices, and see which seem reasonable. The question asks what happens when someone is short of oxygen. Choice (A) says that bone marrow becomes more active. Actually, bone marrow has nothing to do with getting less oxygen. If you realize this, eliminate (A). Some of the answer choices may not only be unreasonable, but also downright silly. Take a look at (C)—an increase in the number of respiratory passages. Can people grow new respiratory passages in response to a lack of oxygen? Obviously, (C) is incorrect. So is (D)—do muscles suddenly grow when you are at a high altitude? Even if you know nothing about biology, you have a 50 percent chance of answering this question correctly. The answer must be either (B) or (E). In fact, the correct answer is (B)—an increase in the respiratory intake occurs with a shortage of oxygen.

To summarize, correct answer choices will make sense. Feel free to use factual information you know to be true to help you eliminate answer choices. But don't go too far, otherwise you'll fall into the trap the next technique discusses.

STICK TO THE PASSAGE

What type of reading passage would you prefer to read—a passage on a topic you are familiar with, or a passage on a topic you know nothing about? Most would answer the former. We enjoy reading about topics we know. It is easy to relate the information to books we've read, personal experiences, and so forth. However, the danger of a familiar topic is that you may insert your own opinions, experiences, and facts about a topic into the information presented. The trap is that you may select or eliminate answer choices that are based upon what you know, rather than upon what is presented in the passage.

Do not try to use outside knowledge to answer a reading question. All correct answers will be supported by information found in the passage.

Everything you need to know has to be found somewhere in the passage. You should always rely on the information in the passage, not what you know about a topic, to answer the question. If you are familiar with a topic, make sure you can "prove" your answer choice. There must be support somewhere in the passage in order for an answer choice to be correct.

What about the passages that you know nothing about? Often, passages you know nothing about can be the easiest because you'll be so focused on the material presented.

APPROACH TO THE READING SECTION

As we've stated throughout this chapter, the questions are your key to the Reading Section. The question type will give you a specific method for solving the problem. You can aid your search by eliminating answer choices according to the rules we've discussed above. Now that we know how to approach a reading passage, is there an ideal order to approach the questions?

First, it is important to recognize that there is no set order of difficulty within the Reading Section. So, proceeding from question 1 to question 50 will help you keep your place; however, it won't provide any advantage for you in terms of order of difficulty. Here are a few things that you should focus on when practicing the Reading Section:

Is time a problem? If you find that the Reading Section takes a large amount of time, you may want to select the passages that are accompanied by the most questions. For example, start with the passages that have four or five questions following the text. This way, you'll maximize the number of questions you answer for the time it takes to dissect one passage. After you've finished these questions, move to passages that have three questions following the text, then two questions, and so on. Of course, if time is a significant problem, review the techniques included in this manual. You also may need to adjust your pacing for each section on the exam.

Do you prefer one question type to another? Unfortunately, one passage can include a number of different types of questions. This makes it difficult to search for specific question types without going back and forth between passages (something you do not want to do). Some students are very comfortable with the "research" questions—questions that involve charts, tables of contents, indexes, etc. If you are comfortable with these questions, make sure you give yourself a chance to do them.

In the chapters that follow, we'll be discussing many techniques for specific types of questions. It is important that you learn to distinguish these types of questions from one another, so that you can maximize your efficiency and effectiveness on the Reading Section.

Summary

- The Reading Section consists of 50 multiple-choice questions based on information provided in passages, graphs, charts, or research material.
- Approximately 40 percent of the reading questions are based on critical analysis and evaluation; approximately 60 percent of the reading questions are based on comprehension and research skills.
- It is not necessary to read the entire passage in order to find the information needed to answer a question. The type of question you are asked will dictate how you approach the passage.
- Reading passages can take many forms—a chart, a one-sentence passage, a passage of 100 words, or a passage of approximately 200 words.
- Questions can be very specific or very general. You will learn techniques for how to approach each type of question.
- Process of Elimination is an important part of the Reading Section. The most common reasons to eliminate an answer choice are that it:
  - is inconsistent with the author's attitude towards the subject
  - is controversial
  - contains strong language
  - is incorrect in scope
  - defies common sense
  - goes beyond the information contained in the passage

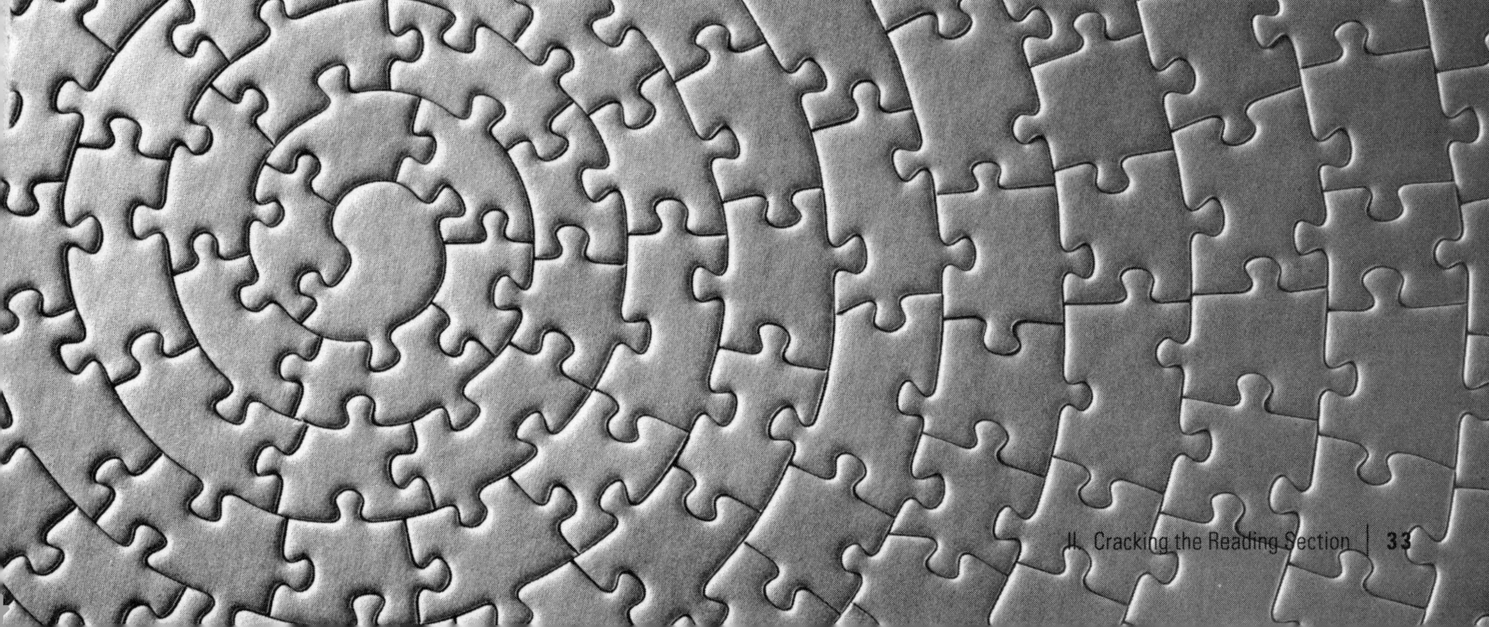

Chapter 3
Critical Analysis and Evaluation Questions

Approximately 40 percent of the reading questions on the CBEST will test "critical analysis and evaluation." Throughout this chapter, we will identify some of the ways in which these questions can be asked. We'll also provide specific instructions for how to find the correct answer for these questions in a passage. Finally, we'll help you distinguish between the different types of questions in the Reading Section. Analysis and evaluation questions can be broken into three major areas:

- **Questions about the author.** We'll go through five different types of questions that ask about the author's attitude, assumptions, audience, evidence, opinions, and techniques.
- **Questions about facts within a passage.** Certain analysis questions will require you to distinguish between facts and opinions, and to identify the relevant facts of an argument.
- **Questions that ask for additional information for a passage.** We will learn how to select statements that will complete the meaning of a passage, weaken the argument made in a passage, or strengthen the argument made in a passage.

KNOW THE AUTHOR

It would be very helpful if there were a quick summary about the author next to each passage in the Reading Section. That way, we could gain some insight into the author's expertise, motivation, opinion, and so forth. Since we won't be given this quick biography, we will need to examine the style, tone, and information presented in a passage to get a feel for who the author is.

How can you recognize questions that ask you for something about the author? Here are some sample question stems:

- Which of the following would be most consistent with the writer's purpose?
- This passage uses which of the following argumentative techniques?
- The primary message of the author is...?
- What is the attitude of the author toward...?
- The author is most likely speaking to what group?
- In what type of publication would the author's work be found?
- The author would most likely agree with which statement below?

We will use the passage below to discuss the different types of "author" questions. Sample passage 1:

> Recent dissatisfaction with the current tax code has inspired local Congressman David Moore to introduce legislation that will get rid of the "marriage tax." The "marriage tax" describes the higher taxes that a married couple currently pays compared to two single individuals. If a married couple and two single individuals together earn the same amount of money, the married couple could pay up to $1,400 more in federal taxes each year. While there are certain benefits in the tax for married couples, especially if one of the individuals does not work, most such couples find themselves disadvantaged due to their married status. Congressman Moore believes that the tax code should treat married couples the same as two single individuals. While some critics argue that the tax system is currently too complicated to simply equate married and single individuals, almost all agree that some revision of the "marriage tax" is necessary.

---

1. Which of the following best describes the author's attitude toward the proposed legislation put forth by Congressman Moore?

   A. Uncertain

   B. Supportive

   C. Opposed

   D. Elated

   E. Disdainful

Here's How to Crack It

Question 1 is an example of an "attitude" question. Often, you may be asked about the author's attitude, opinion, or viewpoint. In order to answer attitude questions correctly, we need to look for certain information in the passage as well as use one of our keys to eliminating answer choices—understanding the author. First, we need to go back to the passage to look for clues about the author's attitude. Start with the first sentence to gain an understanding of the topic at hand, and paraphrase the sentence. From the first sentence, we know that Congressman Moore is looking to get rid of the "marriage tax." After you have a general understanding of the main topic, look for sentences that distinguish the author's opinion from the subject matter. Take a look at the passage above and see if you can identify a sentence that presents the author's opinion. The fourth sentence gives us some clues as to the author's viewpoint: "While there are certain benefits in the tax for married couples, especially if one of the individuals does not work, most such couples find themselves disadvantaged due to their married status." The last part of the sentence indicates that the author is against the "marriage tax." If Congressman Moore is looking to get rid of the tax, the author is going to be in favor of his proposal. Now, let's look at the answer choices. Only two answer choices are positive—"supportive" and "elated." "Elated" is a bit too strong, and therefore not appropriate for this passage. Choices (C) and (E) are very negative, and negative choices are often incorrect answers to CBEST questions. Remember that CBEST authors will usually show respect to professionals. Therefore, (B) is the correct answer choice.

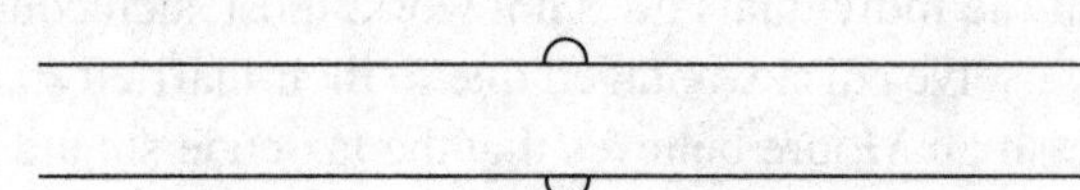

2. In what type of publication might this passage be found?

   A. A law journal

   B. An encyclopedia

   C. A local newspaper section

   D. A history textbook

   E. A book on the tax code

Here's How to Crack It

Technical or general? Determine how the passage is written so you can identify in what publication the passage will most likely appear.

Some questions about the author will ask you to determine where the passage is most likely to be found. Your first key to these questions is to determine whether the passage is technical or general. A technical passage is written with the understanding that the reader possesses a high level of knowledge about the topic at hand. Scientific journals are a very common example of a publication that contains technical passages. In general, any passage that uses complicated language, without explaining or defining most terms, is a technical passage. A general passage involves more simple language, and is often more opinion based. A general passage will define any new concepts for the reader and will strive to do more than provide factual information. These passages can also be persuasive and opinionated.

How do you determine if a passage is technical or general? Scan the passage to take a look at the choice of words used. Is the text complicated? Does the author make assumptions about the reader's knowledge? Does the passage contain an author's viewpoint? Does the passage explain new terms or concepts?

You should be able to identify the passage above as a general passage. There are two ways to spot this. First, the passage explains new concepts in detail (the definition of "marriage tax" is one example). Second, the passage contains the author's argument that the marriage tax is bad (we saw this in our analysis of Question 1). Since this passage is intended for a general audience, we want to eliminate answer choices that mainly include technical pieces of writing. Choices (A) and (E) would require language much more complex than that used in the passage. Choice (B) can be eliminated—an encyclopedia will not include proposed legislation. Further, common sense helps us to eliminate (D)—a history textbook would not cover such recent information; a newly proposed piece of legislation probably wouldn't make its way into a history book. Therefore, (C) is correct. A newspaper could include this passage, possibly in an editorial section. The passage is directed toward a general audience.

Apply the Strategy

Remember POE! Always think about what answer choices you can eliminate on all reading questions.

3. What technique does the author employ to demonstrate a problem with the "marriage tax"?

   A. a quotation

   B. a numerical example

   C. a sarcastic comment

   D. an anecdote

   E. a plea to the reader

Here's How to Crack It

Some questions will ask you what technique an author uses in order to make his or her point. These questions are easy, because all you need to do is go back to the passage in order to find the correct answer. Take a look at the answer choices first to get a feel for the types of things to look for in the passage. We can immediately eliminate (A), because there are no quotations contained in the passage at all. We can also see that (D) is incorrect; there are no anecdotes contained within the passage. Choice (E) is also incorrect; at no point in the passage does the author make a direct statement to the audience. Choice (C) is somewhat more difficult to evaluate; however, not only are there no sarcastic comments in the passage, but also a sarcastic comment could be an example of extreme language. Eliminate it. Choice (B) is correct, the author uses a numerical example (the difference of $1,400 between the tax owed by the married couple and that owed by two single individuals) in order to demonstrate the effect of the "marriage tax."

4. Which of the following statements would the author most likely agree with regarding the "marriage tax"?

   A. The "marriage tax" is inevitable due to complex rules in the tax code.

   B. The "marriage tax" unfairly punishes single men or women since there are tax benefits to being married.

   C. Despite other benefits in the tax system, married individuals are unfairly treated by the "marriage tax."

   D. Critics of the "marriage tax" will be unable to make any changes in the federal tax code.

   E. A $1,400 adjustment in taxes is not significant enough to attempt changing the tax code.

Here's How to Crack It

On an "agree" question, find an answer choice that the author might include in his or her passage.

This type of question asks you to identify a statement that the author would agree with. Therefore, you need to find a statement that supports the main idea within the passage. Note that this type of question is not the same as a similar-looking type of question, called a strengthen/weaken question (which we'll come to later in the chapter). To solve these questions, try fitting each statement somewhere into the passage. Does it agree with information provided in the passage? Does it restate a sentence already found in the passage? If so, you've probably found the correct answer.

Let's begin by analyzing each answer choice. Choice (A) is incorrect. Notice how the CBEST authors will try to trap you by including words and phrases found in the passage. The passage does state that the tax code is complex; however, it does not say the "marriage tax" is therefore *inevitable*. Eliminate (A). Choice (B) states the opposite of what the author claims. The "marriage tax" negatively affects married individuals by taxing them more than single individuals—therefore, eliminate (B). Choice (D) voices the strong opinion that critics will not be able to change the system. This issue is not addressed by the passage; therefore, we cannot make any assumptions about the author's opinion on this issue. Eliminate (D). Choice (E) is also incorrect. The author, by presenting the proposed legislation, argues that the tax penalty gives us a reason to change the tax code. Choice (C) is correct. The numerical example shows how *married* individuals are treated unfairly in the tax system.

5. Which of the following assumptions can be made about the author's view of the current "marriage tax" and the tax system?

   A. The author believes that changes in the tax system are possible through legislation.

   B. The author believes that there should be no benefits in the tax code for married individuals.

   C. The author believes that married individuals should be given favorable treatment in our tax system.

   D. The author believes that Congressman Moore's legislation will pass.

   E. The author believes that the "marriage tax" is the greatest problem with the current tax code.

Here's How to Crack It

First, we need to be clear about what an assumption is. An assumption is something that an author believes to be true (whether it is or it isn't). This belief is necessary in order for the author to establish a point. Assumptions are not stated in the passage; instead, they can be identified by interpreting the information presented in the passage. Therefore, the correct answer to an assumption question cannot be found in the passage; it must be derived from the passage. When you're asked an assumption question, look to eliminate answer choices that contradict the author's main point. Further, make sure that you are not choosing a statement that is presented in the passage. In general, assumption statements are obvious. Don't try to find a very detailed answer—assumptions can be very basic. One trick to finding the correct answer to an assumption question is to negate the answer choice that you think is the credited response. Because assumptions are critical to the author's argument, the reasoning should fall apart.

The correct answer to an "assumption" question will not be written in the passage.

Answer choice (B) is incorrect. We cannot assume that the author is against *any* benefits for married individuals. We know that the author is against the "marriage tax," but we don't know whether or not the author believes in benefits for married couples. Choice (C) is also incorrect. Nothing can be drawn from the passage that would indicate that the author believes this. The passage gives us no clear answer about (D), and (E) is too extreme. We know the author is concerned about the "marriage tax" (why write an article if it wasn't important to the author?), but we can't assume that it is the *most* important issue. Finally, let's take a look at (A). It seems rather obvious, but the author does believe that legislation can be used to change the tax code. By making this assumption, the author moves from discussing Moore's proposal to the tax changes that could result from it. If we negate this statement (the author does NOT believe that changes in the tax system are possible through legislation), the author's reasoning would be invalid and the article wouldn't make sense. Choice (A) is correct.

JUST THE FACTS

On the CBEST, you will be asked to identify statements as either facts or opinions. Further, you will need to identify which facts are the most important to convey the overall meaning of a passage. What is the difference between a fact and an opinion? A fact is a true statement or a real occurrence. An opinion is a belief or conclusion that is held with confidence but cannot be proven. "Bill is wearing the color red" is a fact. "I don't like the color of Bill's sweater" is an opinion. You cannot challenge the fact that Bill is wearing red. But you could dispute whether or not you liked the color of Bill's sweater; this is a matter of taste, which is open to debate. Here is a passage with questions that involve distinguishing between facts and opinions:

> It is disappointing that more individuals are not aware of the effect of insulin on weight gain. Insulin is a critical hormone that allows individuals to absorb simple sugars (like glucose and fructose) from their food as it is digested. Most individuals produce the right amount of insulin. In fact, most individuals are not aware of the presence of insulin in the bloodstream. Recently, nutritionists have discovered that foods known as complex carbohydrates—potatoes, carrots, and pasta among them—break down into simple sugars. Other complex carbohydrates are highly refined foods, like white bread and white rice. Sometimes this breakdown into sugars occurs so rapidly that the sugars may trigger a strong insulin response. This can be problematic. A high level of insulin will inhibit the breakdown of fatty deposits. An accumulation of fatty deposits will lead to increased weight gain. Therefore, eating too many carbohydrates leads to too much insulin, which in turn promotes the accumulation of fat.______________________.

6. Which sentence best expresses an opinion of the author, not a fact?

   A. It is disappointing that more individuals are not aware of the effect of insulin on weight gain.

   B. Insulin is a critical hormone that allows individuals to absorb simple sugars (like glucose and fructose) from their food as it is digested.

   C. Sometimes this breakdown into sugars occurs so rapidly that the sugars may trigger a strong insulin response.

   D. A high level of insulin will inhibit the breakdown of fatty deposits.

   E. An accumulation of fatty deposits will lead to increased weight gain.

Here's How to Crack It

This question type may be labeled "Find the opinion." The question asks us to consider the five statements and identify the one statement that is an opinion. When given this type of question you shouldn't have to go back to the passage at all! Simply evaluate each sentence, and determine whether the statement is opinion or fact. Try to find words in each statement that express an opinion. Look for words that express the author's feelings. If you find that only one statement is an opinion, you've got the correct answer. You may refer to the passage if you have trouble determining if a statement is a fact or an opinion. Choice (A) contains a word that describes the author's feelings. The word "disappointing" is our clue that the statement is an opinion and not a fact. Is this statement universally true? No! While the author may be disappointed that people are not well educated about the effects of insulin on weight-gain, others may be ambivalent or unconcerned. Choice (A) is an opinion of the author. Choices (B), (C), (D), and (E) are all facts that could be verified. Choice (E) is a logical conclusion drawn from previous statements within the passage, so it is not an opinion and thus incorrect. The correct answer is choice (A).

Ask yourself if you can challenge the statement. If so, it is an opinion, not a fact.

7. Which of the following statements is least relevant to the main idea of the passage?

   A. Other complex carbohydrates are highly refined foods, like white bread and white rice.

   B. Sometimes, this breakdown into sugars occurs so rapidly that the sugars may trigger a strong insulin response.

   C. A high level of insulin will inhibit the breakdown of fatty deposits.

   D. An accumulation of fatty deposits will lead to increased weight gain.

   E. Therefore, eating too many carbohydrates leads to too much insulin, which in turn promotes the accumulation of fat.

Here's How to Crack It

Which statement would you be able to eliminate from the passage, and still have the passage clearly convey its message? We want to locate a fact in the passage that, while adding to the depth of the passage, is unnecessary to convey the overall message. Often, these statements are descriptive. How should you approach these questions? First, ask yourself whether the statement reflects the main theme of the passage. If so, then see whether future statements are based upon that information. Locate the statement in the passage, and read a few lines above and below the statement.

Often, the first sentence and last sentence of each paragraph will be relevant. Topic sentences frequently come at the start of each paragraph, and the final thought, or conclusion, often comes at the end of each passage.

Choice (A) provides examples of complex carbohydrates. If we eliminated this statement from the overall passage, would the main point still be made? Yes. Choice (A) certainly adds value to the passage by giving the reader a better understanding of complex carbohydrates, but it is not a crucial part of the passage. Choices (B), (C), (D), and (E) all explain vital steps in the description of how insulin can lead to weight gain. Without one of these statements, the reader would not have a clear understanding of the passage. Choice (A) is the least important statement in the passage and is therefore the correct answer.

MORE INFORMATION, PLEASE!

Sometimes, you will be asked to provide more information than that which appears in the passage. These questions can come in a few forms—they may ask you to complete the meaning of a passage, identify a statement that will strengthen the author's claim, or identify a statement that will weaken the author's claim. Occasionally, you will be asked to complete the meaning of a passage by inserting a phrase or statement into a blank. If you are given a fill-in-the-blank question, read a few lines above and a few lines below the blank to get a feel for the type of sentence that is needed.

Refer to the passage on insulin and weight gain for the following questions:

---

8. Which sentence, if inserted into the blank line, would best complete the passage?

   A. Clearly, insulin's effect on weight gain is more important than its influence in causing diabetes.

   B. Individuals concerned with their weight should concentrate on avoiding large amounts of complex carbohydrates.

   C. Meats and other proteins are not complex carbohydrates.

   D. The FDA needs to take action to make more individuals aware of the effects of insulin.

   E. Exercise is one way to decrease the amount of insulin in your system.

Here's How to Crack It

Since the blank comes at the end of the passage, you will need to select a sentence that provides a final comment on the topic. You may want to look for a conclusion in one of the answer choices (we'll cover conclusion statements in detail in the next chapter). If you read a few statements above the blank, you should be able to get a feel for the main point of the passage—we should be concerned about insulin, since a rise in insulin results in an inability to break down fatty deposits, and will therefore lead to weight gain. Let's analyze the answer choices to find a statement that adequately finishes the passage. Choice (A) is out of scope. Nowhere does the passage address the importance of insulin in causing diabetes; there is no comparison made between the two in the passage, so eliminate (A). Choice (B) will work; it ties the issue of weight gain back to complex carbohydrates. There is no reason to eliminate (B). Choice (C) does not summarize the main point of the passage. Choice (D) is also out of scope. If the passage were several pages long, this very well might be a topic the author would want to address. However, we're looking for the best sentence at the end of our brief passage, and (D) is out of scope. Choice (E) can be eliminated for the same reasons. The passage is concerned with describing why insulin is important, not how to reduce the amount of insulin in the body. Therefore, (B) is correct.

Apply the Strategy

On a "weaken" question, find an answer choice that makes the author's conclusion less convincing.

9. Which of the following, if true, would weaken the author's argument?

A. Meats and other proteins are not complex carbohydrates.

B. Lack of exercise is the major reason doctors cite as the cause of obesity.

C. Complex carbohydrates can have some health benefits.

D. Certain foods, like whole grains and cereals, can counteract the tendency of other complex carbohydrates to raise insulin levels.

E. Most diet books stress intake of vegetables as the key to weight loss.

Here's How to Crack It

This question asks us to weaken the argument presented by the author. In order to do this, we first need to identify the argument. Skim the passage to get an understanding of the main theme presented by the author. We've already discussed the main point of this passage—a high amount of insulin leads to weight gain. Therefore, we should look for an answer choice that will dispute or contradict the author's claim. Choice (A) is useless. It provides no attack on the author's main point; it merely states a fact. Choice (B) is a bit tricky. If lack of exercise is the main reason for obesity, then is the author's claim weakened? Actually, no. The author does not claim that a large quantity of insulin is the primary reason for weight gain. The author simply states that it is one reason. Choice (C) is also appealing. However, in order to weaken the claim, the statement would need to state that carbohydrates do not lead to high levels of insulin. At first, (D) may seem out of scope. Who cares about whole grains and cereals? Well, if these foods counteract the effects of other complex carbohydrates, it may be possible to still eat these foods without worrying about weight gain. Look at one of the statements in the passage: *...eating too many carbohydrates leads to too much insulin, which in turn* *promotes the accumulation of fat.* If statement (D) is true, the author's claim would be weakened, for (D) shows that carbohydrates might *not* lead to more insulin, and thus *not* lead to weight gain. Choice (E) is out of scope. The suggestions from diet books do not weaken the author's claim that carbohydrates lead to more insulin, which in turn leads to weight gain. Choice (D) is the correct answer. It directly weakens one of the statements put forth by the author.

Conversely, if you are asked to identify a statement that *strengthens* the argument, choose the answer choice that adds the best support to a statement already in the passage. Common correct answer choices are those that provide statistical support for an author's claim.

Summary

- Critical analysis and evaluation questions come in roughly three major topic areas: questions about the author, questions about the facts in a passage, and questions that ask you to add meaning to the passage.
- Use Process of Elimination techniques, looking for things like scope and tone.
- Determine whether the passage is technical or general when asked to identify the type of publication in which a passage may be found. Look at the complexity of the writing, and whether or not the author uses opinions to persuade the reader.
- Try to fit each answer choice into the passage to determine which statement the author would agree with.
- For "technique" questions, go back to the passage and look for the method the author uses to make a claim.
- For "assumption" questions, do not select an answer choice that is found in the passage. Look for an obvious statement that an author uses to help build an argument. If you negate an answer choice and the author's reasoning still makes sense, it is probably not the correct answer.
- Look for words that describe the author's feelings when identifying an opinion statement.
- You do not need to go back to the passage to solve a "find the opinion" question. Evaluate each answer choice, and select the one that is not a fact.
- In order to identify a fact as the "least relevant," try removing the statement from the passage, and see if the passage loses meaning or consistency.
- If you are asked to complete a sentence in the passage, choose an answer choice that is consistent with the author's message.
- If you are asked to weaken an author's claim, first find the main point. Then, find an answer choice that directly contradicts that main point.

Chapter 4
Reading Comprehension and Research Skills

Approximately 60 percent of the reading questions on the CBEST will test "comprehension and research skills." In this chapter, we will identify the ways in which these questions can be asked. We'll also provide specific instructions for how to find the correct answer for these questions in a passage. Finally, we'll help you distinguish question types from one another. Comprehension and research questions can be broken into four major areas:

- **What's the point?** Many questions will ask you to identify the main idea, central theme, or conclusion in a passage.
- **Identify the structure.** There are three different types of questions that require you to understand the structure and layout of a passage.
- **Specific questions.** Some questions will ask a very direct question based on a word, phrase, or quote within a passage. These specific questions require different strategies from most of the general questions we discussed in the previous chapter.
- **Research questions.** Through the use of indexes, charts, graphs, and tables of contents, you will be asked questions about the structure and placement of various items.

WHAT'S THE POINT? THE 2-T-2 TECHNIQUE

Proven Technique

The 2-T-2 technique will help you understand the passage without having to read every sentence.

Many questions will ask you to identify the main idea. Some questions are very straightforward ("What is the main point of the passage?"), while other questions will ask you to rephrase the main idea by choosing a title for the passage, or by summarizing the passage. When you are given a main idea question, you may not have to read the entire passage. Instead, you should focus on the crucial parts of the passage—the first two sentences, all topic sentences, and the last two sentences. We call this the 2-T-2 technique (where "2-T-2"stands for the first two sentences, all topic sentences, and the last two sentences). The first two sentences will introduce you to the topic that is being discussed. If there is more than one paragraph, each topic sentence will give you a clue about each paragraph. Further, if there are any transitions in the passage, you will be able to recognize them by reading the topic sentences. The final two sentences will give you a feel for how the passage concludes. The following is a passage that we will use to discuss all possible types of "main idea" questions. As always, read the questions before going to the passage.

One type of fixed-income security is the municipal bond, which is issued by state and local governments. Interest income derived from municipal bonds is exempt from federal, state, and local income taxation. There are two types of municipal bonds. One type, called a general obligation bond, is fully backed by the issuer. The other type, called a revenue bond, is issued to finance particular projects. Revenue bonds are backed by the revenues from a project or from the organization responsible for the project. Typical issuers of revenue bonds are airports, hospitals, or port authorities. Revenue bonds are riskier in terms of default than general obligation bonds. One specific type of revenue bond is the industrial development bond, which is issued to finance commercial enterprises such as the construction of a factory that can be operated by a private firm.

The appeal of municipal bonds to investors is their tax-exempt status. Because investors need not pay federal taxes on the interest proceeds, they are willing to accept lower yields on these investments. This greatly helps state and local governments, which are able to save tremendous amounts of money. Sadly, many investors shy away from municipal bonds, discouraged by the low rate of return. However, if an investor were to study the after-tax returns on municipal bonds compared to other investments, he or she would see that municipal bonds have been one of the most profitable types of fixed-income security over the last 15 years, especially for investors in high tax brackets.

---

1. Which of the following best describes the main topic of the passage?

   A. All about municipal bonds

   B. The role of the industrial development bond

   C. The tax benefits of municipal bonds

   D. An analysis of general obligation versus revenue bonds

   E. Investment choices for investors in high tax brackets

Tip! Scope will be a helpful POE tool on main idea questions.

Here's How to Crack It

Question 1 is an example of the most basic type of main idea question. This question could also be asked in the following ways:

- What is the main point of this passage?
- What is the author's central idea?
- What is the principal message conveyed by this passage?

All of these questions, and others similar to them, mean the same thing—What's the point?! We want to know why the author took the time to write the passage, and what information the author is trying to convey. As we mentioned above, you do not need to read the entire passage in order to get the main point. Let's read the passage, according to the formula mentioned above—the first two sentences, the topic sentences, and the last two sentences:

> One type of fixed-income security is the municipal bond, which is issued by state and local governments. Interest income derived from municipal bonds is exempt from federal, state, and local income taxation. ~~There are two types of municipal bonds. One type, called a general obligation bond, is fully backed by the issuer. The other type, called a revenue bond, is issued to finance particular projects. Revenue bonds are backed by the revenues from a project or from the organization responsible for the project. Typical issuers of revenue bonds are airports, hospitals, or port authorities. Revenue bonds are riskier in terms of default than general obligation bonds. One specific type of revenue bond is the industrial development bond, which is issued to finance commercial enterprises such as the construction of a factory that can be operated by a private firm.~~
>
> The appeal of municipal bonds to investors is their tax-exempt status. ~~Because investors need not pay federal taxes on the interest proceeds, they are willing to accept lower yields on these investments. This greatly helps state and local governments, who are able to save tremendous amounts of money.~~ Sadly, many investors shy away from municipal bonds, discouraged over the low rate of return. However, if an investor were to study the after-tax returns on municipal bonds compared to other investments, he or she would see that municipal bonds have been one of the most profitable types of fixed income security over the last 15 years, especially for investors in high tax brackets.

The first two sentences introduce us to the topic—municipal bonds. We know that they are issued by local governments and are exempt from some taxes. The topic sentence in the second paragraph expands on the subject of taxation. Finally, the last two sentences discuss how people often misinterpret the tax benefits and value of municipal bonds.

From the information we've learned by using 2-T-2, let's look at the answer choices. Choice (A) is extremely broad. Do you think that a 200-word passage can adequately describe everything about municipal bonds? Of course not. (Don't forget to use our scope technique to eliminate answer choices!) By the same rationale, (D) is too broad. Choices (B) and (E) describe topics that are contained within the passage. However, these topics show up too briefly in the passage to be the main focus of the passage. In general, beware of the CBEST authors using these partial answer choices as traps on main idea questions. Did (C) appeal to you? Both paragraphs of the passage discuss the tax implications of municipal bonds. Choice (C) is the correct answer.

Here are a few more questions related to the main idea, but with a twist:

---

2. Which of the following would be the best title for the passage above?

   A. Municipal Bonds

   B. Fixed-Income Securities

   C. Tax-Exempt Investments

   D. Tax Benefits of Municipal Bonds

   E. Airport Use of Revenue Bonds

Apply the Strategy
On a "title" question, ask yourself: Is the title narrow enough so that a CBEST passage could adequately address the topic?

Here's How to Crack It

We've already discussed how to find the main idea by selectively reading the text (using the 2-T-2 technique). In this question, we are asked to select a title for the passage. Approach this problem the exact same way we approached Question 1. Look for an answer choice that incorporates the main idea of the passage into the title. Use scope to eliminate titles that are too broad, and eliminate titles that only speak about a very small part of the passage. Choices (A), (B), and (C) are too broad, and should be eliminated. Be careful with (C): even though it includes the word "tax," which is part of the main idea, it does not discuss municipal bonds. Choice (E) is too narrow; even though an airport bond is mentioned in the passage, it is only a detail and not part of the central theme. Choice (D) adequately titles the passage. The passage primarily talks about the tax benefits of municipal bonds, so (D) is the correct answer.

---

3. Which of the following best summarizes the passage?

   A. There are many different types of municipal bonds, such as general obligation, revenue, and industrial development bonds.

   B. Investors shy away from municipal bonds because they do not look past the low yield.

   C. Airports often raise funds for expansion by offering revenue bonds.

   D. The tax-exempt feature of municipal bonds is one reason that investors and local governments choose them.

   E. Municipal bonds are the best type of investments for individuals in a high-tax bracket.

Here's How to Crack It

Same idea, just another way to ask the question—what's the point?! When you are asked to summarize a passage, first use the 2-T-2 technique. Then, try to eliminate answer choices that are out of scope or that contradict the main idea of the passage. Further, eliminate answer choices that deal with too narrow a topic. Make sure that the answer choice you select does not add anything to the passage. A correct summary will simply restate the passage in a concise and organized fashion.

Choice (A) summarizes the first three sentences of the passage quite well. However, there is much more information in the passage than what is contained in the first three sentences, so (A) is incomplete. Choice (B) is also tempting (it paraphrases parts of the second paragraph), but it does not express the central point of the passage. Choice (C) is wrong because it's beyond the scope of the passage. While the author mentions airports briefly, this passage is not about airports—it's about municipal bonds. Choice (E) reiterates one of the last sentences in the passage, but again, does not provide an overall summary. Choice (D) is the best answer choice. As (D) suggests, the passage mainly describes different features of municipal bonds and their tax-exempt status. Choice (D) is the correct answer.

PASSAGE STRUCTURE

Several questions on the CBEST will require you to understand the organization and structure of a reading passage. There are three types of structure questions—passage arrangement, missing sentences, and useless information. We'll tackle all three types of questions using the passage below. For now, skip the passage and start with Question 4.

Three of the most common sources of energy are fossil fuels, nuclear power, and hydroelectric power. Each of these three methods of energy production has its advantages and disadvantages.

Fossil fuels are the most widely used energy source in the United States. The burning of oil and coal derivatives releases energy that is used to boil water. The released steam turns turbines and produces energy. Today, fossil fuels are relatively abundant, which makes this form of energy production inexpensive. However, one of the problems with fossil fuels is that burning oil and coal derivatives releases chemicals that are harmful to the environment.

Nuclear power harnesses the energy contained in atoms. An atom contains protons, neutrons, and electrons. The energy released is used to convert water to steam, which in turn drives turbines. This form of energy production has proven to be even less costly than fossil fuels, but there is no foolproof method for storing all of the dangerous by-products from nuclear power plants. There is a significant fear that nuclear waste may be released into the environment, and some accidents have already occurred (the Chernobyl incident is just one example).

Hydroelectric power is produced by using the force of water to turn turbines. This is the cleanest of the three methods of energy production. ____. Further, rivers with hydroelectric plants are much more vulnerable to the effects of erosion.

4. Which of the following best describes the structure of the passage?

   A. The passage starts with a central theme, gives three examples, and draws a conclusion.

   B. The passage starts with a question, and then explains the answer to that question.

   C. The passage introduces a topic, then gives a more detailed account of the topic.

   D. The passage presents an argument, then a counter-argument, then refutes the counter-argument.

   E. The passage starts with a statement, which is then analyzed by several different experts.

Here's How to Crack It

You can identify the structure of the passage by using the main idea technique presented at the beginning of this chapter—read the first two sentences, all topic sentences, and the last two sentences. Let's take a look at the passage using this 2-T-2 technique:

Tip! The 2-T-2 technique will help you identify the structure of the passage.

Three of the most common sources of energy are fossil fuels, nuclear power, and hydroelectric power. Each of these three methods of energy production has its advantages and disadvantages.

Fossil fuels are the most widely used energy source in the United States. ~~The burning of oil and coal derivatives releases energy that is used to boil water. The released steam turns turbines and produces energy. Today, fossil fuels are relatively abundant, which makes this form of energy production inexpensive. However, one of the problems with fossil fuels is that burning oil and coal derivatives releases chemicals that are harmful to the environment~~.

Nuclear power harnesses the energy contained in atoms. ~~An atom contains protons, neutrons, and electrons. The energy released is used to convert water to steam, which in turn drives turbines. This form of energy production has proven to be even less costly than fossil fuels, but there is no foolproof method for storing all of the dangerous by-products from nuclear power plants. There is a significant fear that nuclear waste may be released into the environment, and some accidents have already occurred (the Chernobyl incident is just one example).~~

Hydroelectric power is produced by using the force of water to turn turbines. ~~This is the cleanest of the three methods of energy production.~~ ____________________ ____________________. Further, rivers with hydroelectric plants are much more vulnerable to the effects of erosion.

What has been discussed? In the first two sentences, the author describes the three most common sources of energy, and mentions that there are advantages and disadvantages to each. Then, we get a topic sentence about each type of energy source. There is no real conclusion— the last two sentences discuss the disadvantages of hydroelectric power.

Use Process of Elimination to find the correct answer. You may want to glance back at the passage if you find more than one possible answer choice. In the example above, (A) and (B) can be eliminated immediately. There is no conclusion to the passage, nor did the passage begin with a question. The passage does not present an argument, so (D) can be eliminated. If you glance at the next three paragraphs, you will find that no experts are mentioned, which eliminates (E). The best answer is (C); the author introduces the topic of energy sources, and then describes the advantages and disadvantages of the three most common types of energy sources.

Questions requiring this sort of information can be asked in somewhat different ways. See the example below.

5. Which of the following best organizes the information presented in the passage?

A. I. Hypothesis
II. Conclusion

B. I. Introduction
II. Explanation

C. I. Question
II. Analysis

D. I. Quotation
II. Examples

E. I. Theory
II. Research
III. Discussion

Here's How to Crack It

This question is very similar to the first sample question we discussed, only the format of the answer choices is different. Using the same techniques as above, we can quickly eliminate (A), (C), (D), and (E). Choice (B) clearly describes the organizational pattern of the passage.

STRUCTURE—SENTENCES

Some structure questions will deal specifically with individual sentences contained within a passage. You may be asked to identify a sentence that is irrelevant to the overall meaning of the passage, or you may be asked to insert a sentence into a passage in order to strengthen the passage. We'll do an example of each beginning on the next page.

6. Which of the following sentences in the third paragraph is *least* relevant to the main idea of the third paragraph?

    A. Nuclear power harnesses the energy contained in atoms.

    B. An atom contains a proton, neutron, and electron.

    C. The energy released is used to convert water to steam, which in turn drives turbines.

    D. This form of energy production has proven to be even less costly than fossil fuels, but there is no foolproof method for storing all of the dangerous by-products from nuclear power plants.

    E. There is a significant fear that nuclear waste may be released into the environment, and some accidents have already occurred (the Chernobyl incident is just one example).

Here's How to Crack It

First, go directly to the paragraph. Read the topic sentence to get an idea of the information that will be discussed. In the example above, the topic sentence of the third paragraph introduces us to nuclear power. Now read the remaining sentences in the paragraph, and try to identify a sentence that stands out as awkward or unnecessary. If you still have answer choices remaining, then use the 2-T-2 technique, and choose the sentence that is least relevant to the overall meaning of the passage. In the example above, the paragraph describes how nuclear power works, and some advantages and disadvantages to this energy source. The second sentence is out of place. Describing the properties of an atom is unnecessary to the overall meaning of the paragraph. Choice (B) is the correct answer.

Apply the Strategy

If you are having trouble eliminating a sentence, try reading the paragraph without a sentence. If the paragraph does not lose any overall meaning, you've found the correct answer.

7. Which sentence, if inserted into the blank line, would best fit the overall structure of the passage?

   A. Politicians should require more cities to use hydroelectric power, since it is the cleanest method.

   B. However, not all communities have access to rivers, making access to hydroelectric power rare.

   C. Some experts argue that hydroelectric power is up to 50 percent cleaner than fossil fuels.

   D. Cities should take whatever steps are necessary to convert to hydroelectric power.

   E. The depth of the water in the river is not a factor in the ability to turn turbines.

Here's How to Crack It

First, go straight to the paragraph that contains the missing sentence. Eliminate as many answer choices as possible before going to the entire passage. Place each answer choice into the sentence. Determine if the sentence is relevant to the paragraph. Next, make sure the sentence "fits" into the paragraph. Does the paragraph flow? Does the tone of the author remain consistent? If not, eliminate the answer choice. In our question above, (A) and (C) are not consistent with the author's tone. The entire passage has been a straightforward explanation of the pros and cons of energy sources. Inserting an argumentative sentence wouldn't fit the paragraph.

Make sure to read the sentences before and after the missing sentence in order to determine its meaning. Notice how the last sentence starts with the word "further." This sentence explains a problem with hydroelectric power. Therefore, the blank sentence should also describe a problem with hydroelectric power. Choice (B) is the only choice that discusses a drawback to hydroelectric power. Choice (B) is the correct answer.

SPECIFIC QUESTIONS

Up to this point, we've focused on questions that dealt with the overall meaning of the passage. There are also questions on the CBEST that will ask us for very specific pieces of information. These "specific" questions are often easier for students than "general" questions, since the answers can often be found directly in the passage. Some questions will ask you to find a piece of information in the passage; other questions will ask you to find the meaning of a particular word or phrase. In order to learn about specific questions, we'll use the passage below (again, skip to the questions following the passage):

> There has been a great increase in the number of different anticancer drugs for women available in the United States in the past five years. However, the U.S. Food and Drug Administration has warned that certain drugs may be more harmful than they are beneficial.
>
> Tamoxifen, the first of the designer estrogen-based drugs, has been used to treat breast cancer for more than twenty-five years. This derivative of estrogen acts to starve tumors that feed on estrogen. New research suggests that Tamoxifen can not only help reduce the effect of tumors once they appear, but the drug can also decrease the risk of developing tumors by up to 45 percent. While this evidence would seem to indicate that Tamoxifen could benefit all women, additional information shows that Tamoxifen comes with several risks. The research further explained that women who took Tamoxifen developed uterine cancer twice as often as those who did not. There are additional side effects. Others died from blood clots probably triggered by the medication. Further, the effect of Tamoxifen seems to decrease over time. Research shows that its effectiveness starts to decrease after five years, making the decision about when to start taking the drug difficult. Deciding whether women should take Tamoxifen has become so complicated that the National Cancer Institute (NCI) has developed a computer program to help women determine whether they should take the drug.

8. In addition to the risk of uterine cancer, what is a potential side effect of taking Tamoxifen?

   A. increase in tumor development of up to 45 percent

   B. starvation

   C. blood clots

   D. loss of energy

   E. none of the above

Here's How to Crack It

Tip! Use keywords to help you locate the correct answer within a passage.

This first question asks us to identify a specific piece of information in the passage—a danger in the use of Tamoxifen. In attacking these specific questions, try to identify keywords that you can search for in the passage. "Tamoxifen" is certainly a keyword, although it appears so often in the passage that it may not be of tremendous help to you. Another phrase is "side effects." Probably the best key to the question is the phrase "uterine cancer." The correct answer will probably be located near this phrase. Two lines further down, the passage mentions the risk of blood clots. Choice (C) is the correct answer.

Here is an additional specific question about the previous passage:

9. What is the National Cancer Institute's position on Tamoxifen?

   A. The NCI states that no one should take the drug due to its risks.

   B. The NCI believes that only women in the late stages of breast cancer should take the drug.

   C. The NCI is concerned about giving women the proper tools to decide whether or not Tamoxifen is right for them.

   D. The NCI supports any drug approved by the FDA.

   E. The NCI argues that uterine cancer is harder to treat than breast cancer.

Here's How to Crack It

This specific question gives us a great keyword to work with—the National Cancer Institute. This keyword can be found near the end of the passage. When you spot a keyword, read approximately two lines above and two lines below the line on which the keyword appears, in order to get a feel for the context in which it is mentioned. In this case, we find that there are many pros and cons to taking Tamoxifen, and that the NCI has set up a computer program to help women understand the benefits and risks. Choice (C) best paraphrases the information in the passage.

Apply the Strategy

Be sure to read a few lines above and a few lines below the vocabulary word you are searching for in order to understand the overall meaning.

Finally, you may be asked to recognize the meaning of a particular word or phrase within a passage. To find the correct answer to these "vocabulary in context" questions, first locate the word in question. Next, read a few lines above and a few lines below the word to understand its use in the passage. Finally, be careful. CBEST authors will often ask about words that can have multiple meanings. Be sure to select the meaning that best fits the word's use *in the passage*, not the definition you know best. The following is an example using the previous passage.

10. Which of the following is the best meaning of the word "designer" as it is used in the first sentence of the second paragraph of the passage?

    A. fashionable

    B. trendy

    C. pure

    D. altered

    E. planned

Here's How to Crack It

The word "designer" can be found at the beginning of the paragraph, so be sure to read a few lines above and below the line on which it appears. Let's take a look at the answer choices. Is the drug fashionable or trendy? This is probably not the author's intention when describing the drug. Choice (C) is contradicted by the word "derivative" a few lines below. "Designer" must not mean "pure." We're left with (D) and (E). "Planned" does not fit into the passage, leaving "altered" as the remaining answer choice. The drug Tamoxifen has been modified from the natural form of estrogen, making (D) the correct answer.

RESEARCH QUESTIONS

Research questions account for approximately 10 percent of all reading questions on the CBEST. These types of questions are probably the easiest ones on the Reading Section. Most students will treat all research questions as first-pass questions. While some of these questions can be tricky, all of the information can be found in a table, graph, or passage.

There are three basic types of questions that ask you about structure. First, questions will ask you to identify and locate information. For these questions, tables of contents and indexes are most often used. You may also be asked to find information within a section heading, book, chapter, or article. Next, CBEST authors may ask you how a passage is organized. Finally, you may be asked questions about information found in a graph or table. These questions will ask you to either find information within a given table, or to identify conclusions, generalizations, or relationships from the information presented in the table.

The most common type of passage in a structure question is an index. We will use the index to analyze some common types of structure questions.

Use the excerpt from an index to answer the questions that follow:

Video:
- Black, 286–287
- Input, 145–147
- Insert, 150
- Output, 168–169
- Switcher:
  - Distribution, 348
  - Production, 348–353, 396
- Tracks, 277

Videographer, 16

Videotape recorder (VTR), 131–132

Viewfinder, 24, 46–49

Voice-over (VO), 252, 262–263, 343

11. On which pages should one look to find information about a direct video input?

    A. 286–287

    B. 131–132

    C. 46–49

    D. 145–147

    E. 262–263

Here's How to Crack it

This question is an example of the most common type of research question. The question asks us to identify and locate a specific piece of information. First, take a look at the item we are asked to locate (in the example above, we're looking for keywords "direct video input"). Next, glance down the index to see if any of the keywords match topics in the index. In the question above, there aren't any matches for direct, but we do have a location for video input, found on pages 145–147. These pages are listed as (D), which is the correct answer.

These same types of questions can also be asked using a table of contents. Use the table of contents to answer the questions that follow:

Preparing for a Wedding:

12. On what pages would you look to find information on how to reserve a site for a wedding?

 A. 162–175

 B. 21–25

 C. 26–35

 D. 130–134

 E. 2–20

Here's How to Crack It

Using the techniques described above, first identify the keywords of the information we need to find—"reserve," "site," "wedding." Next, try to find a match for one of those words. "Wedding" appears everywhere, so that isn't a big help. However, "site" is another word for "location," and "reserving a site" is similar to "finding a location." The correct answer is (C).

PASSAGE ORGANIZATION

CBEST authors will often ask about the manner in which a topic or table of contents is arranged. Here is an example using the previous table of contents:

13. Which of the following best describes the organizational pattern used in the table of contents?

    A. alphabetical

    B. chronological

    C. by order of importance

    D. by cost

    E. by category

Here's How to Crack It

Process of Elimination is key to answering questions about the organizational structure of an index or table of contents. It is fairly obvious that the topics are not organized alphabetically—eliminate (A). Choices (C) and (D) are impossible to prove, and therefore can be eliminated. Choice (B) may seem correct, because there are some topics that do seem to follow in a chronological order. However, there is a better answer choice. Choice (E) breaks each topic into a different category. The book deals with the different categories of things to be done when planning a wedding. Choice (E) is the correct answer.

GRAPHS AND CHARTS

The CBEST Reading Section may use graphs and charts to ask you structure questions. The only tricky thing about graphs and charts is that the authors may leave some information blank. In this case, try to complete the information (filling in missing figures, labeling graphs) before tackling the questions. Below is an example of a reading question using a line graph.

Use the graph below to answer the question that follows.

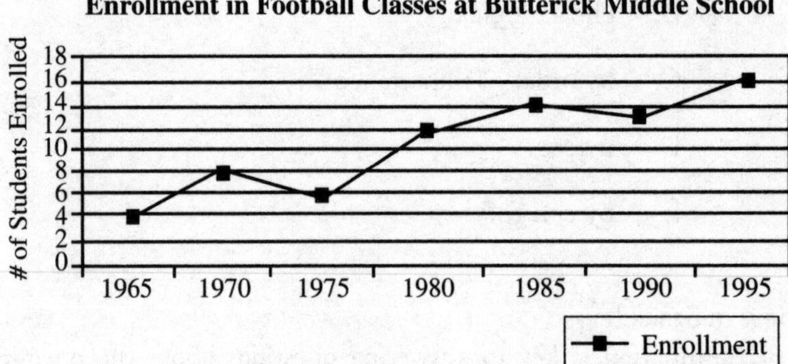

14. Within what five-year period was the increase in enrollment in football classes the greatest?

    A. 1965 to 1970

    B. 1970 to 1975

    C. 1975 to 1980

    D. 1980 to 1985

    E. 1985 to 1990

Here's How to Crack It

The question asks us to identify the period that saw the greatest increase in enrollment. First, look at the graph, and try to identify answer choices that may be eliminated. There are decreases in enrollment between 1970 to 1975, and 1985 to 1990. Therefore, eliminate (B) and (E). Visually, you may be able to identify the correct answer. If not, find the difference between the periods for the remaining answer choices. The correct answer is (C). There was an increase of six students during that time period.

Summary

- When asked for the main idea, read the passage according to the 2-T-2 technique: the first two sentences, all topic sentences, and the last two sentences. Try to get a feel for the main point of the passage.
- Eliminate answer choices that are out of scope on main idea questions. Eliminate any title that gives a description that is too broad for the passage.
- On specific questions, identify keywords to search for the correct answer. Read a few lines above and a few lines below in order to understand the point of the paragraph.
- When asked to find the meaning of a vocabulary word or phrase, be sure to select the definition that is most relevant to the passage, not the most common definition.
- Structure questions require you to understand how the passage is organized. To recognize the structure, read the passage using the 2-T-2 technique.
- On questions that ask you to identify a page number in an index, use keywords and search the index to find one or more of your keywords. Then select the most appropriate index page based upon your remaining choices.
- Fill in any missing information in graphs or charts in order to solve chart questions.

Chapter 5
Reading Section Drills and Answers and Explanations

Read the passage below and answer the question that follows.

Adverse possession is a legal principle by which a person may acquire valid title to a property owned by someone else, provided certain requirements are met. Typically, the law requires that the disseisor hold possession for an extended period of time, openly occupying the property in a hostile or non-permissive manner, and that the possession be continuous and exclusive.

1. To make this passage more clear to a general audience, the author could do which of the following?

   A. Define professional jargon, such as *disseisor*, in simpler terms.

   B. Explain other methods whereby a person can obtain property.

   C. Eliminate the description of the requirements for adverse possession.

   D. Cite the legal precedents for adverse possession.

   E. Note that the typical time requirement for adverse possession is seven years.

Read the passage below and answer the question that follows.

Law enforcement officers and traffic safety experts unanimously agree that texting while driving is always dangerous. Nevertheless, the number of people who admit to texting while driving increases every year.

2. Which of the following is suggested by the passage?

   A. More people admit to texting while driving because it is more socially acceptable to do so.

   B. Using a cellular phone while driving is only acceptable in emergency situations.

   C. Texting while driving is illegal in every jurisdiction.

   D. People who drive dangerously must have compelling reasons for doing so.

   E. Those who text while driving may be ignoring the known risks involved.

Read this excerpt from a book index and then answer the question that follows.

- Music, 215-218
  - Country / Western, 215-218
    - Folk, 216
    - Country Pop, 217-218
  - Pop, 217-218, 220-229, 257-259
    - Adult Contemporary, 222-224
    - Country Pop, 217-218
    - Pop Rock, 257-259
    - Teen pop, 226-229
  - R&B / Soul, 231-240
    - Disco, 232-235
    - Funk, 236
    - Motown, 238-239
  - Rock, 242-262
    - Alternative, 245-250
    - Metal, 254-256
    - Pop Rock, 257-259
    - Punk, 260

3. On which pages would one be most likely to find information about popular disco artists of the 1970s?

A. 217-218

B. 226-229

C. 232-235

D. 245-250

E. 257-259

Read the passage below and answer the question that follows.

Since the 1980s, education experts have increasingly acknowledged the importance of differentiated instruction geared toward different learning modalities. Research has shown that individual students respond differently to visual, auditory, and tactile input. Contemporary teachers have largely embraced this research, and attempt to incorporate different modalities into their lessons in order to better reach their students.

4. One of the main points in the passage is that

   A. prior to the 1980s, no one acknowledged the importance of differentiated instruction.

   B. lessons that do not incorporate different learning modalities will be largely ineffective.

   C. education theories tend to vary frequently over time.

   D. contemporary teachers have learned from studies that support the use of differentiated instruction.

   E. education theories prior to the 1980s supported only one modality of teaching and learning.

Read the passage below and answer the four questions that follow.

Since the early 2000s, digital music consumption has dramatically increased, while physical album sales have decreased by more than 70%. The interest in digital music has largely been fueled by the appearance of peer-to-peer file sharing services in the early 2000s, which have since paved the way for immensely successful online retailers that sell music in digital formats. _____ services have allowed consumers to build their music collections one song at a time, instead of having to purchase full albums.

[1] Another effect of these digital music services is the growing popularity of independent artists. [2] Previously, the only way for artists to gain <u>exposure</u> was through physical album sales and radio play, which typically required the support of a successful record company. [3]Today, the digital music market allows consumers to discover artists that may not have the benefit of any record company resources. [4] Although physical music sales have declined, many music fans are still willing to pay top dollar to attend concert performances. [5] Some artists have gained millions of fans simply by uploading a self-produced video to the internet. [6] _____, we may see a trend toward digital music being offered for free, which would come with the benefit of increased audiences of loyal fans.

5. Which words, if inserted *in order* in the blank spaces in the first and second paragraphs, would provide the most clarity in the sequence of the author's ideas?

   A. Some; Before

   B. Other; Quickly

   C. Those; Afterward

   D. All; Later

   E. These; Soon

6. Which of the following best defines the term <u>exposure,</u> as it appears in the second paragraph of the passage?

   A. Vulnerability

   B. Publicity

   C. Lack of privacy

   D. Access to company resources

   E. Commercials

7. Which of the following numbered sentences has the *least* relevance to the main idea of the passage?

   A. Sentence 1

   B. Sentence 2

   C. Sentence 3

   D. Sentence 4

   E. Sentence 5

8. From the passage, which of the following can be inferred about the music industry prior to the early 2000s?

   A. Independent artists did not have any significant presence in the music industry.

   B. Physical album sales were continually increasing.

   C. Digital music formats did not exist.

   D. The primary way to purchase music was to buy complete albums.

   E. Physical media formats had inferior sound quality compared to today's digital formats.

Read the passage below and answer the question that follows.

Independent practice, such as homework, is an important component of student learning. It allows students the opportunity to reinforce skills and knowledge without the guidance of the teacher.

9. Which of the following is implied by the passage?

A. Students will struggle to learn without the guidance of the teacher.

B. Teachers do not assign as much homework as they should.

C. Homework is most useful when it integrates multiple learning modalities.

D. Students should do at least some regular independent practice to reinforce their learning.

E. Homework is unnecessary if the teacher has provided sufficient guided instruction.

Read the passage below and answer the question that follows.

Credential candidates at Madison College must meet all of the following requirements during their internships.

- Early childhood workshop (required during first or second semester)
- At least 500 total service hours in any primary grades (grades 1-3)
- At least 500 total service hours in any intermediate grades (grades 4-6)
- Three courses in chosen emphasis (Physical Education, Fine Arts, or Science)
- Hold a valid State Substitute Certificate, **or**, passing scores on **both** the Teacher Competency Exam and the Subject Qualification Exam.

10. Which of the following academic plans would meet the requirements at Madison College?

A. Service hours (400 in grade 2, 100 in grade 3, 500 in grade 4); early childhood workshop in first semester; Fine Arts courses 412 and 415; Science course 310; passing scores on Teacher Competency Exam and Subject Qualification Exam

B. Service hours (300 in grade 1, 425 in grade 2, 400 in grade 4); early childhood workshop in second semester; Physical Education courses 301, 305, and 306; State Substitute Certificate

C. Service hours (550 in grade 1, 580 in grade 5); State Substitute Certificate; early childhood workshop in first semester; Fine Arts courses 305, 308, and 312

D. Service hours (250 in grade 2, 255 in grade 3, 500 in grade 6); early childhood workshop in third semester; Science courses 305, 310, and 407; passing scores on Teacher Competency Exam and Subject Qualification Exam

E. Service hours (800 in grade 2); early childhood workshop in second semester; Fine Arts courses 305, 309, and 315; Science course 409; passing score on Subject Qualification Exam.

Read the passage below and answer the questions that follow.

[1]President Theodore Roosevelt signed the Food and Drug Act in 1906. [2]The Act included restrictions on additives that are “filthy” or “injurious to health,” and led to the creation of the Food and Drug Administration (FDA) in 1927. [3]However, after an incident of mass fatality involving a drug called Elixir Sulfanilamide, it was clear that additional regulatory authority was needed. [4]The newer Food, Drug, and Cosmetic Act was signed by President Franklin Roosevelt in 1938. [5]This law required safety reviews of all new drugs, and also banned the use of false claims in labeling.

11. In relation to the passage, Sentence 3 does which of the following?

A. It speculates that lives would have been saved if the 1938 act had been passed sooner.

B. It describes the first mass tragedy involving pharmaceuticals in the United States.

C. It implies that the Act signed in 1938 was mostly indistinguishable from the one signed in 1906.

D. It suggests a reason for the creation of the Food, Drug, and Cosmetic Act in 1938.

E. It supports the author’s argument that expanded regulation is needed in the future.

12. Which of the following sentences, if inserted after Sentence 5, would best fit the tone and sequence of ideas in this passage?

A. Another regulatory agency formed in the 1900s was the Federal Highway Administration.

B. It was the first Act to explicitly grant authority to the FDA to oversee the safety of food, drugs, and cosmetics.

C. These regulations are really helpful for consumers nowadays.

D. The Food, Drug, and Cosmetic act defined and regulated specific food coloring additives, such as “Yellow no. 5.”

E. A cosmetic is a product intended to alter or improve a person’s appearance.

13. This passage would be most likely to appear in which of the following?

    A. A brief essay discussing regulations in US food and drug industries

    B. A biography of President Theodore Roosevelt

    C. A manual of food and drug legislation

    D. A dissertation about the Food and Drug Act of 1906

    E. An argument about the benefits of safety regulations

Use the chart below to answer the question that follows.

GlobalNet Solutions Inc.
Employee Survey Results

Job Status:
Full time: 74%
Part time: 26%

Gender of Employees:
Male: 57%
Female: 43%

Average employee income: $67,292
Highest individual employee income: $156,034

Employees by Department:
Executive: 154
Accounting: 1,238
Sales: 3,952
IT Support: 510

14. All of the following can be determined from the information shown in the chart EXCEPT:

A. Some employees earn less than $67,292 in income.

B. A greater percentage of employees work full time than work part time.

C. Full time employees earn higher income than part time employees.

D. The Executive department has the fewest employees of any department listed.

E. There are more male employees than female employees.

Read the passage below and answer the question that follows.

At Taft Middle School, students have access to the shared computer lab for 40 minutes per week. Teachers report that, during this time, they teach typing and word processing skills. In order to learn the more advanced skills that will be required of them in tomorrow's job market, our students need to spend more time with technology and a staff member who is capable of teaching these concepts. Clearly, an increase in the technology budget is well warranted.

15. Which of the following functions does the first sentence perform?

    A. It is an expression of the author's opinion.

    B. It highlights a contrast with the final sentence.

    C. It includes an unnecessary detail that distracts from the author's purpose.

    D. It sets the author's tone using vivid imagery.

    E. It provides information to support the author's conclusion.

Read the following passage and answer the question that follows.

A calorie (also called kilocalorie or nutritional calorie) is the approximate amount of energy needed to raise the temperature of one gram of water by one degree Celsius.

16. The preceding excerpt would be LEAST likely to appear in which of the following?

    A. An introductory text on physical science

    B. A glossary of scientific terms

    C. A beginner's guide to nutrition

    D. A brief editorial discussing the causes and effects of obesity in the United States

    E. An encyclopedia

READING DRILLS ANSWERS AND EXPLANATIONS

1. **A** This would be the most effective way *to make this passage more clear to a general audience.* Since a general audience would typically not understand specific legal terminology such as *disseisor,* it would help to provide definitions for these terms. Choice (B) is not the correct answer. The addition of *other methods* could be relevant to this topic, but it would not improve the audience's understanding of the existing sentences. This change would not *make this passage more clear to a general audience.* Eliminate (B). Choice (C) is not the correct answer. Eliminating the discussion of requirements would serve to eliminate much of the specialized vocabulary in the passage, but it would not help a general audience to understand what adverse possession is. The description of requirements should be clarified or simplified, not eliminated. Eliminate (C). Choice (D) is not the correct answer. Legal precedents may be of interest to a profession in the legal or real estate industries, but this information would not serve to *make this passage more clear to a general audience.* Eliminate (D). Choice (E) is not the correct answer. The addition of this detail could be relevant to this topic, but it would not improve the audience's understanding of the existing sentences. This change would not *make this passage more clear to a general audience.* Eliminate (E).

2. **E** The statement that *law enforcement officers and safety experts unanimously agree* supports the idea that there are *known risks* to texting while driving. The fact that people are still texting while driving suggests that these people *may be ignoring* the risks. Note the use of "may be" in the answer, which means that the answer is not too extreme. Choice (A) is not the correct answer. The passage does not speculate as to whether or not it is *socially acceptable* to text while driving. Eliminate (A). Choice (B) is not the correct answer. The passage does not indicate that *emergency situations* are considered. Also note the more general situation of *using a cellular phone,* while the passage is specifically about *texting.* Eliminate (B). Choice (C) is not the correct answer. The passage does not reveal the legality of texting while driving. Note that *law enforcement officers* is irrelevant to this answer; their opinion does not necessarily mean that texting while driving is *illegal.* Eliminate (C). Choice (D) is not the correct answer. The passage does not speculate as to the *reasons* that people text while driving. Also note the use of the word *must,* which makes this answer extreme. Eliminate (D).

3. **C** The category of "Disco" is where one could find information about popular disco artists of the 1970s. The other categories list other types of music. Choices (A), (B), (D), and (E) refer to Country music, Teen pop, Alternative, and Pop Rock, respectively. Since these genres are different from Disco, these choices should be eliminated.

4. **D** This answer is best supported by the final sentence, which states that contemporary teachers have *embraced this research, and attempt to incorporate different modalities into their lessons.* Choice (A) is not the correct answer. This answer uses extreme language. The passage does not state that *no one acknowledged the importance of differentiated instruction.* This language is much stronger than the language in the passage. Choice (B) is not the correct answer. This answer uses extreme language. The passage does not indicate that certain types of language will be *largely ineffective.* This language is much stronger than the language in the passage. Choice (C) is not the correct answer. This answer uses extreme language. Although the passage indicates a change in education theory, this

indicates only one change, and there is no indication that the theories *tend to vary frequently.* This language is much stronger than the language in the passage. Choice (E) is not the correct answer. Although the passage reveals a change toward acknowledging different learning modalities, there is no evidence that the former theories *supported only one modality.* This language is much stronger than the language in the passage.

5. **E** The first blank refers directly to the *peer-to-peer file sharing services* and *online retailers* mentioned in the previous sentence. Look for a word that continues the thought. *These* works best. The second blank refers to a prediction: *we may see a trend toward digital music being offered for free.* Look for a word that applies to the future. *Soon* is the best choice, and *Later* may be somewhat acceptable; however, in considering **both** blanks, (E) is the best answer. Don't forget to use Process of Elimination on this question. Choice (A) is not the correct answer. *Some* might be adequate for the first blank. However, *before* is a reversal of what works in the second blank. The second blank needs to refer to the future, not the past. Eliminate (A). Choice (B) is not the correct answer. The word *other* would indicate a contrast. However, we want a word that indicates agreement with the previous sentence. For the second blank, *quickly* does not have the same meaning as *soon* in the context of the sentence. Eliminate (B). Choice (C) is not the correct answer. The difference between *those* and *these* is fairly subtle; in general, *these* indicates a "proximity" to the speaker or idea, whereas *those* indicates more distance. Since the referenced *services* are directly in the previous sentence, *these* is better. Additionally, the word *afterward* does not fit the meaning of the second blank, since the blank refers to a prediction for the future, while *afterward* should refer directly to an event in the preceding sentence. Eliminate (C). Choice (D) is not the correct answer. *All* is too extreme for the first blank. The passage does not refer to *all* music services; rather, the blank refers specifically to the digital music services mentioned in the preceding sentence. *Later* may be somewhat acceptable; however, in considering **both** blanks, this is not the best answer. Eliminate (D).

6. **B** This answer is supported by the statement that exposure is gained through *physical album sales and record play,* which indicates that it may increase the author's success or popularity. Additionally, the following two sentences state that digital music *allows consumers to discover artists, and that some artists have gained millions of fans* through the use of digital media. The word *publicity* best defines *exposure* in the context of the passage. Choice (A) is not the correct answer. This is a trap answer based on an alternate definition of *exposure.* The passage indicates that exposure is gained through *physical album sales and record play,* which would indicate a positive outcome, rather than a negative outcome such as *vulnerability.* Eliminate (A). Choice (C) is not the correct answer. This is another trap answer based on an alternate definition of *exposure.* The passage indicates that exposure is gained through *physical album sales and record play,* which would indicate a positive outcome, rather than a negative outcome such as *lack of privacy.* Eliminate (C). Choice (D) is not the correct answer. This is a trap answer based on the recycled language *company resources.* The passage indicates that artists can gain popularity without company resources, as illustrated by the example of artists gaining *millions of fans simply by uploading a self-produced video to the internet.* Eliminate (D). Choice (E) is not the correct answer. This is a trap answer based on a potential misreading of

the passage. The passage does not refer to direct advertising such as *commercials*, but rather, the popularity gained through *physical album sales and radio play,* as well as *the digital music market.* The word *exposure* in this context most clearly refers to the artists' popularity or success. *Commercials* does not fit here. Eliminate (E).

7. **D** Since the passage is mainly concerned with the increasing popularity of digital music, mentioning concert performances would be irrelevant. This information does not have a meaningful connection to the rest of the passage, and should be omitted. Choice (A) is not the correct answer. Sentence 1 is an appropriate transition between the two paragraphs: paragraph 1 discusses one "effect" being that *physical album sales have decreased by more than 70%,* and paragraph 2 discusses the *growing popularity of independent artists.* Eliminate (A). Choice (B) is not the correct answer. Sentence 2 is relevant to the discussion of the *growing popularity of independent artists.* This paragraph contrasts the historical necessity of *physical album sales and radio play* with the ability of today's consumers *to discover artists that may not have the benefit of any record company resources.* Eliminate (B). Choice (C) is not the correct answer. Sentence 3 is relevant to the discussion of the *growing popularity of independent artists.* Once again, this paragraph contrasts the historical necessity of *physical album sales and radio play* with the ability of today's consumers *to discover artists that may not have the benefit of any record company resources.* Eliminate (C). Choice (E) is not the correct answer. Sentence 5 is relevant to the discussion of the *growing popularity of independent artists.* The action of *uploading a self-produced video to the internet* is mentioned as an example of digital music services contributing to the success of independent artists. Eliminate (E).

8. **D** The statement that primarily supports this answer is that digital music services *have allowed consumers to build their music collections one song at a time, instead of having to purchase full albums.* Since consumers "had" to purchase full albums, it follows that this was the *primary way to purchase music.* Choice (A) is not the correct answer. Although the passage refers to the *growing popularity of independent artists,* there is no indication that *independent artists did not have any significant presence in the music industry.* In other words, we do not know how popular independent artists were in this period; we only know that their popularity is now *growing.* This answer is much stronger than the language in the passage. Eliminate (A). Choice (B) is not the correct answer. Although the passage states that *physical album sales have decreased by more than 70%,* there is no evidence that the sales were *continually increasing* before this time. The passage does not reveal the trend of physical album sales prior to the early 2000s, only that there has been a decrease since then. Eliminate (B). Choice (C) is not the correct answer. The passage discusses *peer-to-peer file sharing services* and *online retailers,* but does not reveal the origin of digital music itself. It is quite possible that digital music formats existed for a long time; the passage only discusses the increased popularity of related services since the early 2000s. Eliminate (C). Choice (E) is not the correct answer. This answer states that the sound quality was *inferior*; however, there is no such comparison made in the passage. The passage does not discuss *sound quality* of music formats, only popularity. Eliminate (E).

9. **D** The text that best supports this answer is the statement that *independent practice... is an important component of student learning.* The passage then continues with additional reasoning in favor of independent practice. Select (D). Choice (A) is not the correct answer. The passage does not indicate that *students will struggle to learn without the guidance of the teacher.* Eliminate (A). Choice (B) is not the correct answer. Although the passage states that independent practice is *an important component of student learning,* the author does not express thoughts on how much homework teachers *do,* or *should,* assign. Eliminate (B). Choice (C) is not the correct answer. The passage does not make reference to *multiple learning modalities.* Eliminate (C). Choice (E) is not the correct answer. The passage does not indicate circumstances in which homework may be *unnecessary.* Eliminate (E).

10. **C** This plan would meet all of the requirements listed. The best approach for this type of question might be to read each requirement one at a time, and eliminate answers that do NOT meet the requirement. Choice (A) is not the correct answer. This plan does not meet the requirement in the fourth bullet (regarding courses). This candidate would take two Fine Arts courses, and one Science course, but these would be from two different emphases, and the requirement is to take *three courses in chosen emphasis.* Choice (B) is not the correct answer. This plan does not meet the requirement in the third bullet (regarding hours in intermediate grades). This candidate will have completed only 400 of the 500 required hours in intermediate grades. Choice (D) is not the correct answer. This plan does not meet the requirement in the first bullet (regarding the early childhood workshop). This candidate will have taken the workshop in his or her third semester; however, the requirement is to take the workshop *during the first or second semester.* Choice (E) is not the correct answer. This plan does not meet the requirements in either the third or fifth bullets. This candidate will have completed zero of the 500 required service hours in intermediate grades, and he or she will not have passed the Teacher Competency Exam.

11. **D** This sentence suggests an event that led to the creation of the Food, Drug, and Cosmetic Act in 1938. The sentence states that *additional regulatory authority was needed,* which indicates that this was a catalyst for the expanded regulation in 1938. Choice (A) is not the correct answer. Although the passage indicates that Elixir Sulfanilamide *killed over 100 people,* the author does not hypothesize that *lives would have been saved if the 1938 act had been passed sooner.* This is a speculation that is not reflected in the text of the passage. Eliminate (A). Choice (B) is not the correct answer. The passage does not indicate that the incident with Elixir Sulfanilamide was the *first mass tragedy involving pharmaceuticals in the United States.* There could have been other previous events. Eliminate (B). Choice (C) is not the correct answer. The passage does not suggest that the *Act signed in 1938 was mostly indistinguishable from the one signed in 1906.* Although they may have had similarities, the word "indistinguishable" is far too strong. Eliminate (C). Choice (E) is not the correct answer. The author does not reveal his/her feelings about the regulations, nor suggest that *expanded regulation is needed in the future.* Eliminate (E).

12. **B** To approach this question, look for an answer that best matches the passage in content, vocabulary, tone, and level of detail. Choice (B) fits well in the context of a brief summary of the legislation discussed. Choice (A) is not the correct answer. Since the passage is about *food and drug* regulations, a sentence about the Federal Highway Administration would be off topic. Eliminate (A). Choice (C) is not the correct answer. The informal vocabulary in this sentence (*really, nowadays*) does not match the moderately academic tone of the passage. Eliminate (C). Choice (D) is not the correct answer. This sentence adds a precise detail that would not fit well in the scope of the passage, which is structured as a brief overview. Eliminate (D). Choice (E) is not the correct answer. Since the passage is mainly concerned with providing a brief overview of the legislation discussed, the definition of *cosmetic* is not very relevant and would be out of place. Eliminate (E).

13. **A** A *brief essay discussing regulations in US food and drug industries* would fit the content, tone, and scope of the passage. Choice (B) is not the correct answer. The information in sentences 3-5 regards legislation under a different president. It would not be relevant in a biography of Theodore Roosevelt. Eliminate (B). Choice (C) is not the correct answer. The passage is structured as a brief overview. A manual of legislation would have significantly more detail. Eliminate (C). Choice (D) is not the correct answer. The passage is structured as a brief overview. A dissertation would have significantly more detail. Eliminate (D). Choice (E) is not the correct answer. This passage does not present an argument on the matter of safety regulations. It is a brief overview of some specific food and drug legislation. Eliminate (E).

14. **C** The chart does not reveal information about full time employee income compared with part-time employee income. Note the word EXCEPT in the question stem. Select (C), since this information is NOT shown in the chart. Choice (A) is not the correct answer. See that the average income is provided, as well as the highest income. It is therefore possible to determine that at least some employees earn less than the average. In other words, if some employees earn higher than the average, then it must be true that some employees earn lower than the average. This confirms that some employees earn less than $67,292 in income. Eliminate (A). Choice (B) is not the correct answer. See the portion of the chart that lists "Job Status," which indicates that 74% of employees work full time, and 26% work part time. This confirms that a greater percentage of employees work full time than work part time. Eliminate (B). Choice (D) is not the correct answer. See the portion of the chart that lists "Employees by Department." Of the departments listed, the Executive department has the fewest employees. Eliminate (D). Choice (E) is not the correct answer. See the portion of the chart that lists "Gender of Employees," which states that 57% of employees are male and 43% are female. This confirms that there are more male employees than female employees. Eliminate (E).

15. **E** The information that students use the computer lab *for 40 minutes per week* supports the argument that *students need to spend more time with technology,* and the conclusion that *an increase in the technology budget* is well warranted. Choice (A) is not the correct answer. The first sentence is not an opinion; rather, it is a statement of information. The author does not state his/her feelings about the situation until later in the paragraph. Eliminate (A). Choice (B) is not the correct answer. The first sentence does not *highlight a contrast with the final sentence.* Rather, it is offered in support of

the final sentence, and the argument that students need more access to technology. Eliminate (B). Choice (C) is not the correct answer. The information that students use the computer lab *for 40 minutes per week* supports the argument that *students need to spend more time with technology.* It is not *an unnecessary detail that distracts from the author's purpose.* Eliminate (C). Choice (D) is not the correct answer. The statement that *students have access to the shared computer lab for 40 minutes per week* would not be considered vivid imagery. Rather, it is straightforward information. Eliminate (D).

16. **D** The definition of a calorie would be out of place in a brief editorial discussing the causes and effects of obesity in the United States. Such an editorial would be expected to be more general in breadth, without going into the level of detail that would include scientific definitions. Since this would be LEAST likely to include the excerpt, select (D). Choice (A) is not the correct answer. The definition of a calorie would be useful in an introductory text on physical science. Such a text would be reasonably expected to explain the terms that are used. Eliminate (A). Choice (B) is not the correct answer. The definition of a calorie would be useful in a glossary of scientific terms. Eliminate (B). Choice (C) is not the correct answer. The definition of a calorie would be useful in a beginner's guide to nutrition. Note that the calorie is also referred to as a "nutritional calorie" in the excerpt. A nutrition guide would explain how calories are relevant to nutrition. Eliminate (C). Choice (E) is not the correct answer. The definition of a calorie is likely to be found in an encyclopedia, under the entry "calorie" or related topics. Eliminate (E).

Part III Cracking the Mathematics Section

The Mathematics Section: sounds somewhat intimidating, doesn't it? When you consider the number of topics that could appear on a math test, your head may start to spin. Not to worry. The writers of the CBEST focus on a limited number of topics, all of which will be covered in detail in the next three chapters. According to the writers of the test, the CBEST "assesses basic skills and concepts that are important in performing the job of an educator." Not sure what this means? Let's take a look.

WHAT THE CBEST TESTS

The CBEST Mathematics Section contains 50 multiple-choice questions. There is no specific time limit, as you have four hours to complete the entire exam. We recommend, however, that you spend about eighty minutes on the Mathematics Section (some students will find they need to adjust this time—see Chapter 2 for a review on pacing). The writers of the CBEST test three major skill areas:

1. **Estimation, Measurement, and Statistical Principles**
   30% (approximately 15 questions)
   - Standard units of length, temperature, weight, and capacity
   - Measure length and perimeter.
   - Estimation of answers using arithmetic
   - Statistical principles such as averages, ratios, and proportions
   - Basic probability
   - Interpret meaning of standardized test scores.

The CBEST Mathematics Section will test you on topics that you may not have studied for several years! We'll get you caught up in the chapters ahead.

2. **Computation and Problem Solving**
   35% (approximately 17–18 questions)
   - Basic operations of addition, subtraction, multiplication, and division with integers, fractions, decimals, percentages, positive, and negative numbers
   - Solve arithmetic word problems.
   - Solve algebraic problems.
   - Determine whether enough information is given to solve math problems.
   - Recognize multiple methods of solving a word problem.

3. **Numerical and Graphic Relationships**
   35% (approximately 17–18 questions)
   - Recognize relationships in numerical data.
   - Recognize the position of numbers in relation to each other.
   - Use the relations less than, greater than, or equal to and their associated symbols to express a numerical relationship.
   - Identify numbers, formulas, and mathematical expressions that are equivalent.
   - Understand basic logical connectives.
   - Identify or specify a missing entry from a table of data.
   - Use information presented in tables, spreadsheets, and graphs to solve math problems.

You need to answer approximately 60% of the questions correctly in order to pass the Mathematics Section of the CBEST.

WHAT THE CBEST DOESN'T TEST

The CBEST does not test any math you may have taken in college—no complex statistics, linear algebra, or calculus. In fact, most of the material tested on the CBEST was covered in your basic high school math classes. Even the geometry that is tested is very basic (in Chapter 6 we cover all the geometry you need)—no proofs, no theorems, no complex figures.

You won't see any complex math questions from trigonometry, calculus, or advanced statistics.

We aren't saying that the Mathematics Section should be easy—many CBEST test takers have not taken a math class in five, ten, maybe twenty years. If you haven't had math in a long time, pay close attention to the information presented in the upcoming chapters. It may take some time to relearn this information.

NO CALCULATOR

Calculators are not allowed on the test. To prepare for test day, make sure to practice completing the problems without a calculator. Some of the techniques covered will help you with this.

POE—MATHEMATICS STYLE

In Chapter 2, and in the reading chapters, we discussed the key technique to eliminating answer choices—Process of Elimination. POE also works very well on the Mathematics Section. As we go through the examples in this book, you may find that we aren't using traditional methods to solve a problem. We won't cite rules of advanced mathematics. We'll be showing you how to use the answer choices to work your way through the problem.

ELIMINATION BY BALLPARKING

Take a look at the following question:

> The area of a gymnasium floor is 3,675 square feet. If the basketball court covers 2,100 square feet, what percent of the gymnasium floor does the basketball court occupy?

Proven Technique

Ballparking is a tried-and-true Princeton Review technique that will help you tackle tough math problems quickly. At the very least, Ballparking enables you to eliminate unrealistic answer choices efficiently.

If you aren't sure how to set up this question, what would you do? You'd probably have to leave it blank and move on to another question. Without any answer choices, guessing doesn't really work, does it? Well, you could choose a number, and hope for the best. (If you aren't sure how to do a percent question, don't worry. We will review percent questions in detail in Chapter 6.)

On the CBEST, they give you five answer choices to choose from. At worst, you would have a one in five chance of getting the question correct. Let's take a look at the question again, this time with answer choices:

> The area of a gymnasium floor is 3,675 square feet. If the basketball court covers 2,100 square feet, approximately what percent of the gymnasium floor does the basketball court occupy?
>
> A. 14 percent
>
> B. 43 percent
>
> C. 50 percent
>
> D. 57 percent
>
> E. 74 percent

At first glance, this may not seem very different from our original problem. However, we now have a lot more to work with—the five answer choices. Sure, we could make a guess right now, and we'd have a one in five chance of getting the question correct. But let's not stop there. Let's see what the answer choices tell us. The first thing you need to ask is:

Does the Answer Choice Make Sense?

The basketball court covers 2,100 square feet out of a possible 3,675 square feet. Try to picture this in your head. Would the basketball court only take up a very small portion of the gymnasium? Would it take up half? More than half? If you estimate, you can tell that 2,100 square feet is more than half the total 3,675 square feet.

Eliminate Answer Choices That Are Out of the Ballpark

Eliminate answer choices on the Math Section by Ballparking the correct answer.

Okay, we know that the basketball court will take up more than half the space in the gymnasium. If we think about this in terms of percentages, we know that the basketball court covers more than 50 percent. Look at (A), (B), and (C). We know that these cannot be correct. So what should we do? Eliminate them! Now, we will choose between (D) and (E)—a 50 percent chance of getting the question correct. This is much better than the original one in five chance. (If you chose (D), you were correct.)

Ballparking is a tool for more than just percentage questions. It can be used for most mathematics questions on the CBEST. In fact, once you read a problem, the first thing you should ask yourself is "Do the answer choices make sense?" You'll find that you can eliminate many incorrect answer choices without doing numerous calculations. You may wonder why the CBEST authors include answer choices that we can eliminate using Ballparking. You can also eliminate partial choices, which CBEST authors often include, and which provide a common trap that students often fall into. Here is an example of a question involving partial answer choices:

> Brian has $250 a month in spending money. If Brian spends 20 percent on movies, and 15 percent of the remaining amount on baseball games, how much money does Brian have to spend after movies and baseball games?
>
> A. $30.00
>
> B. $50.00
>
> C. $80.00
>
> D. $163.50
>
> E. $170.00

Before we go straight to calculating the answer, let's ballpark. Brian is starting with $250, and we need to find out how much money he will have after movies and baseball games. Let's approximate. Is he spending over half his money? No. Thus, we should be able to eliminate (A), (B), and (C).

Here is how the CBEST writers incorporate partial answer choices into a question. This question requires several steps. Let's take the information we are given one step at a time.

Brian spends 20 percent of his money on movies. 20 percent of $250.00 = $50.00. Notice that answer choice (B) is a partial answer choice. If you lost track of what you needed to solve, you'd see that $50.00 number in your scratch work. However, we aren't done with this question!

Next, he spends 15 percent of the remaining amount at baseball games. The remaining amount is also a concept that CBEST writers love to use. What is the remaining amount? Brian started with $250.00; now, after spending $50.00, the remaining amount is $200.00. Thus, we need to find 15 percent of $200.00 (not of the original $250.00). 15 percent of $200.00 = $30.00. Notice again that this is a partial answer choice—eliminate (A).

Our final step is to find the amount of money Brian has left. He started with \$250.00, spent \$50.00 on movies, and \$30.00 on baseball games. If we subtract, we find

$$\begin{array}{r} \$250.00 \\ -\ \$50.00 \\ \underline{-\ \$30.00} \\ =\$170.00 \end{array}$$

(E) is the correct answer. Why did the CBEST writers include three answer choices that we were able to eliminate immediately? Because they wanted to provide partial answer choice traps. We already mentioned how (A) and (B) are answer choice traps. (C) is the total amount that Brian spent on the two activities. CBEST writers want to give you the opportunity to select a number that you've probably written down.

Can Partial Answer Choices Help You?

Absolutely. Because partial answer choices will appear on many of the mathematics questions on the CBEST, you need to learn to take advantage of them. First, if you recognize a partial answer choice as you are going through the problem, it probably means that you are doing the question correctly. Keep working! Second, it is generally a safe bet to eliminate any number you come up with as you are working through the steps of a problem. This will help you eliminate more answer choices.

When Should You Use Ballparking?

All the time. Even if you are absolutely sure how to set up a problem, evaluating the answer choices will give you some clues. Ballparking helps bring some clarity to a problem before you work too hard to find the exact answer. Ask yourself, "Do the answer choices make sense?" If they don't, eliminate them. If you find that your calculations lead you to one of these answer choices, you will know you've made an error. Take a step back, reread the problem, and start again.

Apply the Strategy

Even if you aren't sure how to solve a math question, eliminate as many answer choices as possible by Ballparking.

Common Sense Is Your Friend

Students often get so caught up trying to solve a problem that they simply forget to think. If you have a problem, and aren't sure of the specific formula or the exact method to solve the question, take a step back. Start by looking at the answer choices, and try to ballpark.

Even if you have no idea how to do a problem, don't simply guess and move on. Ballparking is most essential when you don't know how to solve a problem. In the previous examples, we demonstrated the value of being an intelligent guesser. The difference between guessing from among two or three possible choices, as opposed to five, will greatly affect your final mathematics score. Ballparking will help you to avoid careless errors, eliminate partial answer traps, and improve your chances of guessing correctly.

TAKING THE CBEST MATHEMATICS TEST

As we discussed in Chapter 2, there is no order of difficulty presented in the Mathematics Section. It is perfectly natural to start with question number one, then do question number two, question number three, and so on. However, as you proceed through the test, you will find that some questions are harder than others. You will want to maximize your time and effort on the easier questions, and spend less time on the harder questions.

NO ONE QUESTION MAY BEAT YOU

On most tests, there is always that one question that seems to haunt you. No matter how hard you work, you just can't seem to get it right. There are a number of reasons for this: You can't exactly remember the formula, you are miscalculating, or maybe it's just a mental block. We understand how frustrating this can be, especially when deep down inside you just know you can do the problem. Some students will spend unlimited time on a question that stumps them, just to "prove" to themselves they can do it.

Unfortunately, this stubbornness can really hurt your overall score. Precious minutes pass, leaving you rushed to complete the remaining questions. At some point, you will probably need to let a question go. Don't fret. You may have lost that battle, but you can still win the war. In fact, this is so important that we've designed a technique to help you avoid this trap.

Tailor your test toward your strengths—if you love algebra questions, make sure you have time to solve all algebra questions. If you hate geometry, save those as second-pass questions.

FIRST PASS, SECOND PASS

As we've mentioned, you need to get about 60 percent of the mathematics questions correct in order to pass the section. This leaves you with a lot of room to pick and choose the questions you want to spend time on. Of course, regardless of how many questions you do, you will be registering an answer for every question. By focusing on the questions you can handle, you will improve your accuracy and your score. Here is how to use this technique:

On your first pass, start at the beginning and do every problem that, after reading it, makes sense to you right away. If you get to a question that you have no idea how to solve, then you should leave the question and move on. If you're taking the paper-based version of the exam, circle these questions prominently in your test booklet in order to keep track of them. If you're taking the computer-based test, use the "Flag for Review" button provided. After you've answered all the first-pass questions in the section, go back and work on these questions.

Why go through all this trouble? We want to make sure that you are using your time to maximum efficiency. If you find that you can't answer all of the mathematics questions in the time you have, at least you've answered all the problems you know you can do.

Sometimes, when you start your second pass, you'll figure out exactly how to get one of the problems that stumped you on the first pass. Of course, there may still be some questions that, no matter how many times you read them, seem impossible to answer. But remember, no matter how bad a question may be, under no circumstances should you leave it blank. Let's say that one more time:

You may not leave a problem blank!

There is a big difference between leaving a question for later, and simply leaving a question blank. If you have no idea how to do a second-pass question, be sure to use Ballparking as a technique to eliminate answer choices. Eliminate what you can, and then select an answer choice. Before you turn in your bubble sheet, check to make sure that you have selected an answer for every question.

MATH ON PAPER, NOT IN YOUR HEAD

Avoid careless mistakes by writing down all calculations.

If you haven't taken a math class for years, or if you usually rely on a calculator or spreadsheet to do your work, it may take you a while to get comfortable working with numbers again. It is crucial that you do all your work on paper (or on the booklet of erasable sheets provided), and not in your head. Writing down your calculations will do more than improve your accuracy—you'll be able to eliminate partial answer choices based on the numbers you've written in your test booklet as you go through the steps for each problem.

If you're taking the paper-based exam, cross off answer choices in your test booklet when you eliminate them. If you're taking the computer-based version, use your pen and erasable sheets to carefully write down the letters corresponding to eliminated answer choices and cross them out. Doing so will help avoid confusion and, if you need to guess, you'll clearly see which answer choices remain.

PRACTICE CORRECTLY

It is important that you practice these math problems in the same way you will be taking the test. Don't practice using a calculator. Be sure to do calculations in this book, and to mark off incorrect answer choices. It takes a while to adapt, and you don't want to be trying these things for the first time during the actual test. The three tests in the back of this book should provide excellent practice.

Summary

Here are some general points to remember throughout the entire Mathematics Section:

- The CBEST Mathematics Section contains 50 questions on only a few areas of math:
    - Estimation, Measurement, and Statistical Principles—30%
    - Computation and Problem Solving—35%
    - Numerical and Graphic Relationships—35%
- Complicated math topics, such as trigonometry, calculus, proofs, and theorems, are not tested on the CBEST.
- A type of POE, called Ballparking, enables you to eliminate answer choices that don't make sense because they are either too big or too small.
- Ballparking will help you recognize and avoid partial answer choices.
- Do the Mathematics Section using the first-pass, second-pass system:
    - Use the first pass for the problems you recognize and know how to solve.
    - Leave questions you are unsure of until the second pass.
- You must answer every question. There is no penalty for guessing.
- There is guessing, and then there is guessing! Always ask yourself if you can eliminate any answer choices.
- To practice getting ready for the CBEST without the help of a calculator, write all of your calculations on paper.

Chapter 6
Basic Math

MATHEMATICS REVIEW

Before we start reviewing the specific types of questions tested on the CBEST, you should be certain that you are familiar with some basic terms and concepts that you will need to know for the CBEST. This material is not very difficult, and the sample problems are not representative of actual CBEST questions. However, you must know this information backward and forward. If you don't, you'll lose valuable points on the test and have trouble setting up problems correctly.

Math Flashbacks

Is zero a positive number? Is zero an integer? While these may seem more like trivia questions than crucial CBEST information, knowing the basics helps us understand and correctly set up problems. The difficulty, however, is that you learned some of this information in the third grade! We understand that you may be a little rusty, so, let's flash back to the basics. We think you'll be surprised by the number of times you say, "Oh yeah, I remember that."

The Number Line

The number line is a two-dimensional way of looking at positive and negative numbers.

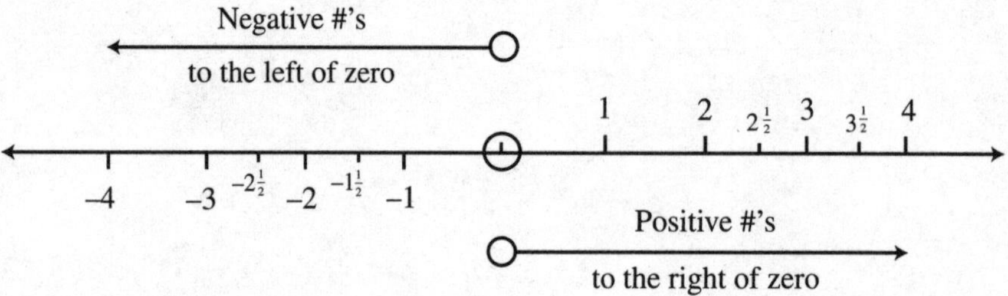

Facts about zero: Zero is neither positive nor negative.

A positive number is defined as any number greater than zero—that is, any number located to the right of zero on the number line. A negative number is any number less than zero—that is, any number located to the left of zero on the number line. What about zero? Zero is neither positive nor negative.

Numbers get larger the farther they move toward the right on the number line. For example, 15 is larger than 2, since it is farther to the right on the number line. Numbers get smaller the farther they move toward the left on the number line. This means that –4 is smaller than –3. It may seem contradictory that a 4 is smaller than a 3, but remember, –4 is farther to the left than is –3.

Combining Positive and Negative Numbers

What's 4 + 3? Seven, of course. We can use the number line to help us add. When you add two positive numbers, you are simply counting to the right on a number line. In our example, we count 4 spaces to the right, and then another three spaces, giving us 7 total spaces to the right. 4 + 3 = 7.

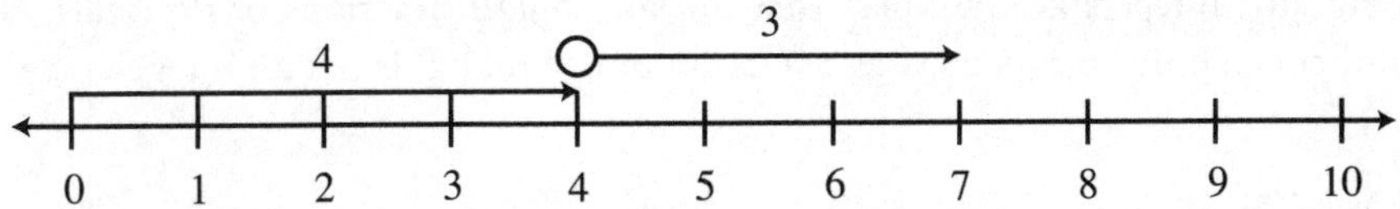

Well, that was probably the silliest paragraph you've read so far. But stay with us. The number line can also help us to add positive and negative numbers together. What if we wanted to find the sum of 6 and –2? To do this, count 6 spaces to the right of zero on the number line (positive 6). Next, to add –2, count over 2 spaces to the left. Where did you stop? 4? Perfect.

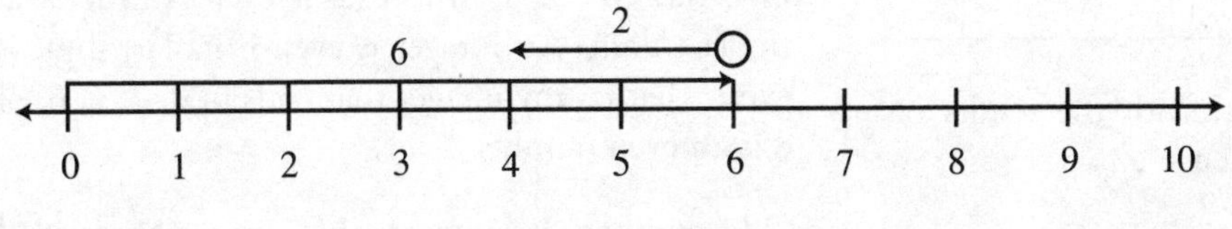

Thus, $6 + (-2) = 4$.

Adding a negative number is the same thing as subtracting a positive number. We could rewrite the addition problem above as the following:

$$6 - 2 = 4$$

Visualize the number line to help you work with positive and negative numbers.

More Great Books
Do you need to brush up on your math basics? Check out *Math Smart*, also from The Princeton Review.

Positive and Negative Numbers—Multiplication Rules

Here are a few rules to remember when multiplying positive and negative numbers together:

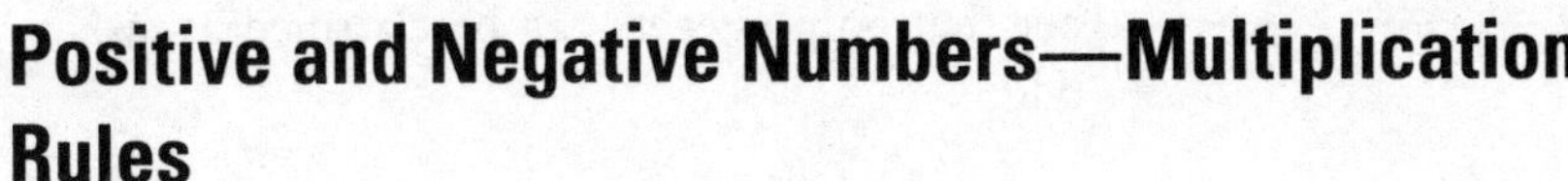

1. positive × positive = positive $\quad 2 \times 3 = 6$
2. negative × negative = positive $\quad -2 \times -3 = 6$
3. positive × negative = negative $\quad -2 \times 3 = -6$

Integers

Integers are a specific type of number. Examples of integers are:

1, 2, 3, 4, 400, 389, 27, –912...

Facts About Zero: Zero is an integer.

Zero is also an integer. Therefore, we can break up the group of integers into positive integers (1, 2, 3, 4, and so on); negative integers (–1, –2, –3, –4, and so on), and zero. There are an infinite number of integers. So what *isn't* an integer? Here are a few examples:

$$332.7, -\frac{33}{2}, 27.246857, \pi \ldots$$

Essentially, integers are numbers that do not contain fractions or decimals. If a number can only be expressed as a fraction or decimal, it is not an integer.

Odd and Even Numbers

The terms odd and even are used to describe certain types of integers. Even numbers are integers that can be divided evenly by 2. Examples of even numbers are:

–24, –2, 0, 4, 8, 12, 416...

One way to tell if an integer is even is to look at the last digit. An integer is even if its last digit is even. That is, any integer that ends in 0, 2, 4, 6, or 8 is an even number.

Odd numbers are integers that cannot be divided evenly by 2. If an integer isn't an even number, it's an odd number. Examples of odd numbers are:

–25, –3, 1, 3, 5, 7, 9, 9245...

One way to tell if a number is odd is to look at the last digit. An integer is odd if its last digit is odd.

Notice that zero is an even number (even though zero is neither positive nor negative). Also, remember that only integers can be classified as even or odd.

Here are some rules that deal with the results of combining even and odd numbers:

1. even × even = even
2. odd × odd = odd
3. even × odd = even
4. even + even = even
5. odd + odd = even
6. even + odd = odd

While it is helpful to have these rules memorized, you can always recreate them by trying an example.

INTEGERS DRILL

Answers can be found at the end of this chapter.

1. Circle the numbers in the list that are **integers**:

1	0.333	1,024	–2.5
2.54	$-\frac{2}{3}$	–62	239
10	0	$\frac{1}{4}$	4.768
24	$-\frac{5}{6}$	1.5	–756
–0.58	–3	98	

2. Circle the numbers in the list that are **even**:

26	1	160	276
557	94	0	1,035
	67	77	

Places and Digits

What are the digits? (We aren't talking about your fingers and toes here.) There are ten digits: 0, 1, 2, 3, 4, 5, 6, 7, 8, 9

Digits are used to create numbers, just like the alphabet is used to create words. The number 324,856 is made up of six different digits. Each of these digits is in a "place." A place indicates where the digit is located within the number. Let's use the following number to review the places of a number:

243.789

The 2 is in the *hundreds* place. Its value is 2×100 or 200

The 4 is in the *tens* place. Its value is 4×10 or 40

The 3 is in the *units* place. Its value is 3×1 or 3

Another term to describe the "units" place is the "ones" place.

The 7 is in the *tenths* place. Its value is $\frac{7}{10}$, or .7

The 8 is in the *hundredths* place. Its value is $\frac{8}{100}$, or .08

The 9 is in the *thousandths* place. Its value is $\frac{9}{1000}$, or .009

Adding all the numbers together gives you 243.789

PLACE VALUE DRILL

Answers can be found at the end of the chapter.

Identify the **place value** of each underlined digit.

1. $\underline{3}0.92$
2. $76\underline{8}$
3. $4{,}\underline{8}65$
4. $6.\underline{7}03$
5. $0.03\underline{1}2$

Arithmetic Operations

There are only a few arithmetic operations that are tested on the CBEST:

1. addition ($4 + 8 = 12$)
2. subtraction ($12 - 8 = 4$)
3. multiplication ($4 \times 8 = 32$ or $8 \times 4 = 32$)
4. division ($32 \div 4 = 8$)
5. raising to a power ($3^2 = 9$)
6. finding a square root ($\sqrt{25} = 5$)

(Note that these last two operations, raising to a power and finding a square root, rarely appear on the CBEST).

You are probably very familiar with the first four math operations. When you use these operations, there is a special name for each result. These are listed below:

1. The result of addition is a **sum.**
2. The result of subtraction is a **difference.**
3. The result of multiplication is a **product.**
4. The result of division is a **quotient.**

PEMDAS

Let's say we wanted to find the result of the following expression:

$$6 + 10 \div 5 - 3 \times 2 + (3 \times 5)$$

There are a number of different operations that we will need to perform in order to simplify this expression. In fact, you will see many CBEST questions that ask you to solve a problem using many different operations. There is a specific order in which these operations must be performed in order to simplify the expression correctly. What is the order? Just remember one thing:

PEMDAS

Many students have learned this as "Please Excuse My Dear Aunt Sally" (although no one seems to remember the story behind the phrase). This acronym stands for the following math operations: Parentheses, Exponents, Multiplication, Division, Addition, and Subtraction.

In other words, the correct order of operations is as follows:

1. **Parentheses** (also known as **brackets**) are always dealt with first. Example:

$$72 \div (2 \times 9)$$
$$72 \div 18 = \mathbf{4}$$

2. **Exponents** have the highest priority after parentheses. Example:

$$72 \div 3^2$$
$$72 \div 9 = \mathbf{8}$$

3. **Multiplication and Division** have higher priority than addition and subtraction. Example:

$$18 \times 2 - 5$$
$$36 - 5 = \mathbf{31}$$

Also, remember to solve multiplication and division together, from **left to right**. Example:

$$18 \div 2 \times 3$$
$$9 \times 3 = \mathbf{27}$$

4. **Addition and Subtraction** have the lowest priority. Remember to solve addition and subtraction together, from **left to right**. Example:

$$15 - 5 + 3$$
$$10 + 3 = \mathbf{13}$$

Most CBEST questions will be designed to give you a clear understanding of the order in which you must perform the operations. However, if you are unsure of exactly the order in which to solve a problem, be sure to use the rules of PEMDAS.

Let's go back to the previous expression, and solve it using the rules of PEMDAS:

$$6 + 10 \div 5 - 3 \times 2 + (3 \times 5)$$

Step 1: Solve all work inside the parentheses. $3 \times 5 = 15$, so our problem now looks like:

$$6 + 10 \div 5 - 3 \times 2 + 15$$

Step 2: There are no exponents, so we move to multiplication and division, moving from left to right in the expression:

$$6 + 2 - 6 + 15$$

Step 3: We finish the problem by using addition and subtraction, moving from left to right in the expression:

$$8 - 6 + 15$$
$$2 + 15$$
$$17$$

ORDER OF OPERATIONS DRILL

Here are some additional problems to practice the correct order of operations. Answers can be found at the end of this chapter.

1. $310 + (200 - 194) =$ _____
2. $(5 + 3) \times 7 =$ _____
3. $5 \times 7 - 3 \times 5 =$ _____
4. $2 \times [7 - 6 \div 3] =$ _____
5. $12 - 5 \times 3 + 7 =$ _____
6. $13 + 6 \times 3 =$ _____
7. $121 - 6 + 10 =$ _____
8. $(21 + 17) / (11 + 8) =$ _____
9. $6(7 + 1) \div 3 =$ _____
10. $23 \times 0 + 15 \times 1 =$ _____

Factors

Factors are defined as numbers that divide evenly into your original number. For example, the factors of 24 are: 1, 2, 3, 4, 6, 8, 12, and 24.

Factors = the smaller numbers that divide into your original number

If you are asked to find the factors of a number, the best way to make sure you don't leave any out is to find them in pairs. For instance, if you are asked to find the factors of 36, count in pairs, starting with (1 × 36).

The pairs that make 36 are: (1 × 36), (2 × 18), (3 × 12), (4 × 9), and (6 × 6). Thus, the factors of 36 are 1, 36, 2, 18, 3, 12, 4, 9, and 6.

FACTORS DRILL

Answers can be found at the end of this chapter.

List all of the **factors** of each number.

1. 18
2. 105
3. 90
4. 156
5. 76

Multiples

Multiples are defined as numbers that your original number will divide into evenly. For example, the multiples of 4 are 4, 8, 12, 16, 20, 24, etc. One way to remember multiples is to think of your "times tables." To find the multiples of 4, start with 4 × 1 = 4, then 4 × 2 = 8, 4 × 3 = 12, and so on.

Students often have trouble remembering the difference between factors and multiples. When you think of factors, think of fractions, or the smaller pieces of a number; when you are asked to find multiples, think of multiplying, and use the times tables in order to calculate the multiples.

- What are the *multiples* of the number 12? 12, 24, 36, 48, and so on.
- What are the *factors* of the number 12? 1, 2, 3, 4, 6, 12.

Multiples = the larger numbers (think multiply)
Factors = the smaller numbers (think fractions)

MULTIPLES DRILL

Answers can be found at the end of this chapter.

List the first five **multiples** of each number.

1. 12
2. 15
3. 20
4. 9
5. 11

Fractions

Fractions = Division

A fraction is defined as a part of a whole. A fraction is just another way of expressing division. $\frac{x}{y}$ is the same thing as x divided by y. The expression $\frac{1}{2}$ is the same thing as 1 divided by 2. The top part of the fraction (x in the example above) is known as the **numerator**. The bottom part of the fraction (y in the example above) is known as the **denominator**. These terms aren't tested on the CBEST, but you should be familiar with them for the explanations that will follow.

Reducing Fractions

A fraction can be expressed in many different ways. For example:

$$\frac{50}{100}=\frac{25}{50}=\frac{10}{20}=\frac{4}{8}=\frac{2}{4}=\frac{1}{2}$$

When you add or multiply fractions, you will often end up with a big fraction that may not appear in the answer choices. In order to find the correct answer, you will need to know how to reduce a fraction to its simplest value.

To reduce a fraction, divide both the numerator and the denominator by the same factor. This process may take several steps. While it may save time to find the largest number that will divide into both numbers, try to keep your pencil moving. Don't worry about whether two numbers will both divide by 24! Start with nice, small numbers. See if both parts of the fraction can be divided by 2, 3, or 5. If you find that you need to reduce again, fine. You'll get to the final result in no time.

Take, for example, the fraction $\frac{12}{60}$. What can we divide numerator 12 and denominator 60 by? If you saw that they are both divisible by 12, great! The fraction will reduce to $\frac{1}{5}$. If you didn't see that right away, don't panic. Start with an easy number. Both 12 and 60 are even, so start with 2. This will result in $\frac{6}{30}$. Try reducing by 3—now we're down to $\frac{2}{10}$. Divide by 2 again, and you've got $\frac{1}{5}$. This might take a few more steps, but it will get you the correct answer nonetheless.

If possible, try to reduce fractions before performing operations with them. This will help you save time, and avoid errors that come up when you start to manipulate large numbers.

REDUCING FRACTIONS DRILL

Answers can be found at the end of this chapter.

Reduce each fraction to its simplest form.

1. $\frac{4}{12}$
2. $\frac{10}{75}$
3. $\frac{18}{21}$
4. $\frac{45}{120}$
5. $\frac{99}{117}$

Adding or Subtracting Fractions with the Same Denominator

In order to add two or more fractions with the same denominator, simply add the numerators of each fraction. The denominator will be the common denominator in each fraction. Here is an example:

$$\frac{3}{4}+\frac{1}{4}=\frac{3+1}{4}=\frac{4}{4}=1$$

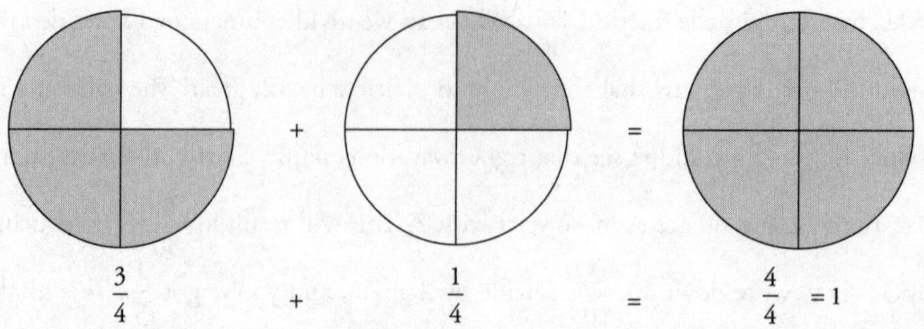

$$\frac{3}{4} + \frac{1}{4} = \frac{4}{4} = 1$$

Subtraction works in exactly the same way:

$$\frac{3}{4}-\frac{1}{4}=\frac{3-1}{4}=\frac{2}{4}=\frac{1}{2}$$

Converting Mixed Numbers to Fractions

The CBEST loves to use mixed numbers—that is, a number that contains both a whole number and a fraction. An example of a mixed number is $3\frac{4}{5}$. When you come across a mixed number, you should usually convert it into a fraction (often referred to as an improper fraction, since the numerator will be greater than the denominator). Let's convert $3\frac{4}{5}$ into a standard fraction.

First, convert the integer part of the number into a fraction with the same denominator as the fraction part of the number. In this example, we want to turn the integer 3 into a fraction with a denominator of 5:

$$3=\frac{3}{1}=\frac{15}{5}$$

Next, add the two fractions with a common denominator together:

$$\frac{15}{5}+\frac{4}{5}=\frac{19}{5}$$

Often, CBEST questions will require you to perform operations involving two different mixed numbers. Converting mixed numbers into fractions will help make your calculations easier.

The Bowtie

Unfortunately, not all fraction problems will contain fractions with the same denominator. There is a way to add and subtract fractions with different denominators. Remember the phrase "least common denominator?" This is the method used most often to teach fractions. To use it, you need to find the smallest number that is a multiple of both denominators. This generally involves a lot of counting (the multiples of 4 are 4, 8, 12, 16, 20...; the multiples of 5 are 5, 10, 15, 20...), and is occasionally a frustrating experience.

Welcome to the Bowtie. The Bowtie is a powerful tool to help simplify the process of adding, subtracting, and comparing fractions. The example below will show you how the Bowtie is used:

$$\overset{4}{\frac{1}{3}} + \overset{9}{\frac{3}{4}} = \overset{13}{\frac{13}{12}}$$

The first step is to multiply in the direction of each arrow. Write each number on top of the fraction at the top of the arrow. Next, use the sign (in this case, addition) to combine the two numbers you just wrote down. In the example above, we added 4 and 9 together, giving us 13 as the numerator. Finally, in order to find the denominator, multiply the two denominators together. The resulting fraction is $\frac{13}{12}$.

The beauty of the Bowtie is that you don't have to sit there trying to come up with a common denominator. Simply multiply, add (or subtract), and you're done!

Multiplying Fractions

To multiply fractions, line them up and multiply straight across:

$$\frac{4}{5} \times \frac{5}{6} = \frac{20}{30} = \frac{2}{3}$$

We performed one multiplication problem above another. Across the top of the fractions, we multiplied 4 and 5; across the bottom of the fractions, we multiplied 5 and 6.

However, there is an even easier way to solve the fraction problem above.

When multiplying two fractions, always look to see if you can reduce first. In the problem above, we can cancel the 5 from the numerator and denominator, because $\frac{5}{5} = 1$.

$$\frac{(4 \times \cancel{5})}{(\cancel{5} \times 6)} \times \frac{(4 \times 1)}{(1 \times 6)} = \frac{4}{6}$$

Multiplying two fractions will yield a product less than the original fractions.

Generally, when we think of multiplying two numbers, we think of the product being larger than the original numbers (for example, 10 × 7 = 70). But with fractions, the product is smaller than the original numbers: $\frac{1}{10} \times \frac{1}{7} = \frac{1}{70}$, a number much smaller than $\frac{1}{10}$ or $\frac{1}{7}$.

Next, we can divide the numerator and denominator by 2.

$$\frac{4}{6} = \frac{2}{3}$$

In general, your calculations will be easier if you take a moment to reduce before you multiply.

Dividing Fractions

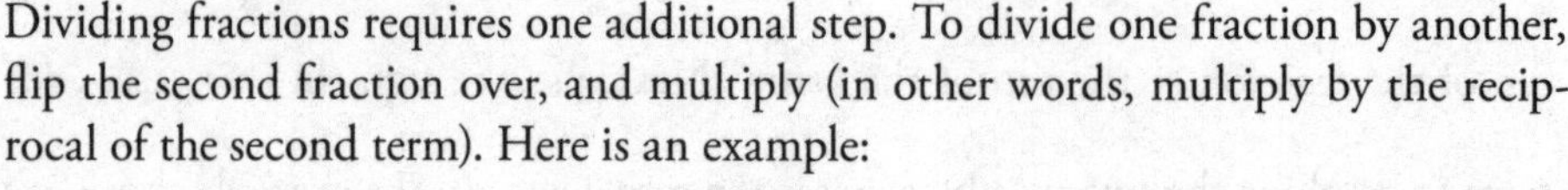

Dividing fractions requires one additional step. To divide one fraction by another, flip the second fraction over, and multiply (in other words, multiply by the reciprocal of the second term). Here is an example:

Remember

When you divide, don't ask why—just flip it over and multiply!

$$\frac{4}{5} \div \frac{3}{10} =$$

$$\frac{4}{5} \times \frac{10}{3}$$

Now we can reduce the 10 and the 5, and get the final result $\frac{8}{3}$.

Make sure that you reduce only after you have flipped the second fraction. Sometimes students get confused when whole numbers are involved, such as

$$\frac{6}{\frac{2}{3}}$$

Remember, a whole number can be a fraction, by placing the whole number over 1.

In this problem, we have $\frac{\frac{6}{1}}{\frac{2}{3}}$, which is the same as $\frac{6}{1} \div \frac{2}{3}$. Now, we can flip the second fraction, giving us $\frac{6}{1} \times \frac{3}{2}$. The final result is $\frac{18}{2}$, or 9.

Pay careful attention before identifying the larger fraction.

It is easy to recognize that 6 is greater than 2. Remember, though, that $\frac{1}{6}$ is much less than $\frac{1}{2}$. If you are unsure which fraction is larger, remember to use the Bowtie to compare.

Comparing Fractions

The CBEST sometimes contains problems that require you to identify which of two fractions is larger. When fractions have the same denominator, it is easy to tell which amount is bigger. For example, which fraction is larger, $\frac{1}{4}$ or $\frac{3}{4}$? The answer is $\frac{3}{4}$. 3 parts out of 4 is clearly larger than 1 part out of 4. When two fractions have the same denominator, simply choose the fraction with the larger numerator.

Comparing fractions becomes somewhat more difficult when the fractions do not have a common denominator. Which fraction is greater, $\frac{4}{7}$ or $\frac{3}{5}$? The most efficient way to compare these fractions is to use the Bowtie again. Here, we'll use the first step of the Bowtie—cross multiply as the arrows indicate below:

The Bowtie can also be used to compare two fractions.

$$^{20}\frac{4}{7} \times \frac{3}{5}^{21}$$

The result of 4 × 5 is 20, so we write this above the fraction $\frac{4}{7}$; the other arrow gives us a result of 21. Now, compare the two products we just calculated. Which one is bigger? 21. Since 21 is the larger product, the fraction underneath, $\frac{3}{5}$, is the larger fraction!

Once again, the Bowtie will save you time when working with fractions. This is much more efficient than turning these fractions into decimals, or finding a common denominator.

COMPARING FRACTIONS DRILL

Answers can be found at the end of this chapter.

Indicate which fraction is **larger**.

1. $\frac{3}{8}$ or $\frac{5}{8}$
2. $\frac{5}{7}$ or $\frac{5}{12}$
3. $\frac{4}{9}$ or $\frac{6}{13}$
4. $\frac{3}{5}$ or $\frac{8}{11}$
5. $\frac{10}{7}$ or $\frac{14}{9}$

FRACTION DRILL

Answers can be found at the end of this chapter.

1. $\frac{6}{4} \times \frac{5}{9} =$ _____
2. $\frac{22}{45} \times \frac{15}{33} =$ _____
3. $\frac{7}{12} \div \frac{28}{3} =$ _____
4. $\dfrac{\frac{3}{5}}{\frac{9}{10}} =$ _____
5. $\frac{2}{9} + \frac{3}{4} =$ _____
6. $\frac{5}{4} - \frac{1}{3} =$ _____
7. $\frac{7}{9} + \frac{5}{2} - \frac{5}{6} + \frac{2}{3} =$ _____
8. $2\frac{3}{8} - 1\frac{4}{5} =$ _____
9. $\frac{3}{8} \div \frac{9}{7} =$ _____
10. $\dfrac{\frac{1}{4}}{\frac{3}{8} + \frac{4}{5}} =$ _____
11. $5\frac{3}{7} + 2\frac{7}{12} =$ _____
12. $\frac{2}{5} + \frac{4}{11} + \frac{5}{6} + \frac{7}{11} + \frac{1}{6} + \frac{3}{5} =$ _____

Decimals

You will learn more about decimals in Chapter 9, Numerical and Graphical Relationships.

As we mentioned earlier, fractions are simply a way to indicate division. Fractions can also be expressed as decimals. Any fraction can be converted into a decimal, and vice-versa. You probably know some already ($\frac{1}{2} = .5; \frac{1}{4} = .25$, etc.). In order to find the decimal equivalent of a fraction, simply divide the numerator by the denominator. For example,

$$\frac{3}{4} = 3 \div 4 = .75$$

Adding and Subtracting Decimals

In order to add or subtract decimals, you must align the decimal places of all the numbers. Then simply add or subtract. Some examples are:

Align the decimal points before adding or subtracting decimals.

$$\begin{array}{r} 2.72 \\ +\underline{3.46} \\ =6.18 \end{array} \qquad \begin{array}{r} 8.19 \\ -\underline{1.54} \\ =6.65 \end{array}$$

If you are trying to add or subtract two decimals, and the two numbers do not have the same number of digits, you will need to add zeros to fill out the places in each number. For example, if we want to find the difference between 8.3 and 2.784, we first need to set up the problem:

$$\begin{array}{r} 8.3 \\ -\underline{2.784} \end{array}$$

To make the problem complete, add zeros to the end of the first number (in the hundredths and thousandths places). The problem should look like:

$$\begin{array}{r} 8.300 \\ -\underline{2.784} \\ =5.516 \end{array}$$

Multiplying Decimals

The best way to multiply decimals is to ignore any decimal points until you have completed the multiplication. Once you complete the problem, count the number of digits that are located to the right of all decimal points. Then place the decimal point that number of places to the left in the final result. Let's look at the following example:

$$\begin{array}{r} 2.45 \\ \times\ \underline{3.2} \\ =\ 490 \\ +\underline{7350} \\ 7840 \end{array}$$

Now, there are three numbers located to the right of the decimal point, so we need to move the decimal three places to the left. Starting with the 0, count over three places to the left. The final result is 7.840.

Dividing Decimals

When diving decimals, you need to make sure that the divisor (the number you are dividing by) is a whole number. For example, if you are given the problem:

Before dividing decimals, make sure the denominator is a whole number.

$$1.86 \div .3$$

The easiest way to solve this is to put it into fraction form:

$$\frac{1.86}{.3}$$

Now we must first turn the divisor (.3) into a whole number. In order to make .3 a whole number, we move the decimal point one place to the right. Whatever you do to the bottom part of the fraction, you must do to the top part. So, we need to move the decimal point in 1.86 one to the right, resulting in 18.6. Now, our division problem looks like:

$$\frac{18.6}{3} = 6.2$$

DECIMAL DRILL

Answers can be found at the end of this chapter.

1. $8.654 - 3.27 =$ _____
2. $1.354 + 8.207 =$ _____
3. $12.9 \times 25.8 =$ _____
4. $12.8 \div 6.25 =$ _____
5. $21.6 \div 8 =$ _____
6. $\frac{12.9 \times 3.1}{0.3} =$ _____
7. $2.561 - 3.45 =$ _____
8. $15.86 \times 0.2 =$ _____
9. $\frac{6.34 \times 5.18}{0.6} =$ _____
10. $5.954 + 0.014 =$ _____

PERCENTAGES

A percent is a number out of 100.

Percentages are very similar to fractions and decimals. In fact, a percent is really just a fraction whose denominator is 100. The word "percent" means "out of 100."

$$50\% = \frac{50}{100} = .5$$

$$47\% = \frac{47}{100} = .47$$

As you can see, percentages can be converted into fractions and decimals, and vice versa. In order to convert a fraction into a percentage, usually the easiest thing to do is to first convert the fraction into a decimal. Then, multiply the decimal by 100 in order to get the percentage. For example:

$$\frac{3}{4} = 3 \div 4 = .75(\times 100) = 75\%$$

$$\frac{6}{10} = 6 \div 10 = .6(\times 100) = 60\%$$

This process will work for any fraction. However, it does require a few steps. There are a few fractions that show up often on the CBEST and are worth memorizing. Review the chart below.

Fraction	Decimal	Percent
$\frac{1}{100}$	.01	1%
$\frac{1}{8}$	.125	12.5%
$\frac{1}{5}$	.2	20%
$\frac{1}{4}$	.25	25%
$\frac{1}{3}$	.333...	33.3%
$\frac{2}{5}$	.4	40%
$\frac{1}{2}$	.5	50%
$\frac{3}{5}$	.6	60%
$\frac{2}{3}$	.666...	66.7%
$\frac{3}{4}$	.75	75%
$\frac{4}{5}$	.8	80%

Quick and Easy Percent Calculation

Break down a complex percent question into easy percentage calculations.

Percent problems can often be solved by calculating "easy" percentages such as 1% and 10%. Instead of immediately doing detailed calculations, break down the work into these "easy" percentages. For example,

What is 23% of 520?

We can answer this question by first finding 20% of 520, and then adding 3% of 520. To find 10% of a number, simply move the decimal point one place to the left.

To find 1% of any number, just move the decimal point of that number over two places to the left. So, we have:

$$10\% \text{ of } 520 = 52$$
$$1\% \text{ of } 520 = 5.2$$
$$23\% \text{ of } 520 = 52 + 52 + 5.2 + 5.2 + 5.2 = 119.6$$

With a little practice, you'll find that you'll be able to solve percentage questions with minimal calculation.

In general, when solving for a quantity of people, the answer should be a whole number. Ask yourself if it makes sense to have fractions of people in a classroom. The same is true for objects such as cars (can there be fractions of cars in a parking lot?).

1. A school district is proposing a 15% decrease in the number of students per classroom. Currently there are 20 students per classroom. How many students per classroom would there be with the proposed decrease?

A. 23 students

B. 19 students

C. 18.5 students

D. 17 students

E. 16 students

Here's How to Crack It

We need to find 15% of 20. Using the techniques discussed above, we can break 15% down into 10% and 5%. 10% of 20 is 2. Half of that is 1. Thus, 15% is 2 + 1, or 3 students. Since the school district is proposing to decrease the number of students, subtract 3 from 20. The new total would be 20 – 3 = 17. Choice (D) is the correct answer.

Translating Percentages

Many percent questions will be in the form of a word problem. In order to set up the problem correctly, you'll need to be able to translate words into their mathematical equivalents. Here are some key terms to translate:

Tip! Translate percent word problems into their mathematical equivalents.

Of = Multiply ("$\frac{1}{3}$ of 24" translates to: $\frac{1}{3} \times 24$)

Percent = # out of 100 ("30%" translates to: $\frac{30}{100}$)

What = Variable ("30% of what" translates to: $\frac{30}{100}x$)

Is, Are, Were = Equals Sign ("$\frac{1}{3}$ of x is 12" translates to: $\frac{1}{3}x = 12$)

2. Teresa took a science test with 40 questions. If she missed 7 questions, and left 9 unanswered, what percent of the questions did Teresa answer correctly?

   A. 9%

   B. 16%

   C. 27%

   D. 40%

   E. 60%

Here's How to Crack It

In order to set up a math equation for the above problem, translate the last sentence.

"What percent" translates to: $\frac{x}{100}$.

"Of the questions" translates to: $\times 40$

"did she answer correctly" translates to: $= 24$ (the number of questions she answered correctly can be found by subtracting 7 and 9 from 40). Thus, the equation reads:

$$\frac{x}{100} \times 40 = 24$$

Now, we can manipulate the equation to find the percent.

$$\frac{x}{100} \times 40 = 24$$

$$\frac{x}{100} = \frac{24}{40}$$

$$\frac{x}{100} = \frac{3}{5}$$

$$x = \frac{300}{5}$$

$$x = 60$$

Choice (E) is the correct answer. Notice that there are several partial answer choices, including 40% (the amount of questions Teresa did *not* answer correctly).

Don't forget that Ballparking, as always, is helpful on this problem. If you recognized that Teresa answered over half of the questions correctly, then only (E), will work.

Percent Change

Some CBEST questions will ask you to find a percent increase or decrease between two values. Whether you're solving for percent increase or percent decrease, you should use the percent change formula:

$$\%\text{Increase or Decrease} = \frac{\text{Difference}}{\text{Original Amount}} \times 100$$

3. In 1995, Company X sold a total of 40,000 computers. In 1996, Company X sold a total of 50,000 computers. By what percent did sales of computers increase for Company X from 1995 to 1996?

   A. 20%

   B. 25%

   C. 50%

   D. 65%

   E. 80%

Here's How to Crack It

The question asks for a percent increase, so we need to use the percent change formula. Your equation should look like:

$$\%\text{Increase} = \frac{10{,}000}{40{,}000} \times 100$$

It can often be confusing to determine which of the following numbers is defined as the original amount. In this case, we are asked to solve a percent increase, so our original amount is the lower number (the number from 1995).

Once we've set up the problem as above, we have $\frac{1}{4} \times 100 = 0.25 \times 100 = 25$, so our percent is 25%. Choice (B) is the correct answer.

An easy rule to remember is this: If the question asks for a percent decrease, the original amount is the *higher* number. If the question asks for a percent increase, the original amount is the *lower* number.

Beware of partial answer choices! Notice that 20% is also an answer choice. If you incorrectly made 50,000 the original amount, you would have gotten 20% as the correct answer. Be careful on these questions—CBEST writers will always include these trap answer choices.

MEASUREMENT

According to the authors of the CBEST, you will be required to "understand and use standard units of length, temperature, weight, and capacity in the U.S. measurement system." In order to solve measurement questions, you will need to learn two things: conversions, and how to set up a conversion equation. First, here are a number of common measurements that you should know for the test:

Length:	12 inches	=	1 foot
	3 feet	=	1 yard
Therefore,			
	36 inches	=	1 yard

Temperature: In any temperature question, the equation $F = \frac{9}{5}C + 32$ will be provided. Common temperature questions will give you a temperature in one scale, and ask you to find the temperature in the other scale.

Weight:	16 ounces	=	1 pound
	2,000 pounds	=	1 ton
Capacity:	2 cups	=	1 pint
	2 pints	=	1 quart
	4 quarts	=	1 gallon
Time:	60 seconds	=	1 minute
	60 minutes	=	1 hour
	24 hours	=	1 day
	7 days	=	1 week
	52 weeks	=	1 year

Now that you've learned these conversions, let's see how to solve a typical conversion problem:

4. Kathleen jogs for exactly $1\frac{1}{2}$ hours per day. How many seconds does Kathleen spend jogging each day?

A. 90

B. 150

C. 1,800

D. 3,600

E. 5,400

Here's How to Crack It

We are given an amount of time expressed in hours and need to convert it to seconds. One way to solve is with a proportion. Some problems take more than one proportion step.

Here, we can start by converting hours to minutes. Be certain that your units are the same in each fraction!

For more on proportions, see page 144.

$$\left(\frac{1 \text{ hour}}{60 \text{ minutes}} = \frac{1.5 \text{ hours}}{x \text{ minutes}}\right)$$

$$\text{Cross multiply: } 60 \times 1.5 = 1 \times x$$

$$x = 90 \text{ minutes}$$

Next, we need to convert minutes to seconds. Simply use a second proportion (note that we used a different variable y this time, just to avoid confusion):

$$\left(\frac{1 \text{ minute}}{60 \text{ seconds}} = \frac{90 \text{ minutes}}{y \text{ seconds}}\right)$$

Cross multiply: $60 \times 90 = 1 \times y$

$y = 5400$ seconds

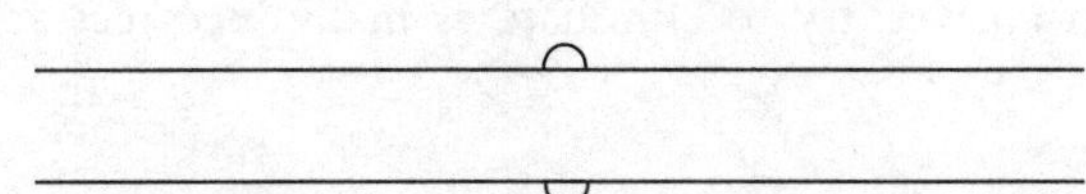

5. Fiona is preparing her favorite appetizer. If the recipe calls for 4 pounds of ground beef for one serving, how many ounces of ground beef will she need for two servings?

A. 12

B. 16

C. 64

D. 128

E. 140

Here's How to Crack It

First, convert pounds to ounces, using a proportion:

$$\left(\frac{1 \text{ pound}}{16 \text{ ounces}} = \frac{4 \text{ pounds}}{x \text{ ounces}}\right)$$

You should calculate the result to be 64 ounces.

Reading the problem carefully, we see that this is the amount for 1 serving; however, Fiona needs two servings. Multiply $64 \times 2 = 128$.

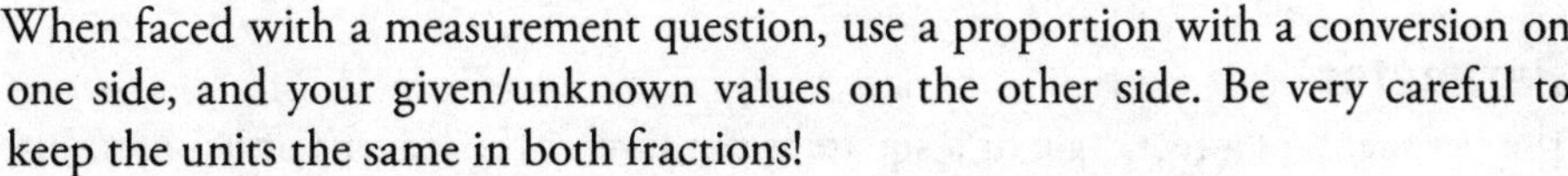

When faced with a measurement question, use a proportion with a conversion on one side, and your given/unknown values on the other side. Be very careful to keep the units the same in both fractions!

There will be no proofs or theorems on the CBEST.

GEOMETRY

This title might have made you cringe. Relax, the most difficult parts about geometry —proofs, theorems, and complicated formulas—will *not* be tested on the CBEST. There are a few basic rules you will need to relearn in order to handle the two to four questions you will see on the test. All of the formulas and rules will be covered below. However, the key to geometry is Process of Elimination! It is easy to recognize bad answer choices in geometry questions. Even if you aren't sure how to get the correct answer, try to eliminate as many incorrect answer choices as possible.

We've reduced the size of the geometry review from prior editions of *CBEST Prep* because students are no longer tested on area and volume. Instead, you will be asked questions that require you to "measure length and perimeter." Below, we'll review common geometric shapes that appear on the CBEST and how to calculate the length/perimeter of each one. Therefore, don't panic if you don't see some of the formulas you used to use in geometry—they simply won't be covered on the actual exam!

Perimeter

The perimeter of a triangle is the sum of the lengths of its sides.

Finding the perimeter of a triangle is quite simple—add up the lengths of the three sides.

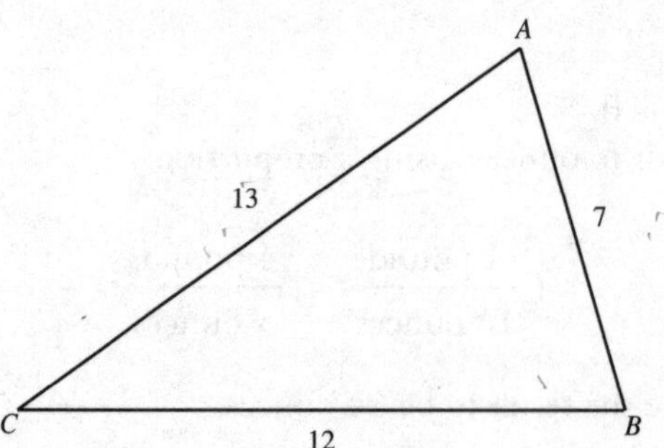

In the figure above, the perimeter of triangle *ABC* is 32 (7 + 12 +13).

Rectangles and Squares

Perimeter

The perimeter of a rectangle or a square is the sum of the lengths of its sides. Just add them up.

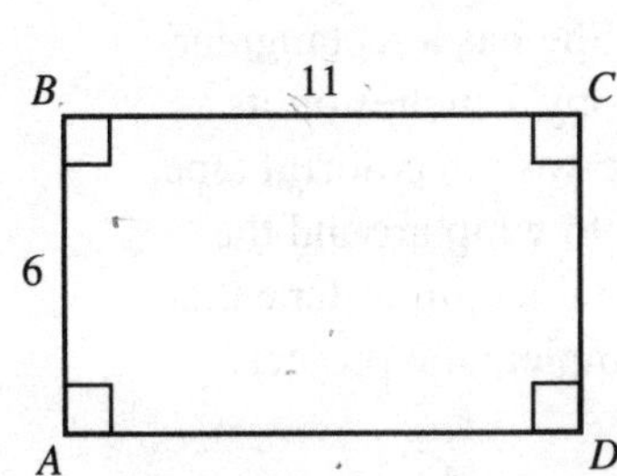

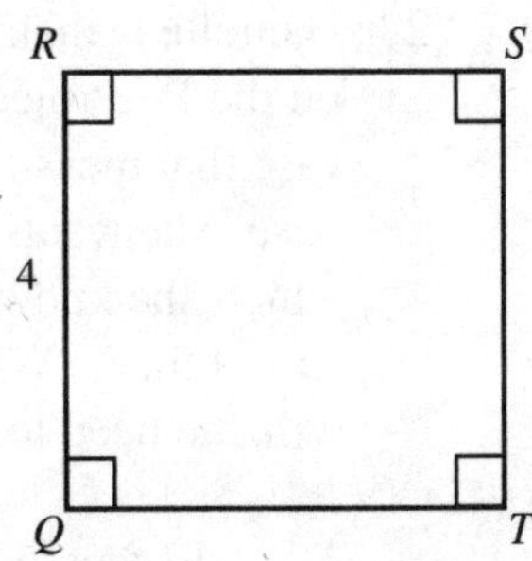

A rectangle has two pairs of equal sides. Therefore, we know that the rectangle *ABCD* has side lengths 11, 6, 11, and 6, for a total perimeter of 34.

A square has four equal sides, so we know that the square *RSTQ* has side lengths 4, 4, 4, and 4, for a total perimeter of 16.

GEOMETRY DRILL (LENGTH & PERIMETER)

Answers can be found at the end of this chapter.

1. Alvaro builds a gazebo for his yard. What is the perimeter of the gazebo?

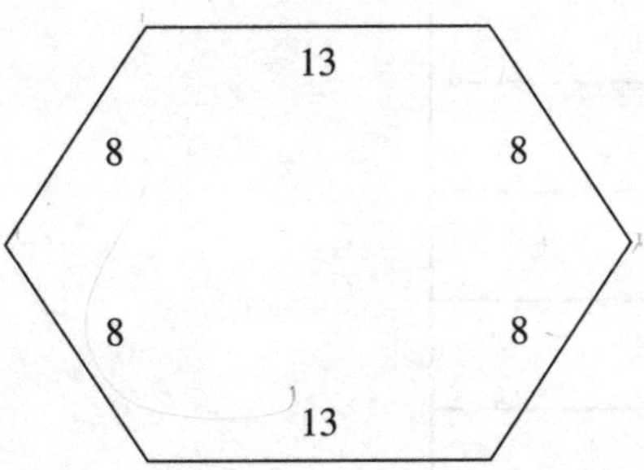

A. 48

B. 58

C. 68

D. 78

E. 88

2. Danielle is making a flower vase that she saw on the PinProject website. She has a rectangular vase that measures 4 inches by 7 inches on its base. She wants to wrap the vase in colorful tape, which she knows will have to wrap around the vase 9 times. What is the total length of tape that will she need to have to complete the project?

   A. 12 feet, 5 inches

   B. 14 feet, 6 inches

   C. 16 feet, 5 inches

   D. 16 feet, 6 inches

   E. 18 feet, 5 inches

3. The bookshelf shown has seven shelves, and each shelf is 24 inches long. If your books average 3 inches in width, how many books can you fit on all the shelves?

   A. 56

   B. 76

   C. 98

   D. 128

   E. 168

4. The figure below is a regular octagon. What is the perimeter of the octagon?

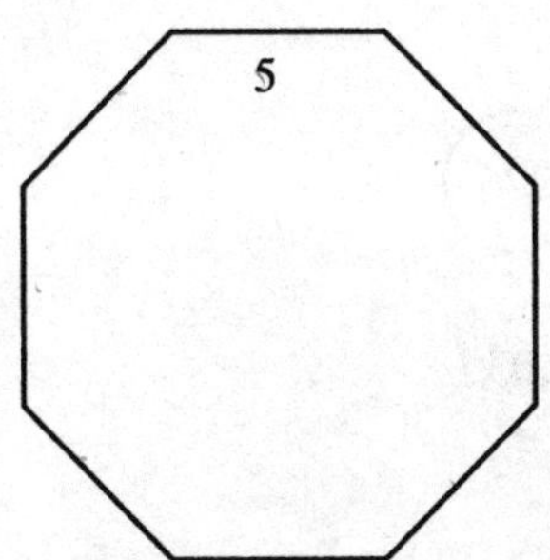

A. 25

B. 30

C. 35

D. 40

E. 45

ANSWERS TO DRILLS

Integers Drill

From page 104

1. Integers are numbers that do not have fraction parts or decimal parts. The correct answers (integers) are circled below.

 (1)	0.333	 (1,024)	–2.5
2.54	$-\frac{2}{3}$	(–62)	(239)
(10)	(0)	$\frac{1}{4}$	4.768
(24)	$-\frac{5}{6}$	1.5	(–756)
–0.58	(–3)	(98)	

2. Even numbers are integers that are divisible by 2. You can remember that even numbers always end in 0, 2, 4, 6, or 8. The correct answers (even integers) are circled below.

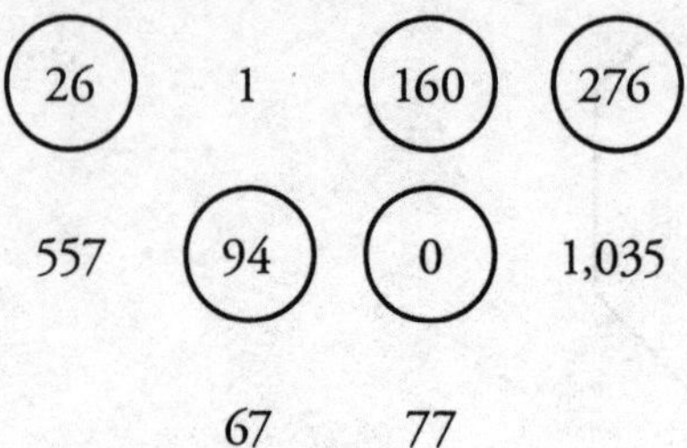

Place Value Drill

From page 106

1. tens
2. ones, or units
3. hundreds
4. tenths
5. thousandths

Order of Operations Drill

From page 108

1. 316
2. 56
3. 20
4. 10
5. 4
6. 31
7. 125
8. 2
9. 16
10. 15

Factors Drill

From page 109

1. 1, 2, 3, 6, 9, 18
2. 1, 3, 5, 7, 15, 21, 35, 105
3. 1, 2, 3, 5, 6, 9, 10, 15, 18, 30, 45, 90
4. 1, 2, 3, 4, 6, 12, 13, 26, 39, 52, 78, 156
5. 1, 2, 4, 19, 38, 76

Multiples Drill

From page 110

1. 12, 24, 36, 48, 60
2. 15, 30, 45, 60, 75
3. 20, 40, 60, 80, 100
4. 9, 18, 27, 36, 45
5. 11, 22, 33, 44, 55

Reducing Fractions Drill

From page 111

1. $\frac{1}{3}$
2. $\frac{2}{15}$
3. $\frac{6}{7}$
4. $\frac{3}{8}$
5. $\frac{11}{13}$

Comparing Fractions Drill

From page 115

1. $\frac{5}{8}$
2. $\frac{5}{7}$
3. $\frac{6}{13}$
4. $\frac{8}{11}$
5. $\frac{14}{9}$

Fraction Drill

From page 116

1. $\frac{5}{6}$
2. $\frac{2}{9}$
3. $\frac{1}{16}$
4. $\frac{2}{3}$
5. $\frac{35}{36}$
6. $\frac{11}{12}$
7. $3\frac{1}{9}$
8. $\frac{23}{40}$
9. $$=\frac{3}{8}\div\frac{9}{7}$$
   $$=\frac{3}{8}\times\frac{7}{9}$$
   $$=\frac{1}{8}\times\frac{7}{3}$$
   $$=\frac{7}{24}$$

10. $$\frac{\frac{1}{4}}{\frac{3}{8}+\frac{4}{5}}$$

$$=\frac{\frac{1}{4}}{\frac{15}{40}+\frac{32}{40}}$$

$$=\frac{\frac{1}{4}}{\frac{47}{40}}$$

$$=\frac{1}{4}\times\frac{40}{47}$$

$$=\frac{1}{1}\times\frac{10}{47}$$

$$=\frac{10}{47}$$

11. $$5\frac{3}{7}+2\frac{7}{12}$$

$$=5+2+\frac{3}{7}+\frac{7}{12}$$

$$=7+\frac{3}{7}+\frac{7}{12}$$

$$=7+\frac{36}{84}+\frac{49}{84}$$

$$=7+\frac{85}{84}$$

$$=7+1+\frac{1}{84}$$

$$=8\frac{1}{84}$$

12. $$\frac{2}{5}+\frac{4}{11}+\frac{5}{6}+\frac{7}{11}+\frac{1}{6}+\frac{3}{5}$$

$$=\frac{2}{5}+\frac{3}{5}+\frac{4}{11}+\frac{7}{11}+\frac{5}{6}+\frac{1}{6}$$

$$=\frac{5}{5}+\frac{11}{11}+\frac{6}{6}$$

$$=1+1+1$$

$$=3$$

Decimal Drill

From page 118

1. 5.384
2. 9.561
3. 332.82
4. 2.048
5. 2.7
6. 133.3
7. −0.889
8. 3.172
9. 54.74
10. 5.968

Geometry Drill (Length and Perimeter)

From page 127

1. **B** $13 + 13 + 8 + 8 + 8 + 8$
$= 26 + 32$
$= 58$

2. **D** Base perimeter $= 4 + 4 + 7 + 7$
$= 8 + 14$
$= 22$ inches

The tape wraps 9 times, so we have
$22 \times 9 = 198$ inches

198 inches $\div$ 12 = $16\frac{1}{2}$ feet, or 16 feet, 6 inches

3. **A** There are a total of 24×7 inches of shelves, or 168 inches.
Each book is 3 inches, so we have
$168 \div 3 = 56$ books

4. **D** $5 \times 8 = 40$
Note: "regular" means that all sides are congruent

Summary

- PEMDAS helps us remember the order of operations in a sequence. Simplify anything found in the parentheses; then solve any exponents; then multiply and divide, from left to right; finally, add and subtract, from left to right.
- **Factors** are numbers that divide into your original number evenly. When counting the number of factors, use factor pairs so that you don't leave any out.
- **Multiples** are numbers that your original number will divide into evenly. When finding multiples, think of multiplication tables, and remember to start by multiplying the number by 1.
- Use the Bowtie to help you add, subtract, and compare fractions.
- A **percentage** is a number out of 100.
- Use translation techniques to turn percentage word problems into math expressions.
- Review the basic measurements of length, weight, capacity, and time.
- The **perimeter** of a shape is the total length of its sides—just add them up.
- A square has four equal sides. A rectangle has two pairs of equal sides.

Chapter 7
Estimation, Measurement, and Statistical Principles

ESTIMATION

CBEST writers state that there may be some math questions where you will need to "estimate the results of problems involving addition, subtraction, multiplication, and division prior to computation." This should sound familiar. In Part III, we discussed how Ballparking can help you eliminate answer choices. Sounds like the CBEST authors want to give us a few free points here! Before we move on to some more complicated statistical principles, let's take a look at a few questions where estimation will be the key to quickly finding the correct answer.

Apply the Strategy
Tip! Always look at the answer choices to see if you can Ballpark before doing any calculations.

1. Oliver sells the following items at his coffee shop:

   \$3.00 for a quesadilla
   \$1.25 for a cup of coffee
   \$1.75 for nachos

   Laura purchases 3 quesadillas, 2 orders of nachos, and 2 cups of coffee. How many quesadillas would Leo have to purchase in order to spend the same amount of money as Laura?

   A. 1

   B. 2

   C. 3

   D. 5

   E. 10

Here's How to Crack It

This is one of the easier math questions that you would find on the CBEST. Therefore, the key to this question is doing your work accurately and quickly. If you look at the answer choices before doing numerous calculations, you will recognize that this question can be solved without any work. Can we eliminate any answer choices immediately? Yes. Choices (A), (B), and (C) won't be the correct answer. Laura ordered three quesadillas, and additional food. Thus, Leo will need to order more than the three Laura ordered. Immediately, we are down to two answer choices—5 and 10. Ten quesadillas would equal \$30, which seems much more than Laura's total cost. Choice (D) is the correct answer.

STATISTICAL PRINCIPLES

Averages

There are a number of ways to describe an average—you may see the terms average, arithmetic mean, or mean. They all describe the same thing. An average is defined as follows: in a set of *n* numbers, the average is the total of the numbers divided by *n*. Let's make that a little easier. There are three parts to an average: the total, the number of things, and the average. To solve average questions, use the average circle:

Use the average circle to keep track of the three parts of an average.

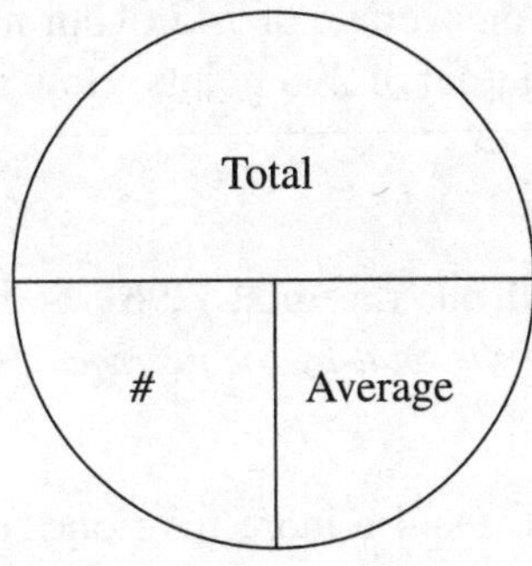

When you get an average question, fill out the circle. You will be given two pieces of information—your job is to find the third. The average circle helps you see how to get the correct answer.

> You probably remember
> Total ÷ Number = Average
>
> From this, we also know
> Total ÷ Average = Number and Average × Number = Total

Example 1

You take three tests and score a 90, 80, and an 82. What is your average score for the three tests?

Solution: Fill in what you know. The total, or sum, is 252. The number of things is 3. *To find the average, divide the total by the number of things.* 252 ÷ 3 is 84.

Example 2

> You score an average of 84 on five tests. What is the sum total of all five tests?

Solution: You can fill in the average (84), and the number of things (5). *To find the total, multiply the two numbers together.* 84 × 5, or 420, is the correct answer.

Example 3

> You score an average of 74 in your history class, and have a total of 296 points. How many tests did you take?

Solution: Here, we can fill out the total (296), and the average (74). *To find the number of things, divide the total by the average.* 296 ÷ 74, or 4 is the correct answer.

Some average questions will require more than one step, or ask for information that won't be contained in the average circle; regardless, always find the third piece of your average circle. Here is a more challenging average question:

Example 4

> If Paula-Ann scored an average of 86 on her first 5 tests, what is the minimum she must score on her 6th test in order to have an overall average of 88?
>
> A. 84
>
> B. 88
>
> C. 90
>
> D. 96
>
> E. 98

Solution: Like the previous examples, let's fill out our average circle first. We have the average and the number of things, so we need to find the total. Multiplying 5 by 86 gives us a total of 430. Next, let's fill in another average circle with the information we want in the second part of the question. There are six things, and we want an average of 88. The total here is 528. The difference between the totals on the first five tests and all six tests is 98 (528 – 430). (E) is the correct answer.

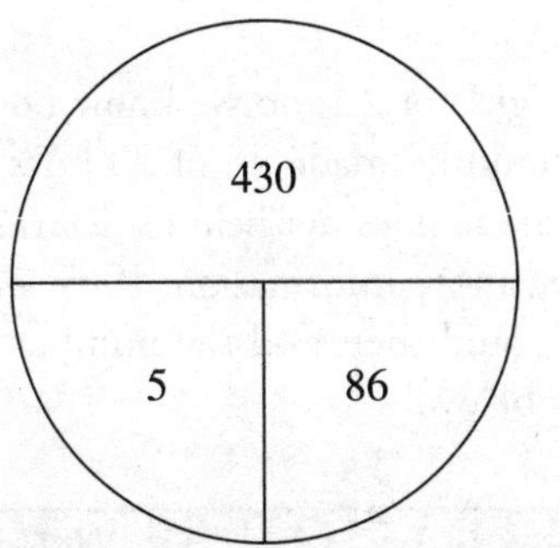

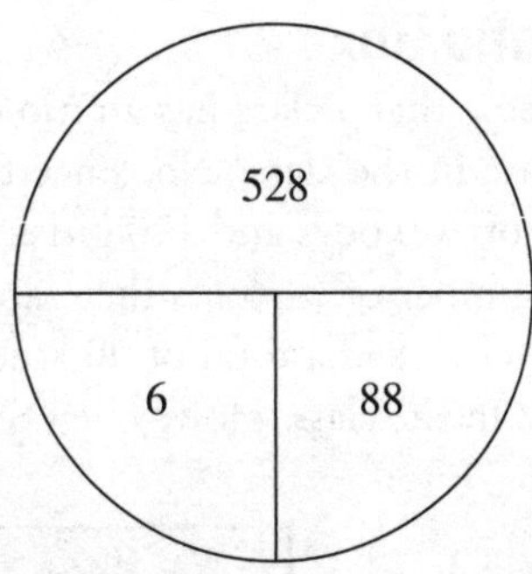

Take all average problems one step at a time, and always fill out the average circle.

Ratios

A ratio is a form of comparison. At first, it may seem that ratios are just like fractions. However, a fraction compares part of something to the whole thing. A ratio compares part of something to another part. Ratios can be written in three formats. The ratio of *a* to *b* can be written as:

$\frac{a}{b}$, or the ratio of *a* to *b*, or *a*:*b*

When expressing a ratio, order matters. 16:20 is different from 20:16.

To understand the difference between ratios and fractions, let's work with the following example: In a third-grade class, there are 20 boys and 16 girls.

The ratio of *boys* to *girls* can be written as $\frac{20}{16}$, or 20:16.

Ratios, like fractions, can also be reduced, or turned into decimals or percentages. The ratio of *girls* to *boys* is not 20:16 but 16:20. Be careful with the order of the ratio. A ratio of 20:16 is different from a ratio of 16:20.

What fractional part of the class is boys? To find a fraction, we are looking for the part over the whole. There are 20 boys, and a whole, or total, of 36 students. Thus, the fractional part of the class which is boys is $\frac{20}{36}$, which may be reduced to $\frac{5}{9}$.

The Ratio Box

If we know that a class has a ratio of boys to girls of 2:1, do we know how many people are in the class? No, since the class could be made up of 20 boys and 10 girls, or of 200 boys and 100 girls. The ratio alone does not help us determine the actual number of students there are. We need more information. If we were told that the class had a total of 90 students, we could then find the number of boys and girls in the class. How? Use the ratio box below.

	Boys	Girls	Whole
Ratio (parts)	2	1	3
Multiply By			
Actual Number			90

If we treat the initial ratio as "parts," we could find the total number of parts. In this example, we know the class is composed of 2 parts boys and 1 part girls, for a total of 3 parts. We filled in the "whole" number as 3.

Our next step is to determine how we can make the jump from 3 parts to the whole class of 90 students. In order to solve this, we need to find out what number we need to multiply by in order to transform 3 into 90. You can see that we need to multiply by 30. Therefore, let's fill in every space in the second row with the number 30 (the second row will always contain the same number—we multiply evenly across all parts of the ratio):

	Boys	Girls	Whole
Ratio (parts)	2	1	3
Multiply By	30	30	30
Actual Number			90

Use the ratio box to turn an initial ratio into actual numbers.

Our final step is to determine the actual number of boys and the actual number of girls in the class. We can do that by multiplying the two numbers in the boys column (2 × 30), and the two numbers in the girls column (1 × 30). The completed ratio box appears below.

	Boys	Girls	Whole
Ratio (parts)	2	1	3
Multiply By	30	30	30
Actual Number	60	30	90

From our work, we have found that in a class of 90 students, with a ratio of 2 boys to 1 girl, there are 60 boys and 30 girls in the class.

Here are a few points on how to use the ratio box:

- Always use the Ratio Box on ratio questions— you will be given an initial ratio, and one "actual number."
- Start by filling in the initial ratio and the actual number; take the sum of the initial ratio to get the whole number of "parts"; determine the multiply number, and write that number in for every column.
- Find the actual numbers by multiplying down each column.

The Ratio Box helps you keep track of all the information you need for any type of ratio question. Practice using the ratio box, and ratios will be a breeze. Here is a final example:

> CORE Education services produces two types of products—notebooks and binders. If CORE has an inventory of notebooks and binders in a 3:2 ratio, and a total of 100 products in stock, how many notebooks does CORE have in inventory?
>
> A. 5
>
> B. 30
>
> C. 40
>
> D. 60
>
> E. 80

Solution: After reading the question, here is what the initial ratio box should look like:

	Notebooks	Binders	Whole
Ratio (parts)	3	2	5
Multiply By			
Actual Number			100

Next, we need to find the multiplier. What do you multiply 5 by in order to get 100? The answer is 20. Here is what the completed ratio box looks like:

	Notebooks	Binders	Whole
Ratio (parts)	3	2	5
Multiply By	20	20	20
Actual Number	**60**	40	100

The correct answer is (D), 60. Be careful not to select 40, which is the total number of binders in inventory.

Proportions

Some CBEST questions will define a relationship between two things, and ask you to use this relationship to find other proportional values. Let's take a look at a sample proportion question:

2. If Chris can iron three shirts in 18 minutes, how long will it take him to iron 12 shirts?

   A. 1 hour 4 minutes

   B. 1 hour 12 minutes

   C. 1 hour 18 minutes

   D. 1 hour 44 minutes

   E. 3 hours 18 minutes

Here's How to Crack It

Every proportion question will contain two relationships—one that is given to you, and one with a missing piece of information. In this example, we're given the relationship:

$$\frac{3 \text{ (shirts)}}{18 \text{ (minutes)}}$$

Set this relationship equal to the one we want to find:

$$\frac{3 \text{ (shirts)}}{18 \text{ (minutes)}} = \frac{12 \text{ (shirts)}}{x \text{ (minutes)}}$$

Make sure your units match when calculating a proportion.

In order for a proportion equation to be correct, notice that the units must be in the same order (in this example, both fractions contain shirts over minutes). Further, the units must always be the same (you can't have minutes in one fraction and hours in the other). Now, we can cross multiply to solve the question:

$$3x = (12)(18)$$
$$x = (4)(18)$$
$$x = 72 \text{ minutes}$$

Thus, it takes Chris 72 minutes to iron 12 shirts. While 72 minutes is not an answer choice, we can reduce to find the correct answer of 1 hour, 12 minutes. Choice (B) is the correct answer.

PROBABILITY

The CBEST will test your knowledge of basic probability. Below, we'll show you everything you need to know about probability for purposes of this test. Probability can get quite complicated (some schools offer yearlong courses that explore probability in great detail), but we'll keep it simple by breaking down the four basic things you need to know for the CBEST.

Probability is Expressed as a Fraction Between 0 and 1

Probability defines the likelihood that an event will occur. A probability of 0 means that there is no chance the event will occur. A probability of 1 means that it is certain that an event will occur. Outside of these extremes, probability is expressed as a fraction between 0 and 1.

Probability is a fraction in which:

$$\frac{\text{\# of desired outcomes}}{\text{total \# of outcomes}}$$

Let's look at a few examples. What if we want to find the probability of throwing a single six-sided die and getting a 4? There are a total of 6 **possible** outcomes for one such roll—1, 2, 3, 4, 5, and 6. There is just one **desired** outcome—that we get a 4. Thus, the probability of rolling a 4 is $\frac{1}{6}$. What about the probability of flipping a coin and having it turn up heads? Here, the probability is $\frac{1}{2}$. There are two possible outcomes—heads or tails, and our one desired outcome is that we flip heads.

An event is defined as **independent** if it is not affected by previous events.

Let's talk about rolling a die again. Let's say you throw the die and it comes up a 4. Does this mean that the probability of a 4 appearing next time will be less than $\frac{1}{6}$? Absolutely not! The probability of rolling a 4 on the next turn is still $\frac{1}{6}$, since the two rolls are independent events and one does not affect the outcome of the other.

To find the probability of more than one independent event occurring, multiply the probability of each event together.

Multiply the probability of independent events to find the combined probability.

What is the probability of throwing a 4 two times in a row? Well, the probability of throwing a 4 is $\frac{1}{6}$. This probability does not change on the second throw. Thus, the probability is $\frac{1}{6} \times \frac{1}{6}$, or $\frac{1}{36}$.

The following examples are sample questions that will test the concepts you need to know for the test.

3. David throws a six-sided die and gets a 3. What is the probability that his next throw will NOT be a three?

A. $\frac{1}{6}$

B. $\frac{1}{4}$

C. $\frac{1}{2}$

D. $\frac{5}{6}$

E. 1

Here's How to Crack It

The probability of not getting a three is $\frac{5}{6}$. There are five rolls which would not give us a 3—namely, if we were to roll 1, 2, 4, 5, or 6. There is a total of six possible outcomes. The probability is not affected by the fact that David rolled a 3 on his previous throw. Choice (D) is the correct answer.

4. A bag of marbles contains 8 red marbles, 6 blue marbles, and 4 green marbles. If one marble is chosen at random from the bag, what is the probability that this marble will be blue?

   A. $\frac{2}{9}$

   B. $\frac{1}{3}$

   C. $\frac{4}{9}$

   D. $\frac{1}{2}$

   E. $\frac{3}{4}$

Here's How to Crack It

There are a total of 18 marbles (the total number of **possible** outcomes). There are 6 blue marbles (the number of **desired** outcomes). Therefore, the probability of selecting a blue marble is $\frac{6}{18}$, which reduces to $\frac{1}{3}$. Choice (B) is the correct answer.

STANDARDIZED TEST SCORES

As you know, tests can be graded and evaluated in a number of ways. We've all experienced different grading systems—letter grades, percentile scores, and scores specific to a test (like the CBEST scores of 20-80 in this section!). Below, we will review the two most common types of standardized test scores. Your job is to interpret these scores, and understand how individuals performed relative to other students.

Percentile Scores

Percentile scores provide a measure of how a test taker performs relative to other test takers. Percentiles can be understood as a rank within 100, and percentile scores range from 1 to 99 (the highest percentile is 99, and the lowest is 1). For example, if a student scored in the 78th percentile on a test, that student achieved a score that is higher than 78 percent of the other students who took the test (and lower than 21 percent of the students who took the test). So, if 200 students took the test, the student in the 78th percentile scored higher than 156 students who also took the same test. A score in the median (or middle) of all scores would receive a score in the 50th percentile.

Do not confuse percentile with percentage correct scores. Percentile scores allow you to compare one student's scores with those of a group of students who took the test. If a student scores in the 75th percentile, it does NOT necessarily mean that the student got 3 out of every 4 questions correct on the test! In fact, without more information, we have no idea how many questions the student answered correctly—all we know is that the student performed better than 75 percent of the students who took the exam.

Below is an example of how you may be tested on interpreting percentile scores:

---

5. On a recent statistics quiz, Lisa scored in the 82nd percentile. Her friend Kendra scored in the 65th percentile. The quiz contained 150 questions, and Lisa answered 111 questions correctly. Which of the following statements must be true?

   A. Kendra answered 39 questions correctly.

   B. Kendra answered 94 questions correctly.

   C. 17 students received scores between Lisa and Kendra.

   D. Kendra's score is greater than the score of 65 other students.

   E. Kendra answered fewer than 111 questions correctly.

Here's How to Crack It

The correct answer is (E)—because Kendra scored in a lower percentile than Lisa, she must have answered fewer questions correctly than Lisa did. Thus, she answered fewer than 111 questions correctly. Let's look at the other answer choices. First, do we know how many questions Kendra answered correctly? We do not. All we are given is her percentile score. We have no idea how many questions Kendra got right (only that the number is less than 111). That eliminates (A) and (B). Next, do we know how many test takers there are? We do not. Choices (C) and (D) assume that there are 100 test takers. We are not given this information anywhere in the statement above.

Stanine Scores

"Stanine" is short for standard nine. The name comes from the fact that stanine scores range from a low of 1 to a high of 9. So while percentile scores range from 1 to 99, stanine scores range from only 1 to 9. Stanine scores provide less detail for students about test performance relative to other students than do percentile scores. Stanine scores often are given with verbal descriptions of the student's performance. A stanine score of 1, 2, or 3 is below average; 4, 5, or 6 is average; and 7, 8, or 9 is above average. The median (or middle) score is a 5.

Relating Stanine Scores to Percentile Scores

How is it determined who gets a stanine score of 4, and how many students will receive such a score? Stanine scores assume a normal distribution, meaning that for a particular stanine score, you can approximate the range of percentile scores that equate to that score. Look at the normal distribution curve below:

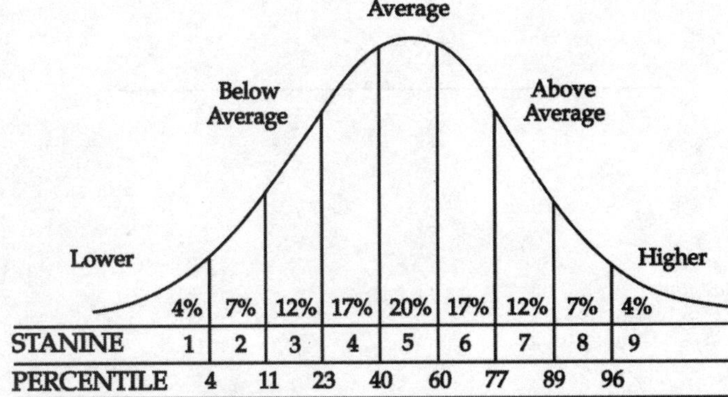

Approximately 17% of test takers will receive a stanine score of 4—and this number corresponds to a percentile score between 23% and 40%. Notice that the same number of students will receive a 4 as will receive a 6; the same is true for 3 and 7; 2 and 8; and 1 and 9.

6. Brent received a stanine score of 5 on the Chemistry exam. Angie received a stanine score of 4 on the same exam. Which of the following statements must be true?

   A. Brent received a percentile score at least 10 points higher than Angie.

   B. Brent answered 20% of the questions correctly.

   C. Brent received the exact average score of all test takers.

   D. Over 50% of the test takers received a higher stanine score than Angie.

   E. Brent scored in the 50th percentile on the exam.

Here's How to Crack It

Let's evaluate each statement one at a time. Statement (A) is possible, but it does not have to be true. For example, Brent could receive a score in the 42nd percentile, and Angie could receive a score in the 38th percentile. Statement (B) is false—we have no information about how he did on the questions themselves. We don't know if he got most of the test questions right or wrong! Statements (C) and (E) are possible, but a stanine score of 5 indicates a wide range of scores (40th percentile to 60th percentile). Statement (D) is true. According to the chart, 60 percent of the test takers will receive a stanine score of 5 or higher. Choice (D) is the correct answer.

Summary

- Estimating the correct answer can solve some questions on the CBEST. Use Ballparking techniques to eliminate answer choices and avoid needless calculations.
- Use the average circle to find any of the three parts of an average—the number of things, the total, and the average.
- A ratio compares a part to a part. Use the ratio box to solve most ratio questions.
- To find a proportion, set the equation you are given equal to the one you want to find.
- Probabilities are expressed as fractions between 0 and 1. Probability is defined as the number of desired outcomes over the total number of possible outcomes.
- Percentile scores and stanine scores describe the performance of a test taker relative to the performance of other test takers who took the same exam. Remember that these scores do not indicate the number of questions a student answered correctly— they simply place a student's score in relation to all other scores.

Chapter 8
Computation and Problem Solving

Approximately 35 percent of the questions on the Mathematics Section will fall under the category of computation and problem solving. Of these questions, we've already covered two important areas:

- Questions that require you to add, subtract, multiply, or divide whole numbers.
- Questions that require you to add, subtract, multiply, or divide fractions, decimals, and percentages.

In addition to solving word problems using the order of operations, you will have to solve questions involving algebra. You may not like algebra. You may remember, with sadness, the last time you sat through an algebra class. Well, there is some good news. In the pages ahead, we'll show you how to solve algebra questions without having to write an equation! Here is an outline for the algebra concepts that will be covered in this chapter:

- Manipulating an equation. Okay, so there will be some algebra. We'll show you what to do if you are asked to solve an equation.
- Solve an inequality. We'll show you how to handle a math sentence that has a > or < sign, instead of an equals sign.
- Backsolving. Worried about trying to turn a word problem into an equation? Don't be. With this technique, we'll show you how to solve an algebra question without algebra!
- What numbers are needed? We'll show you how to crack a specific algebra question on the CBEST by identifying the numbers you'll need to use to solve a problem.
- What can be determined? Some CBEST questions will ask you to identify what, if anything, can be known given certain pieces of information.
- There's got to be another way. Some math questions will require you to find an alternative method of solving a problem.

MANIPULATING AN EQUATION

Believe it or not, you've already set up a number of algebraic equations. In the last chapter, we set up equalities when using proportions. When we set up a proportion, we had several numbers and one unknown, or variable. A sample equation question could look something like the following question.

1. If $3x + 18 = 24$, what is the value of x?

   A. 2

   B. 6

   C. 14

   D. 15

   E. 45

Here's How to Crack It

The question can be asked in many ways: "what is the value of x," "solve for x," "x equals?" No matter how the CBEST authors phrase the question, you have to do one thing—isolate the variable x from all the other numbers. This means getting the variable on one side of the equation, and all the numbers on the other side of the equation. In order to do this, you need to know **the golden rule of equations:**

The golden rule of equations—whatever you do to one side of the equation, you must do to the other side of the equation.

> Whatever you do to the left side of the equation, you have to do the same to the right side of the equation.

Let's take a look at how to solve the equation above.

First, the variable is found on the left side of the equation. Thus, we need to get all the values on the right side of the equation. The first step is to move any numbers not attached to variables, in this case, the 18.

$$\begin{array}{r} 3x+18=24 \\ -18\;-18 \\ \hline 3x-\;0=\;6 \end{array}$$

In order to move the 18, we needed to subtract 18 from the left side of the equation. Therefore, we also need to subtract 18 from the right side of the equation. After simplifying each side of the equation, our new equation is:

$$3x=6$$

Next, we need to move the number 3 from the variable x. Currently, 3 and x are to be multiplied together. In order to eliminate the 3 from the left side of the equation, we need to divide by 3. Following the golden rule, we also must divide the right side of the equation by 3.

$$\begin{array}{cc} 3x & =6 \\ \div 3 & \div 3 \\ & x=2 \end{array}$$

The number 3 cancels out on the left side of the equation and we are left with the variable x. On the right side of the equation, we can simplify the operation 6 divided by 3. Our final equation is that $x = 2$; answer choice (A) is the correct answer.

Occasionally, you will be presented with an equation that has more than one variable. Don't worry. You won't be asked to try to solve for multiple variables. Instead, the CBEST writers will give you a value to enter into the equation, as in the following example:

---

2. If $4a + 2b = 32 - a + b$, find the value of a when $b = 12$.

   A. 2

   B. 4

   C. 6

   D. 10

   E. 12

Here's How to Crack It

Start this problem by rewriting the equation, substituting the number 12 wherever you see b:

$$4a + 2(12) = 32 - a + (12)$$

Next, using the order of operations, simplify the equation:

$$4a + 24 = 32 - a + 12$$

$$4a + 24 = 44 - a$$

Now you can solve this equation using the same techniques we described in the previous example. Isolate the variable a from all the other numbers. In this case, both the left side and the right side of the equation contain the variable a. While you can choose to put the variable on either side of the equation, it is usually easier to move the smaller value. In this example, we'll move the $-a$ to the left side of the equation:

$$\begin{aligned} 4a + 24 &= 44 - a \\ +a \quad\;\; &\quad\;\;\;\; +a \\ 5a + 24 &= 44 \end{aligned}$$

Next, move the number 24 away from the variable to the right side of the equation:

$$\begin{array}{r} 5a + 24 = 44 \\ -24 - 24 \\ 5a = 20 \end{array}$$

Finally, divide by 5:

$$\begin{array}{r} 5a = 20 \\ \div 5 \quad \div 5 \\ a = 4 \end{array}$$

Choice (B) is the correct answer.

If you have questions with more than one variable, the CBEST authors will need to give you additional information in order to solve the equation. Most often, they will simply give you the value of one of the variables, and ask you to find the other. The following drill includes additional equations that will allow you to practice manipulating and solving.

EQUATION DRILL

Answers and explanations can be found at the end of this chapter.

1. If $6y - 3 = -9$, then y equals

   A. –2

   B. –1

   C. 1

   D. 2

   E. 6

2. If $n + 2b + p = h - r$, what is the value of h when

$n = 8,\ b = \frac{1}{2},\ p = \frac{3}{4}$, and $r = 6$?

A. $9\frac{3}{4}$

B. 15

C. $15\frac{1}{2}$

D. $15\frac{3}{4}$

E. $18\frac{3}{4}$

3. If $8c - 12 = 12$, what is twice the value of c?

A. 0

B. 3

C. 6

D. 32

E. 96

4. If $5z = 10 + 2z$, what is the value of $9z$?

A. $\frac{10}{3}$

B. 10

C. 16

D. 21

E. 30

5. Solve the equation: $3n + 7 = 4 - 5n$

A. $n = -\frac{11}{2}$

B. $n = \frac{3}{8}$

C. $n = -\frac{3}{2}$

D. $n = -\frac{3}{8}$

E. $n = \frac{3}{2}$

6. If $4a + 8b = 36$, what is the value of a if $b = 5$?

A. -1

B. 2

C. 4

D. 7

E. 19

7. If $g = 2h$ and $8 = 3h - 7$, what is the value of g?

A. $\frac{2}{3}$

B. $\frac{5}{2}$

C. 5

D. 8

E. 10

8. If $5t + 8 = 3s$, which of the following is equivalent to $10t$?

A. $\frac{3s+8}{5}$

B. $3s - 16$

C. $6s - 16$

D. $\frac{3s-8}{5}$

E. $6s + 16$

INEQUALITIES

Inequalities are very similar to equations. Instead of providing a specific value for a variable, an inequality defines a range of values for a variable. For example, an inequality may tell you that $x < 5$. You don't know exactly what the value of x is, but you do know its range. It could be any value less than 5.

Let's review the symbols for inequalities. These will be helpful not only for solving inequalities, but also for relating numbers to one another (covered in Chapter 7):

$>$	**greater than**	$9 > 5$	"9 is greater than 5"
$<$	**less than**	$5 < 9$	"5 is less than 9"
$\geq$	**greater than or equal to**	$x \geq 5$	"x is greater than or equal to 5"
$\leq$	**less than or equal to**	$y \leq 9$	"y is less than or equal to 9"

Let's use a variation of our first example to see how to solve an inequality:

---

1. If $3x + 18 > 24$, which of the following expressions gives all the possible values of x?

A. $x > 2$

B. $x < 6$

C. $x > 14$

D. $x < 15$

E. $x \geq 45$

Here's How to Crack It

When solving an inequality, treat the inequality like an equal sign. Remember to use the golden rule of equations (whatever you do to one side, you must do the other side).

$$\begin{aligned} 3x + 18 &> 24 \\ -18 &\quad -18 \\ 3x &> 6 \\ \div 3 &\quad \div 3 \\ x &> 2 \end{aligned}$$

Choice (A) is the correct answer.

As you can see, an inequality is just like an equation, with one notable exception:

> If you are multiplying or dividing by a negative number, you must flip the sign of the inequality.

Here is an example that illustrates this rule:

2. If $-7a + 3 < 24$, then which of the following expressions gives all the possible values of a?

A. $a = 3$

B. $a < -3$

C. $a > -3$

D. $a > \frac{27}{7}$

E. $a = -3$

Here's How to Crack It

With any inequality or equation, try to isolate the variable from all the other numbers. In this case, start by subtracting 3 from both sides of the equation; this leaves us with the inequality:

$$-7a < 21$$

At this point, we need to divide by –7 in order to isolate the variable:

$$\frac{-7a}{-7} < \frac{21}{-7}$$

Remember that when you multiply or divide by a negative number you must flip the inequality sign.

Here, we are dividing by a negative number. Thus, we must proceed with division as normal, but flip the sign:

$$a > -3$$

Choice (C) is the correct answer. Be careful when selecting your answer choice! The CBEST writers will almost always include an answer choice that looks correct, except that the sign is pointing in the wrong direction.

INEQUALITY DRILL

Answers and explanations can be found at the end of this chapter.

1. If $-3x + 6 \geq 18$, which of the following must be true?

   A. $x \leq -4$

   B. $x \leq 6$

   C. $x \geq -4$

   D. $x \geq -6$

   E. $x = 2$

2. If $5x + 3 < 28$, then which of the following expressions gives all the possible values of x?

   A. $x < 5$

   B. $x < -5$

   C. $x > 0$

   D. $x > 5$

   E. $x = -5$

3. If $-5x - 21 < 14$, which of the following must be true?

   A. $x > 7$

   B. $x > -7$

   C. $x < 7$

   D. $x < -7$

   E. $x = 7$

Multiplying Or Dividing by a Negative Number

If it helps you remember, you can flip the sign as a separate step.

Example:

$$-7a < 21$$
$$-a < 3$$
$$a > -3$$

4. Solve the inequality: $4 + 2w > 5$

A. $w < \frac{1}{2}$

B. $w > \frac{1}{2}$

C. $w \geq \frac{9}{2}$

D. $w \leq \frac{9}{2}$

E. $w < 4$

5. If $3f + 11 \leq 32$, which of the following must be true?

A. $f \geq -7$

B. $f \leq -7$

C. $f > 7$

D. $f < 7$

E. $3f = -7$

6. If $6p - 5 > p + 11$, which of the following could be a value of p?

A. -16

B. $-\frac{16}{5}$

C. $\frac{6}{5}$

D. $\frac{16}{5}$

E. 16

BACKSOLVING

Let's take a look at a typical algebraic word problem.

1. Marcello has 34 more dimes than nickels. If he has a total of 76 coins, how many nickels does Marcello have?

   A. 21

   B. 40

   C. 42

   D. 84

   E. 110

You might be thinking that you need to set up an equation to solve this problem. In fact, you would need two equations, each with two variables. But there is a better way!

When you notice this type of problem, with numbers in the answer choices, it's the perfect opportunity to use the Backsolving technique. Instead of solving algebraically, you can try one of the answer choices, and see if it works. If it doesn't work, you try another choice, until you find the one that does work. Here's how.

Let's solve the sample problem above, using this Backsolving technique.

---

1. Marcello has 34 more dimes than nickels. If he has a total of 76 coins, how many nickels does Marcello have?

   A. 21

   B. 40

   C. 42

   D. 84

   E. 110

Here's How to Crack It

Start by making a table of the information you need. In this case, "nickels," "dimes," and "total" makes sense. Include the answer choices in the "nickels" column, since the question asks *how many nickels does Marcello have?*

Start with (C), and work through the steps of the problem. If Marcello has 42 nickels, he must have 76 dimes. That makes a total of 118 coins.

Nickles	Dimes	Total
21		
40		
42	42 + 34 = 76	118
84		
110		

Apply the Strategy

When we eliminate one wrong answer using the Backsolving technique, we can often eliminate two more!

The problem stated that Marcello has a *total* of 76 coins. Which means (C) cannot be the right answer, since we came up with a total of 118.

There's a reason we started with (C). Notice that the choices are in order, and (C) is in the middle. Now that we've eliminated (C), we can decide whether to try a larger number next, or a smaller one. In this case, choosing a smaller number will get us a smaller total, which is what we want. We can eliminate (D) and (E)—they are too large—and try (B) next.

When we plug in (B) 40 nickels, we can see that the total is still too large. That means that the correct answer must be (A). Feel free to test it to be sure! If Marcello has 21 nickels, then he must have 55 dimes, for a total of 76 coins. This matches the information given in the problem. Select (A).

Nickles	Dimes	Total
21	21 + 34 = 55	21 + 55 = 76
~~40~~	~~40 + 34 = 74~~	~~40 + 74 = 114~~
~~42~~	~~42 + 34 = 76~~	~~42 + 76 = 116~~
~~84~~		
~~110~~		

To summarize:

Backsolving Technique

1. Identify the opportunity to use Backsolving—the problem has numbers in the answer choices, and you might have been tempted to solve algebraically.
2. Start with (C), and plug it in to the problem. Work through all the given information, and see if (C) is correct.
3. If (C) is ***not*** correct, you should be able to eliminate two other answers (too large or too small). Then try another answer.
4. Once you've identified the answer that matches all the given information in the problem, you're done.

Backsolving turns difficult algebra questions into arithmetic problems. Rather than worry about creating equations, sometimes with more than one variable, focus on using the answer choices to your advantage.

Proven Technique

Tip! When Backsolving, always start with choice (C), the middle number.

We'll cover two more typical Backsolving questions to be sure you're familiar with this technique.

---

2. Adam is half as old as Bob and three times as old as Cindy. If the sum of their ages is 40, what is Bob's age?

A. 3

B. 6

C. 12

D. 18

E. 24

Here's How to Crack It

Again we have an algebra question with numbers in the answer choices. Backsolve! The answer choices tell us Bob's age. We start with Bob's age at 12, (C). If Bob is 12, then Adam is 6, and Cindy is 2. The sum of their ages is 20. We're looking for the sum of their ages to be 40, so eliminate (C).

Apply the Strategy
If (C) is incorrect, try to determine if you need a larger value or a smaller value. If you aren't sure, just choose another answer choice and keep working.

Now which way should we go? Should we increase Bob's age to 18 (answer choice (D)) or decrease his age to 6, (B)? When we tried Bob at the age of 12, the sum of their ages was much less than we wanted. We need to increase the total of the three individuals. Therefore, we should increase Bob's age to 18, and try (D). Before trying (D), eliminate (A) and (B)—they will give us even smaller totals.

If Bob is 18, then Adam is half his age, or 9. Cindy is a third of Adam's age, so she is 3. If we take the sum of their ages, we get 18 + 9 + 3 = 30. But the sum of their ages should be 40, so (D) is not correct. Eliminate it.

We're left with only one answer choice, so (E) must be the correct answer. Want to see the work? If Bob is 24, then Adam is half his age, 12. Cindy is a third of Adam's age, so she is 4. The sum of their ages, 24 + 12 + 4, equals 40. We have correctly solved the problem.

3. If there are four times as many women as men employed by the Acme Insurance Company, then how many of the 75 workers are women?

A. 80

B. 75

C. 60

D. 45

E. 15

Here's How to Crack It

Did you recognize this question as a Backsolving problem? We have a statement in which an algebraic equation could be written, as well as numbers in the answer choices. Before Backsolving, be sure to use another great math technique, Ballparking. The question tells us that there are a total of 75 workers. Thus, (A) and (B) don't make sense. We can't have the number of women in the company greater than or equal to the total number of employees.

In general, we have always said to start with (C). In this case, since we have eliminated (A) and (B) due to Ballparking, start with the middle remaining value, (D). By using the remaining middle value, we'll be as efficient as possible when solving this question.

Choice (D) tells us that there are 45 women in the work force. If there are 45 women, and a total of 75 employees, then there must be 30 men (75 – 45). Are there four times as many women as men? In this case, 45 is not 4 times 30.

We can eliminate (D). There needs to be a greater number of women in order to make a ratio of 4 times as many women as men. Let's move to (C), which has more women.

Choice (C) tells us that there are 60 women in the work force. If there are 60 women, and a total of 75 employees, then there must be 15 men (75 – 60). Are there four times as many women as men? Yes. 60 is four times greater than 15. Choice (C) is the correct answer.

Will Backsolving Work for Every Question?

Unfortunately, no. Many questions on the CBEST will have to be solved by manipulating the information that is given to you in the question. Backsolving is just one of a number of techniques we have shown you throughout these math chapters. Remember the keys to identifying a Backsolving question:

- There are numbers in the answer choices.
- Does it seem like an algebra question? That is, do you feel like you need to start writing an algebraic equation in order to solve the problem traditionally? If so, you've probably identified a Backsolving question.
- The question asks for a specific amount. Backsolving questions will typically end in concrete statements, such as "what is the value of *x*," "how many tools does Bill have," or "how many tickets were purchased?"

How to Recognize a Backsolving Question:

1. Numbers in the answer choices.
2. The question is a word problem.
3. The question asks for a specific amount.

BACKSOLVING DRILL

Answers and explanations can be found at the end of this chapter.

1. Kathleen and Elizabeth jog a total of 23 miles today. If Kathleen jogs 5 more miles than Elizabeth, how many miles did Elizabeth jog?

   A. 5

   B. 9

   C. 14

   D. 16

   E. 18

2. Forty-two people have registered for a raffle. If there are twice as many children as adults signed up, how many children are registered for the raffle?

A. 14

B. 18

C. 20

D. 28

E. 32

3. If $2x - 7 = 3$, then $x =$

A. 1

B. 2

C. 3

D. 4

E. 5

IDENTIFY THE INFORMATION NEEDED

So far in this chapter, we've talked about how to solve algebraic equations and inequalities. We've also talked about how to solve an algebra word problem without setting up an equation by using Backsolving. In this next type of algebra question, we'll need to identify the information needed to solve an equation. Let's look at the following example:

1. **Read the problem below; then answer the question that follows.**

> In Priyah's English class, the students scored an average of 48 points on the last exam. Ashley's score was in the 80th percentile, and Yuan's score was in the 75th percentile. If Priyah scored 55 points on the exam, was her score higher than Ashley's?

What single piece of information is necessary to solve the problem above?

A. Priyah's average exam score for the semester

B. The number of students in the class

C. The class's median score for the exam

D. Priyah's percentile score for the exam

E. The number of questions on the exam

Here's How to Crack It

This question asks about scores and percentiles. Keep in mind that we won't need to solve the question indicated in the box. We only need to know *what information* is necessary to solve the question.

When solving a question about percentiles, remember that percentiles provide a ranking. For example, Ashley's 80th percentile ranking means that she scored higher than 80% of students in the class. However, this does not tell us her actual score on the exam. (If most students did poorly, Ashley's point score may have been quite low). So, in order to compare Priyah's score with Ashley's, we would need to know Priyah's percentile score, *or* Ashley's actual score. Only one of these is listed as an answer choice: (D).

Tip! If you are asked to identify the information needed in a problem, you do not need to solve the problem.

Using Process of Elimination, we can get rid of the answer choices that do not provide the necessary information. Priyah's *average exam score* (A) will not tell us about her ranking on this past exam. The *number of students in the class* does not help us to compare scores, so eliminate (B). The *class's median score* (C) would not provide enough detail for the given question (we only know that the median score equals the 50th percentile). Finally, the *number of questions* on the exam is not enough information to compare the two scores. (Remember that percentile is not the same thing as percent score).

Solving the problem won't get you any bonus points. Let's try the following example:

---

2. **Read the problem below; then answer the question that follows.**

> At a game store, customers can spin a prize wheel to win a collectible figurine from a selection. There is a 10% chance of winning a Dragon figurine, a 20% chance of winning a Troll figurine, and a 25% chance of winning a Wizard figurine. How many Dragon figurines are there in the prize selection?

What single piece of information is necessary to solve the problem above?

A. The number of customers who spin the wheel

B. The number of Troll figurines

C. The number of Barbarian figurines

D. The total number of figurines

E. Either B or D

Here's How to Crack It

This question asks about percentages. Keep in mind that we won't need to *solve* the question indicated in the box. We only need to know *what information* is necessary to solve the question.

When solving a percentage question, we can use **part ÷ whole = percent**. In this case, Dragon figurines ÷ total figurines = 10%. (The 10% was given in the problem.) We would be looking for the number of Dragon figurines, so we would need to know the total. (D) looks like a good choice.

However, notice that (E) includes two answers—(B) and (D). Looking at (B), if we knew the total number of Troll figurines, we could solve for the total number of figurines, using similar steps. From there, we could also obtain the total number of Dragon figurines, as shown above. Choice (E) is correct—either piece of information would allow us to obtain the answer.

The number of customers (A) is not necessary to solve this question. Also, *the number of Barbarian figurines* (D) would not give us the information needed, since we do not know the percent of Barbarian figurines. (We don't know which types of figurines were left unmentioned).

When asked to identify the information needed to solve a problem, remember the following keys:

1. Identify the type of question. Chances are good that the question will fall into a category you are familiar with. Is it a ratio? A percentage? An average? Once you identify the question, try to set up the problem.
2. Do **not** actually solve the problem. You only need to identify the information that is **needed** to solve the problem. Solving the problem will waste time and distract you from your focus on the answer choices.
3. Look out for misleading information. There will usually be some numbers given to you in the question that are not needed to find the correct answer.

WHAT CAN BE FOUND?

Another type of question on the CBEST asks you to identify what kind of information you *could* solve for given the information in a question. You can recognize these questions by the phrase "What can be determined?" If you see this phrase in the question, you won't need to worry about doing any formal calculations—you'll simply need to identify what could be known based on the information you are given. Let's take a look at the following example to better understand these types of questions.

> Each of 51 students is asked to select one and only one class as an elective. There are 13 spaces available in music, 18 spaces available in football, and 30 spaces available in art. As of 3:00 P.M., 21 of the total spaces have been filled.

3. Which of the following facts can be determined from the information given above?

   A. the number of students that selected music

   B. the average number of students registering per hour

   C. the total number of students at the school

   D. the number of spaces remaining in football

   E. the number of students in the group that have not yet chosen an elective class.

Here's How to Crack It

There are two key things to remember when solving these types of questions:

1. **Process of Elimination.** Of course! Often the best way to choose the correct answer is to eliminate answer choices that you know are wrong. With these types of questions, evaluating the answer choices will also give you a clue as to what the CBEST writers are looking for.

2. **Stay focused *only* on the information presented.** The biggest trap on these questions is to make assumptions that are not contained in the information (much like the trap of making assumptions in the Reading Section of the test). A correct answer must be proven by the information you are given. You cannot bring in any outside information—stick to what is written!

Let's use these two techniques to solve the example above. What information are we given? We know that each member of a group of students needs to choose one elective class from the following: music, football, and art. We also know that by 3:00 P.M., 21 of the spaces have been filled. Use Process of Elimination thoughtfully, and get rid of any answers that are not certain based on the given information. Choices (A) and (D) are incorrect—we do not know how many students registered for each class, only the total for all the classes. Choice (B) is incorrect, because we aren't told how many hours have passed for registration. Choice (C) is incorrect, since we know nothing about how many students attend the school—we only know about the particular group of students being discussed. Choice (E) is correct—we know that 21 spaces have been filled, and that there are a total of 51 students—and thus we can determine how many students still need to choose an elective.

Let's try one more example:

> Dave and Melissa travel from their home to the theater, each taking a different route. Dave makes it to the theater in 25 minutes. Melissa travels 7 miles, and makes it to the theater in 42 minutes.

4. Which of the following facts can be determined from the information given above?

   A. The speed at which Dave made the trip, in miles per hour

   B. Whether Dave or Melissa arrived at the theater first

   C. By what percent the duration of Melissa's trip exceeded that of Dave's trip

   D. The time it took Dave to return home from the theater

   E. None of the above can be determined

Here's How to Crack It

First, summarize the information that you are given. We know that Dave and Melissa are each traveling to the theater—Dave takes 25 minutes (we do *not* know how many *miles* he traveled), and Melissa took 42 minutes to go 7 miles. Choice (A) asks for Dave's speed—a calculation that would require knowing both the time and the distance. Since we do not know the distance Dave traveled, we can eliminate (A). Choice (B) is tricky—it *seems* like Dave would arrive at the theater first, but we are not told that the two left for the theater at the same time. Therefore, while (B) may be true, we cannot prove it, so we must eliminate (B). Choice (C) is a percent increase question. Since we have both the time it took Dave and the time it took Melissa, we could set up an equation to find this percentage.

Choice (C) is correct. Choice (D) is incorrect because we are told nothing about the return trip home from the theater. And finally, since we have an answer that works, (C), choice (E) is not correct.

So, we know that the correct answer in the problem above is (C). By the way, what is the percentage difference in the duration of the two trips? Don't know? Good! Don't worry about doing formal calculations on these questions. Your job is simply to determine what information can be found, not to actually solve the problem. Solving will only waste time.

Choice (E) in the above example may appear as an answer choice on some questions you encounter on the CBEST. Only select this answer choice once you've eliminated all the others, and be careful! It is very tempting to pick this answer choice if the question is difficult. Make sure you've evaluated all other answer choices before selecting the "It cannot be determined" answer choice.

There's Got to be Another Way—Alternative Solution Questions

Some questions on the CBEST will ask you to identify an alternative method to solving a question. In the question, the authors will present one formula for solving a desired problem, and ask you to identify another possible way of setting up the equation. Before we talk about the keys to solving these problems, let's take a look at what one looks like.

---

5. Joe buys a hot dog with ketchup, mustard, and relish. A hot dog costs $1.75, and toppings are $.35 each. Joe pays with a five–dollar bill. Joe uses the following expression to calculate the amount of money he should receive back for the purchase:

   $5.00 – ($1.75 + $.35 + $.35 + $.35)

   Which of the following expressions could Joe have also used?

   A. 3 × ($5.00 – $1.75 – $.35)

   B. $3.25 – 3 × $.35

   C. $1.75 + (3 × $.35) – $5.00

   D. $.35 – $5.00 + $1.75

   E. 3($5.00 – $.35) + ($5.00 – $1.75)

Here's How to Crack It

Before we solve the problem, let's talk about how the problem is structured. First, you will be given a description of the problem. Then, you will be given one correct method of solving the problem. Finally, you will be asked to identify an answer choice that gives you an alternative way of solving the problem.

So, how do you approach this type of question? First, you may be able to identify or set up your own equation after reading through the information. This may help you immediately identify the correct answer. However, if you aren't sure about how to set up the problem, you can still get the correct answer because:

Make sure your answer choice equals the expression given in the problem.

> The Value of the Correct Answer Will Equal the Value of the Given Equation!

If you aren't sure how to identify the other equation, no problem! Simplify the initial equation, solve each answer choice, and select the answer choice that gives you the same result as the initial equation. Let's do this for Example 1.

If we solve the equation given to us, we have \$5.00 – \$2.80 = \$2.20. Therefore, the correct answer needs to produce a value of \$2.20. Choice (A): 3 × (\$5.00 – \$1.75 – \$.35) = 3 × \$2.90 = \$8.70, so we can eliminate (A).

Choice (B): \$3.25 – 3 × \$.35 = \$3.25 – \$1.05 = \$2.20. Perfect! This equation yields the same value as the given equation, so (B) is the correct answer.

Of course, you will save more time if you are able to recognize the correct alternative equation without doing calculations. In this case, the total amount of change that Joe will receive back is \$5.00 minus the total cost of the hot dog with the toppings. In the given equation, each additional cost is subtracted from \$5.00. Choice (B) simplifies this equation by subtracting the cost of the hot dog from the \$5.00.

In summary, if you can identify the alternative equation, great. If not, don't worry. Solve each answer choice, and stop when you find one that equals the result of the given equation.

Here is one more example:

6. Oliver makes business trips between San Diego and San Francisco. Within the last year, Oliver took 6 trips by train, and 6 trips by plane. The cost of a train ride is $53, and the cost of a flight is $102. Oliver uses the following expression to calculate the amount of money he spends on these trips:

   (6 × $53) + (6 × $102)

   Which of the following expressions could Oliver have also used?

   A. 6($53 + $102)

   B. (12 × $53) + $102

   C. 36 × $155

   D. (6 + 6)($53 + $102)

   E. 12 ÷ $153

Here's How to Crack It

Try to manipulate the given expression to fit an expression in the answer choices.

In order to find the total cost Oliver spent on travel, we need to multiply the number of trips by the cost of each trip. The given equation does this for us by taking the sum of the cost of 6 plane trips and 6 train trips. If you look at the expression, you may be able to tell that this expression can be factored (you might even shout out "the distributive property!").

Yes, the expression can be simplified by removing the 6 from each individual expression:

(6 × $53) + (6 × $102)
= 6($53) + 6($102)
= 6($53 + $102)

Choice (A) is the correct answer. If you were not familiar with this factoring method, don't worry. Solve the expression:

(6 × $53) + (6 × $102)
= 318 + 612
= 930

Then go to the answer choices, and find a value that gives you 930. You'll find that only (A) will equal 930 (you should stop as soon as you find the first equation that yields the same result).

ANSWERS TO DRILLS

Equation Drill

From page 157

1. **B** First, add 3 to each side of the equation: $6y = -6$

   Now, divide each side of the equation by 6: $y = -1$.

2. **D** Here is the equation we are given: $n + 2b + p = h - r$

   Now, substitute the values we are given for n, b, p, and r:

   $$8 + 2(\frac{1}{2}) + \frac{3}{4} = h - 6$$

   $$8 + 1 + \frac{3}{4} = h - 6$$

   $$9\frac{3}{4} = h - 6$$

   $$15\frac{3}{4} = h$$

3. **C** If you got answer choice (B), reread the question! The question asks for twice the value of the variable c. Solve to find that c is 3; twice c is 6, which is the correct answer.

4. **E** Rewrite the equation as $3z = 10$. Since we are asked to find the value of $9z$, multiply the equation by 3 to get $9z = 30$. 30 is the correct answer.

5. **D** $3n + 7 = 4 - 5n$

   $8n + 7 = 4$ add $5n$ to both sides

   $8n = -3$ subtract 7 from both sides

   $n = -\frac{3}{8}$ divide both sides by 8

6. **A** Substitute $b = 5$:

   $4a + 8(5) = 36$

   $4a + 40 = 36$ simplify

   $4a = -4$ subtract 40 from both sides

   $a = -1$ divide both sides by 4

7. **E** First, we must solve $8 = 3h - 7$:

   $15 = 3h$ add 7 to both sides

   $5 = h$ divide both sides by 3

   Then, substitute $5 = h$ into the first equation:

   $g = 2(5)$

   $g = 10$

   The question asks for the value of g, which is 10.

8. **C** Careful! The question asks for an expression equal to $10t$. We could rewrite the equation in terms of t:

   $5t + 8 = 3s$

   $5t = 3s - 8$

   But wait! This equation is in terms of $5t$, and we want to end up with $10t$. We can simply multiply the whole equation by 2:

   $10t = 6s - 16$

Inequality Drill

From page 163

1. **A** Simplify the inequality to get $-3x \geq 12$. Divide by -3 to get that $x \leq -4$. Remember that the sign will change when multiplying or dividing by a negative number.
2. **A** Subtract 3 from both sides of the inequality to get $5x < 25$. Divide by 5 to get $x < 5$.
3. **B** Add 21 to each side of the inequality to get $-5x < 35$. Divide by -5 to get $x > -7$.
4. **B** $4 + 2w > 5$

   $2w > 1$ subtract 4 from both sides

   $w > \frac{1}{2}$ divide both sides by 2

5. **A** $-3f + 11 \leq 32$

   $-3f \leq 21$ subtract 11 from both sides

   $-f \leq 7$ divide both sides by 3

   $f \geq -7$ divide both sides by -1; flip the inequality sign

6. **E** You can solve normally:

$6p - 5 > p + 11$	
$6p > p + 16$	add 5 to both sides
$5p > 16$	subtract p from both sides
$p > \frac{16}{5}$	divide both sides by 5

Since p must be greater than 16/5, the only correct answer is (E) 16. Another option is to backsolve. Some of the fractions aren't particularly easy to work with, however. When you plug in the correct answer (E), you have:

$6(16) - 5 > (16) + 11$	
$96 - 5 > 27$	simplify
$91 > 27$	TRUE. Could you have estimated here?

Backsolving Drill

From page 169

1. **B** Start with (C). If Elizabeth jogs 14 miles, then Kathleen jogs 19. This total of 33 is too high, so eliminate (C), (D), and (E), and move to (B). If Elizabeth jogs 9 miles, and Kathleen jogs 14, then the total is 23.

2. **D** Start with (C). If 20 children register for the raffle, then 10 adults register. Since this total does not equal 42, the number of children is too small. Eliminate (C), (B), and (A), and move to (D). If 28 children are registered, then 14 adults are registered. This gives us the total of 42 we are looking for.

3. **E** It is possible to backsolve on equations. If you ever have a complicated equation, simply backsolve to find the correct value of the variable. In this case, starting with (C) will yield you a negative value, not the value of 3. Eliminate (C), (B), and (A). Choice (D) is also too small. Choice (E) gives us the correct value of x.

Summary

- When manipulating an equation, remember the golden rule of equations: Whatever you do to one side of the equation, you must do to the other side.
- When manipulating an equation, isolate the variable from all numbers.
- Treat inequalities just like equations, with one exception: Whenever you multiply or divide by a negative number, you must flip the sign.
- Backsolving is a powerful technique on algebra questions; rather than setting up your own equation, try Backsolving to see which one "fits" the problem.
- You can backsolve on any algebra question that has the following features:
    - numbers in the answer choices
    - a question that asks for a specific amount
- When Backsolving, start with the middle answer choice (C). If this answer choice does not work, you will often have a clue as to whether the correct answer will be smaller or larger.
- Use POE in conjunction with Backsolving to automatically eliminate answer choices that cannot work in the problem.
- When asked to identify the numbers needed to solve a problem, don't worry about solving the problem—simply set up the equation and identify the needed numbers.
- When given a "Which of the following can be determined?" question, be sure to not make any assumptions about what you can solve—stick to only the provided information.
- There are two ways to solve an alternative method problem. You can set up another equation, or you can calculate the value of the given equation, and see which one of the answer choices gives you the same value.

Chapter 9
Numerical and Graphical Relationships

About 35 percent of the mathematics problems on the CBEST will involve the question types described below. Some information, especially the logic rules, may be new to you. Don't worry—there will be very little information to memorize in this chapter. The following topics will be covered:

- Numerical relationships. Recognizing the position of numbers in relation to each other.
- Rounding. Using the rules of rounding when solving problems.
- Solving problems with graphs. Taking information contained in tables and graphs to solve math problems.
- Recognizing trends in information presented in graphs.
- Finding missing information in graphs.
- Rules of logic. Understanding and applying basic logical connectives.

POSITION OF NUMBERS

In the review chapter, we discussed the number line and how numbers are plotted on the line. On the CBEST, you will often be asked to recognize the position of numbers in relation to each other. Sample types of questions are:

- Which of the following numbers is greatest?
- Which of the following numbers is closest to zero?
- Which of the following numbers, when multiplied by 3, would yield the smallest product?

In order to handle these types of questions, here are a few rules to remember about the position of numbers.

FRACTIONS

If two fractions have the same numerator, the fraction with the larger denominator is the *smaller* fraction. For example, of $\frac{1}{4}$ and $\frac{1}{3}$, which fraction is larger? The larger fraction is $\frac{1}{3}$ (it has the smaller denominator).

Remember to use the Bowtie to compare two fractions (see page 112).

What about trying to find the larger of two fractions with different numerators and denominators? Remember, when trying to determine which fraction is larger, use the Bowtie. The Bowtie is especially useful when two fractions have different numerators and denominators.

1. Which of the following fractions is between $\frac{1}{4}$ and $\frac{1}{2}$?

   A. $\frac{1}{6}$

   B. $\frac{2}{3}$

   C. $\frac{1}{3}$

   D. $\frac{3}{4}$

   E. $\frac{1}{8}$

Here's How to Crack It

Before looking at the answer choices, take a look at the two fractions that we are given in the question. Which one is larger? $\frac{1}{2}$. Which one is smaller? $\frac{1}{4}$. So, we need to find an answer choice that is larger than $\frac{1}{4}$ and less than $\frac{1}{2}$. (If you are more comfortable with decimals, you may choose to look for a number that is greater than .25 and less than .5. However, this will require much more time, as you'll need to translate all of the answer choices into decimals as well). First, eliminate any answer choice that is not greater than $\frac{1}{4}$. We can eliminate (A) and (E). Next, eliminate any answer choice that is greater than $\frac{1}{2}$. From this step, we can eliminate (B) and (D). Choice (C), or $\frac{1}{3}$, is the correct answer.

NEGATIVE NUMBERS

The further a number is to the left in the number line, the smaller the number.

When comparing two negative numbers, the larger value is the number that is closer to 0 on the number line.

For example, which number has the larger value, –12 or –3? While we generally think of a value of 12 being larger (it just seems bigger), remember that the negative sign makes it smaller than –3. The number –3 is closer to zero on the number line than is –12.

---

2. Which of the following numbers is smallest?

   A. $-\frac{12}{5}$

   B. –4

   C. $\frac{2}{3}$

   D. 0

   E. $-\frac{19}{3}$

Here's How to Crack It

First, Ballpark using the answer choices. Eliminate any number that is not negative—(C) and (D). Next, we need to compare the remaining answer choices to each other, using the Bowtie. – 4 is smaller than $-\frac{12}{5}$. (Using the Bowtie, we get –20 above – 4, and –12 above $-\frac{12}{5}$.) Eliminate (A). Next, compare – 4 to $-\frac{19}{3}$. Using the Bowtie, you can tell that $-\frac{19}{3}$ is the smallest number. (E) is the correct answer.

DECIMALS

When comparing decimals, start by comparing numbers using the largest place. For example, which decimal is greater, 2.461 or 2.409? To find the correct answer, we start with the units digit. Each number has a units digit of 2, so move to the next greatest place, the tenths place. Each number has a tenths digit of 4, so move to the next greatest place, the hundredths place. In this place, the number 2.461 has a larger value than 2.409 (a 6 compared to a 0). Therefore, 2.461 is the larger decimal. Once you find a difference, the problem is solved (there's no need to compare the values in the thousandths place).

3. If the value of y is between .0045 and .023, which of the following could be the value of y?

   A. .0036

   B. .06

   C. .0261

   D. .018

   E. .0236

Here's How to Crack It

First, eliminate any answer choice that is not greater than .0045. This will eliminate (A). Next, eliminate any answer choice that is not less than .023. This will eliminate (B), (C), and (E). The remaining choice, (D), is the correct answer. The number .018 is located between .0045 and .023.

When asked about the position of numbers, remember the rules of fractions, negatives, and decimals. Further, POE is the key tool to solving these questions. Use the answer choices to help you eliminate incorrect answers, and to thereby find the correct answer.

ROUNDING NUMBERS

Rounding rules: If the following value is 5 or greater, round up. If the following value is 4 or lower, round down.

The CBEST test writers will sometimes ask you to round a number. Sample questions might read "...rounded to the nearest thousand" or "...if the result is rounded to the nearest tenth." Whenever you are asked to round a number, look at the next digit to the right. For example, if you are asked to round to the nearest tenth, then look at the hundredths digit. If the digit is 5 or higher, round up. Otherwise, round down.

Here is a sample question that you might see on the CBEST:

4. Students scored an average of 73.4861 on a recent test. What is the average score of the students, rounded to the nearest hundredth?

   A. 100

   B. 73.5

   C. 73.49

   D. 73.486

   E. 73.48

Here's How to Crack It

First, eliminate (A), (B), and (D). None of these answer choices are rounded to the nearest hundredth. To round 73.4861 to the nearest hundredth, we need to look at the digit in the thousandths place. The digit is 6. Rounding tells us that if a digit is 5 or greater, round up. Thus, we need to round the digit in the hundredths place from 8 up to 9. The correct answer is 73.49, (C).

ONLY ROUND ONCE!

Perform all calculations with complete numbers before rounding the final result.

It is important that you wait until all calculations have been finished before you round the numbers off. Rounding too early can lead to an incorrect answer choice. Here is an example in which rounding too early will lead to a mistake:

5. When the sum of 1.324 and 3.743 is rounded to the nearest tenth, the result is:

   A. 5.0

   B. 5.067

   C. 5.07

   D. 5.08

   E. 5.1

Here's How to Crack It

First, the answer must be rounded to the nearest tenth, so eliminate (B), (C), and (D). Next, add the two values together. Do *not* round yet! We're looking to round the **sum**, not the individual numbers. The equation: 1.324 + 3.743 yields a result of 5.067. Now we can round to the nearest tenth; the 6 digit in the hundredths place indicates that we need to round up. The correct answer is 5.1, (E). (Note that if you rounded each number initially, the values would be 1.3 and 3.7, and the sum would be 5.0—(A). Be careful!

ROUNDING DRILL

Answers can be found at the end of this chapter.

1. What is 2.019 rounded to the nearest tenth? To the nearest hundredth?

2. What is 438,172 rounded to the nearest hundred?

3. What is 173,893 rounded to the nearest thousand?

4. What is .4954 rounded to the nearest hundredth?

5. To the nearest ten, what is 186?

GRAPHS

The size of a graph will not indicate the level of difficulty of the questions. Don't let a large graph intimidate you!

Most types of math questions on the CBEST are presented as word problems. The CBEST writers will also ask you to solve various math problems using graphs. These graphs can take many forms—a table of information, a bar chart, a line chart, or a pie chart.

Often, questions using graphs can be intimidating to students, simply because of the size or amount of information presented in a graph. Yet graph questions are no more complicated than any other type of math question. Simply find the information that you need from the graph, use that data for any necessary calculations, and you're done. Finally, some students feel that the more complicated the graph, the more difficult the problem will be. This simply isn't true. Don't let the size of a graph intimidate you! Let's use the chart below to evaluate the questions that follow.

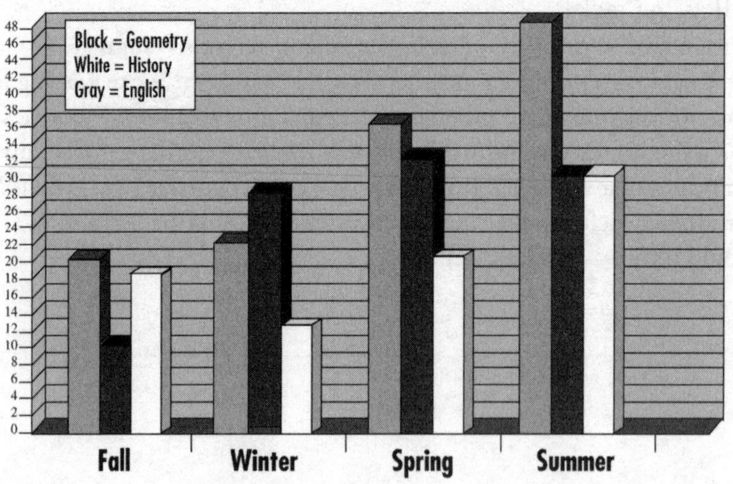

1. How many more students took geometry in the winter than took history in the fall?

   A. 3

   B. 10

   C. 18

   D. 19

   E. 28

Here's How to Crack It

In this graph question, we are asked to find the difference between two values on the graph. First, locate the value of each group. As you can see, 28 students took geometry in the winter and 18 students took history in the fall. After finding these two pieces of information, the problem is straightforward. Subtract 18 from 28 to get 10, or (B), as the correct answer. (Note: partial answer choices will always appear on problems using graphs, so be careful!)

As you can see, graph questions are not that complicated once you identify the type of information you need from the graph. In the example above, all the numbers we needed to use were presented in the graph. On some more challenging graph questions, you may need to do a few extra steps before finding the correct answer. Here is an example:

---

2. The percent of geometry students that took geometry in the spring is how much greater than the percent of history students that took history in the spring?

   A. 7%

   B. 12%

   C. 20%

   D. 30%

   E. 32%

Here's How to Crack It

This question asks us to compare two percents. In the graph above, no percentages are given, so we'll need to calculate the percentages first. To find the percent of geometry students that took geometry in the spring, we need two pieces of information—the total number of geometry students for the year, and the number of geometry students in the spring.

If we add up all geometry students for the year, there are 100. 32 took geometry in the spring. To express this as a percentage, we have $\frac{32}{100} = 32\%$.

If we follow the same procedure to determine the percent of history students that took history in the spring, we get:

$$\frac{20}{80} = \frac{1}{4} = 25\%$$

The difference between the two values is 32% –25%, or 7%. Choice (A) is the correct answer. Again, watch out for the numerous partial answer choices.

RELATING DATA FOUND IN GRAPHS

In the previous two examples, we had to take information from the graph and perform certain operations on the numbers. On some CBEST questions, you will be asked to compare numbers to each other. Sample questions include:

- "What was the percent increase from Year X to Year Y?"
- "In order to equal the amount of sales of Company X, Company Y needs to increase its sales by what percent?"
- "What year saw the greatest increase in production for Company X?"

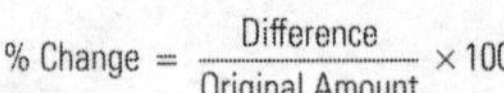

Remember the percent change formula? This formula is often helpful when asked to compare data within a graph. Using the graph from the previous page, let's examine one of these types of questions.

3. Which class saw the largest percent change in enrollment from spring to summer?

   A. English

   B. Geometry

   C. History

   D. English and History have the same percent increase

   E. It cannot be determined by the information given

Here's How to Crack It

We need to find the largest percent change from the spring term to the summer term. In order to find a percent change, use the percent change formula:

$$\% \text{ Change} = \frac{\text{Difference}}{\text{Original Amount}} \times 100$$

For English, the percent change is

$$\frac{(48-36)}{36} = \frac{12}{36} = \frac{1}{3} = 0.33$$

Then, multiply by 100 to get the percent: 33.33%.

For Geometry, the percent change is

$$\frac{(32-30)}{30} = \frac{2}{30} = \frac{1}{15} = \textit{less than}\, 10\%$$

For History, the percent change is

$$\frac{(30-20)}{20} = \frac{10}{20} = \frac{1}{2} = 0.5$$

Then, multiply by 100 to get the percent: 50%.

From these calculations, you can see that (C) is the correct answer choice.

FILL IN THE MISSING DATA

Another type of graph question asks you to supply information that has been left off of a graph. Some graphs may leave off totals, subtotals, etc. When asked to find the "missing piece," first try to identify any pattern in the data. This will help you ballpark your answer, as well as give you clues as to how to calculate the correct answer.

Use the table below to answer the question that follows:

Day	Starting Price of Stock X	Ending Price of Stock X
Monday	$3\frac{1}{2}$	6
Tuesday	6	$8\frac{1}{2}$
Wednesday	$8\frac{1}{2}$	11
Thursday	11	
Friday		16

4. The chart above shows the starting price and ending price of stock X for one week. If the same growth occurs throughout each day of the week, what was the starting price of stock X on Friday?

A. 11

B. $12\frac{1}{4}$

C. $13\frac{1}{2}$

D. $14\frac{1}{2}$

E. 16

Here's How to Crack It

Each day the stock gains $2\frac{1}{2}$ units (from "starting price of stock X" to "ending price of stock X"). If we add this to Thursday's starting price, the ending price on

Thursday will be $13\frac{1}{2}$. This is also the same starting price as the start total on Friday. Therefore, (C) is the correct answer.

LOGICAL CONNECTIVES

You may see a few questions dealing with fundamental rules of logic. While these questions may be unfamiliar to you, they aren't very complicated. There are only a few rules that will be tested on the CBEST, and we'll review them all.

If-Then Statements

An "If-Then" statement is a type of logical claim. It can be abbreviated "If A, then B." Consider the following statement:

> "If the children do their homework, then they will receive ice cream."

This statement can be broken into two parts. The "If" portion of the statement is "If the children do their homework" (the part of the statement represented by "A"). The "Then" statement is "they will receive ice cream" (the part of the statement represented by "B").

Only one other statement logically follows from an If-Then statement. This is called the contrapositive. If we have a statement of the form

If A, then B

the contrapositive form is

If not B, then not A

If we translate this to our statement above, the contrapositive tells us "If the children did not receive ice cream, then they did not do their homework."

On the CBEST, you may be asked to identify an answer choice that logically follows from a prior statement. The way to do this is always to find the contrapositive.

As an aside, you may be wondering if there are other possible truths in the statement above. Other statements, like "If the children did not do their homework, they did not receive ice cream" may seem correct, but cannot be proven (maybe someone decided to give them ice cream anyway). Also, the statement "The children received ice cream, so they must have done their homework" does not logically follow. All we know for certain is that if the children did not receive ice cream, they did not do their homework.

Memorize the contrapositive rule: Given If A, Then B, we know that If Not B, then Not A must be true.

A common problem with these types of questions is that students try to use too much information to solve the problem. Don't think of examples in everyday life, or whether or not children should get ice cream for doing their homework! Simply identify the contrapositive, and find it among the answer choices.

Here are some more example of If-Then statements:

---

5. Consider the following statement: If Ben scores a goal, his team will win. Which of the following answer choices must be true?

   A. Ben's team won, so he must have scored a goal.

   B. Ben's team lost, and he scored a goal.

   C. If Ben does not score a goal, his team will lose.

   D. If Ben's team lost, he didn't score a goal.

   E. Ben is the only member of his team who can score a goal.

Here's How to Crack It

The statement is an If-Then statement. Identify the contrapositive. In this example, the contrapositive is (D). Choice (D) is the correct answer. Choice (A) is incorrect, because it is not necessary that Ben score in order for his team to win. Choice (B) is incorrect, because our statement tells us that if Ben scores his team will win. Choice (C) is incorrect (it takes the form If not A, then not B—which is not always true). And (E) is out of scope.

---

6. Consider the following statement: If Paula orders tacos for dinner, she will not eat a salad. Which of the following statements must be true?

   A. Paula ate tacos and a salad for dinner.

   B. If Paula ate a salad for dinner, she did not order tacos.

   C. If Paula did not eat a salad, she must have ordered tacos.

   D. Paula will eat a salad for dinner.

   E. Paula does not like salad.

Here's How to Crack It

Again, you have been given an If-Then statement. This one is a little tricky since the second part of the argument is negative (If tacos, then *not* salad). Still, find the contrapositive to identify the correct answer. The contrapositive is: If salad, then no tacos. Choice (B) says exactly this, and is the correct answer. Choice (A) is impossible according to the information in the question. Choices (C) and (D) are possible, but cannot be proven. Choice (E) is a silly answer choice. Expect to see one of these per logic question, and be sure to eliminate it!

QUANTIFIERS—SOME, ALL, NONE

If-Then statements are not the only type of logic question that you may see on the CBEST. Other logic questions will involve quantifiers—terms that describe the members of a group. We'll take the three main quantifiers—all, some, and none—individually in the examples below.

All

Consider the following statement: "All integers are numbers." This statement tells us that every integer is also a number. But it does not follow that all numbers are integers. (In fact, we know that is false. There are other numbers, like decimals and fractions, which are not integers.)

On an "all" question, use the same rules that you would in a contrapositive question to find the correct answer.

So, if you are asked a question which includes the term "all," treat the statement the same way you would treat an If-Then statement. Use the contrapositive to find what logically follows.

7. Consider the following statements: "At Sequoia High School, all members of the basketball team are at least six feet tall."

   Which of the following statements must be true?

   A. Everyone at Sequoia High School is at least six feet tall

   B. All students at Sequoia High School who are at least six feet tall are on the basketball team.

   C. Students at Sequoia High School who are under six feet tall are not on the basketball team.

   D. Some students at Sequoia High School are under six feet tall.

   E. The tallest students at Sequoia High School are members of the basketball team.

Here's How to Crack It

We are told that all members of the basketball team are at least six feet tall. With an "all" quantifier, find the contrapositive. The contrapositive tells us that if a student is under six feet, then he or she is not a member of the basketball team. Choice (C) states the contrapositive, and is the correct answer. Choice (D) may seem correct, and is probably very likely, but it does not logically follow from the information in the question.

Some

"Some" tells us that at least one item fits a particular category.

Questions with the quantifier "some" are another type of logic question. Let's evaluate the following statement:

"Some of the students are wearing red shirts today."

What can we logically deduce from this statement? We could speculate about what the other students are wearing. We might speculate about the popularity of red shirts at school. However, the only thing we know for *certain* is that *at least one* of the students is wearing a red shirt. The quantifier "some" tells us that certain members of the group fit into one category. Here is an example:

8. All students must enroll in one math class. This year, students may choose between calculus, geometry, or statistics. Some of the students are enrolled in calculus. Which of the following must be true?

   A. Some students are enrolled in geometry.

   B. Some students are enrolled in statistics.

   C. All students are taking calculus.

   D. More students are taking calculus than geometry or statistics.

   E. Not all of the students are enrolled in statistics.

Here's How to Crack It

We are given the statement that some students are enrolled in calculus. Therefore, all we know is that at least one student is taking calculus. We don't know whether any students at all are enrolled in geometry or statistics, or how many are enrolled in each subject. In fact, it is possible that *all* of the students are taking calculus, but we can't be certain— therefore, eliminate (C). Choices (A) and (B) could be true, but we don't know whether students are enrolling in other subjects. Choice (D) is incorrect—we don't know the exact number of students enrolled in each subject. Choice (E) simply restates what we are told in the problem—if some of the students take calculus, we know that at least one student is studying calculus. Therefore, *all* students cannot be taking statistics. Choice (E) is correct.

None

A final type of quantifier you may see is "none." Consider the following example:

"At a reception, none of the soft drinks are diet sodas."

What do we know for certain given this statement? All we can deduce is that, of all the soft drinks at the reception, none of them are diet sodas. This is equivalent to saying that *all* soft drinks at the reception are *not* diet sodas.

Below is a sample question using all types of quantifiers.

9. Mitch has a collection of marbles. None of his marbles are colored green. Some of the marbles are colored red. The marbles are colored red, blue, orange, or yellow; but no marble has more than one color on it.

Which of the following statements must be true?

A. Mitch has more marbles colored red than any other color.

B. Mitch has more blue marbles than green marbles.

C. Mitch has more red marbles than green marbles.

D. Mitch's favorite marble is colored orange, red, and yellow.

E. If Mitch has a blue marble, then he has an orange marble.

Here's How to Crack It

The sample question has provided us with several statements about Mitch's collection of marbles.

Look at each answer choice, and eliminate those that are incorrect. Choice (A) might seem likely, but we are not given any information about the number of red marbles that Mitch has (or the number of marbles of any other color). We can't prove (A), so eliminate it. Next, we don't know if Mitch has any blue marbles at all, so eliminate (B). Choice (D) is incorrect—we are told in the problem that each marble has only one color. Choice (E) tries to trap you (it's an If-Then statement) but nothing like this is stated in the question. Choice (C) is true—it restates the two facts we are given in the problem. Mitch has at least one red marble, and has no green marbles. Therefore, he has more red marbles than green marbles.

ANSWERS TO ROUNDING DRILL

From page 189

1. 2.0, 2.02
2. 438,200
3. 174,000
4. 0.50
5. 190

Summary

- Topics presented in this chapter will account for approximately 35 percent of the questions you see on the Mathematics Section of the CBEST.
- Use the number line as a guide to the position of numbers in relation to each other. Be sure to review the rules of negative numbers, fractions, and decimals—often the CBEST writers will use these types of numbers in these types of questions.
- When rounding, look at the digit beyond the place to which you are to round. If the digit is from 0–4, round down. If the digit is 5 or greater, round up.
- Only round numbers *after* all calculations have been performed. Rounding numbers before working with them can lead to rounding errors and incorrect answers.
- Questions involving graphs are no more complicated than other math questions. Find the information you need to do the problem. The size or complexity of the graph does not relate to the difficulty of the problem.
- You will often need to use the percent change formula on graph questions.
- Look for a pattern in order to identify how to calculate any missing information in a graph.
- When given an If-Then statement, the only logical deduction you can make is the contrapositive.
    - Logic: If *a*, Then *b*.
    - Contrapositive: If Not *b*, Then Not *a*.
- The CBEST will include quantifiers, such as "all," "some," and "none" in logic questions. Use POE on all questions to find the correct logical answer choice.
- Use the rules of If-Then statements when given a question that has an "all" quantifier.
- When you see the quantifier "some" (i.e., "some of *x* are *y*"), then the only conclusion you can draw is that at least one member of *x* belongs to *y*.

Part IV Cracking the Writing Section

INTRODUCTION TO THE WRITING SECTION

The CBEST Writing Section contains two essays, an "Issue" essay and an "Experience" essay.

You will be asked to compose two essays in the Writing Section of the CBEST. One of the topics asks you to analyze a situation or statement. We'll call this essay the "Issue" essay. The other topic asks you to write about a personal experience. We'll call this the "Experience" essay. There is no specific time restriction for the Writing Section. As we've mentioned, you will have four hours to complete the entire CBEST; our pacing plan allots approximately 30–40 minutes per essay. Note that if you are taking the paper-based version of the exam, your essay must be written in pencil. Therefore, when you practice composing essays for the CBEST, be sure to use a pencil.

There is a tremendous difference between writing a good essay for one of your classes and writing a good essay for purposes of the CBEST. Most composition assignments in school require you to write essays that are several pages long. Most require you to demonstrate some specialized knowledge on a particular topic. If a teacher were to assign you a ten-page paper on a specific topic, he or she would probably evaluate your essay on a number of factors—command of the material, insight, analysis, and overall writing ability. Obviously, this same set of criteria won't be applied to the impromptu essays you write for the CBEST.

CBEST scorers have a very specific way of reading and evaluating each of your essays. The scorers who will read and score your essays are usually teachers, trained to read these essays "holistically." Holistic scoring means that the teachers will evaluate your essays not only on the basis of your ideas, but also by the quality of your writing. We'll outline these scoring criteria, and then design a specific approach to each of the two essays on the CBEST.

HOW ARE ESSAYS SCORED?

Two graders will read each of your essays. Each essay will be given a score from 1–4. We'll describe what each of the scores represents in a moment. Graders will evaluate your essays based on the following criteria:

1. **Rhetorical Force**—the clarity with which the central idea or point of view is stated and maintained; the coherence of the discussion and the quality of the writer's ideas.
2. **Organization**—the clarity of the writing and the logical sequence of the writer's ideas.
3. **Support and Development**—the relevance, depth, and specificity of supporting information.
4. **Usage**—the extent to which the writing shows care and precision in word choice.
5. **Structure and Conventions**—the extent to which the writing is free of errors in syntax, paragraph structure, sentence structure, and mechanics (spelling, punctuation, and capitalization).
6. **Appropriateness**—the extent to which the writer addresses the topic and uses language and style appropriate to the given audience and purpose.

Scoring Description

A score of 4, or pass, describes a well-formed writing sample that effectively communicates a whole message to the specified audience. An essay of this caliber has the following characteristics:

- The writer clearly presents a central idea and/or point of view and maintains focus on that topic; the response is well reasoned.
- Ideas or points of discussion are logically arranged, and their meaning is clearly communicated.
- Assertions and generalizations are supported with relevant and specific information.
- Word choice is precise and usage is careful and accurate.
- The writer composes well-formed sentences and paragraphs, with only minor flaws in mechanical conventions.
- The response completely addresses the topic and uses language and style appropriate for the given audience.

A score of 3, or marginal pass, is an adequately formed writing sample that communicates a message to the specified audience. An essay that receives a score of 3 has the following characteristics:

- The writer presents a central idea and/or point of view and generally maintains focus. The response is adequately reasoned.
- Organization of ideas is generally clear and effective, and the meaning is generally clear.
- Assertions and generalizations are adequately supported, although sometimes unevenly.
- Word choice and usage are adequate. Some errors are present, but they do not take away from the overall meaning.
- The response may have errors in paragraphing, sentence structure, and/or mechanical conventions, but they are neither frequent nor serious enough to impede overall meaning.
- The response may not fully address the topic.

A score of 2, or marginal fail, is a partially formed writing sample that attempts to communicate a message to the specified audience, and has the following characteristics:

- The writer may state a central idea or opinion, but loses focus. Reasoning may be too simplistic.
- Organization of ideas may be present, but is ineffective, leaving the reader confused.
- Assertions are only partially supported. Some comments may be irrelevant or insufficient.
- Word choice and usage are unclear, and are a distraction to the reader.
- The writer's response may have distracting errors in paragraphing, sentence structure, and mechanical conventions.
- The response incompletely addresses most tasks of the assignment, and/or uses language inappropriate for the audience and purpose.

A score of 1, or fail, is an inadequately formed writing sample that fails to communicate a message to the specified audience. In order to fail, your essay would have the following characteristics:

- The writer fails to state a central idea or opinion. The response lacks coherence and reason.
- Organization of ideas is ineffective and seriously flawed, impeding the meaning throughout.
- Assertions are not supported or are very underdeveloped; the presentation of details is confused.
- Word choice and usage contain serious and frequent errors.
- The response demonstrates little or no understanding of any of the assignment's tasks. Language may be inappropriate for the audience and purpose.

OUR APPROACH TO THE ESSAYS

Apply the Strategy

We'll help you develop a strategy to construct a format for your essays before you begin writing.

Throughout the remainder of this chapter, we will show you how to develop a specific plan to compose an essay on the CBEST. We'll identify specific strategies for the Issue essay and the Experience essay. Further, we will go back to the scoring criteria above, and ensure that you follow the six keys to a strong essay. Finally, we'll point out some of the most common errors and traps that students fall into when writing their essays.

Preparing for the Essay

We've just spent four chapters reviewing the key concepts and strategies you'll need for the Mathematics Section. Many students think there is no way to prepare for the essays, though. They often feel that since they won't know the essay topics in advance, preparation is impossible. After all, are there key concepts and strategies when it comes to an essay?

It is true that you'll see the topic for the first time on the day of the CBEST; however, you CAN walk into the test with a specific plan for how you will compose your essays. You can prepare the structure of your paragraphs, including how they will relate to one another. In short, you will have a blueprint for composing an essay on any topic.

ISSUE ESSAY

There are a number of things you will need to do in order to create a successful Issue essay:

1. **Read the entire topic and question at least once.** Identify what the authors are asking you to discuss. Are you simply asked if you agree or disagree with an issue, or are the writers asking you to respond to a number of questions? Does the question ask you to use examples? If so, do the writers want specific examples (from school, recent events, literature, etc.)?
2. **Take a stand. Are you for or against the issue?** Taking a clear stand on the issue is crucial to the framework of your entire essay.
3. **Support your claim.** Now is the time to come up with examples. Take down notes on your test booklet, and come up with three to five reasons/examples that support your claim. You will need to expand on these in order to explain and defend your thesis to the reader. Spend up to five minutes brainstorming and taking notes. Don't worry just yet about the strength of your examples.
4. **Rank your supporting work.** Choose the best three or four examples/reasons that support your claim.
5. **Compose your essay.** This step will be discussed in much more detail. In short, you'll be inserting your claim and supporting ideas into a general template.
6. **Review your essay.** Once your essay is complete, you will need to review it to be sure you have avoided the traps and mistakes that students frequently make.

Tip! It is imperative that you take a stand in an "Issue" essay. You must decide if you are for or against the topic.

Successful Issue Essays

CBEST authors are looking for an essay that takes a stand. You must take a strong position on the issue. It will not matter which side of an issue you take—there are no "right" or "wrong" answers on these essays. Certainly, you will want to present good evidence to support your position, but authors will never deduct points for choosing a particular position. In addition to taking a stand, authors will grade you on how well you support your position. Finally, the essay must be engaging—well organized, easy to read, and structurally sound.

An Issue Essay Template

Typically, but not always, a good essay will have five paragraphs: an introduction, three body paragraphs, and a conclusion. As you practice writing, you may find that you want to come up with your own template. The template presented here is just one example of how to write a successful Issue essay. It does, however, provide you with a systematic way to organize and construct a successful essay. Keep in mind that you can always alter your format if it doesn't suit the requirements of a particular essay prompt.

Paragraph 1: The issue of ______________________________

____

is a controversial one. Some believe that ______________

Others believe that ______________________________

____

After careful thought, I believe that ________________

____

Paragraph 2: One reason for this belief is that ____________

____

Paragraph 3: Another reason for this belief is ____________

____

Paragraph 4: The best reason for this belief is ____________

____

Paragraph 5: In the final analysis, ____________________

____

Paragraph 1—The Introduction

Your introduction needs to do the following things:

1. Introduce/restate the issue.
2. Address the two sides of the issue.
3. State your thesis. A thesis sentence is the sentence that states your overall position on the issue, and tells the readers what you are going to discuss. Use your thesis to state your position, and introduce the supporting reasons that you will use in the paragraphs to follow.

More Great Books

Improve your vocabulary in order to write a stellar essay by checking out *Grammar Smart* and *Word Smart* from your friends at The Princeton Review.

Let's use some sample Issue essay questions in order to practice writing the first paragraph in our essay:

Essay Topic 1

The school board at High School X is considering raising the number of years of required physical education classes. The board will be voting on a proposal to raise the number of years students need to take physical education from one year to three years. Do you think the school board should increase the physical education requirement to three years? Support your opinion with specific examples.

Here is an example of a first paragraph that uses the sample template provided above:

> The issue of increasing the required number of physical education classes in high school is a controversial one. Some believe that physical education classes are a crucial part of the high school experience, where students learn lessons of competition and cooperation. Others believe that physical education activities can be done after the school day in extracurricular activities, and that the increase in the number of required classes would take away from more traditional learning. After careful thought, I believe that the school board should increase the physical education requirement to three years in order to benefit student health, teach general cooperation skills, and provide a necessary break from a long day indoors.

Notice how the same template can be used to take different stands on an issue. Regardless of what you write about, the template does not change.

As you can see, we used the template format above to write our introductory paragraph. To finish our essay, we would then use the following paragraphs to develop the reasons we presented in our thesis statement (student health, cooperation skills, and a break from the classroom). Is it possible that we could use this template, but take the other side of the issue? Of course! Here is a sample paragraph that takes the other position:

> **The issue of** increasing the required number of physical education classes in high school **is a controversial one. Some believe that** physical education classes are not as important as more traditional subjects like math and history. **Others believe that** physical education activities help to teach competition and cooperation, skills that students need to learn for their experiences beyond the classroom. **After careful thought,** I believe that the school board should not increase the physical education requirement to three years because students would lose the opportunity to take other electives, which, unlike physical education, cannot easily be done after school hours.

You may have noticed in the two examples above that in making this particular template work most effectively, "some believe that..." introduces a position that you are ultimately going to support. The "others believe that..." introduces some counter arguments to your position. The sentence beginning "after careful thought..." will return to the point of view you believe in, and is where you will state your thesis.

Now that the first paragraph is complete, we will begin to focus on the next step of the essay—supporting your claim.

Brainstorming

Spend a few minutes listing as many examples and reasons you can think of to support your claim.

You've taken a stand on one side of an issue. Now, you need to support it. Before you begin writing your essay, take notes on your scratch paper, coming up with several examples and reasons to support your position. This is often called brainstorming. Don't worry about the quality of these examples. The goal in brainstorming is to come up with as many examples as possible.

If you are having trouble coming up with reasons, don't panic. Reread the question, and think about the people who would be affected by the issue being discussed. In the example above, who would be affected? Certainly the students would face a new curriculum in school. Administrators, parents, and teachers would also have opinions on the issue. Consider some of the arguments these groups would make. Would they be happy with the position you've taken? Why, or why not?

Once you have spent a few minutes brainstorming, you then need to start going through what you have written to determine which ideas are most compelling. The template we've provided includes three paragraphs to support your claim. In general, three examples are sufficient to support your thesis. Now, plan the order in which you want to present these ideas. Save your strongest example for the final supporting paragraph.

Paragraphs 2, 3 and 4—Your Supporting Paragraphs

Your goal is to support your thesis with specific compelling examples. Try to add depth and clarity to your examples. Err on the side of thoroughly explaining a statement, rather than simply making assertions without the facts to support them. Make sure that each paragraph focuses on one idea, as the readers will grade your essay based in part on your ability to organize your ideas logically into separate paragraphs.

Paragraph 5—Writing Your Conclusion

The appearance of your essay is important. If you are taking the paper-based test, be sure to write neatly! If you are taking the computer-based test, be sure that your paragraphs are properly formatted.

A conclusion paragraph needs to restate your central claim, and leave the reader with a final point to consider. First, summarize your thesis. *Although there are some benefits to increasing physical education requirements, the proposal to do so should not be approved.* After another sentence or two, leave the reader with a final sentence that states your opinion. Try to make this final sentence powerful, as it is the final thing your reader will see when evaluating your essay. *While students may increase their physical fitness, are we willing to decrease their classroom experiences?* Remember that the conclusion is for summing up: don't introduce new examples or basic ideas in your final paragraph. However, it is desirable to rephrase your thesis, as opposed to simply reproducing it verbatim from the introduction (which is less interesting and can appear mechanical).

Review Your Essay

Once you complete your essay, read it over again. Check for the common traps and errors we'll identify later in this chapter. Do any necessary editing. Then, take a deep breath, and start the next essay.

THE EXPERIENCE ESSAY

There are a number of things you will need to do in order to write an effective Experience essay. You'll already be familiar with some of the steps below from the Issue essay.

Most "Experience" essays will ask you about your teaching experience, or your motivation to become a teacher. Spend some time before test day thinking about your teaching background.

1. **Read the entire topic and question at least once.** Identify what the authors are asking you to discuss. Are you asked to describe an event from your life? Does the essay ask how the event has affected you? Are you asked to identify important people in your life? How did they help influence you?
2. **Choose a topic.** If you can immediately identify an experience (event, person, etc.), move on to step 4. If you don't immediately recognize a topic, move to step 3 to brainstorm.
3. **Develop your story.** Now is the time to come up with an experience to describe. Do not try to make up a story that you feel will reflect what the readers want to read. The questions will be general enough so that you will be able to draw an experience from your life. Your challenge will be to communicate the details, importance, and impact that your experience had on you. Take down notes on your test booklet, and come up with details to support your experience. You will need to describe your experience in detail in order to support and explain your thesis to the reader. Spend up to 5 minutes brainstorming and taking notes.
4. **Answer a reader's questions.** Before you begin to write your essay, be sure that your essay will answer the following questions:
   - Who was involved?
   - How long did the event last?
   - Why did the event occur?
   - What were your emotions during the event?
   - What were the effects of the event?
   - How has the event changed you?

   These questions, of course, won't apply to all essays. In general, though, be sure that your essay conveys not only what happened, but also your feelings about the event.

5. **Compose your essay.** After spending 5-7 minutes on the steps above, compose your essay. We will provide a sample template on the next page.
6. **Review your essay.** Once your essay is complete, you will need to review it as with the Issue essay to be sure you have avoided the traps and mistakes that students frequently make.

Successful Experience Essays

CBEST authors are looking for an essay that grabs their attention. Try to compose an essay that describes an important or symbolic moment in your life. Writing about how you learned to walk and chew gum at the same time is probably not as compelling as how you learned to overcome your fear of public speaking. When you describe your experience, keep in mind that the reader does not have any background knowledge about the event or people involved in your story. Be sure to fully describe the characters and supporting information in your experience. Finally, like the Issue essay, the Experience essay must be appealing to read—well organized, clearly written, and structurally sound.

An Experience Essay Template

We've covered the basics of a template when we wrote the Issue essay, but the Experience essay requires a different set of criteria. There are innumerable formats that you can use to compose your essay, so organize your ideas whatever way seems the most logical. Again, five paragraphs will typically work best.

Sample Template 1

Paragraph 1: Introduction and thesis.
Paragraph 2: Describe the event.
Paragraph 3: Describe the immediate effects of the event.
Paragraph 4: Describe the long-term effects of the event.
Paragraph 5: Conclusion.

Sample Template 2

Paragraph 1: Introduction and thesis.
Paragraph 2: Describe any background information/events leading up to your experience.
Paragraph 3: Describe the choices you felt you needed to make.
Paragraph 4: Describe the results of your actions.
Paragraph 5: Conclusion.

Any variation will work; just make sure that your essay is constructed in a logical format. In any case, the two most important paragraphs of your essay are the first and last, the introduction and conclusion.

The Introduction

Your introduction needs to do the following things:

1. Introduce/restate the topic.
2. Provide any information that the reader would need in order to understand your thesis.
3. State your thesis. For an Experience essay, a thesis should introduce the event you are about to discuss, and how it may have shaped you as a person.

Let's use a sample Experience essay question in order to practice writing the first paragraph:

> **Essay Topic 2**
>
> At some point in our lives, all of us have faced some sort of rejection or defeat. Write an essay about a time in your life when you experienced such a rejection. How did the experience affect you?

Here is a sample first paragraph:

> Most people think of rejection as a negative experience. We are quick to become discouraged when we are defeated. However, there are many valuable lessons to be learned in the face of rejection. The state championships in water polo were the occasion of my greatest humiliation and rejection. I suffered many defeats during the water polo playoffs, but these defeats helped me to refocus my efforts and improve my performance considerably.

As you can see, we used the template format above to write our introductory paragraph. To finish our essay, we would then use the following paragraph topics to explain the event (what happened at the state championships?), the immediate effects (anger, sadness, etc.), and the long-term effects (refocus, improvement, rededication to the sport). Remember to ask yourself the why, what, how, when, and where questions to ensure you are delivering a vivid picture of the event to the reader.

Concluding the Experience Essay

A conclusion paragraph should first summarize the event about which you wrote. "It was devastating to sit on the bench during the playoffs after having been a starter for the entire regular season." After another sentence or two, leave the reader with a final sentence that states your opinion about how the event has changed you or your life. Try to make this final sentence powerful, as it is the final thing your reader will see when evaluating your essay. "I often speculate on what type of player I would be if the coach had let me play on that June afternoon, but I am certain I wouldn't be as dedicated and focused as I am today."

SIX KEYS TO A STRONG ESSAY

So far, we've discussed how to construct templates for each type of essay you will write on the CBEST. Now, let's revisit the scoring criteria to make sure that your essays will include all of the items a reader looks for when evaluating your response.

1. Answer the Question, and Only the Question—Rhetorical Force

Some essay prompts contain more than one question. Be sure your essay answers all of the questions.

As Sergeant Joe Friday would say, "Just the facts, ma'am." In order to compose a successful essay, you must present an essay that answers the question. Make sure your thesis addresses all questions presented to you. If an essay question asks you to describe an experience and the influence it had on you, you must address both parts. Writing only about the experience, and not about the effects of the experience, will lower your score.

Further, do not stray from the topic to add information that does not directly address the question. Sure, sometimes you may need to write a paragraph that provides background information on an issue, but don't write a paragraph that has nothing to do with the question. A strong essay is focused, complete, and to the point. As a final review of your essay, take each paragraph, and make sure it ties back in to your thesis.

2. Organization

Our templates give you a specific framework to present your thoughts in a clear, logical way. Use paragraphs 2, 3, and 4 to explain your topic of choice. Readers will appreciate an essay that flows from one paragraph to the next, and transition sentences help to join two paragraphs together. Your first sentence (which is usually your topic sentence) should identify with the information presented in the previous paragraph. For example, referring to the essay about physical education requirements, the second paragraph could describe the health benefits. The third paragraph could describe the lessons of cooperation and teamwork learned through physical education classes. How could these be tied together? Quite easily. In fact, check out the sentence below.

> The increase in physical education classes would not only improve the general health of a student, but would also improve cooperation and teamwork skills.

This sentence helps to connect one paragraph to the next, and tells the reader what the paragraph will be describing. Transition sentences do not need to be fancy, so don't waste time trying to come up with elegant connections from one point to the next.

3. Development of Ideas

CBEST scorers will want you to provide support for your ideas. Stating an opinion is not enough. The scorers will want to see if you have legitimate explanations for your ideas. On the CBEST scoring criteria, the "depth" of supporting information is important. Compare the following two explanations:

> **No depth:** Under the new requirements, students would miss valuable class time.
>
> **Depth:** Consider the effects of two more years of physical education classes. Currently, students are able to take only four "elective" classes during their sophomore through junior years. If students need to take two more years of physical education classes, they will lose 50 percent of their elective classes. Most students cite elective classes as the most rewarding classes in school.

Which do you think the CBEST readers prefer? If you are going to state an opinion, be sure you have enough information to explain your reasoning. CBEST scorers will never penalize you for stating an opinion, only for opinions that are not fully explained.

4. Usage

CBEST scorers are looking for two things regarding the composition of your essay: Intelligent word choice, and correct usage of words. Try to vary your word choice when writing your essay. If you have an essay topic that asks you to describe an event that occured when you were happy, do not use the word "happy" fifty times during your response. Further, if you are not sure what a word means, don't use it. An improperly placed word can stall an essay, or contradict a point you are trying to convey. Be sure to avoid common diction errors as well! These include confusing "your" (the possessive pronoun) with "you're" (the contraction of "you are") and "its" (the possessive pronoun) for "it's" (the contraction of it and is). In order to receive a good score on this part of the essay, make sure you avoid the word-choice traps.

For more on fundamental grammar rules and sentence construction, check out *Writing Smart*, by The Princeton Review. It's a great resource if you're looking to improve your writing skills.

5. Structure and Convention

A strong essay will be both grammatically correct and easy to read. One way to make an essay easier to read is by changing the form and look of your sentences. Effective writing mixes up short and long sentences for variety. If you find that all of your sentences are about the same length and tone, try to adjust the sentence length.

6. Appropriateness

You are writing to an experienced group of teachers. Consider your audience when composing your essays.

Finally, a strong essay will appeal to the person evaluating your essays. Since CBEST scorers are veteran teachers who have been trained to grade these essays, consider what you would write to a veteran teacher. In general, if you write within a strong template, and explain yourself, the readers will easily understand your essay. However, be sure to avoid using any jargon, acronyms, or language that may be unfamiliar to the reader.

ESSAY WRITING PITFALLS

Here are some of the most common mistakes that students make when writing essays for the CBEST. Read through them to make sure you aren't doing the same types of things when writing your essays.

The "I Believe" Syndrome

Whenever an essay asks for your opinion on an issue, it is very natural to state "I believe" or "I think." There is no problem with this, as long as you only do it once in a while. However, if you qualify every opinion statement with "I think," the essay will become very dull to read. We know that everything you write is what you think. After all, you're writing the essay.

Big Word Syndrome

Some test takers believe that if they can insert challenging vocabulary into their essays, they will receive a high score. Often, these attempts fail miserably. Don't panic if you feel you are composing your essay in simple, conversational text. The important thing is how well your essay flows, not whether you can insert the words "anthropomorphic" and "catastrophic" into the same sentence. It's great to use impressive vocabulary words if you can, but make sure that you're using them correctly. When in doubt, leave them out!

Redundancy Syndrome

There is nothing worse than reading the same idea over and over again, written in a number of different ways. Economy of words is important on the CBEST. Don't write a sentence unless it has something unique to add to the essay. Don't write a sentence unless it has something unique to add to the essay. Don't write a sentence unless it has something unique to add to the essay.

Ugly Essay Syndrome

CBEST scorers will read several hundred essays at one time. Imagine how your essay will be treated if it is messy, illegible, and without proper indentations. Be respectful to your readers. They appreciate a neat, well-formatted essay. Write neatly if you are taking the paper-based test. If you are taking the computer-based test, be sure to indent properly.

Summary

- You will be asked to compose two essays on the CBEST—one Issue essay and one Experience essay. While there is no specific time limit for each essay, our pacing plan suggests you spend between 30–40 minutes for each.
- CBEST scorers will evaluate your essays on a number of criteria, and give you an overall score from 1–4 for each essay. Two readers will grade each essay.
- Have a plan for constructing your essays. Use a template, if possible, so that you will know ahead of time how your essays will be organized.
- For a successful Issue essay: Step 1: Read the entire topic and question at least once. Step 2: Take a stand. Step 3: Brainstorm. Step 4: Rank your supporting work. Step 5: Compose your essay. Step 6: Review your essay.
- For a successful Experience essay: Step 1: Read the entire topic and question at least once. Step 2: Choose a topic. Step 3: Develop your story. Step 4: Answer a reader's questions. Step 5: Compose your essay. Step 6: Review your essay.
- Your thesis statement should be stated in the introductory paragraph of each essay.
- Avoid the common essay syndromes—"I believe," big words, redundancy, and the ugly essay.

Part V Taking the CBEST

Test day is coming. After all the hours of studying, memorizing math rules and practicing your essays, it is time for the real thing. No problem! By the time you've completed this book, you will have studied all of the types of problems that will appear on this test, learned key strategies and techniques for maximizing the number of questions you can get correct, and taken and reviewed up to four full-length practice tests. In this chapter, we're going to talk about how to get ready for test day—what you'll need, how to handle the day of the test, and what to do after you've completed the test.

Know All Procedures, Policies, and Test Center Rules

Be sure to thoroughly familiarize yourself with the CBEST website and all the current regulations governing the test. These rules can be strictly enforced. Violating procedure could result in your being ejected from the testing center, your scores being voided, or even your teaching credentials being revoked. Know which items are prohibited from the testing center, which forms of ID are acceptable, what constitutes cheating, etc. Something as minor as having a middle initial on your ID—but not on your admissions ticket—could be a serious issue. Policies may change, so be sure to stay well-informed!

If you arrive to the exam significantly late you will likely not be admitted. Give yourself more than enough time to get to the test center on schedule!

The Night Before

Students often try to do something dramatic the night before the CBEST. Don't. You've probably been told to make sure you get lots of sleep the night before the exam. If you are accustomed to sleeping only six hours a night, trying to get twelve hours of sleep the night before will not benefit you. You'll probably be sitting in bed for hours wondering why you're trying to get so much sleep, and won't think about anything except the test!

Pack a bag the night before the test with everything you will need (e.g., admissions ticket, ID, medications, snacks for breaks, pencils and sharpeners, etc.)!

Another common mistake is to "cram" the night before the CBEST. If you've studied the techniques we've presented, and have taken the practice tests, cramming will do absolutely nothing except raise your level of anxiety about the test. If you want to do a few practice problems, great. Go over problems you've already solved. If you think that you can improve your math score by doing 300 math questions the night before, think again.

In short, stick to your normal routine. Have a relaxing evening (maybe watch a good comedy), and you'll be ready to go on test day.

Nerves

It is absolutely natural to be nervous going in to take the test. The CBEST is an important hurdle in your quest to be a teacher and should be taken seriously. It shouldn't scare you, however. We don't want you to get so nervous about passing the test that you just sit there for four hours and stare blankly at the test booklet.

The actual CBEST will be just like the practice tests you have taken. Walk into the testing center on test day knowing that you have seen this material before.

How do you avoid this? Well, you're already doing it. The best way to avoid getting nervous is to become familiar with the test. For this reason, it is extremely important that you take the practice tests under the same conditions as an actual CBEST. Give yourself four hours in a quiet environment. Don't watch TV when you take the tests, and don't break out a calculator for those difficult calculations. Familiarity with the test is a key component to gaining confidence on the CBEST. You'll be able to practice dealing with the fatigue that will set in during the four hours. Sure, the actual CBEST will be somewhat more stressful than the practice tests you take, but you want to be sure you're familiar with how the day will work. You may still be nervous, and that's fine. You just don't want to be panicked.

It is also important to remember that you have learned many techniques and strategies that leave you in control of the CBEST. You control the order in which you complete the sections. You control which questions you want to attack. You can use the tools of Process of Elimination, Scope, and Ballparking to leave you in better control of the answer choices. These techniques will help you greatly increase your chances of solving the problem correctly.

Use the practice tests to refine your control of the CBEST. In Chapter 2, we talked about the recommended pacing on each section. Make sure to modify this pacing after each diagnostic test so that by test day you'll have a clear plan for how much time you should spend on each section.

Four Hours Is a Long Time

Feel free to take a few breaks during the test to compose yourself.

Be sure to use all four hours of the testing period when taking the CBEST. Your pacing plan should allow an extra 10 to 15 minutes to do the following: relax between sections, use the restroom, sharpen pencils, and so forth. Don't feel like you have to continually be working at a furious pace during these four hours. Give yourself "mini-breaks" throughout the test. Closing your eyes, and taking five deep breaths, can often be all that you need to clear your mind before moving on to the next section.

Also remember that this is not a race! You will likely see other test takers leave the room before the end of the four hours. Remember that some test takers will only be taking one or two sections of the exam; others will take the test as quickly as possible. When the room gets half-empty, it can be very tempting to start to rush, with hopes of starting your Saturday afternoon a little early. Stay focused. A few more minutes in the testing room can mean never having to go back to take the CBEST again.

Testing Conditions

As a test taker, you have a right to a fair and accurate administration of your test. If you encounter anything that you feel is unsatisfactory, don't be afraid to ask your proctor or test supervisor to change it. Certain examples of unsatisfactory conditions are: a room with an uncomfortable temperature, excessive noise surrounding the classroom, or incorrect timing of the test. If you feel that your test was not administered in the correct way, be sure to document the incident after the test, and contact NES to discuss your rights as a test taker.

Receiving Your Scores

You can access your scores online at **www.cbest.nesinc.com**. When you register to take the CBEST you can also request that your scores be emailed to you. Scores for the computer-based version may be available within a few days after you take your test (depending upon when during the CBT testing period you sit for the exam). Scores for the paper-based version are generally available after about two weeks (consult the website for the applicable score release dates). In addition to receiving your scores, you will receive a detailed breakdown of your performance on each of the skills measured by each section of the test.

Should You Ever Cancel Your Score?

It is possible that you may leave the test center feeling that you did not perform as well as you had hoped. Unfortunately, many students in that situation feel that the correct thing to do is cancel their scores. No matter how you think you performed on the exam, **DO NOT** cancel your scores on the CBEST. Here are just a few reasons why:

1. **You only have to pass**. Unlike other standardized tests, where your score can be used as an evaluative measure, you only have to pass the CBEST. Your scaled scores are inconsequential— a 41 equals a pass, as does an 80. So, you shouldn't be concerned about how well you performed, only about whether you passed.
2. **You may pass some (or all) of the sections!** Typically, when students cancel their scores, it is because they feel that they performed horribly on one section. Well, if you cancel your score, you will not receive the results of any section on the test. Remember, if you pass a section of the CBEST, you'll never need to take that section again. For example, if Chris passed the essays and Reading Section, but not the Mathematics Section, he would only need to take the Mathematics Section during the next administration of the CBEST. If he cancels his scores, he would need to take all three sections again.
3. **Your score report can help you in the future.** If you did not pass one of the sections, the information provided on your CBEST score report can help you when you take the test again. When you receive your scores, you will also receive a category breakdown within the Reading and Mathematics Sections. This feedback can help you narrow your focus when you study for a particular section again.

Since you only need to pass the CBEST, we recommend that you do not cancel your scores.

If you are taking the computer-based version of the CBEST, canceling your score may not be an option.

And Finally . . .

Be sure to celebrate after completing the test. You deserve it.

Congratulations! You are on your way to becoming a teacher.

Chapter 10
Practice Test 1

SECTION I: TEST OF READING

Directions: Each question in the Reading section of the practice test is a multiple-choice question with five answer choices. Read each question carefully and choose the ONE best answer. Record each answer on the answer sheet provided in the back of this book.

You may work on the multiple-choice questions in any order that you choose. You may wish to monitor how long it takes you to complete the practice test. When taking the actual CBEST, you will have one four-hour test session in which to complete the section(s) for which you registered.

Read the passage below; then answer the four questions that follow.

Imagine going to a fast food restaurant a few years from now. You order a burger, and before you receive your order, the burger is placed through gamma-ray treatment. Order some fish, and you'll have to wait for the fish to be placed under a pressure three times higher than the pressure found in the deepest part of the ocean. Why would restaurants go to such lengths? Simply, to make sure your food is safe.

The threat of bacteria entering into our food is at an all-time high. New bacteria such as *Escherichia coli* and *Vibrio vulnificus* have alarmed many food handlers and have caused an increasing number of food poisoning deaths over the last five years. As a result, food processors are adopting rigorous standards of cleanliness. Food scientists are helping. Many scientists are proposing radical alternatives to common food treatment, such as some of the examples described above. While the new techniques are costly, they are not as costly as the potential lawsuits, bad publicity, and human loss that one outbreak could cause.

The real price of this new technology may not be in dollars, but in overall taste. Scientists admit that tastes may vary in certain foods depending on their processing treatment. As a layman, it seems that placing an oyster under 90,000 pounds of pressure sure seems likely to have some effect on the taste. I just hope that when the gamma rays remove any bacteria, they'll leave me with the wonderful joy of eating a delicious burger.

1. The writer's main purpose in writing this passage is to:

   A. demonstrate a love for hamburgers.

   B. explain why some food processing techniques will change in the future.

   C. perform a cost analysis of a food outbreak.

   D. demonstrate recent scientific advancements.

   E. predict popular foods in the twenty-first century.

2. Which of the following best defines the word "layman" as it is used in the passage?

   A. non-scientist

   B. expert

   C. private citizen

   D. clergyman

   E. carpenter

3. This passage is most likely taken from:

   A. a scientific journal.

   B. a cookbook.

   C. an economics textbook.

   D. a newspaper column.

   E. a legal journal.

4. Which of the following best describes the author's attitude toward the new food processing techniques?

   A. delighted

   B. terrified

   C. angry

   D. frustrated

   E. whimsical

Read the passage below; then answer the three questions that follow.

High Definition Television, or HDTV, is finally available to consumers, approximately ten years after most companies promised it. Consumers love the new system. More than 10,000 people appeared at a local store on the first day that HDTV became available. The appeal of HDTV is the clearer picture that an HDTV signal produces. The signal holds approximately three times as many horizontal and vertical lines as a standard television, resulting in a picture that rivals movie screens. Further, HDTVs are quite large—current versions range from 56 inches to a 64 inch-wide screen unit.

Despite these benefits, consumers who purchase these sets now may be disappointed with the results. There are very few digitally produced programs on television, and the number of these programs is unlikely to increase in the near future. The major networks plan to offer only five hours of digital programming per week next year, and only in the top ten markets. It will not be until 2004 that more than 50 percent of network television is broadcast in digital form. Further, cable companies are not under any regulation to carry digital programming. Since two-thirds of Americans receive their television through cable, the delay may be even longer.

5. The main point of the passage is that:

   A. Current HDTV sets are much larger than most standard televisions.

   B. Consumers love HDTV.

   C. The cable television industry is thriving.

   D. HDTV provides a clearer resolution picture.

   E. HDTV is available, although there is little programming that utilizes HDTV technology.

6. Which of the following would be the best title for the passage?

   A. HDTV Is Here to Stay

   B. Network and Cable Broadcasting

   C. HDTVs Are Here—Is the Programming?

   D. Television in 2004

   E. Why I Love HDTV

7. Which of the following best describes the word "major" as it is used in the passage?

   A. officer

   B. large

   C. subject

   D. legal

   E. important

Read the passage below; then answer the question that follows.

Whenever a major train accident occurs, there is a dramatic increase in the number of train mishaps reported in the media, a phenomenon that may last for as long as a few months after the accident. Railroad officials assert that the publicity given to the horror of major train accidents focuses media attention on the train industry, and that the increase in the number of reported accidents is caused by an increase in the number of news sources covering train accidents, not by an increase in the number of accidents.

8. Which of the following, if true, would seriously weaken the assertions of the train officials?

   A. The publicity surrounding train accidents is largely limited to the country in which the crash occurred.

   B. Train accidents tend to occur far more often during certain peak travel months.

   C. News organizations have no guidelines to help them determine how severe an accident must be for it to receive coverage.

   D. Accidents receive coverage by news sources only when the news sources find it advantageous to do so.

   E. Studies by regulators show that the number of train accidents remains relatively constant from month to month.

Read the passage below; then answer the four questions that follow.

In Roman times, defeated enemies were generally put to death as criminals for having offended the emperor of Rome. During the Middle Ages, however, the practice of ransoming, or returning prisoners in exchange for money, became common. Though some saw this custom as a step toward a more humane society, the primary reasons behind it were economic rather than humanitarian.

In those times, rulers had only a limited ability to raise taxes. They could neither force their subjects to fight, nor pay them to do so. The promise of material cooperation in the form of goods and ransom was therefore the only way of inducing combatants to participate in a war. In the Middle Ages, the predominant incentive for the individual soldier was the expectation of spoils. Although collecting ransom clearly brought financial gain, keeping a prisoner and arranging for his exchange could be expensive. Consequently, procedures were devised to reduce transaction costs.

One such device was a rule asserting that the prisoner had to assess his own value. This compelled the prisoner to establish a value without too much distortion; indicating too low a value would increase the captive's chances of being killed, while indicating too high a value would either ruin him financially or create a prohibitively expensive ransom that would also result in death.

9. The primary purpose of the passage is to:

   A. discuss the economic basis of the medieval practice of exchanging prisoners for ransom.

   B. examine the history of the treatment of prisoners of war.

   C. emphasize the importance of a warrior's code of honor during the Middle Ages.

   D. explore a way of reducing the costs of ransom.

   E. demonstrate why warriors of the Middle Ages looked forward to battles.

10. From the passage, it can be inferred that a medieval soldier:

   A. was less likely to kill captured members of opposing armies than was a soldier of the Roman Empire.

   B. was similar to a twentieth-century terrorist.

   C. had few economic options and chose to fight because it was the only way to earn an adequate living.

   D. was motivated to spare prisoners' lives by humanitarian rather than economic ideals.

   E. had no respect for his captured enemies.

11. Which of the following best describes the change in policy from executing prisoners in Roman times to ransoming prisoners in the Middle Ages?

A. Roman emperors demanded more respect than medieval rulers, and thus Roman subjects went to greater lengths to defend their nation.

B. It was a reflection of the lesser degree of direct control medieval rulers had over their subjects.

C. It became a show of strength and honor for warriors of the Middle Ages to be able to capture and return their enemies.

D. Medieval soldiers believed that executing prisoners was immoral.

E. Medieval soldiers demonstrated more concern about economic policy than did their Roman counterparts.

12. The author uses the phrase "without too much distortion" in the final paragraph in order to:

A. indicate that prisoners would fairly assess their worth.

B. emphasize the important role medieval prisoners played in determining whether they should be ransomed.

C. explain how prisoners often paid more than an appropriate ransom in order to increase their chances for survival.

D. suggest that captors and captives often had relationships.

E. show that when in prison a soldier's view could become distorted.

Read the passage below; then answer the four questions that follow.

In recent years, Americans have gotten the message—eat more vegetables! However, we're still not eating enough of the leafy green vegetables, such as spinach, broccoli, and Brussels sprouts that do the most to promote good health. Currently, half of all the vegetable servings we consume are potatoes, and half of those are French fries.

Research reported at the Nurses' Health Study confirms the benefits of leafy greens. Researchers determined that women who consumed at least 400 micrograms of folic acid daily in either leafy green vegetables or multivitamin pills reduced their risk of colon cancer as much as 75 percent over fifteen years. Remember not to simply substitute vitamins for vegetables, because there are thousands of healthy compounds present in green leafy vegetables that cannot be duplicated in a pill.

13. The main point of the passage is:

A. multivitamin pills contain folic acid, as do leafy green vegetables.

B. recent studies help confirm that leafy green vegetables help to promote good health.

C. eating more vegetables can reduce the risk of colon cancer.

D. important research was just presented at the Nurses' Health Study.

E. almost half of the vegetables consumed by Americans are potatoes.

14. The author argues that vitamins may not be an ideal replacement for leafy vegetables because:

A. increasing dependence on multivitamins can lead to poor nutritional habits.

B. multivitamins are not proven to fight against colon cancer.

C. folic acid is not contained in multivitamins.

D. a vitamin supplement may not replace the thousands of compounds found in leafy green vegetables.

E. caloric intake may decrease sharply.

15. The passage states that leafy green vegetables are helpful because:

A. they help to reduce the risk of contracting colon cancer, but little more.

B. they contain more compounds than potatoes.

C. they contain more folic acid than any other food.

D. they contain numerous compounds that are helpful to the body, such as folic acid.

E. multivitamins are not very helpful.

16. Which of the following changes would the author most likely wish to see in the way Americans consume vegetables?

A. a lower overall consumption in vegetables

B. an increase in the number of potatoes consumed

C. an overall increase in the number of leafy green vegetables consumed

D. a switch from leafy green vegetables to carrots

E. more spinach and fewer Brussels sprouts

Read the passage below; then answer the four questions that follow.

[1]We should elect Josie president of our French club at the annual meeting this Friday. [2]That office has been vacant for over a month since Pierre, our former president, graduated. [3]Josie is the only current member who not only speaks fluent French, but who has also lived in France and is familiar with the culture. [4]__________, Josie is extremely likeable and it's always a pleasure to work with her. [5]Archie, the other nominee for president, is certainly pleasant enough. [6]____________, he only speaks minimal French, having taken just French 101 (the introductory course). [7]Even Principal Smith believes that Josie should be elected, having advocated for her at the last meeting. [8]If even Principal Smith believes that Josie is the right student for the job, surely we should elect her on Friday. [9]Electing anyone else would not only be a disservice to Josie, but to us members of the French club as well.

17. Which of the following is a statement of fact?

    A. Sentence 1

    B. Sentence 3

    C. Sentence 5

    D. Sentence 8

    E. Sentence 9

18. Which of the following pairs of words, if inserted in order into the blanks in the passage, would best help the reader understand the author's sequence of ideas?

    A. However; But

    B. In addition; Moreover

    C. Moreover; However

    D. Although; Similarly

    E. In contrast; In addition

19. Upon which of the following questionable persuasive techniques does the author of the passage rely?

    A. The author attacks Archie personally based on irrelevant factors.

    B. The author rejects Archie's candidacy because he has not taken advanced French classes.

    C. The author asserts that Josie should be elected but fails to offer any evidence to support this assertion.

    D. The author rejects Archie's candidacy without giving any reasons for doing so.

    E. The author relies in part on the authority of Principal Smith.

20. Which of the following sentences from the passage is least relevant to the main idea?

    A. We should elect Josie president of our French club at the annual meeting this Friday.

    B. That office has been vacant for over a month since Pierre, our former president, graduated.

    C. Josie is the only current member who not only speaks fluent French, but who has also lived in France and is familiar with the culture.

    D. If even Principal Smith believes that Josie is the right student for the job, surely we should elect her on Friday.

    E. Electing anyone else would not only be a disservice to Josie, but to us members of the French club as well.

Read the passage below; then answer the four questions that follow.

Recent findings from paleontologists have sparked great debate about the possibility of birds evolving from dinosaurs. Two new species of small dinosaur have been found, each of which was clearly covered with feathers. This has led many in the scientific community to believe the increasingly popular theory that birds are descended directly from dinosaurs.

Some have suggested that even the famed velociraptor may have been covered with its own feathers. If the dinosaur–bird connection was convincing before, it is now almost certain. With any new discovery come skeptics, and this recent finding is no exception. Even these startling discoveries do not impress some scientists. These scientists contend that both birds and dinosaurs evolved from the same older common ancestor. They assert that any similarities between birds and dinosaurs are due to the common parentage, not due to a direct evolutionary relationship.__________

21. What is the best summary of the passage?

    A. Whenever a new anthropological study is done, it will be subject to controversy and debate.

    B. The velociraptor was covered with feathers.

    C. New evidence lends greater weight to the theory that birds are descended from dinosaurs.

    D. Critics of recent studies contend common parentage links birds and dinosaurs.

    E. Evolutionary relationships are difficult to define with certainty.

22. What is the author's attitude toward the belief that birds are descended directly from dinosaurs?

    A. skeptical support

    B. unwavering conviction

    C. indifference

    D. confident support

    E. utter disbelief

23. Which of the following is the best definition for the author's use of the word "sparked" in the first paragraph?

A. started

B. glittered

C. ended

D. resolved

E. burned

24. Which of the following sentences, if inserted into the blank at the end of the passage, would best fit in with the author's logical pattern of ideas?

A. So it is clear that the issue of whether or not birds are related to dinosaurs will forever remain a mystery.

B. Accordingly, the fact that some dinosaurs had feathers is simply a random coincidence, as they are unrelated to birds.

C. Other recent fossil discoveries also support the view that dinosaurs are the direct descendants of birds.

D. Thus, the issue of whether birds evolved directly from dinosaurs has finally been resolved.

E. These scientists point out the many differences between dinosaurs and birds that suggest only a remote evolutionary connection.

Analyze the index below; then answer the two questions that follow.

Shakespeare, William	59, 199–215, 245–284
Comic plays of	203–207
Films on plays of	179
History plays of	197–198
Romantic plays of	189 and 193
Poetry of	211–213
Tragic plays of	208–211

25. On what pages would you look to find information on *Macbeth*, which critics call "Shakespeare's best written tragedy"?

A. 203–207

B. 197–198

C. 189 and 193

D. 211–213

E. 208–211

26. Which of the following best describes the organizational pattern used in the section of the book dealing with Shakespeare?

A. chronological

B. alphabetical

C. by category

D. by literary importance

E. from least influential to most influential

Read the passage below; then answer the three questions that follow.

Despite years of publicity about the problem, the percentage of college students who binge drink, that is, consume five or more drinks in one sitting, has declined only from 44 percent to 43 percent. Further, half of all students who binge drink do so regularly—at least three times within a two-week period. Finally, 33 percent more students admit that they drink just to get drunk. Dangerous drinking is at its worst in fraternities and sororities, where four out of five members acknowledge that they binge.

Public pressure has shown some previous influence regarding students' drinking habits. A University of Michigan researcher says the percentage of drinkers who binged dropped through the late 1980s and early 1990s, largely because of the widespread publicity about the dangers of drunken driving. ____.

27. Which of the following sentences best summarizes the overall message of the passage?

    A. According to statistics, binge drinking is on the decline.

    B. Dangerous drinking remains prevalent on college campuses

    C. Fraternity and sorority binge drinking is most problematic.

    D. Too many students drink just to get drunk.

    E. Efforts to curb drunk driving seem to be more successful than efforts to curb binge drinking.

28. Which of the following sentences, if inserted into the blank, would best complete the passage?

    A. Currently, there seems to be no way of stopping binge drinking.

    B. We should therefore only encourage college students to drink if they are not going to drive.

    C. So the problems caused by drunk driving are worse than the problems caused by binge-drinking.

    D. University officials should evaluate how to use public pressure more effectively to help curb the current binge-drinking problem.

    E. If schools first reduce the number of fraternity students who binge drink, the rest of the campus will follow.

29. Which of the following statements, if true, would weaken the claim that publicity efforts helped to curb binge drinking in the late 1980s?

A. Drunk driving convictions decreased 12% over that time period.

B. Students did not watch as much television as other groups, decreasing the number of times they heard those ads.

C. New state laws for drunk driving became much more severe—one conviction went from a suspended license to three years in jail.

D. Binge drinking was listed as a "favorite activity" by many college students.

E. Membership in a designated drivers program at Michigan increased by 500 percent during the late 1980s.

Read the passage below; then answer the question that follows.

Zinc lozenges have gained great popularity among adults as a means to reduce the duration and severity of colds. Unfortunately, the lozenges do not work for children. ______________________________ ______________________________. Even if they knew and could alter the medicine, children may not be too excited about taking them. Children complain about the taste of the lozenges; many children vomit if taking one on an empty stomach.

30. Which of the following sentences would best complete the passage when inserted into the blank above?

    A. Scientists are unable to explain why the lozenges do not work for children.

    B. Nonetheless, children should take them.

    C. Be careful of products that promote zinc lozenges for children.

    D. New lozenges are currently being tested for animals.

    E. The severity of children's colds should be monitored closely.

Read the passage below; then answer the four questions that follow.

The United States is currently home to an unprecedented 4,000 non-native plant species and 2,300 alien animal species. These plants and animals arrive by air and by sea from other continents, often in the bilge water of tankers and as stowaways on aircrafts. Previously, very little was done to stop this transport of alien plants and animals. But now, aliens are so out of control that they are threatening the very existence of America's native species. Of the 1,900 imperiled American species, 49 percent are being endangered by aliens. Aliens are currently the leading threat to species populations, next to habitat destruction. In some locations, the influence of aliens is already as bad as it can be. In Hawaii, more than 95 percent of the 282 imperiled plants and birds are threatened by aliens.

In general, a plant or animal is kept in check by species that compete with it, eat it, or sicken it. On new grounds, though, aliens often have no such constraints. Many foreign creatures have flourished in delicate ecosystems. Our environment cannot quickly adapt to a new plant species.

A crucial preventative measure is to outlaw the release of ballast water (water used to balance a ship) in ports. Some ports, like the port in San Francisco Bay, are populated by almost 99 percent alien species. Legislators need to take action to enact the pertinent legislation quickly—before the situation gets even worse. Yet, limiting the inclusion of alien species will not be easy. Many new species enter undetected. Further, some alien species provide great help to our environment. America's economy thrives on many of our immigrants—soybeans, wheat, cotton, rye, and fruiting trees all originated on other continents and were brought over by colonists. Without any data or observations, it is difficult to predict if an alien species will be beneficial or harmful to our environment.

31. Which of the following is the best summary of the passage?

    A. The United States is home to over 6,000 alien plant and animal species.

    B. Alien species provide a number of problems for our ecosystems, which do not have easy solutions.

    C. Alien animals and plants can help our environment.

    D. Our environment cannot easily adapt to alien species.

    E. It is difficult to predict the effects of an alien species in our environment.

32. The author specifically mentions the state of Hawaii in the passage because it has:

    A. benefited the most from alien species.

    B. been greatly hurt by alien species.

    C. been largely unharmed by alien plants or animals.

    D. new laws outlining the entry of alien species.

    E. a port which contains 99 percent alien species.

33. From paragraph 2 to paragraph 3 the author shifts from:

A. argumentation to explanation

B. opinion to explanation

C. recommendation to explanation

D. explanation to recommendation

E. persuasion to recommendation

34. What would be an appropriate title for the previous passage?

A. Hawaii's Ecological Trouble

B. Bad Ballast Water!

C. Aliens—Changing Our Ecosystems

D. Ecosystems in Trouble

E. Solutions to Alien Invasions

Read the passage below; then answer the four questions that follow.

Mounting evidence suggests that any musical stimulus, from Beethoven to Beyoncé, can have therapeutic effects. Whether you've had heart surgery or a bad day at the office, some soothing sounds may help to lessen stress and promote well-being. Music therapy isn't mainstream health care, but recent studies suggest it can have a wide range of benefits. Most studies have been done with patients recovering from various illnesses, such as a stroke and Parkinson's disease.

No one really knows how music helps the body. We do know that listening to music can directly influence pulse, and the electrical activity of muscles, as well as lower blood pressure. Neuroscientists suspect that music can actually help build and strengthen connections among nerve cells. This is probably why listening to Mozart before an IQ test boosts scores by roughly nine points.

35. Which of the following is NOT mentioned as a benefit to listening to music?

    A. relieved stress

    B. increased neural activity

    C. aided recovery

    D. increased coordination

    E. lower blood pressure

36. Which of the following best summarizes the content of the passage?

    A. Music therapy has become so widely accepted, many health care organizations are adding music therapy sessions to their insurance policies.

    B. A detailed analysis on how music helps the body.

    C. Neuroscientists are tracking the neurological effects of music on the body.

    D. Evidence suggests that music therapy helps the body, even if we aren't sure exactly how.

    E. Students can perform better on standardized exams if they listen to more classical music.

37. The author's use of the word "mainstream" in the first paragraph means:

    A. conventional

    B. radical

    C. musical

    D. medicinal

    E. experimental

38. In which of the following would this passage most likely be found?

    A. A neurology journal

    B. A medical students' textbook

    C. A magazine article about Mozart

    D. An article in a psychology journal discussing intelligence testing

    E. A pamphlet at a health fair

Read the passage below; then answer the three questions that follow.

My little brother, Emmet, has loved airplanes since before he was born. He pores over books from the library and can easily identify the type of an aircraft as it flies overhead. While our family doesn't share his enthusiasm, we indulge it. Our family has frequented almost every air and space museum in the United States. Within seconds of my parents' sharing our next vacation destination, Emmet produces an itinerary <u>replete</u> with destinations marked by their aeronautic significance. Last summer we were surprised when a water park made the top of his list for an upcoming trip to Oregon. It all made sense when we pulled into the parking lot and saw a 747 on the roof with a waterslide protruding from its side.

39. Which of the following best describes the author's attitude toward Emmet's passion for airplanes?

    A. anger

    B. concern

    C. jealousy

    D. affection

    E. hatred

40. Which of the following statements best expresses the main idea of the passage?

    A. My little brother, Emmet, has loved airplanes since before he was born.

    B. He pores over books from the library.

    C. Our family doesn't share his enthusiasm.

    D. A water park made the top of his list.

    E. It all made sense when we pulled into the parking lot.

41. Which of the following is the best meaning of replete as it is used in the passage?

    A. stuffed

    B. empty

    C. filled

    D. significant

    E. time-consuming

Read the passage below; then answer the four questions that follow.

The koala is one of the most misunderstood animals. Although it is sometimes called a koala bear, or Australian bear, and is somewhat bear-like in appearance, it is not related to true bears. Once abundant, it is now found in much-reduced numbers in Queensland, Victoria, and New South Wales. It has thick, grayish fur, a tailless body 2 to 2 1/2 ft (60–75 cm) long, a protuberant, curved, black nose, and large, furry ears. The five sharply clawed toes on each foot enable it to grasp and climb. A slow-moving, nocturnal animal, the koala has perhaps the most specialized diet of any living mammal. It feeds on leaves and shoots of a particular species of eucalyptus at a specific stage of maturation. The single cub is about 3/4 in (1.9 cm) long at birth and is nursed in the mother's pouch, from which it emerges for the first time at about six months old. Until it is approximately eight months old a koala continues to ride in the pouch, and until about one year of age it is carried on its mother's back or in her arms. The harmless and defenseless koala has been ruthlessly hunted, chiefly for fur but also for food. Disease and the clearing of the eucalyptus forests have also taken a heavy toll. Protective measures have been adopted to prevent the extinction of the koala.

42. An appropriate title for this passage would be:

A. Koalas Face Extinction

B. Koala—It's Not a Bear!

C. The Unique Koala Diet

D. Get to Know the Koala

E. Victorian Koalas

43. The following passage would most likely be located in:

A. a newspaper article.

B. an editorial column.

C. a scientific journal.

D. a doctoral dissertation.

E. an encyclopedia.

44. Which of the following is NOT one of the reasons the koala is facing extinction?

A. It is hunted for fur.

B. It is hunted for food.

C. Many are isolated as pets, away from other koalas.

D. Disease in their natural habitat.

E. Destruction of their natural habitat.

45. Why does the author believe that the koalas are often linked to bears?

A. Their diet is similar to those of true bears.

B. Both true bears and koalas raise their young in a pouch.

C. Both bears and koalas are facing extinction.

D. Bears and koalas are both nocturnal.

E. They are often referred to as koala bears or Australian bears.

Read the passage below; then answer the three questions that follow.

One effect of a moist, warmer-than-usual spring is the increase in the number of ticks. Ticks, no larger than the size of a pinhead, are reason for concern since they can transmit Lyme disease. Lyme disease is spread by ticks that usually live on mice and deer. However, ticks can also attach themselves to other creatures, including people. If a tick bites someone, a large rash will usually appear at the site of the bite within a month. In addition, many will suffer from chills, fever, headache, and mild conditions of arthritis shortly after a rash appears. Untreated, Lyme disease can cause severe arthritis, and an irregular heartbeat.

Antibiotics used to be the only treatment for Lyme disease. Now, recent advances have led to the creation of a vaccine. In order for the vaccine to work, individuals must take three shots over a period of twelve months. Many people find this treatment highly unpleasant. A dose of tick-repellent should help the casual outdoor-bound individual avoid the danger of ticks.

46. According to the passage, what is the first sign of a tick bite on humans?

    A. an irregular heartbeat

    B. arthritis

    C. chills and fever

    D. headaches

    E. a large rash

47. Which of the following facts from the passage is *least* relevant to the central theme of paragraph 1?

    A. Ticks can transmit Lyme disease.

    B. Lyme disease is spread by ticks that usually live on mice and deer.

    C. Ticks can attach themselves to people.

    D. Lyme disease can cause arthritis.

    E. Lyme disease can cause an irregular heartbeat.

48. According to the passage, the vaccine against Lyme disease is appropriate only for those who:

    A. plan on going outside during a warm day.

    B. occasionally spend time hiking and traveling outdoors.

    C. do not like the smell of tick repellent.

    D. live in the Northeastern United States.

    E. are outdoors so often that they must constantly protect themselves against ticks.

Use the graph below to answer questions 49 and 50.

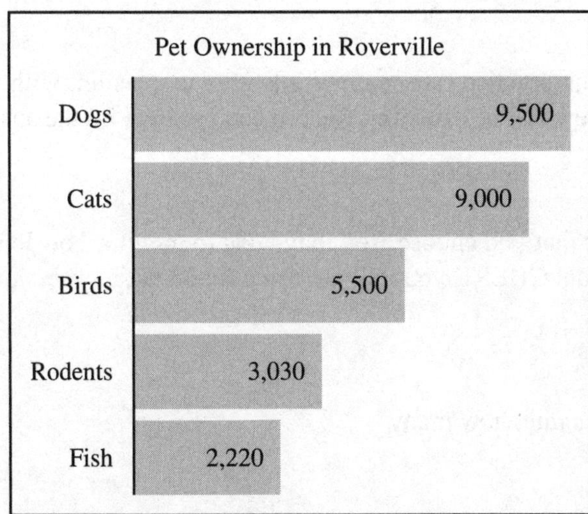

Number of Households in Roverville Owning 1 or More (By Specific Type of Pet) in 2018

49. Which of the following can be determined from the information in the chart above?

    A. There were more pet dogs than pet cats in Roverville in 2018.

    B. There were fewer pet rodents than pet birds in Roverville in 2018.

    C. In 2018 more than twice as many Roverville households owned at least 1 pet bird than owned at least 1 pet fish.

    D. At least one household owned both a pet dog and a pet cat in 2018.

    E. In 2018 more than three times as many Roverville households owned at least 1 pet dog than owned at least 1 pet bird.

50. If each pet in Roverville belongs to one household only, one can conclude from the chart that:

    A. Roverville residents like dogs more than cats.

    B. Most Roverville residents owned a dog in 2018.

    C. All the Roverville residents combined owned at least 9,500 dogs in 2018.

    D. Dog ownership increased in 2018 from the previous year in Roverville.

    E. Few Roverville residents like rodents.

SECTION II: TEST OF MATHEMATICS

Directions: Each question in the Mathematics Section of the practice test is a multiple-choice question with five answer choices. Read each question carefully and choose the ONE best answer. Record each answer on the answer sheet provided in the back of this book.

You may work on the multiple-choice questions in any order that you choose. You may wish to monitor how long it takes you to complete the practice test. When taking the actual CBEST, you will have one four-hour test session in which to complete the section(s) for which you registered.

1. Richard can write 2 test questions in 10 minutes. At this rate, how many questions can he write in 2 hours?

A. 24

B. 36

C. 40

D. 80

E. 120

2. A delivery driver drove the following distances on Monday: $4\frac{3}{4}$ miles, $5\frac{1}{3}$ miles, 3 miles, $7\frac{2}{3}$ miles, and $5\frac{1}{4}$ miles. What was the average distance the driver drove, in miles, on Monday?

A. 5

B. $5\frac{1}{5}$

C. 6

D. $6\frac{1}{5}$

E. 26

3. If 16 is the average of three numbers x, 12, and 15, what is the value of x?

A. 24

B. 21

C. 18

D. 12

E. 9

Questions 4 and 5. Read the information below, then answer the questions that follow.

> Before recess, a vending machine contains 42 items. There are 13 candy bars, 14 bags of pretzels, and 15 packs of gum. After recess, there are 11 items remaining in the vending machine.

4. Which of the following facts can be determined from the information given above?

A. the number of candy bars sold

B. the cost of a bag of pretzels

C. the total capacity of the vending machine

D. the amount of money collected by the vending machine during recess

E. the number of items that were sold during recess

5. In order to calculate the total value of the items sold during recess, what additional information would be needed?

A. the cost of a bag of pretzels, the cost of a candy bar, and the cost of a pack of gum

B. the number of candy bars left in the vending machine after recess

C. the number of bags of pretzels left in the vending machine after recess

D. (A), (B), and (C)

E. it cannot be determined without more information

6. A dress that normally sells for $250 is on sale for $175. The sale price is approximately what percent of the original price?

A. 70%

B. 60%

C. 50%

D. 40%

E. 30%

7. A bank charges a fee of $4.25 for every $100 that is used for cash advances. What was the amount used for cash advances if the total fee equaled $63.75?

A. $15

B. $150

C. $1,150

D. $1,500

E. $1,555

8. Of the following, which is the largest in value?

A. .02

B. .024

C. .076

D. .063

E. .0025

9. **Use the diagram below to answer the question that follows.**

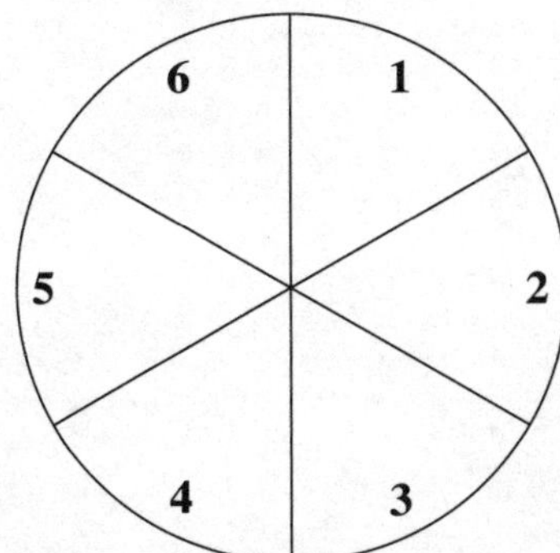

The spinner has an equal probability of landing on any number from 1-6. If you spin the spinner two times, what is the probability that the sum of the two numbers will equal 7?

A. $\frac{1}{12}$

B. $\frac{1}{6}$

C. $\frac{1}{4}$

D. $\frac{1}{3}$

E. $\frac{1}{2}$

10. Consider these two statements:

Some dolls have brown hair.
All dolls with black hair have a red bow.

If these two statements are true, which of the following statements must also be true?

A. There are no dolls with red hair.

B. No dolls with brown hair have a red bow.

C. Some dolls with red bows have brown hair.

D. Not all dolls have black hair.

E. Not all dolls have red bows.

11. Pam needs to order ribbon to decorate her gifts. Each gift requires 31 inches of ribbon. If she has 22 gifts, what is the total length of ribbon that Pam needs to order?

A. 10 feet, 6 inches

B. 31 feet

C. 56 feet, 10 inches

D. 62 feet, 4 inches

E. 682 feet

12. **Use the diagram below to answer the question that follows.**

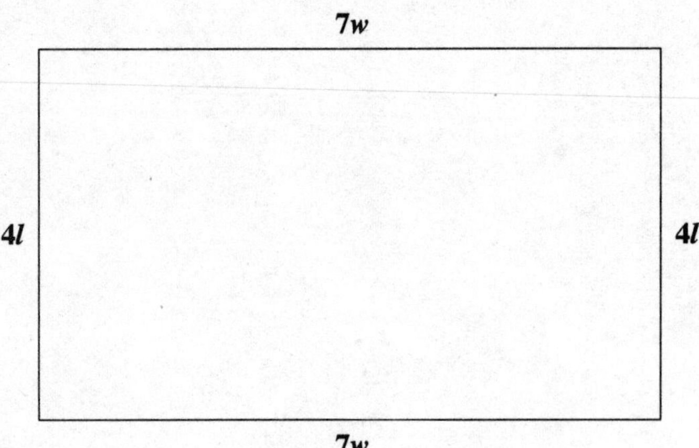

The length of a rectangle is $4l$ and the width is $7w$. Which of the following expressions represents the perimeter of the rectangle?

A. $22lw$

B. $28lw$

C. $11lw$

D. $4l + 7w$

E. $8l + 14w$

13. Julie can grade 20 spelling tests per hour. She starts grading tests at 9:00 A.M. At this rate, which of the following is the best estimate as to when she will be finished grading 134 tests?

A. 12:30 P.M.

B. 1:30 P.M.

C. 2:00 P.M.

D. 3:30 P.M.

E. 5:00 P.M.

14. 3 less than 8 times a number is 37. What is the number?

A. 34

B. 29

C. 21

D. 5

E. 4

15. $\frac{1}{2}$ is how many times greater than $\frac{1}{4}$?

A. $\frac{1}{2}$

B. 2

C. 4

D. 6

E. 8

16. At a certain company, 65% of employees work in the sales department. If the company has 5,020 employees, how many employees do not work in the sales department?

A. 3,765

B. 3,263

C. 2,761

D. 1,757

E. 1,255

17. Anne, Sue, and Jen want to go to the amusement park together. They agree to combine their money. Anne has $11.00, Sue has $15.00, and Jen has $16.00. Admission is $21 per person. How much more money will they each need to obtain, on average, in order for everyone to be able to go to the amusement park?

A. $5.00

B. $6.00

C. $7.00

D. $10.00

E. $14.00

18. Which of the following expressions is *not* equivalent to 6×52?

A. $6 + (26 \times 2)$

B. 12×26

C. $6 \times (40 + 12)$

D. 24×13

E. $(2 \times 3) \times (13 \times 4)$

19. The school library moved some of its books from the first floor to the second floor. If the school originally had 1,035,726 books on the first floor, and if after the move there are 924,192 books on the first floor, approximately how many books were moved to the second floor?

A. 100,000 books

B. 75,000 books

C. 10,000 books

D. 7,500 books

E. 1,000 books

20. **Use the information below to answer the question that follows.**

> Jessica's monthly rent is \$50 more than $\left(\frac{1}{2}\right)$ of Michael's monthly rent.
>
> If Jessica's monthly rent is \$640, what is Michael's monthly rent?

If r represents Michael's monthly rent, which of the following equations can be used to solve the preceding problem?

A. $\$640 + 50 = \left(\frac{1}{2}\right) r$

B. $\$640 = 50 + \left(\frac{1}{2}\right) r$

C. $2(\$640) = 50 + r$

D. $\left(\frac{1}{2}\right) \$640 = r - 50$

E. $640 = 25r$

Questions 21 and 22: Use the chart below to answer the questions that follow.

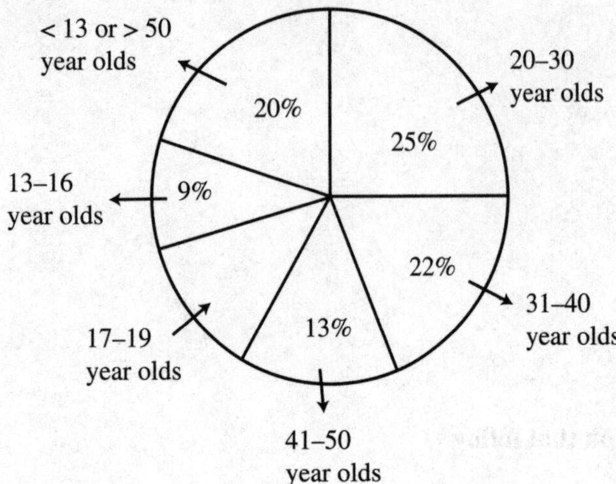

21. What percent of the total population of Town C is made up of teenagers (ages 13–19)?

 A. 12%

 B. 14%

 C. 17%

 D. 19%

 E. 20%

22. If there are 125,000 people in Town C, how many people are between the ages of 20 and 50, inclusive?

 A. 25,000

 B. 33,575

 C. 50,000

 D. 75,000

 E. 82,500

23. The sum of 3.468 and 7.397, when rounded to the nearest tenth, is:

A. 11

B. 10.9

C. 10.8

D. 10.0

E. 3.6

24. If a cafe purchases eggs for $2 per dozen and sells a three-egg omelet for $4, what is the cafe's profit on 4 dozen of these omelets?

A. $24

B. $64

C. $144

D. $168

E. $192

Questions 25 and 26. Use the table below to answer the questions that follow.

Population of State X		
City	**1996 population**	**1997 population**
Town A	200,000	250,000
Town B	150,000	150,000
Town C	30,000	60,000
Town D	145,000	160,000
Town E	75,000	65,000

25. Which Town saw the largest percent increase in population from 1996 to 1997?

A. Town A

B. Town B

C. Town C

D. Town D

E. Town E

26. By approximately what percent did State X increase in population in 1997 from 1996?

A. 14%

B. 25%

C. 33%

D. 45%

E. 85%

27. Howard currently earns $6.00 per hour and works 12 hours per week. If Howard wants to raise his weekly gross pay to $114.00 how many additional hours must he work per week?

A. 4 hours

B. 5 hours

C. 6 hours

D. 7 hours

E. 8 hours

28. Paula-Ann needs to ship two packages. The first package weighs $16\frac{1}{4}$ pounds, and the second package weighs $23\frac{3}{8}$ pounds. What is the total-weight of the packages that Paula-Ann needs to ship?

A. $7\frac{1}{8}$ pounds

B. $38\frac{8}{9}$ pounds

C. $39\frac{5}{8}$ pounds

D. 40 pounds

E. $40\frac{5}{8}$ pounds

29. Ben's garden has a collection of roses, tulips, and carnations, in a ratio of 3:2:1. If Ben has a total of 72 flowers in his garden, how many roses are in his garden?

A. 6 roses

B. 12 roses

C. 24 roses

D. 28 roses

E. 36 roses

30. If the value of y is between .00268 and .0339, which of the following could be y?

A. .00175

B. .0134

C. .0389

D. .268

E. 2.6

Questions 31 and 32. Use the information below to answer the questions that follow.

- If the distance to a destination is at least 15 miles from home, Bob will take the bus.
- If the distance to a destination is greater than 4 miles but less than 15 miles from home, Bob will ride his bicycle.
- If the distance to a destination is up to 4 miles from home, Bob will walk.

31. If Bob rode his bicycle to Kathleen's apartment, which of the following statements could be true?

A. Bob's home is 4 miles from Kathleen's apartment.

B. Bob rode over 30 miles round trip to Kathleen's apartment.

C. Kathleen's apartment is at least 15 miles from Bob's home.

D. Kathleen's apartment is within 2 miles from Bob's home.

E. Kathleen's apartment is 11 miles from Bob's home.

32. Using the information above, which of the following facts could be determined?

A. the total number of miles Bob rode on his bike on Tuesday

B. the total number of miles Bob walked on Tuesday

C. the method of transportation Bob used to get to a destination 20 miles away

D. the number of miles from Bob's home to any destination

E. Bob's speed on a bicycle

33. $3x + 12 = 7x - 16$. What is x?

A. 3

B. 7

C. 12

D. 16

E. 28

34. Tommy rides his bicycle at a constant rate of 12 miles per hour. At this rate, how much time, in days, will it take him to ride 360 miles?

A. 1.25 days

B. 1.5 days

C. 1.75 days

D. 2.25 days

E. 2.75 days

35. Multiplying a number by $\frac{1}{2}$ is the same as dividing that number by

A. $\frac{1}{2}$

B. $\frac{1}{4}$

C. 1

D. 2

E. 4

36. Marge has a jar of coins (quarters, dimes, nickels, and/or pennies) totaling $24.70. What is the largest number of quarters that Marge could have in her jar?

A. 247

B. 118

C. 98

D. 49

E. 24

37. If $3z + 6 = 16$, what is the value of $9z$?

A. $\frac{10}{3}$

B. 10

C. 20

D. 22

E. 30

38. **Use the information below to answer the question that follows.**

> Risa was asked to evaluate the expression $(3x + 2)(x + 5)$. Although she was given the value of –5 for x, she was unsure of her answer.

If Risa evaluated the expression correctly, substituting –5 for x, what answer should she have given?

A. –13

B. 0

C. 75

D. 325

E. 425

39. What is the value of 623,499 rounded to the nearest thousand?

A. 600,000

B. 620,000

C. 623,000

D. 623,500

E. 624,000

40. Lara is scheduled to perform 24 surgeries this week. If she performs four surgeries on Monday, how many must she perform each day, on average, to finish by Friday?

A. 2

B. 3

C. 4

D. 5

E. 6

41. How long would it take a jogger averaging 6 miles per hour to reach her destination 5 miles away?

A. 30 minutes

B. 40 minutes

C. 50 minutes

D. 60 minutes

E. 70 minutes

42. Steve has a jar of coins containing 23 quarters, 15 nickels, 36 dimes, and 42 pennies. Steve removes one quarter from the jar and spends it. What is the probability that the next coin Steve takes from the jar will be a nickel or a dime?

A. $\frac{5}{12}$

B. $\frac{51}{116}$

C. $\frac{10}{23}$

D. $\frac{64}{115}$

E. $\frac{51}{115}$

43. **Use the table below to answer the following question.**

Week 1	–2°
Week 2	17°
Week 3	4°
Week 4	–11°
Week 5	9°
Week 6	22°

A website recorded the average temperatures in Springfield for six consecutive weeks. What is the difference between the highest and lowest temperatures recorded during these six weeks?

A. –9

B. –13

C. 33

D. 36

E. 39

44. Mitch makes $2,000 each month. His bills for the month are: $600.00, $250.00, $200.00, $180.00, $140.00, $120.00, and $86.00. If there are four weeks in a month, how much money, on average, does Mitch have left each week after paying his bills?

A. $106.00

B. $242.00

C. $318.00

D. $424.00

E. $500.00

45. If a is a positive integer, and b is a negative integer, which of the following statements could be true?

I. $a + b = 0$
II. $a + b < 0$
III. $a \times b > 0$

A. I only

B. II only

C. III only

D. I and II only

E. II and III only

<u>Questions 46 and 47</u>. Use the table below to answer the questions that follow.

List of Television Shows		
Television Show	**Start Time**	**End Time**
Show A	9:30	
Show B	10:15	10:45
Show C	11:00	11:20
Show D	12:00	12:45
Show E		2:30

46. If Show A is 20 minutes longer than Show C, what time does Show A end?

A. 9:50

B. 10:10

C. 10:20

D. 10:30

E. 11:40

47. If Show E is the longest of all five shows, what is one possible start time for Show E?

A. 2:20

B. 2:10

C. 2:00

D. 1:45

E. 1:40

48. In Allison's class, there are 23 more boys than girls. If there are a total of 81 students in the class, how many girls are in the class?

A. 23

B. 29

C. 40

D. 52

E. 58

49. Consider this statement:

Every student in Julie's class likes to play chess.

Which of the following statements must also be true?

A. No one in Julie's class likes to play checkers.

B. Everyone that likes to play chess is in Julie's class.

C. Some students in Julie's class don't like to play chess.

D. If a student does not like chess, the student is not in Julie's class.

E. Only students in Julie's class like chess.

50. Given the formula $F^\circ = \frac{9}{5}C^\circ + 32^\circ$, where F = Fahrenheit temperature and C = Celsius temperature, which of the following is closest to the temperature in Celsius degrees when the temperature is 95° Fahrenheit?

A. 203°

B. 113°

C. 71°

D. 35°

E. 20°

SECTION III: TEST OF WRITING

Directions: The Writing section of the CBEST assesses basic skills and concepts that are important in performing the job of an educator in California. This section includes two topics that assess your ability to write effectively. One of the topics asks you to analyze a situation or statement; the other asks you to write about a personal experience. You will not be expected to demonstrate any specialized knowledge in your responses.

You should be sure to write only on the topics presented, respond to both topics, address all of the points presented in the topics, and support generalizations with specific examples. Before you begin writing, read each topic and organize your thoughts carefully

Your written response must be your original work, written in your own words, and must not be copied or paraphrased from some other work.

When you take the actual CBEST, scorers will read and evaluate each of your responses using a standard set of criteria, which are outlined in the writing score scale (see Part IV of this book).

The following written performance characteristics, which are incorporated in the CBEST Writing Score Scale, are evaluated during scoring.

I. *Rhetorical Force:* the clarity with which the central idea or point of view is stated and maintained; the coherence of the discussion and the quality of the writer's ideas

II. *Organization:* the clarity of the writing and the logical sequence of the writer's ideas

III. *Support and Development:* the relevance, depth, and specificity of supporting information

IV. *Usage:* the extent to which the writing shows care and precision in word choice

V. *Structure and Conventions:* the extent to which the writing is free of errors in syntax, paragraph structure, sentence structure, and mechanics (e.g., spelling, punctuation, capitalization)

VI. *Appropriateness:* the extent to which the writer addresses the topic and uses language and style appropriate to the given audience and purpose

WRITING TOPICS

Topic 1

A local public school system is considering a plan to convert Jefferson High into an all-male school, and Franklin High into an all-female school. Students in the district would be required to attend a same-sex school. Many in the school system think that all-male and all-female high schools would benefit students and provide a more educational atmosphere. To what extent do you agree or disagree with the supporters?

Support your opinion with specific reasons.

Topic 2

All of us have at some point in our lives had someone whom we've admired, someone we've looked up to. Write about your hero. Identify who the person is, and why he or she is your hero. What qualities does he or she possess that you admire? What have you learned from your hero that has influenced who you are today?

Chapter 11
Practice Test 1: Answers and Explanations

ANSWER KEY

Reading

1.	B	26.	C
2.	A	27.	B
3.	D	28.	D
4.	E	29.	C
5.	E	30.	A
6.	C	31.	B
7.	B	32.	B
8.	B	33.	D
9.	A	34.	C
10.	A	35.	D
11.	B	36.	D
12.	A	37.	A
13.	B	38.	E
14.	D	39.	D
15.	D	40.	A
16.	C	41.	C
17.	B	42.	D
18.	C	43.	E
19.	E	44.	C
20.	B	45.	E
21.	C	46.	E
22.	D	47.	B
23.	A	48.	E
24.	E	49.	C
25.	E	50.	C

Mathematics

1.	A	26.	A
2.	B	27.	D
3.	B	28.	C
4.	E	29.	E
5.	D	30.	B
6.	A	31.	E
7.	D	32.	C
8.	C	33.	B
9.	B	34.	A
10.	D	35.	D
11.	C	36.	C
12.	E	37.	E
13.	D	38.	B
14.	D	39.	C
15.	B	40.	D
16.	D	41.	C
17.	C	42.	E
18.	A	43.	C
19.	A	44.	A
20.	B	45.	D
21.	E	46.	B
22.	D	47.	E
23.	B	48.	B
24.	D	49.	D
25.	C	50.	D

SECTION I: TEST OF READING

1. **B** The passage tells us that new steps are being taken to ensure food safety because of the increasing threat of new diseases. Choice (A) is partial—the author's feelings are expressed, but this is trivial to the overall message. Choices (D) and (E) are too broad, and out of scope. Choice (C) is mentioned in the passage, but is not the central point. The author focuses more on a description of new processing techniques rather than the costs associated with an outbreak.

2. **A** The author is using sarcasm in this sentence. The word is used to indicate that while the author does not have a technical understanding of placing an oyster under 90,000 pounds of pressure, the author assumes something must be happening. Only (A) and (C) are possible definitions of the word. In this case, (A) is a better answer, because it is more specific to the author's intent.

3. **D** This passage includes factual knowledge, as well as the author's opinion and sense of humor. The information is not technical enough to be found in either a scientific journal or a legal journal. While the subject is about food, the passage is unlikely to be found in a cookbook. Finally, the passage does not present enough financial information for it to be found in an economics textbook.

4. **E** The author presents a playful tone within the passage. Choices (B), (C), and (D) are all negative, and (B) is way too extreme. Choice (A) is wrong because the author expresses concern about negative effects on the taste of food rather than any delight. The author jokes about worrying over the taste of food, but never states that he or she is in any way against the new techniques.

5. **E** In the passage, the author praises the features of HDTV, but goes on to announce the programming challenges of HDTV. Choices (A), (B), and (D) are all true, but do not address the central theme. Choice (C) might be true, but it is also secondary to the main point of the passage.

6. **C** The title correctly addresses the two main issues presented in the passage—the description of what HDTV is, and the analysis of when digital programming will arrive. Be careful about titles that use words or phrases that can be found in the passage. Choice (D) is a perfect example of such a trap choice. However, that title is too broad to be correct—it doesn't mention HDTV.

7. **B** The author uses the word "major" to describe how the large networks will not increase their HDTV programming, thereby limiting the effectiveness of an HDTV set. The words "top ten" also suggest that "major" indicates a large amount. While the larger networks may be more "important" (E) than the smaller ones, the context makes it clear that the number of programs broadcast is the issue here.

8. **B** This is one of the more difficult questions on this test. First, we need to be very clear about the argument of the railroad officials. They argue that there is in fact no increase in actual mishaps, just an increase in the number of news sources reporting the mishaps. Choices (C), (D), and (E) would all strengthen this claim, so eliminate those three answer choices. Choice (A) neither strengthens nor weakens the argument, as the phenomenon of increased news stories about train mishaps may be limited to the country wherein the initial accident occurred. Choice (B) weakens that claim by implying that certain months are more likely to have more accidents due to high volume of train rides.

9. **A** This answer choice clearly reflects the overall main idea of the passage. Choice (D) describes the main point of one of the paragraphs, but not of the entire passage.

10. **A** The word "however" in the first paragraph shows the difference between soldiers in the Roman era and those in the Middle Ages. Choice (D) is wrong because it contradicts the passage; medieval soldiers were motivated to spare prisoners' lives for *economic* reasons. Choices (B), (C), and (E) all involve leaps of logic and are unsupported by the passage.

11. **B** Paragraph 2 describes how rulers could neither force nor pay soldiers to fight. They therefore had to entice soldiers with economic incentives.

12. **A** When asked to find the definition of a phrase, be sure to read a few lines above and a few lines below. In the paragraph, it is mentioned that the device was used to create a value that was neither too low nor too high.

13. **B** The passage discusses the importance of leafy green vegetables, then describes a study that supports the author's claim.

14. **D** Multivitamins do contain folic acid that is contained in leafy green vegetables, and appear to help fight colon cancer—(B) and (C) are wrong. However, leafy green vegetables contain many more beneficial compounds.

15. **D** While the passage focuses mostly on the study about colon cancer, in the final sentence the author does state that leafy green vegetables are beneficial for a number of reasons. Part of (A) is incorrect (the phrase "but little more").

16. **C** In the first paragraph, the author is satisfied with the increase in the overall consumption of vegetables, but encourages us to eat more leafy green vegetables.

17. **B** Josie's fluency in French, past residency in France, and familiarity with French culture are all matters of fact. Choices (A), (D), and (E) are all statements of opinion to the effect that Josie should be elected. Moreover, the statement that Archie is "pleasant enough" is also a matter of opinion. Whether or not someone has a pleasing manner or personality is subjective, not a matter of fact (choice C is wrong as well).

18. **C** Sentence 3 states positive information about Josie in that she is fluent in French, knows French culture, etc. Then sentence 4 states more positive information about her in that she is likeable, etc. Accordingly, a word indicating continuity (such as "moreover") is required for the first blank. "However," "Although," and "In contrast" all signify a change in direction, so choices (A), (D), and (E) can be eliminated. For the second blank, sentence 5 states positive information about Archie in that he is pleasant, and then sentence 6 states negative information about him in that his French skills are minimal. A word indicating a change in direction is therefore required, so choice (B) ("moreover") can also be eliminated.

19. **E** The author relies on Principal Smith's authority to bolster the argument that Josie should be elected. Just because Principal Smith believes that Josie is the better candidate doesn't mean that it's true. However, the author attempted to discredit Archie (quite properly) based on the relevant fact that his French skills are minimal, so choice (B) is wrong. Choices (A) and (D) are wrong because the author doesn't do either of these things. Choice (C) is wrong because the author does offer evidence as to why Josie should be elected.

20. **B** The main idea of the passage is that the French club should elect Josie president. Choice (A) is a statement to that effect, and choices (C), (D), and (E) offer highly relevant evidence in support of this assertion. The fact that the office has been vacant for a month is least relevant to this idea. If the author failed to mention that fact, it wouldn't affect the quality of the argument.

21. **C** The topic sentence of the first paragraph states similar information. Choices (B) and (D) are too specific, while (A) and (E) are too broad.

22. **D** The last line of the first paragraph states the author's opinion on the topic. The phrase "almost certain" makes (B) too extreme, while (A) is too wishy-washy. Choice (D) finds a nice balance. Choices (C) and (E) can be easily eliminated.

23. **A** The new studies started great debate. If you were unsure of the correct answer, remember to try inserting the answer choices back into the passage.

24. **E** Choices (A) and (B) are wrong because even the skeptics think that dinosaurs and birds are at least distantly related. Choice (C) is wrong because the author is discussing the skeptics' view at the end of the passage, so evidence of direct descendance would not fit in logically. Choice (D) is wrong because nothing in the second paragraph suggests that the controversy has been resolved; the skeptics' view suggests the opposite.

25. **E** *Macbeth* was a tragic play, and tragic plays can be found on pages 208–211.

26. **C** The section of the book is broken up into the different types of works that Shakespeare produced.

27. **B** Choice (A) is factually true, but actually contains the opposite message of the passage. Choice (C) is true but too specific; (D) is an opinion that is not the primary focus of the passage. Choice (E) also seems to be true, but the main focus of the passage is on current drinking statistics, not a comparison between efforts.

28. **D** The second paragraph states that public pressure has worked in the past. The sentence concludes the paragraph by tying it back into the original point—current efforts to curb binge drinking are not successful. Choice (A) is wrong because the bleak conclusion is not supported and would be logically out of place, and (E) is completely speculative. The passage does not compare drunk driving to binge-drinking—(C) is wrong—nor does it suggest that drinking is acceptable so long as students do not drive; (B) is wrong as well.

29. **C** The researcher claims that public pressure against drunk driving led to a decrease in binge drinking incidents. In order to weaken this claim, you would need to show that another factor helped to decrease binge drinking incidents. Choice (C) does this. Stiff law penalties, not public pressure, may be the primary reason for the decrease in binge drinking.

30. **A** At first glance, it appears that a few sentences would fit into the passage. However, make sure you read beyond the blank line. The start of the next sentence, "Even if they knew..." provides a clue that the previous sentence talks about scientists.

31. **B** The passage describes the negative effects of alien species in our environment, and explains the difficulty of finding solutions.

32. **B** Read a few lines above the word "Hawaii." The author uses Hawaii as an example of an ecosystem that has been ravaged by alien species.

33. **D** In the first two paragraphs the author's tone is neutral; he or she is simply explaining the facts about alien species. In the third paragraph, however, the author expresses a viewpoint by recommending that the release of ballast water be outlawed.

34. **C** Choices (A) and (B) are too narrow in scope, while (D) is too broad. Choice (E) is wrong because only one possible solution is discussed.

35. **D** All of the other four answer choices can be found within the passage. On a "NOT" question, eliminate an answer choice once you find that it works.

36. **D** The first paragraph states that music therapy helps a number of different people in different conditions. The second paragraph attempts to give some information on how music may help the body.

37. **A** The author uses the word mainstream to point out how music therapy is beyond the normal practices in medicine. This "alternative medicine" is having successful results.

38. **E** The content is not scientific enough to be found in a scholarly journal or a medical textbook (choices A, B, and D are wrong). Note that choice (D) is wrong also because IQ testing is only briefly mentioned in the passage. Similarly, Mozart is only incidentally mentioned (choice C is wrong). The passage is aimed at the general public and concerns music to promote one's health, so choice (E) is the best fit.

39. **D** The author's tone is positive as he affectionately recounts his brother's fondness for airplanes. All the other answer choices are negative and therefore wrong.

40. **A** The primary focus of the passage is Emmet's love of airplanes. Choices (D) and (E) deal with details of the trip to the Oregon water park, which is simply offered as an example of Emmet's preoccupation. Choice (B) is wrong because the author is describing Emmet's fascination with airplanes in general, not just his tendency to read books about them. Choice (C) is wrong because the fact that the family doesn't share Emmet's enthusiasm for airplanes is only mentioned once; it is not the main idea of the passage.

41. **C** The word "replete" means "filled" or "stuffed." However, "stuffed," (A), would not make sense in this context. One cannot stuff an itinerary with destinations, so (C) is the better choice. None of the other answer choices are definitions of the word, nor would they make sense in context.

42. **D** Choices (A), (C), and (E) are too specific. Choice (D) is better than (B) since (D) implies that it will provide an introduction to the koala, which is what the passage as a whole is designed to do.

43. **E** The passage is mostly facts, so (B) does not fit. The passage is very general, so (C) and (D) do not fit. The passage is a basic description of a koala, not describing an event involving koalas. Therefore, (A) is wrong and (E) is the best answer choice.

44. **C** Choices (A), (B), (D), and (E) are mentioned in the last few sentences of the paragraph.

45. **E** The beginning of the passage mentions that despite their name, koalas are not related to other bears. The similarity of their names is the primary reason for the confusion.

46. **E** In the first paragraph, the author states that the first sign of a tick bite is a large rash. Other conditions may follow after the rash appears.

47. **B** The central theme of paragraph 1 is that ticks can cause Lyme disease, which can have negative health consequences. Choices (A) and (C) together explain how ticks transmit Lyme disease to people, so they are wrong. Choices (D) and (E) concern the negative health effects of Lyme disease, so they are wrong as well. The fact that ticks that transmit Lyme disease usually live on mice and deer is not a critical fact; if the author were to omit it, this would not affect the line of reasoning.

48. **E** The author encourages the occasional traveler to use traditional methods. Thus, choices (A) and (B) are wrong. Choices (C) and (D) are never mentioned in the passage. Choice (E) is an example of someone who must constantly be on guard against Lyme disease.

49. **C** The chart shows how many Roverville households owned *at least 1 of each pet*. The data does not reveal how many animals of each species were present; residents could own more than 1 of each type (choices A and B are wrong). Choice (D) is unsupported and the math does not work out for choice (E). The chart does indicate that more than twice as many households owned at least 1 pet bird (5,500) than owned at least 1 pet fish (2,220), so choice (C) is correct.

50. **C** The chart reveals statistics concerning ownership only, not how many residents *liked* any given animal (choices A and E are wrong). We only have data for 2018, so choice (D) is unsupported. Moreover, we do not know how many households there were in Roverville in 2018, so we can't know if the majority owned dogs (choice B is wrong). We can conclude that the residents collectively owned at least 9,500 dogs in 2018.

SECTION II: TEST OF MATHEMATICS

1. **A** Richard's rate is 2 questions / 10 minutes. Be sure to compare the same units—minutes to minutes, or hours to hours.

   2 hours is equal to 120 minutes.

   Make an equation:

   $$\frac{2}{10} = \frac{x}{120}$$

   $$\frac{2}{10} \times 120 = x$$

   $$24 = x$$

2. **B** Add the values: $4\frac{3}{4}$, $5\frac{1}{3}$, 3, $7\frac{2}{3}$, and $5\frac{1}{4}$.

   The integer parts of these numbers (4, 5, 3, 7, and 5) add up to 24.

   The fractional parts of these numbers $\left(\frac{3}{4}, \frac{1}{3}, \frac{2}{3}, \text{ and } \frac{1}{4}\right)$ add up to 2.

   (Notice that $\frac{1}{3} + \frac{2}{3} = 1$, and $\frac{3}{4} + \frac{1}{4} = 1$.) The total is 26 miles.

   The question asks for the average, so now divide by 5 (the number of values in the list).

   $$\frac{26}{5} = 5.2, \text{ or } 5\frac{1}{5}.$$

3. **B** To find an average, we find the sum, and divide by the number of items. An equation to solve this question is:

$$\frac{(x+12+15)}{3}=16$$

Then, multiply both sides by 3 to get $(x + 12 + 15) = 48$. Subtract 12 and 15 from both sides to get $x = 48 - 12 - 15 = 21$

Another method for this question is Backsolving. If we begin with (C), then we find the average of 18, 12, and 15: $\frac{(18+12+15)}{3}=\frac{45}{3}=15$. This average is too small, so try (B), 21, next. $\frac{(21+12+15)}{3}=\frac{48}{3}=18$. The correct answer is (B).

4. **E** We know that the vending machine contained 42 items, and was left with 11 items. We can subtract to find that 31 items were sold during recess.

5. **D** In order to calculate the value of the items sold during recess, we need to know the cost of each item, plus the number of items sold. Choice (A) gives us the cost of each item. By using the information in (B) and (C), we can find out how many of each type were sold during recess. What about the number of packs of gum remaining in the machine? We know that there are eleven items left, so we can find this number by subtracting the totals given in (B) and (C).

6. **A** To solve this problem, translate the question into a mathematical equation:

"The sale price is approximately what percent of the original price?" can be translated as

$$175=\left(\frac{x}{100}\right)\times 250$$

Then, solve.

$$\frac{175}{250}=\frac{x}{100}$$

$$\frac{175}{250}\times 100=x$$

$$.7\times 100=x$$

$$70=x$$

7. **D** You can use a proportion to solve this problem.

$$\frac{\$4.25}{\$100} = \frac{\$63.75}{x}$$

$$\frac{4.25}{(100 \times 63.75)} = \frac{1}{x}$$

$$\frac{4.25}{6375} = \frac{1}{x}$$

$$\frac{6375}{4.25} = x$$

$$1500 = x$$

8. **C** When comparing decimal numbers, it helps to line them up by place value, and start with the left-most digits. In this case, all the answers have the same value in the tenths place (all 0). The largest value in the hundredths place is in (C), 0.76, with a 7 in the hundredths place.

9. **B** There are 36 total possible combinations to spin (1 & 1, 1 & 2, 1 & 3, and so on). Of these, there are six possible combinations that would total 7: (1 & 6), (2 & 5), (3 & 4), (4 & 3), (5 & 2), (6 & 1).

$$\frac{6}{36} = \frac{1}{6}$$

Note: since 1 & 6 is different from 6 & 1 (for instance), they need to be counted separately.

10. **D** From the problem, we have "some dolls have brown hair." Thus, not all dolls have black hair. The other answers *could* be true based on the given information; however, (D) is the only answer that *must* be true.

Note: if you practiced using the contrapositive for the second statement, that would be *If a doll does not have a red bow, then it does not have black hair.* However, this does not match any of the answer choices in this case.

11. **C** First, try Ballparking. 31 inches is pretty close to 3 feet, so the correct answer is somewhere close to 3×20 feet, or about 60 feet. We can eliminate (A), (B), and (E), since they aren't close enough to our estimate.

To calculate this problem, multiply $31 \times 22 = 682$ inches. Then, we need to convert this number to feet. (Remember that 12 inches = 1 foot). If we divide 682 by 12, the result is 56, remainder 10.

We could have ballparked the conversion step as well. $12 \times 50 = 600$, and $12 \times 60 = 720$. So our answer is definitely between 50 and 60 feet, which only leaves (C). Notice that (E) is a trap answer (feet instead of inches).

12. **E** To calculate the perimeter of the rectangle, add the lengths of all sides. Remember that rectangles have two pairs of congruent sides.

$4l + 4l + 7w + 7w$
$= 8l + 14w.$

13. **D** Julie must grade 134 tests, which we can estimate at 130 tests. It takes 6.5 hours to grade 130 tests ($\frac{130}{20}$), so Julie will finish a short time after 3:30 P.M. Be sure to approximate during the problem. The phrase "best estimate" is your key to approximate.

14. **D** The equation can be written as follows: $8x - 3 = 37$. Translate the statement. "3 less" becomes -3; "8 times a number" becomes $8x$; "is 37" becomes $= 37$. Further, if you have trouble setting up the equation, you can backsolve. Plug the answer choices into the question to see which answer choice will give you the correct value.

15. **B** Backsolving is the easiest way to solve this problem. Starting with (C), multiply $\frac{1}{4}$ by 4. The result is 1, which is too high. Eliminate (C) and try a smaller number. Try (B). Multiply $\frac{1}{4}$ by 2, and the result is $\frac{1}{2}$. Choice (B) works.

16. **D** Calculate 65% of 5020, which equals 3263. That means that 3,263 employees work in the sales department. Since the question asks how many employees do NOT work in the sales department, eliminate (B). To finish the problem, subtract 3,263 from the total.

$5020 - 3263 = 1757.$

You can also recognize that, if 65% of employees work in the sales department, that means that 35% do not work in the sales department ($100\% - 65\% = 35\%$).

$5020 \times .35 = 1757$

17. **C** Together, the three have \$42.00 (\$11 + \$15 + \$16). The total amount of money they need is \$63.00 (\$21 × 3). The amount remaining is \$63 – \$42 = \$21. The question asks how much they will each need on average, so divide \$21 ÷ 3 = \$7.00 per person.

18. **A** Order of operations dictates that parenthesis and multiplication be performed first. This means that $6 + (26 \times 2)$ is the same as $6 + 52$. Since that is NOT equivalent to the expression in the question (6×52), select (A). Eliminate (B), (C), (D), and (E), since they are equivalent to (6×52). Choice (B) is equivalent to 6 x 52, since the associative property shows: $2 \times 3 \times 2 \times 2 \times 13 = (2 \times 3 \times 2) \times (2 \times 13) = 12 \times 26$. Choice (D) is equivalent, since $2 \times 3 \times 2 \times 2 \times 13 = (2 \times 3 \times 2 \times 2) \times 13 = 24 \times 13$. Choicie (C) is equivalent. Using the correct order of operations, parentheses must be performed first. $6 \times (40 + 12) = 6 \times 52$. Choice (E) is equivalent, since $(2 \times 3) \times (13 \times 4) = 6 \times 52$. Note that it is not necessary to actually calculate the values of these expressions; only to know whether or not they are equivalent.

19. **A** The difference between approximately 1,000,000 and 900,000 is 100,000. Approximate to save time and needless calculation.

20. **B** Translate the problem into an equation.

"Jessica's monthly rent is \$50 more than $\frac{1}{2}$ of Michael's monthly rent."

$\$640 = \$50 + \frac{1}{2}r$

21. **E** We are told that 9% of the population is made up of 13–16 year olds. To find the number of 17–19 year olds, we need to add the percentages for all the other age groups, and subtract the total from 100%. This number is 11%, making the percent of teenagers equal to 20%.

22. **D** First, we need to calculate the percentage of people in this group. The total is 25% + 22% + 13%, or 60%. 60% of 125,000 is equal to 75,000.

23. **B** Before rounding, add the two numbers together. The sum of 3.468 and 7.397 is 10.865. To round to the nearest tenth, look at the digit in the hundredths place, in this case 6. Since the number is 5 or greater, round up. The correctly rounded number becomes 10.9.

24. **D** It may be easiest to first figure out how many eggs the cafe needs for 4 dozen omelets. 4 dozen omelets is 48 omelets (4 × 12). Each omelet uses three eggs, for a total of 144 eggs. The purchase cost of these eggs is \$2 per dozen, so, for 12 dozen eggs, they pay \$24 total (144 eggs = 12 dozen). The sale price of 48 omelets is \$192 total. (48 × \$4). The profit is \$192 – \$24, or \$168.

25. **C** First, eliminate any answer choice that does not increase. Towns B and E do not see an increase. Next, calculate the percent increase using the percent change formula. Town C has the largest increase, with a percent increase of 100%. Note that the largest change in population doesn't automatically indicate that largest percent increase. Town A increases by 50,000 people, but that is only a 25% increase.

26. **A** To find the percent increase, we first need to find the total state population for each year. The total in 1996 is 600,000, and 685,000 in 1997. Our percent change fraction is $\frac{85{,}000}{600{,}000}$. Only (A) is close. (Approximate—a third of 600,000 would be 200,000; a fourth of 600,000 is 150,000; we know that (C) and (B) are too large.)

27. **D** First, we need to calculate the current amount of money that Howard earns per week. By multiplying 12 by \$6.00/hr, we find that Howard earns \$72.00 per week. To get to \$114.00 per week, Howard wants to increase his weekly pay by \$42.00. Divide this total by his rate of \$6.00 per hour, and we get the answer—7 more hours.

28. **C** Add the two fractional amounts together. In order to get the same denominator for each fraction, change $\frac{1}{4}$ to $\frac{2}{8}$. Then, sum the numbers. The result is $39\frac{5}{8}$ pounds.

29. **E** This is a ratio question, so we should use the ratio box to write down all the given information. Unlike most ratio questions, here we are given information about three things (roses, tulips, and carnations). No problem—we just need to add another column to the ratio box. A completed ratio box will look like this:

	Rose	**Tulips**	**Carn.**	**Whole**
Ratio (parts)	3	2	1	6
Multiply By	12	12	12	12
Actual Number	36	24	12	72

Be careful to select the total number of roses, which is what the question is asking for.

30. **B** Choice (A) is too small. It is smaller than .00268. Choice (B) fits between the two values. Choices (C), (D), and (E) are all larger than .0339.

31. **E** If Bob rode his bicycle, we know that the distance between Bob's home and Kathleen's apartment must be between 4 miles and 15 miles. Only (E) meets this requirement.

32. **C** The information given tells us how Bob will get to a given destination, depending on the number of miles it is away from his home. If we know that a destination is 20 miles away, we know that Bob will take the bus. Without additional information, we don't have any way of calculating the number of miles Bob traveled on his bicycle, or on foot. We also can't calculate the speed at which Bob travels.

33. **B** Rearrange the equation to get:

$$28 = 4x$$
$$7 = x$$

34. **A** We know Tommy's rate in miles per hour. First, find the total number of hours it will take Tommy to ride 360 miles. We can solve this using a proportion:

$$\frac{12 \text{ miles}}{1 \text{ hour}} = \frac{360 \text{ miles}}{x \text{ hours}}$$

After cross-multiplying, we find that $12x = 360$. $x = 30$ hours. However, we want the answer in days, not hours. Let's convert hours to days. There are 24 hours in one day, so we have:

$$\frac{30 \text{ hours}}{1 \text{ day}} = \frac{1 \text{ day}}{24 \text{ hours}} = \frac{5}{4} \text{ or } 1.25 \text{ days}$$

35. **D** If you have any questions about this problem, choose any number. If you select the number 10, and multiply it by $\frac{1}{2}$, the result is 5. What number do you divide 10 by to get 5? 2. Remember, the fraction bar is a shorthand way to express division. $\frac{1}{2}$ means 1 divided by 2.

36. **C** The best approach for this problem would be Backsolving. Since the question asks for the largest possible number of quarters, start by plugging in the largest number. If Marge has 247 quarters, that would mean that she has \$61.75 ($247 \times .25 = 61.75$). This number is too large, since the question states that Marge has \$24.70. Eliminate (A). 118 quarters would total \$29.50. This number is also too large. Eliminate (B). 98 quarters would total \$24.50. This is just under Marge's total amount of \$24.70. She would have 20 cents left over, which could be pennies, nickels, or dimes. Select (C). One other approach for this question would be to recognize that the total amount in quarters should be \$24.50, since that is the largest number (up to \$24.70) which is evenly divisible by quarters. If she has \$24.50 in quarters, that means she has 98 quarters ($24.50 / .25 = 98$).

37. **E** If we simplify the equation, we find that $3z = 10$. Rather than solve for z, simply multiply the entire equation by 3. That gives us $9z = 30$. You can save time and calculations by looking for $9z$ only—don't worry about the value of z.

38. **B** Plug in (–5) for x:

$$(3 \times (-5) + 2) \times ((-5) + 5)$$
$$= ((-15) + 2) \times (0)$$
$$= (-13) \times (0)$$
$$= 0$$

39. **C** To round to the nearest thousand, take a look at the hundreds place. In this example, the hundreds digit is a 4, meaning that we should not round up the number. The correctly rounded number is 623,000.

40. **D** First, subtract the surgeries she performs on Monday. This leaves Lara with 20 surgeries to perform, and 4 days left. Divide 20 by 4 to get the correct answer of 5 surgeries per day.

41. **C** You can use a proportion to set up this problem.

$$\frac{60}{6} = \frac{x}{5}$$

$$\frac{300}{6} = x$$

$$50 = x$$

You can also estimate that 5 miles is almost as long as 6 miles, so the time should be a little less than 1 hour. Eliminate (D) and (E), as they are too large.

42. **E** The total number of coins is initially 116. Once Steve removes a quarter from the jar, there are 115 coins. To find the probability of choosing a nickel OR a dime, we need to count all the nickels and dimes: 15 nickels + 36 dimes = 51 coins. So the probability of choosing a nickel or a dime is $\frac{51}{115}$.

$$\left(\frac{15}{115}\right)+\left(\frac{36}{115}\right)=\left(\frac{51}{115}\right).$$

You can eliminate (B) once you realize that it is a trap answer based on a misreading of the question (note the denominator 116).

43. **C** The highest temperature shown in the table is 22°, and the lowest is -11°. To find the difference, subtract the smaller number from the larger number: 22 – (–11), or 22 + 11.

44. **A** Mitch must spend a total of $1,576.00 each month, leaving him with $424.00 in spending money. If we divide this total by 4, there is $106.00 available per week.

45. **D** The question asks what *could* be true. This means that we keep answers that are possible, and eliminate answers that are impossible. It's possible for two integers to add to zero, so (I) could be true. It might help to try your own example numbers: for instance, 5 + –5 = 0. Eliminate (E), since it doesn't include (I). It's also possible for two integers to add to a negative number, so (II) could be true. For example, 5 + –8 = –3. Since (I) and (II) are both possible, the answer must be (D). Additionally, (III) is impossible, and can be eliminated. The product of a positive number and a negative number is always negative, so it can't be greater than zero.

46. **B** Show C runs for 20 minutes, meaning that Show A runs for a total of 40 minutes. 40 minutes after 9:30 is 10:10.

47. **E** The longest show is Show D, which runs for 45 minutes. If Show E ends at 2:30, it must start at least 45 minutes earlier, or before 1:45. Only (E) works. Note: We didn't necessarily need the information from question 46 here. Either way, Show E has to be longer than 45 minutes, leaving only one possible answer.

48. **B** This question is best solved by Backsolving. First, we can eliminate (C), (D), and (E). If there are more boys in the class, then the class will have less than 50 percent girls. These three answer choices are too high. To backsolve, start with one of our remaining answer choices. If we select (B), we're saying that there are 29 girls in the class. This would mean that there are 23 more boys, for a total of 52 boys. 29 girls and 52 boys give us the desired total of 81 students in the class.

49. **D** (D) is the contrapositive of the statement (If not B, then not A). Choice (A) is incorrect—the problem has nothing to do with checkers. (B) is false—students outside of Julie's class can enjoy chess. Choice (C) is false—the statement says that everyone in the class likes chess. Choice (E) is false for the same reasons as (B).

50. **D** To solve this problem, plug in 95° for F, and don't forget to Ballpark. $\left(\frac{9}{5}\right)$ is almost equal to 2, and 32° is close to 30°.

$$F \approx 2C + 30$$
$$95 \approx 2C + 30$$
$$65 \approx 2C$$
$$32.5 \approx C$$

You could also backsolve by plugging in for C in the formula. Starting with choice (C),

$$F \approx 2 \times 70 + 30$$
$$F \approx 140 + 30$$

Choice (C) is too large. Try (D) next:

$$F \approx 2 \times 35 + 30$$
$$F \approx 70 + 30$$

This is very close to 95°.

SECTION III: TEST OF WRITING

Topic 1

A local public school system is considering a plan to convert Jefferson High into an all-male school, and Franklin High into an all-female school. Students in the district would be required to attend a same-sex school. Many in the school system think that all-male and all-female high schools would benefit students and provide a more educational atmosphere. To what extent do you agree or disagree with the supporters? Support your opinion with specific reasons.

Sample Essay #1: Overall Score = 4 (Pass)

Dividing high school students into same-sex schools is certainly not a new concept and has been attempted in many countries with varying degrees of success. The concept assumes that separating the sexes will help improve the students' ability to learn by reducing distractions. After all, the model assumes, if students aren't thinking about making eyes at the girl or boy at the adjoining desk, they're more likely to have their attention on the teacher. But is this necessarily true, especially considering that some students experience same-sex attraction? And might splitting up students by sex create more problems than are solved by doing so? Some students identify with a gender other than the biological sex they were assigned at birth, for example. After careful thought, I oppose the conversion of Jefferson and Franklin High Schools into same-sex schools, both for the logistical problems of the conversion, and the potential for injustice that such a move would create.

First, I'm assuming that the current school system is the more traditional co-educational setup, where all students attend the same classes. If we are to split them up, does this mean we'll have to bus them to their new school? If we implement this plan we may inadvertently add time and stress to their daily commute to school, which is not necessarily conducive to learning.

Second, we have to ask if the programs, facilities, and the teachers are similar enough in each school to justify separating the students. We certainly wouldn't want to put one group of students in a less desirable learning environment than another. For example, do both schools have the same budgets for sports? Are the classrooms, computer facilities, and playgrounds the same? Are the teachers equally competent, and competent enough, in fact, to teach in the new sex-divided model? Call me cynical, but I'm also concerned that the women's programs in particular will suffer if the female students are moved to a separate school.

Third, such a separation would be problematic for transgender students and those with non-binary gender identities. Even if students could attend the school that corresponds to the gender with which they identify, that would still force some young people to make a choice that they should not have to make. For example, which school would a bi-gender student (one who identifies with two genders) or a gender-fluid student (one whose gender identity changes) choose to attend? If these students were forced to go to a same-sex school, it would be a clear violation of their fundamental right to self-expression. Any benefit gained by a same-sex school system could not make up for the injury suffered by students with non-traditional gender identities.

In the final analysis, I think the benefits are far outweighed by the deficits. The "distractions" of the other sex attending the same school are less disruptive than those caused by wrenching them away from their friends, and moving at least half of each population to a new setting. And most importantly, students with non-traditional gender identities would suffer greatly if they were forced to conform to a same-sex school system. The benefits gained by separating the sexes would clearly be outweighed by the hardships and problems that such action would cause.

Sample Essay #2: Overall Score = 3 (Marginal Pass)

Eight to ten years before I entered my high school, it was a unisex school. However at the time the school couldn't survive so it had to merge with its sister school. Today, I could see why the people would think unisex schools would create a more academic environment for students. I would agree with the supporters of same-sex schools. The academic benefits seem to outweigh the negatives.

There are so many pressures on students today to "fit in." If you don't have the "cool" clothes you are an outcast and often considered unpopular. By having same-sex schools, girls won't have pressure to impress boys. I remember stressing more about whether boys thought I was "cool" than about my algebra homework. Peer pressure will always exist in schools, even with a same-sex school. However, I don't think the pressure will be nearly as great. Students, especially girls, would benefit from relaxed social pressures in a same-sex school. Instead of focusing on what they look like and who is wearing what, some girls can focus more on school.

Some people may argue that having unisex schools would hurt students. The concern may arise that the lack of interaction with the other sex may cause problems later. However, through my experience with friends who attended same sex schools, this was not a problem. The unisex schools often had dances where both sexes would attend (or sporting events that both sexes would support). I don't think this would be a problem if events were organized that would include both sexes. Also, school is for learning and social events after school would only enhance a focus on academics during the school hours.

Although many may disagree that same-sex schools would help student academics, I think it would help. Having same-sex schools takes away many pressures students encounter in co-ed schools. By taking these pressures away, students then can focus more on their academics.

Sample Essay #3: Overall Score = 2 (Marginal Fail)

I am thinking that considering converting the Jefferson High School into an all-male school and Franklin High School to an all-female school is a very bad idea. I am unsure what benefits would be here. Maybe people think boys and girls shouldn't be together because they would distract from each other. This may be true but this is not a reason to keep them in different schools. Boys will still distract boys and girls will also be distracting girls and so what is the point? It seems better to have boys and girls altogether.

First, if the school district makes Jefferson into an all-male school, and Franklin into an all-female school, getting to the schools might take a really long time. Instead of just going to the school you are closest to, some students will have to travel to the farther school. That could be costly for students in more time lost, and they might have to be bussed. Then schools have to spend more money on bussing and drivers, instead of other costs. Some boys and some girls will spend more time traveling to and from school then they should. Also, how can the boys learn about girls if they never see them? Of course, it is that we don't want them seeing to much of the girls, but in class where is their harm? And the same thing for the girls. The girls should be seeing the boys also and know them every day. This makes students very happy, and happy students learn much better.

Therefore, I think the educational atmosphere can be achieved in a school where the boys and girls are all together. They can take classes together and learn together and play sports and everything and I do not see the problem where there is a lesser education as a result. The boys and girls are also in fact used to seeing each other every day. What will happen when they always don't? This could be bad for there development into adult persons. Adults do not go to different jobs just because they are male and female. Thus, I believe that one should leave things as they will be and let boys and girls go to class together.

Sample Essay #4: Overall Score = 1 (Fail)

Im not really sure if the school district should convert Franklin and Jefferson into same-sex schools. I guess it depends on what kind of student you are. If you are comfortable in an environment with both males and females, then you probably don't want same-sex schools. But if you have trouble and feel pressure dealing with members of the opposite sex, a same-sex school may help you focus more on your studies.

I remember that when I was in high school I really wanted to ask out this girl in my math class. It sounds kind of dumb but all I thought about in class was her, you know, one of those silly crushes. But that's all I thought about, and I didn't do well in math class at all. Maybe it was because I never really liked math, but I think that to some extent my bad grade was because I wasn't focusing on the teacher but instead on her. So, maybe I would have done better if she wasn't in that class, and there were only guys there. On the other hand, a friend of mine had a girlfriend that went to another school, and when things weren't going well for him, he still thought about it in classes and stuff. So it might not be as bad if it were a guy only school, but I'm not saying that everything would be perfect with the schools that way.

So, as I have shown there are some advantages and disadvantages to the idea by the school bored. Ultimately, it should go to a vote, and allow the people in the district to decide. I'm not sure what I would vote, cause each side has some points. I don't really care if the schools stay the same or change.

Topic 2

All of us have at some point in our lives had someone whom we've admired, someone we've looked up to. Write about your hero. Identify who the person is, and why he or she is your hero. What qualities does he or she possess that you admire? What have you learned from your hero that has influenced who you are today?

Sample Essay #1: Overall Score = 4 (Pass)

In northwest Fresno, California, there are still a few remaining acres of old-growth fig trees. These gnarled old trees, looking dusty even after a healthy spring rain, march along in rows as straight and even as the strings on a guitar. There were hundreds of acres of fig trees at one time, but homes and businesses gradually have replaced them until there are just a few fields left. What most people don't know is that for each and every one of these trees, someone had to dynamite a hole in the hardpan that lies under all of the alluvial soil that makes up the bedrock of the San Joaquin Valley. That someone was my grandfather, and he's my hero.

He'd go out each day and meticulously dig down where the new tree would go, measure his fuse, crimp the blasting cap (often with his teeth), and set off the charge. Oftentimes, when blasting canals for irrigation, he'd have to place his charge in an old innertube filled with dirt, light the fuse, seal the tube and swim with the dynamite to the location of the blast, dive down and place the charge, then swim away to safety. That I'm here to tell the story testifies to his expertise.

I had the opportunity to see him use this skill once when I was just seven years old. My parents had purchased a new home, and in the days before professional landscapers, were planning to put in the yard themselves. My grandfather, without asking (and being a firm believer in trees) came out to our new house one Saturday morning with some dynamite and a selection of flowering trees to plant.

I watched him carefully measure out the fuses and then test a length to determine how fast they burned. I asked him if he was doing that so he'd have time to run away. Then, as he was threading the blasting cap through the dynamite, he told me something I'll never forget. He said, "You never run away from dynamite, Brett. You might slip and fall and get hurt when the charge goes off. No, you make sure you plan carefully, measure everything twice, then walk away." And that's just what he did. He lit the fuse, looked down to make sure it was burning true, turned around and strolled back to the corner of the house where Dad and I had taken cover. Just as he stepped around the corner, there was a "whump" (not too big, you understand, just enough to do the job), and the tree was ready to plant.

When he headed up the Fresno Unified School District in the 1950s, he had a different kind of planting to do. The district had no money and no classrooms. He got some old Quonset huts from an abandoned army base and set up classrooms in fields that belonged to rancher friends of his, many times in fig orchards if you can believe it. The parents would take the kids out to wherever the classes were held. The county, while being sympathetic, would turn a blind eye for a while, but then would come out and condemn the structures. My grandfather would apologize, take them down and move then to another location. He performed this sleight of hand until the bond issues finally passed and the district had enough money to build actual classrooms.

What did I learn from this man? My grandfather taught me that hard work, intelligently planned and for a good cause is its own reward. He taught me to plan carefully, measure exactly, and to persevere in the face of adversity. And, the man after whom they named the Carroll H. Baird School, taught me to never run away from a sputtering fuse, but to walk.

Sample Essay #2: Overall Score = 3 (Marginal Pass)

A hero in my mind is someone to look up to and admire. Some people's heroes are movie stars or athletes. My hero, however, is my mom. She possesses qualities that not many people have. My mom is truly an amazing person, and I hope someday, I will be as good a mother, friend, co-worker, and wife as she is.

I have been lucky to have such a wonderful mom. Growing up, she always was there to cart my brother and I to various sports games or dance lessons. She never complained, but was always at the sidelines, cheering us on. Not only did she take us places, she made sure every night we had a warm meal on the table.

However, it wasn't until recently when I learned what a strong and positive person my mom was. During a recent year, my mom suffered many family tragedies, losing her husband and both her parents. This would cause most people to go into a deep depression, but not my mom. Instead, she lent my brother and me her shoulder to cry on when we needed it and taught us that "all things happen for a reason."

My mom's outstanding qualities don't stop there. She went to work full time so we could have insurance benefits, and continued with a second business at night in order to contribute to our college tuition. My mom has become "mom" to many of my friends because she treats them like they too are her kids. There's usually no debate when a bunch of my friends are trying to figure out where to stay when we are traveling in the area. "Let's go stay at Ann's house," they say, "because her mom is the coolest!" It's pretty rare to find an adult that all of us enjoy so much.

I'm proud to say that my mom is my friend. Our daily interactions together have helped me realize just how special she is. She may not have a great jump shot, or be a leading actress or model, but she is the most important person in my life. She is my hero because I hope to be as strong and loving as she has been. I try to model myself after her. I admire her composure, her compassion, and her friendship. She is an inspiration to us all.

Sample Essay #3: Overall Score = 2 (Marginal Fail)

At 4:00 A.M. my friend gets a page. As he struggles to find his glasses, he knows that he only has thirty seconds to get ready. Five minutes later, he is in the intensive care unit helping to save the life of a newborn child. My hero is my friend Chris (actually, I should call him Dr. Chris). What he does is so amazing!

I can't believe that he is only twenty five and already a doctor. That is something everyone could look up to. Not like Doogie Howser or something dumb like that, but in a real way. I admire how hard he has studied and practiced to become a doctor. His hours are insane, but his drive is even greater. I hope to one day have the dedication to my teaching profession that he has in his medical career. These are the skills that he possesses that I admire so much—drive, dedication, and a never-give-up attitude. When I'm struggling, I think of what he goes through, and that motivates me to work harder.

Chris chose to specialize in cancer treatment. That seems so difficult for me. I'm not sure if I could handle dealing with cancer patients. It seems so dark. I mean, it must be really hard to try to help people that might not have a good chance of living. But Chris has chosen to do that. I guess someone needs to do the difficult jobs, and I'm glad that people like Chris are willing to do them.

If Chris wasn't my hero, I'd probably have to choose my favorite baseball player. But I chose Chris. I'm lucky to have him as a friend.

Sample Essay #4: Overall Score = 1 (Fail)

I have from time to time admired a guy but I have always been disappointed. It seems to me that us Americans spend to much time and energy in unwarranted hero worship which could be spent in better ways. I have had my hopes built up by admiring sports figures, statesmen, and politicians, but the admirable qualities I thought I saw always turned out to be majorly flawed. In fact, I think spending to much time admiring the qualities of other people can lead to other problems. In the past I have admired the honesty of politicians, only to be disappointed when they finally get to office, then don't do what they said. They may be crooks or thieves. Sports figures have disappointed me when I find out they use drugs to make there performance better than it should be, or cheat at the game there supposed to be playing. Sometimes a historical figure seems to be admirable, but they eventually aren't—they usually have faults only that come out later. So I think hero worship is a bad idea. Better instead would be to admire yourself and only judge your actions against you. If one can't admire yourself, you might as well give up and that's why I no longer try to find admirable qualities in other people. The only thing I ever learned from a "hero" is not to learn from them.

Chapter 12
Practice Test 2

SECTION I: TEST OF READING

Directions: Each question in the Reading section of the practice test is a multiple-choice question with five answer choices. Read each question carefully and choose the ONE best answer. Record each answer on the answer sheet provided in the back of this book.

You may work on the multiple-choice questions in any order that you choose. You may wish to monitor how long it takes you to complete the practice test. When taking the actual CBEST, you will have one four-hour test session in which to complete the section(s) for which you registered.

Read the passage below; then answer the three questions that follow.

One of the most daring deep-space missions NASA has ever planned is about to be launched. Deep Space 1, or DS1, will be unique for two reasons—its ion propulsion engine, and its self-navigation system. If DS1 goes well, it will become the model for a new generation of spacecraft.

DS1 is unique in the way in which it will get from place to place. DS1 will be pushed through space by an engine that works by ionizing electrons. Electrons will be fired into xenon gas, stripping the xenon elements of an electron and giving the atoms an electric charge—ionizing them. The ions are then accelerated through an electric field and emitted from thrusters at up to 65,000 m.p.h. This constant push will add 15–20 miles per hour daily to the spacecraft's speed. That will add up. Thanks to this process, the spacecraft requires about one-tenth the weight of fuel used in a conventional aircraft.

Possibly more innovative is the navigation system. The "brain" of the system will scan stars and asteroids to map its location, allowing it to know precisely where it is, and make any necessary adjustments. What would these innovations mean to an automobile? Well, imagine your car finding its own way from San Diego to New York, to a specific shopping mall, at only one gallon of gas per 300 miles!

Note: This passage was written in 1998.

1. Which one of the following statements would the author most likely agree with regarding NASA's view of the DS1 spacecraft?

   A. NASA believes that the DS1 will eventually lead to cars that can drive themselves.

   B. NASA believes that the DS1 spacecraft, if successful on its mission, will become the model for future space travel technology.

   C. NASA will use DS1 until ion propulsion technology is too costly.

   D. NASA believes that DS1 technology will be the leading pioneer in artificial intelligence.

   E. NASA hopes that DS1 technology can be used for passenger trips to the moon.

2. The author puts the word "brain" in quotations in the third paragraph in order to:

   A. imply that NASA has created a new type of intelligent being.

   B. show how similar the navigation system is to a human brain.

   C. indicate that the navigation system will make decisions, similar to decisions a human would make.

   D. show that the system is incapable of any decision making without human influence.

   E. state a belief that new aliens may be found by the DS1 spacecraft.

3. Which of the following techniques does the author use to help the reader better understand the DS1 system?

   A. a technical breakdown of ion propulsion technology

   B. a counterexample

   C. a hypothetical story that describes the spacecraft

   D. a metaphor that relates DS1 technology to a machine we know how to use

   E. a parable

Read the passage below; then answer the question that follows.

Millions of students taking out college loans just received more financial aid. Earlier this year, Congress passed legislation, retroactive to July 1, that lowered the interest rate on new, federally guaranteed student loans to 7.46% from the previous rate of 8.25%. Further, the legislation states that those with more than $30,000 in debt may soon have an extra fifteen years to repay outstanding loans.

4. The passage answers all questions below EXCEPT:

   A. What is the new interest rate for federal student loans?

   B. Who is eligible to receive additional time to repay college debts?

   C. When does the new loan program begin?

   D. How much will a student who is $30,000 in debt save as a result of the new laws?

   E. What was the old interest rate for federal student loans?

Read the passage below; then answer the three questions that follow.

I'm not much of a tennis player. Sure, I can go out and hack like any <u>weekend warrior</u>, but I don't need to be worried about new advances in equipment, or having the best technology. Yet, that's exactly what I have. Last week, I went out and purchased a new, oversized-head, titanium-based racquet. I may not be a good player, but boy, do I look good.

Apparently, I'm not alone. New racquet technologies have led to a number of advances in the past few years, and sales have exploded. New racquets feature larger heads, longer necks, and lighter body weight. All of this comes at a cost. New racquets range from $175 to $300. Of course, a player of my caliber probably doesn't need to purchase such a racquet, but then again, isn't it cool to tell a fellow competitor you are playing with PX2 technology (whatever that is!)?

My local tennis pro, someone who could actually use this technology, claims that the new racquets will help all players. The larger racquet size allows greater court coverage, and more power and stability. Lighter weight racquets are easier to move around; however, that comes with the risk of less control of the ball coming off the racquet. In the end, though, I didn't make my decision based on lighter weight versus string control versus a larger racquet head. I made my decision based on the racquet that sounded the most intimidating!

5. The author uses the phrase <u>weekend warrior</u> to describe himself as:

   A. a top-flight athlete.

   B. a recreational player.

   C. a temperamental competitor.

   D. a tennis professional.

   E. a racquet manufacturer.

6. The author's main point of the passage is:

   A Advances in technology have harmed the tradition of tennis.

   B. Oversized racquets provide more reach for players.

   C. Only professional athletes should be concerned about new advances in racquet technology.

   D. Looking good is more important than playing well.

   E. Although some players may not need new tennis racquets, they may enjoy having the best equipment.

7. An appropriate title for this passage is:

   A. The History of Tennis Racquets

   B. New Tennis Technologies: I Don't Need Them, but I Like Them

   C. Impact of Oversized Racquets on Tennis Serves

   D. Technology in Sports

   E. One Man's Tennis Journey

Read the passage below; then answer the four questions that follow.

Forced to hunt for new prey, killer whales are devastating sea otter territory off the Alaskan coast, disrupting the food chain and setting off an ecological cascade. The whales have created damage with such alarming efficiency that a vast ecosystem now seems to be at risk of collapse.

The problem began when fish stocks started to decline in the Bering Sea, probably as a result of commercial fishing, or changes in the ocean currents and temperatures. Because of this lack of food, seals and sea lions are thinning out, losing some of their insulating blubber. Killer whales, therefore, aren't getting the same diet from seals and sea lions as they used to, forcing them to feed on sea otters. The otter populations have collapsed, allowing their prey, sea urchins, to multiply out of control. Sea urchins have now begun to devour the kelp forests on the ocean floor at an alarming rate. The kelp forests are crucial to a number of habitats.

8. Otter populations have declined off the Alaskan coast primarily because:

   A. Sea urchins are multiplying at record rates.

   B. The kelp forests are being destroyed.

   C. Whales have been forced to search for additional food in their diets.

   D. Commercial fishing is killing otters.

   E. Global warming is making the otter population sick.

9. This passage would most likely appear in:

   A. a newspaper article.

   B. the journal of marine biology.

   C. an editorial.

   D. a biology textbook.

   E. a doctoral thesis.

10. Which of the following best outlines the structure of the passage?

    A. A statement is made, then supported through an example.

    B. A conclusion is stated, followed by detailed explanatory evidence.

    C. A question is raised, then answered.

    D. An experiment is described, followed by the conclusion of the experiment.

    E. An argument is stated, then refuted.

11. Which of the following is the best definition for the author's use of cascade?

    A. a waterfall

    B. an arrangement

    C. a chain of events

    D. a fabric

    E. a tool

Read the passage below; then answer the question that follows.

I want to buy my sister a gift for her birthday that she really likes. I saw some pretty sweaters for sale, but it's still hot out and she won't be able to wear them for at least a couple of months. I did see a gorgeous red dress on sale at a good discount, but my sister hardly ever wears red. The store does sell the same dress in blue, and my sister wears blue all the time, but it costs considerably more than the red one. However, why buy the red dress if my sister won't really like it? I'm going to spend the extra money and buy her the blue dress for her birthday. At least that way I'll know she'll be getting a gift that she really likes.

12. Which of the following is an assumption that influenced the author's reasoning?

A. Most people prefer blue clothing to red clothing.

B. Her sister will appreciate the blue dress more because it is more expensive.

C. Her sister likes dresses more than she likes sweaters.

D. The red dress is on sale at a good discount because red is a less popular color.

E. Her sister's tendency to wear blue more than red is her own choice.

Read the passage below; then answer the question that follows.

It simply isn't fair that big banks continue to charge user fees for customers using "foreign" ATMs. Now, in addition to being charged for using a machine that does not belong to your bank, you must pay an additional fee to the institution that owns the machine. ____ ________________________________. At least those institutions understand how much I dislike all these extra charges.

13. Which of the following sentences, inserted into the line above, would best complete the meaning of the passage?

    A. While small banks can't offer as many services, they do offer checking without ATM fees.

    B. Sometimes, calling a customer service manager will help you eliminate the charges.

    C. Congress has considered making these user transactions illegal.

    D. Banks just make me so angry.

    E. If we all boycott banks that include these charges, they will be forced to change their practices.

Read the passage below; then answer the four questions that follow.

[1]Tom, twenty-nine, leaves his job on Wednesday nights at 6 P.M. to go back to school. [2]Even with a bachelor's degree in biology, and a master's degree in computer science, Tom still felt he needed to go back to school to further his career. [3]His company agreed, and will be paying the $2,000 per semester tuition.

[4]Tom's story is not unique. [5]More and more, Americans are returning to school for quick, practical courses that allow them to keep up with the competition and with rapid changes in technology and business. [6]The rush to these types of "quickie" courses does not mean that graduate degrees are no longer popular. [7]Instead, these courses are used to supplement any employee's education. [8]There is no longer a natural end to when one should complete his or her education. [9]Further, these new courses allow working individuals to learn and work at the same time, eliminating the difficult decision of whether or not to go back to school full time.

[10]The "classroom" is changing as well. [11]More and more, companies are customizing courses for their employees in conjunction with major universities. [12]Classes are held at the workplace, and the curriculum is determined jointly by both leading professors from the university and company administrators. [13]Together, a curriculum is created that provides new information relevant to the workplace. [14]Clearly, adult education has never been better.

14. Which of the following sentences represents an opinion of the author rather than a fact?

    A. 3

    B. 11

    C. 12

    D. 13

    E. 14

15. Which of the following provides the best outline for the passage?

    A. A topic is introduced, then supported by examples.

    B. An example is given, followed by counter-arguments against the example.

    C. A specific story is told, followed by general explanations.

    D. A general story is told, followed by specific explanations.

    E. A theory is tested, then refuted, and another theory is created.

16. Which of the following statements would the author most likely support?

    A. Only professional scholars should develop course curricula.

    B. Continuing education in the workplace allows employees more flexibility than traditional postgraduate classes.

    C. Education ends after any postgraduate degrees are completed.

    D. Companies allow employees to take additional courses strictly to keep them at their current jobs longer.

    E. Adult education is on the decline.

17. The passage implies that many companies are supporting employees' decisions to go back to school because:

    A. Companies believe continued education will benefit the companies.

    B. Companies fear losing employees to other companies that provide additional training.

    C. Companies need to use federal education grants before they expire.

    D. Companies consider most undergraduate education inadequate and of poor quality.

    E. Companies prefer to control the curricula of their employees' classes.

Read the index below; then answer the two questions that follow.

Experiments	
Experiment basics	753–765
Models	741–750
Observation experiments	784–785
Screening experiments	751–752
Two-factor experiment	768–780
2K experiment	768–780
Laboratory experiments	785-790

18. On what pages would you find information about the ways to study and calculate experiments?

    A. 734

    B. 753–765

    C. 784–785

    D. 751–752

    E. 781–783

19. Which of the following best describes the primary organizational pattern used in the section of the book dealing with experiments?

    A. alphabetical

    B. chronological

    C. from easiest to hardest

    D. by type of experiment

    E. by invention

Read the passage below; then answer the three questions that follow.

Stung by broken industry promises, farmers are livid at massive crop failure and crop damage caused by "genetically superior" seeds. In the American Southeast, growers who used genetically manipulated cotton seeds suffered some of the worst crop failure ever. Farmers' organizations around the world are linking up to stop genetically modified seeds from being introduced.

20. Which of the following, if true, would weaken the farmers' claim that genetically modified seeds are to blame for their poor crop production?

A. The seeds were only tried for one season, which had poor weather conditions.

B. The growers of the American Northwest experienced the same type of problems with genetically modified seeds.

C. Cotton seeds are regarded as the best type of genetically modified seeds.

D. Growers in the Southwest were pleased with genetically modified seeds in tomato and corn production.

E. Genetically modified seeds are endorsed by the government.

21. From the passage, it can be inferred that:

A. Currently, the greatest concern for farmers in the American Southeast is the problem with genetically modified seeds.

B. It was once believed that genetically modified seeds would be successful in crop production.

C. Farmers have strong lobbying influences at the national level.

D. Genetically modified seeds are the future of cotton farming.

E. Genetically modified seeds are currently in use throughout all of the United States.

22. The author's use of the words linking up is best defined as:

A. attaching.

B. collaborating.

C. molding.

D. building.

E. connecting.

Read the passage below; then answer the four questions that follow.

An eminent geneticist and his colleagues at Genetics and IVF Institute have created a recent breakthrough that will allow parents to choose the sex of their future child. The process involves using a method to stain sperm with fluorescent dye. Female-producing sperm, which carry more genetic material than male-producing sperm, will glow more brightly. A machine can be used to automatically sort brighter sperm from dimmer ones. So far, the procedure has worked. Of 14 pregnancies involving couples who wanted girls, 13 produced females.

This novel approach to baby-making does pose a number of ethical questions. While few argue against gender selection in order to avoid sex-linked genetic diseases, many people are concerned about using this technology more casually. Some families may choose to have a child to balance out families, or simply because some parents have gender preferences. Could such choices eventually lead to an imbalanced sex ratio?

____.

23. Which of the following best summarizes the central theme of the passage?

    A. IVF has created a successful new fertility drug.

    B. An imbalanced sex ratio may be a result of allowing parents to choose the sex of their children.

    C. It now may be possible to avoid creating children with known sex-linked genetic defects.

    D. New methods in science may allow for parents to choose the sex of their children, which could lead to many ethical concerns.

    E. Fluorescent dye helps to identify different types of sperm.

24. Which of the following best outlines the structure of the passage?

    A. I. Statement
       II. Facts
       III. Quotations

    B. I. Theory
       II. Examples

    C. I. Research
       II. Implications

    D. I. Question
       II. Answer

    E. I. Quote
       II. Thesis
       III. Examples

25. Which of the following provides the best definition for the author's use of the word breakthrough?

A. insight

B. division

C. crack

D. law

E. promotion

26. Which of the following sentences, when inserted into the blank above, would best complete the meaning of the passage?

A. The best solution is to let the government set a policy.

B. Regardless, this technology should become available to the common household in the very near future.

C. Not in my opinion, because a perfect family has one boy and one girl.

D. Before this technology becomes common, we need to take a long look at the possible societal and moral implications of selecting a child's sex.

E. I guess we'll have to wait and see.

Read the passage below; then answer the three questions that follow.

"Top-100" lists have been popular for years, and I assume that they will continue to be for decades. For some reason, everyone seems to be making a list—everything from the top movies, to the top rock albums, to the top cartoon shows.

What most people don't realize is that these lists really tend to be nothing more than publicity stunts. The local bookstore lists its "Top-100" books? Wow, what a great way to boost sales of 100 books within the store! The CEO of that bookstore acknowledges that fact, expressing the list as "a way to bring attention to some of the country's most important books." Further, who are these so-called "experts" that create these lists? I'm concerned about people viewing these lists as facts, not subjective opinions from a group of pundits. ____ ____.

Nonetheless, we play along, and I must concede that at times it can be quite fun, if not sophomoric. As I'm writing this, I can overhear two colleagues debating their favorite movies. We all have our lists, and it's fun to compare and contrast (of course, mine are truly the best). It's even more fun to point out what is wrong with other, more "professional" lists.

27. What would be an appropriate title for the passage?

    A. Top-100 Lists—Harmless Fun For Us All

    B. What's Our Obsession with Rankings?

    C. Top-100 Lists—Academic Merit or Shameless Promotion?

    D. New Promotional Methods in Bookstores

    E. Why I Love Rankings

28. The author's tone can be best described as:

    A. somewhat angry.

    B. incredibly elated.

    C. seriously concerned.

    D. playfully sarcastic.

    E. deeply despairing.

29. Which of the following, if inserted into the blank, would best complete the meaning of the second paragraph?

    A. There are no correct answers to these lists, just the opinions of those lucky enough to have a vote.

    B. Pundits would have come up with a very different list of the "Top-100" books.

    C. Pundits are better informed than you or me to determine what books or movies belong on these lists.

    D. Your favorite book is probably different than my favorite book.

    E. Those who do not agree with the lists probably received a different education than the authors of the lists.

Look at the graph below; then answer the question that follows.

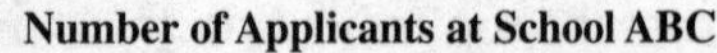

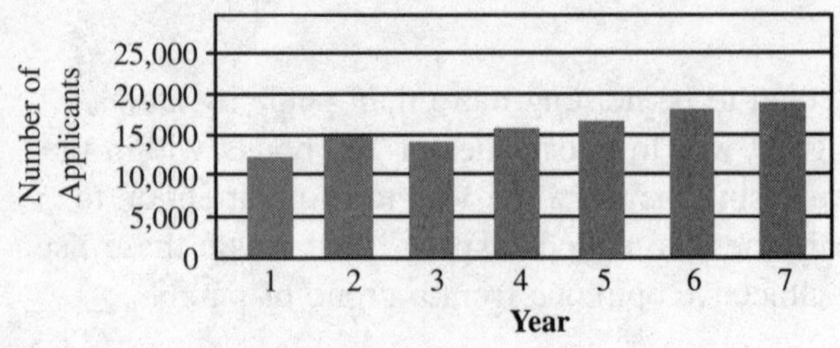

30. Which of the following can be determined from the chart above?

 A. the number of spaces available at School ABC

 B. an approximate number of applicants to ABC from Year 1 to Year 7

 C. the percentage of males applying to ABC

 D. the percentage of females applying to ABC

 E. which year "Year 7" represents

Read the following passage; then answer the three questions that follow.

We in the twentieth century tend to romanticize the Victorian age and view the lives of our ancestors through rose-tinted glasses. There are countless fads and movements that encourage us to live as though it were the nineteenth century, thus presumably simplifying our hectic and highly regulated modern lives. The glorified image of the 1800s is often perpetuated by period films that extol the virtues of this era, magnifying its elegance as only Hollywood can do. We have a collective image of graceful ladies dressed in exquisite attire riding in genteel horse-drawn carriages to serene picnics in the park.

What we don't realize, __________, is that the stench of thousands of horses traipsing around town, coupled with inadequate sanitary measures, was almost unbearable. ___________, that lovely ensemble that the Victorian lady was wearing (properly corseted – of course!) was so unnaturally and uncomfortably tight that it may have been seriously and irreparably damaging her internal organs. And the quaint picnic basket filled with wholesome unprocessed delicacies? It likely contained food that was dangerous or even lethal. In the absence of regulatory agencies to oversee food production, thousands of Victorians became seriously ill or died from contaminated or adulterated food. What we need to remember about the "good old days" is that they really weren't all that great.

31. Which of the following pairs of words or phrases, if inserted *in order* into the blank lines in the passage, would best help the reader understand the author's sequence of ideas?

    A. consequently; Therefore

    B. nonetheless; Thus

    C. however; In addition

    D. so; Nevertheless

    E. therefore; Further

32. Which of the following persuasive techniques does the author use to make his or her main point?

    A. The author attacks the motives of Hollywood filmmakers.

    B. The author uses statistics to disprove a claim.

    C. The author uses an analogy.

    D. The author attacks a viewpoint by introducing additional information that contradicts it.

    E. The author refutes two competing theories by introducing and supporting a third theory.

33. Which of the following facts, if included within the passage, would NOT fit into the author's logical pattern of reasoning?

A. Films about the Victorian age are currently very popular.

B. Regulatory agencies that oversee food production are a twentieth-century invention.

C. Victorian women often cared more about fashion than about their health and comfort.

D. Horses were the most popular means of transportation in the eighteenth century.

E. Rich Victorians could typically afford to have their own servants produce their food, ensuring that is was free of adulterants.

Read the passage below; then answer the two questions that follow.

Judith Rich Harris has written a new controversial book called *The Nurture Assumption.* Although it has been out for only one month, it has already been provoking passionate debate among scientists and therapists. It argues that parents make only a single, lasting contribution to their children's future—their genes. Harris argues that peer groups, not parents, determine the sort of people children will become. Her conclusions are based on her analysis of scientific research, especially with twins. Identical twins raised in the same home are no more alike than those raised apart. And two children adopted by the same parents turn out no more alike than a duo raised separately.

Harris's implications are profound. Does this mean that a parent's love and affection don't matter? Harris, a grandmother and writer of psychology textbooks, without any academic affiliations or a Ph.D., claims that "good parents sometimes have bad kids." Child development experts tend to disagree. It looks as if *The Nurture Assumption* will be the focus of great debate in psychology.

Note: This passage was written in 1998.

34. In which publication would this passage most likely appear?

    A. a book review publication

    B. a psychology journal

    C. a child development textbook

    D. an editorial page

    E. a parenting book

35. Which of the following best describes the main point of the passage?

    A. Parents do not have an influence on their children's behavior.

    B. Harris's book is selling well.

    C. Harris's book contains new theories about parental influence on children that will likely spark much debate in child psychology.

    D. Harris is not affiliated with an academic institution.

    E. Twins are the best indicators of the influence parents have on children.

Read the passage below; then answer the question that follows.

Many pregnant women avoid eating fish because of the mercury levels found in many common freshwater and saltwater fish. Doctors recently conducted a study of 720 women who ate saltwater fish as often as 12 times per week while pregnant, which found no evidence of harm to mothers or their children up to age five.

36. Which of the following best describes the results of the study described in the passage above?

    A. Pregnant women may safely consume seafood.

    B. Freshwater fish contain more mercury than saltwater fish.

    C. Pregnant women who consume saltwater fish have not shown any problems associated with mercury intake during pregnancy, nor have their children.

    D. Children who consume saltwater fish are in danger of mercury poisoning.

    E. Children are in danger of contracting certain diseases later in life if their mothers ate saltwater fish while pregnant.

Read the passage below; then answer the three questions that follow.

In California, countless radio and television ads that oppose Proposition 200 are appearing. From the way the campaign sounds, it seems as though many small local groups are opposed to Proposition 200. Yet a closer look reveals a disturbing trend in political advertising. Large utility companies, who figure to suffer the most if Prop. 200 passes, have carefully crafted a misleading message designed to sap the Prop. 200 effort. The opponents of the measure, the ads proclaim, are small, grassroots consumer and environmental groups—the little guys who really care about utility regulation and its impacts on our community. What the ads don't tell you is that many of the groups and individuals that claim to be against Prop. 200 are actually on the payroll of these large utility companies. More careful research needs to be done to find out exactly who is and who is not funding these initiatives. If "Citizens against Prop. 200" is just a front for the big utility companies who are afraid the proposition will pass, the public will continue to be misled.

37. Which of the following best describes the main point of the passage?

A. Prop. 200 should not be approved.

B. Utility deregulation is a complex initiative.

C. Advertising plays a key role in determining the outcome of state propositions.

D. "Citizens against Prop. 200" includes big businesses.

E. Advertisements and groups opposing Prop. 200 have misled the public by implying that a grassroots effort is the force behind Prop. 200 opposition.

38. Which of the following can be properly inferred from the information in the passage?

A. The author is in support of the proposition.

B. The author is opposed to the proposition.

C. The author supports utility deregulation.

D. The advertising practices of those opposed to Prop. 200 are of great concern.

E. The author will vote for Prop. 200 to show anger toward the advertisements against Prop. 200.

39. The author uses the word sap in the passage above to mean:

A. weaken.

B. strengthen.

C. lengthen.

D. underline.

E. postpone.

Read the passage below; then answer the four questions that follow.

[1]A toy magazine recently promoted "Reference Boy" as the new interactive toy of the year. [2]Like many other blockbuster hits of the last five years, Reference Boy's rise to fame provides evidence that children don't decide what is popular for the holidays. [3]That decision is predetermined by toy executives looking for the next "must-have" product. [4]Buying a popular toy has become a status symbol for parents, sometimes resulting in chaotic shopping conditions. [5]Last year, demand for the popular Young Mike Action Figure was so great that parents resorted to nothing short of guerilla tactics to secure the popular toy for their son or daughter. [6]Limited supplies pushed the market value of the toy as much as twenty times over the list price.

[7]It appears the hype for these toys will come to a quick end. [8]Today, you can walk into any store and purchase dozens of Young Mike Action Figures, at retail cost. [9]Those parents who previously paid up to $400 for one Young Mike last holiday season would be lucky to resell it today for $10.

[10]As the hype for the "cool" toys continues, toy makers are using it to their advantage, and profit. [11]The Reference Boy release didn't hit store shelves quietly—after an appearance on a network morning show, and an afternoon talk show, the rush began. [12]Toy company executives are planning product releases similar in glitz and glamour to movie or album releases. [13]If the trend continues, toy executives may see record profits this holiday season. [14]Toy executives hope the economy will stay strong.

40. Which of the following best summarizes the passage?

A. Popular toys are more the result of parental and company influence than children's opinions about the toys.

B. Product releases are the new trend in toy promotion.

C. Toys may sharply decrease in value, even after a record year of profits and high demand.

D. If a toy is mentioned on a network sales will increase immediately.

E. Reference Boy is the hot new toy for this holiday season.

41. According to the passage, why are toy executives planning large-scale product releases?

A. Sales are always greatest at a large product release party.

B. Large-scale exposure of certain toys has recently meant an immediate explosion in sales.

C. Toys should be able to compete financially against music and books.

D. Executives want to promote new toys only for very limited periods.

E. Executives hope these product releases will keep demand for a product high for several years.

42. Which of the following sentences is least relevant in the third paragraph?

A. Sentence 10

B. Sentence 11

C. Sentence 12

D. Sentence 13

E. Sentence 14

43. Which of the following statements would the author most likely support?

A. The toy market cannot sustain itself at its recent rate of growth.

B. Children must be asked which toys they enjoy before parents determine which toys are "cool."

C. Lately, "cool" toys seem to affect parents as much as, or more than, children.

D. Reference Boy will not be popular next fall.

E. For many years, the toy industry has quietly promoted its products, and for long term growth, it should not deviate from that formula.

Read the table of contents below; then answer the question that follows.

Getting Around San Francisco:

44. On what page would you look to find information on how to get from the airport to a hotel by cab?

A. 67

B. 68

C. 72

D. 74

E. 78

Read the passage below; then answer the three questions that follow.

It's hard to learn to play catch. In the beginning, you use your arms to cradle the ball against your chest; then you use both hands; then one. Soon, you're an expert. You're running down fly balls with ease, and firing throws across your body. I'm not sure if you ever become an expert on parenting. ______________________ ____.

A game of catch is an essential gesture of parenthood, too, I believe, when families are working well. Everyone tosses to be understood. The best part of the game is the silence. I enjoy playing catch with my son. Just like catch, our relationship is one that moves back and forth. I take what I can get from my son, and he takes what he can get (or get away with) from me. We make compromises and adjustments when we are able to, but for the most part things come and go, back and forth, just like a ball when we're sharing a nice day of playing catch.

45. Which of the following sentences, if inserted into the blank above, would best complete the meaning of the first paragraph?

A. Parenting can never be perfected.

B. Like playing catch, parenting is hard to learn.

C. But just as I have become more comfortable playing catch, I have become more comfortable being a parent.

D. Few ballplayers are both great athletes and great fathers.

E. My son is great at playing catch.

46. Which literary technique does the author use to describe her relationship with her son?

A. alliteration

B. a metaphor

C. a parable

D. a myth

E. a fable

47. The author's tone is best described as:

A. reflective.

B. remorseful.

C. forgiving.

D. proud.

E. temperamental.

Read the passage below; then answer the three questions that follow.

[1]Most teachers receive tenure status and lifetime job protection after three years on the job, after which terminating a teacher becomes a very difficult and long process. [2]Teachers faced with termination have a long time before any serious action can be taken—principals seeking to dismiss them must usually file several written reports, wait a year for improvement, file additional poor evaluations, appear at a hearing, and maybe even show up in court to defend the firing. [3]During this process, the teacher still gets paid. [4]This entire process results in few terminations—just 44 of 100,000 tenured teachers were dismissed between 1991 and 1997 in the state of Illinois. [5]Fortunately, many states are moving to streamline their firing procedures. [6]Next year, Florida will cut the time a teacher has to show improvement before a dismissal hearing to 90 days. [7]Firing procedures are unnecessary for an overwhelming majority of the fine men and women teaching our children. [8]However, ____.

48. Which of the following sentences is a statement of opinion?

    A. Sentence 1

    B. Sentence 2

    C. Sentence 3

    D. Sentence 4

    E. Sentence 5

49. Which of the following best summarizes the main point of the passage?

    A. Teachers deserve tenure due to their hard work for low salaries.

    B. Florida is changing its policies regarding teacher dismissal.

    C. There is a debate among teachers about being tenured after only three years.

    D. Most current teacher termination procedures involve many steps, and extend for months, even years.

    E. Teachers' unions are concerned about wrongful terminations of teachers who have done nothing wrong.

50. Which of the following phrases, if inserted into the blank above, would best complete the meaning of the passage?

    A. teachers should be given every benefit of the doubt before termination.

    B. firing procedures need to allow more time for appeals.

    C. if teachers aren't fired, there should be a law that protects them from having to go through termination procedures again.

    D. a swift procedure will ensure equality for all.

    E. when they are necessary, it is important that bottlenecks do not slow down the process.

SECTION II: TEST OF MATHEMATICS

Directions: Each question in the Mathematics Section of the practice test is a multiple-choice question with five answer choices. Read each question carefully and choose the ONE best answer. Record each answer on the answer sheet provided in the back of this book.

You may work on the multiple-choice questions in any order that you choose. You may wish to monitor how long it takes you to complete the practice test. When taking the actual CBEST, you will have one four-hour test session in which to complete the section(s) for which you registered.

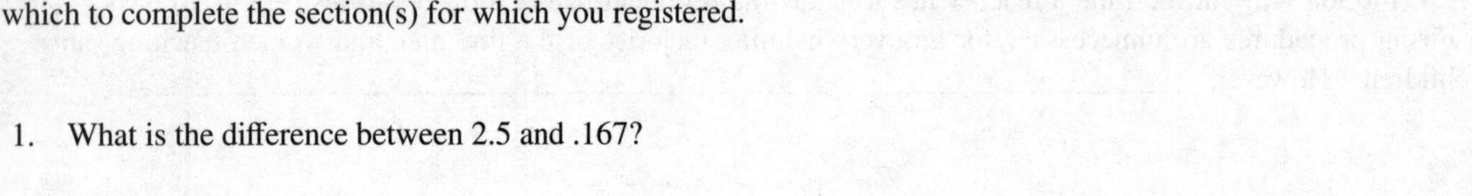

1. What is the difference between 2.5 and .167?

A. .83

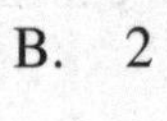

B. 2

C. 2.333

D. 2.667

E 4.17

2. Nancy and May played volleyball for 63 hours in June, and for 89 hours in July. The number of hours in June is approximately what percent of the number of hours in July?

A. 29%

B. 53%

C. 71%

D. 83%

E. 141%

3. What number could be added to the following set of data so that the median and mode of the set are equal?

42, 36, 59, 23, 61, 30, 75

A. 42

B. 36

C. 33

D. 23

E. 10

4. **Read the information below and then answer the question that follows.**

Christopher is preparing a nursery that requires a variety of potting soil. He purchases $27\frac{3}{4}$ pounds of Desert soil and $8\frac{5}{6}$ pounds of Garden soil.

What is the total amount of soil purchased?

A. $39\frac{5}{12}$ pounds

B. $36\frac{7}{12}$ pounds

C. $35\frac{7}{12}$ pounds

D. $35\frac{5}{12}$ pounds

E. $33\frac{7}{12}$ pounds

5. In his sociology class, Adam took three tests. He scored a 78 on his first test, and a 90 on his second test. If Adam had an average of 81 in his class, what did Adam score on his third test?

A. 75

B. 81

C. 83

D. 90

E. 243

6. Frank is going to buy turkey sandwiches for his employees. A sandwich costs \$3.25, and each topping or condiment costs an extra \$.25. Each order of cheese costs an extra \$.50. Here is the list of what Frank will buy:

2 sandwiches without cheese, with 2 condiments each
2 sandwiches with cheese, with 1 condiment each

Assuming no tax, what is the total cost of the sandwiches?

A. \$14.75

B. \$15.00

C. \$15.50

D. \$16.00

E. \$16.50

7. What is the best estimate of $50 + 49 + 48 + 47 + 46 + 45 + 44 + 43 + 42 + 41 + 40$?

A. 550

B. 500

C. 450

D. 400

E. 300

8. **Read the information below and then answer the question that follows.**

> Monica drives to several different students' homes every day for tutoring. During the first full week in September, her daily mileage ranges from a low of 36 miles to a high of 102 miles.

From the preceding information, which of the following must be true regarding Monica's average daily mileage for the week?

A. Her average for all 7 days is between 36 and 102 miles.

B. Her average for all 7 days is 69 miles.

C. Her average for all 7 days is greater than 69 miles.

D. Her average for all 7 days is lower than 69 miles.

E. Her average for all 7 days is any number between 0 and 100 miles.

9. Multiplying a number by $\frac{3}{4}$ is the same as dividing that number by

A. $\frac{9}{16}$

B. $\frac{3}{4}$

C. 1

D. $\frac{4}{3}$

E. 4

10. **Use the chart and information given below to answer the question that follows.**

InterTech Employee Roster

Department	Total
Engineering	64
Marketing	123
Product Design	56

As an employee is preparing the employment roster above, she notices that her own department, Human Resources, has not been included in the report. She also knows that there are a total of 282 employees in these four departments.

Based on the chart above and the given information, what is the accurate number of Human Resources employees at InterTech?

A. 19

B. 27

C. 39

D. 87

E. 282

11. At a school supplies store, the price of a blackboard is reduced from $70.00 to $56.00. By what percent is the price of the blackboard decreased?

A. 10%

B. 14%

C. 20%

D. 56%

E. 86%

12. At his office, Adam did a survey on what his employees wanted for lunch, sandwiches or pizza. Adam received 34 more votes for pizza than sandwiches. If Adam received a total of 76 votes, how many votes did he receive for sandwiches?

A. 21 votes

B. 40 votes

C. 42 votes

D. 84 votes

E. 110 votes

13. The price of a dress is $120.00. If during a sale the price is marked down 15%, what is the new price of the dress?

A. $18.00

B. $90.00

C. $102.00

D. $105.00

E. $135.00

14. What is the value of 654,322 rounded to the nearest thousand?

A. 654,000

B. 654,300

C. 654,400

D. 655,000

E. 655,300

15. Mike and Julie collect pictures. They want to place all of their pictures into photo albums. If Mike and Julie own 412 pictures, and each album holds a maximum of 34 pictures, what is the minimum number of photo albums Mike and Julie must purchase so that every picture is contained in a photo album?

A. 11 albums

B. 12 albums

C. 13 albums

D. 20 albums

E. 34 albums

<u>Questions 16 and 17</u>. Use the information below to answer the two questions that follow.

Chris, Fiona, and Rich are at a baseball game.
They ate a total of 7 hot dogs, 3 bags of peanuts, and 4 soft drinks.
Rich ate more hot dogs than Chris.
Fiona ate 1 bag of peanuts and 1 hot dog.
Hot dogs cost $.75 more than peanuts, but less than soft drinks.

16. Which of the following facts can be determined from the information given above?

A. who ate the most hot dogs

B. how many bags of peanuts Rich ate

C. the total cost of all the food

D. the cost of a hot dog

E. the number of soft drinks Chris drank

17. If peanuts cost $.50, what is one possible total for the cost of the peanuts, hot dogs, and soft drinks eaten by Rich, Chris, and Fiona?

A. $10.25

B. $11.75

C. $13.25

D. $15.25

E. $16.50

18. In a recent store promotion, customers received three game stamps for every purchase of a large drink. If Rick has collected sixty game stamps, how many large drinks has he purchased?

A. 3

B. 18

C. 20

D. 26

E. 57

19. Joe needs to add the fractions $\frac{1}{2}$, $\frac{3}{4}$, and $\frac{2}{5}$. Which of the following methods should Joe use to add these fractions most efficiently?

A. Use the "subtract from one" technique.

B. Multiply the denominators.

C. Use a common denominator of 10.

D. Use a common denominator of 40.

E. Use a common denominator of 20.

20. What is the best estimate of the following expression:

$$\frac{(282.4) \times (11.85) \times (9.2)}{(3.11) \times (70.35) \times (8.827)}$$

A. 3.5

B. 9.2

C. 15.8

D. 20.3

E. 70.35

21. **Use the chart and information given below to answer the question that follows.**

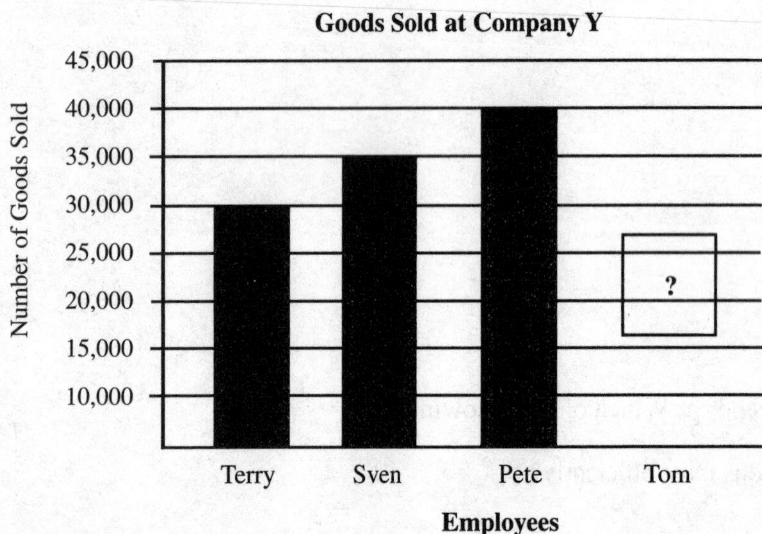

In order for the total amount of goods sold to equal 150,000, how many goods were sold by Tom?

A. 30,000

B. 35,000

C. 40,000

D. 45,000

E. 47,000

22. $10y - 36 + 4y - 6 + y = 3$. What is the value of y?

A. 3

B. 4

C. 6

D. 10

E. 36

23. The value $\frac{3}{8}$ falls between which of the following pairs of percents?

A. 15% and 20%

B. 25% and 30%

C. 35% and 40%

D. 45% and 50%

E. 55% and 60%

24. If the value of x is between $-.345$ and $.008$, which of the following could be the value of x?

A. -1.1

B. $-.45$

C. $-.08$

D. $.08$

E. $.345$

25. Rick, Marty, and Ben all own baseball cards. There are a total of 3,500 cards between them. If Marty owns 70% of the baseball cards, how many cards does Marty have?

A. 1,050 cards

B. 1,225 cards

C. 2,450 cards

D. 2,800 cards

E. 3,430 cards

26. Oliver is building a fence around his yard. When finished, the fence will be 170 feet long. For five days straight, Oliver builds 25 feet of the fence each day. After these five days, how much is left for Oliver to build?

A. 25 feet

B. 45 feet

C. 50 feet

D. 65 feet

E. 70 feet

27. James wants to send 300 thank-you cards. He can write 12 per day. If he begins February 1, when would he expect to be finished?

A. February 12

B. February 13

C. February 25

D. February 26

E. March 12

28. **Use the following chart to help answer the question the follows.**

Student	Questions Answered Correctly	Percentile Score	Stanine Score
Kristen	32	52%	
Jen		44%	
Debbie		82%	
Amy	37		7

Place the order of students' scores from lowest to highest:

A. Amy, Kristen, Debbie, Jen

B. Kristen, Debbie, Amy, Jen

C. Jen, Kristen, Amy, Debbie

D. Debbie, Kristen, Amy, Jen

E. Debbie, Amy, Jen, Kristen

29. Arash walked 485 yards from class to the cafeteria. How many feet did Arash walk?

A. 40 feet

B. 161 feet

C. 1,455 feet

D. 2,100 feet

E. 5,820 feet

30. During Johnna's freshman year of college, she attended class for 3 hours each day. If there are 165 days of class, how many hours of class did Johnna attend?

A. 325 hours

B. 348 hours

C. 425 hours

D. 468 hours

E. 495 hours

31. At a high school, 2 out of every 5 students go to Butterick College. If there are 240 students, how many are expected to go to Butterick College?

A. 24 students

B. 96 students

C. 120 students

D. 144 students

E. 180 students

32. **Use the table given below to answer the question that follows.**

SupplyMart Price List	
Ream of paper	$ 2.00
Box of crayons	$ 3.45
Dry erase marker	$ .65

A teacher purchased the following: 2 dozen reams of paper, 17 boxes of crayons, and 33 dry erase markers. Which answer represents this purchase?

A. 24($2.00) + 17($.65) + 33($3.45)

B. 2($2.00) + 17($.65) + 33($3.45)

C. (24 + 17 + 33) + ($2.00 + $.65 + $3.45)

D. (2 × 12) + $2.00 + 17($3.45) + 33($.65)

E. 24($2.00) + 33($.65) + 17($3.45)

33. What percent of 20 is 5?

A. 1%

B. 5%

C. 25%

D. 40%

E. 75%

34. A designer dress is discounted 15% to \$425. Which of the following equations could be used to determine its original price, p?

A. $.85p = \$425$

B. $.85p + .15p = \$425$

C. $p = \$425 + .15$

D. $.15p = \$425$

E. $p = \$425 - .15$

35. In 1996, the total number of CDs sold at Brandt's record store was 250,000. In 1997, that number rose to 300,000. What was the percent increase in the number of CDs Brandt's record store sold?

A. 17%

B. 20%

C. 50%

D. 75%

E. 105%

36. Which of the following numbers is smallest?

A. .25

B. .0088

C. .325

D. .0067

E. .111

37. The school board is proposing a 5% increase in the number of students per classroom. Currently, there are 20 students per class. How many students would there be per class with the proposed increase?

A. 21

B. 22

C. 23

D. 24

E. 25

38. Use the figure below to answer the question that follows.

Which answer best represents the shaded part of the box shown above?

A. $\frac{3}{4}$

B. $\frac{2}{3}$

C. $\frac{2}{5}$

D. $\frac{1}{3}$

E. $\frac{1}{4}$

39. There are 120 books in Ms. Wilson's classroom library. If $\frac{1}{3}$ of the books are nonfiction, and $\frac{3}{8}$ of the nonfiction books are about animals, how many nonfiction books in the library are about animals?

A. 45

B. 40

C. 25

D. 15

E. 5

40. $\frac{3}{4} = \frac{9}{x}$. What is the value of x?

A. 3

B. 4

C. 9

D. 12

E. 36

41. In her biology class, Brooke took seven tests. On her first six tests, Brooke received test scores of 90, 88, 87, 92, 85, and 92. If her total on seven tests was 612, what did she score on her seventh test?

A. 78

B. 85

C. 88

D. 90

E. 92

Questions 42 and 43. Use the graph below to answer the two questions that follow.

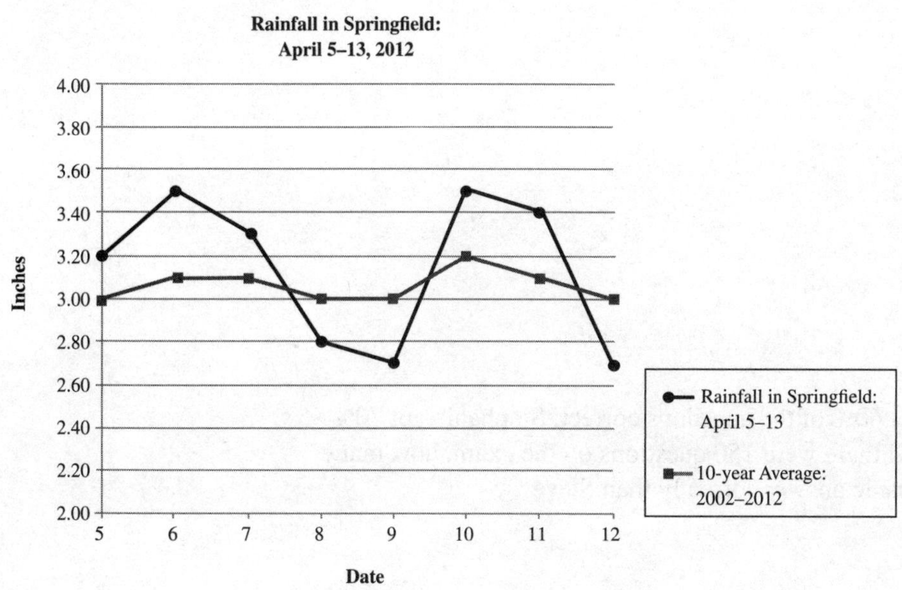

42. Of the eight days shown, on approximately what percent of the days did the rainfall exceed the 10-year average rainfall?

A. 12%

B. 25%

C. 38%

D. 63%

E. 75%

43. Between which two dates in 2012 shown did the greatest decrease in rainfall occur?

A. April 5-6

B. April 6-7

C. April 7-8

D. April 9-10

E. April 11-12

44. How many boxes are needed to hold 52 cupcakes if each box holds 12 cupcakes?

A. $3\frac{1}{3}$

B. 4

C. $4\frac{1}{3}$

D. 5

E. $5\frac{1}{3}$

45. On a recent test, Steve got 60% of the questions correct. Stephanie got 70% of the questions correct. If there were 150 questions on the exam, how many more questions did Stephanie answer correctly than Steve?

A 1 question

B. 10 questions

C. 15 questions

D. 25 questions

E. 90 questions

46. Mike has a bucket containing 13,086 marbles. He buys half that number of marbles, and adds them to his bucket. Approximately how many marbles does he now have in his bucket?

A. 6,500 marbles

B. 13,000 marbles

C. 20,000 marbles

D. 26,000 marbles

E. 39,000 marbles

47. Fiona is playing with a complete deck of 52 cards (13 spades, 13 clubs, 13 diamonds, and 13 hearts). If she draws one card at random, what is the probability that she will select a heart?

A. $\frac{1}{4}$

B. $\frac{1}{2}$

C. $\frac{1}{8}$

D $\frac{1}{13}$

E $\frac{1}{20}$

48. −7 is greater than which of the following numbers?

A. −10

B. −4

C. 0

D. 1

E. 8

49. A rectangular yard, measuring 50 feet long by 40 feet wide, contains a rectangular swimming pool. If the yard is 10 feet wider than the swimming pool on each side, what is the perimeter of the swimming pool?

A. 100 feet

B. 120 feet

C. 140 feet

D. 160 feet

E. 180 feet

50. Consider this statement:

If Mitch directs the movie, then he will also appear in it.

If this statement is true, which of the following statements must also be true?

A. If Mitch did not appear in the movie, then he did not direct it.

B. If Mitch did not direct the movie, then he did not appear in it.

C. If Mitch appeared in the movie, then he directed it.

D. If Mitch appeared in the movie, then he did not direct it.

E. If Mitch did not direct the movie, then he appeared in it.

SECTION III: TEST OF WRITING

Directions: The Writing section of the CBEST assesses basic skills and concepts that are important in performing the job of an educator in California. This section includes two topics that assess your ability to write effectively. One of the topics asks you to analyze a situation or statement; the other asks you to write about a personal experience. You will not be expected to demonstrate any specialized knowledge in your responses.

You should be sure to write only on the topics presented, respond to both topics, address all of the points presented in the topics, and support generalizations with specific examples. Before you begin writing, read each topic and organize your thoughts carefully.

Your written response must be your original work, written in your own words, and must not be copied or paraphrased from some other work.

When you take the actual CBEST, scorers will read and evaluate each of your responses using a standard set of criteria, which are outlined in the writing score scale (see Part IV of this book).

The following written performance characteristics, which are incorporated in the CBEST Writing Score Scale, are evaluated during scoring.

I. *Rhetorical Force:* the clarity with which the central idea or point of view is stated and maintained; the coherence of the discussion and the quality of the writer's ideas

II. *Organization:* the clarity of the writing and the logical sequence of the writer's ideas

III. *Support and Development:* the relevance, depth, and specificity of supporting information

IV. *Usage:* the extent to which the writing shows care and precision in word choice

V. *Structure and Conventions:* the extent to which the writing is free of errors in syntax, paragraph structure, sentence structure, and mechanics (e.g., spelling, punctuation, capitalization)

VI. *Appropriateness:* the extent to which the writer addresses the topic and uses language and style appropriate to the given audience and purpose

WRITING TOPICS

Topic 1

The amount of money available from the state budget for school district X has not increased in the last three years, despite the increasing number of students and rising administrative costs. As a result, members of the school board have formed partnerships with local businesses. Some of these partnerships involve free books, maps, and textbooks from a particular company. Others involve food from local fast-food establishments. Supporters of these partnerships argue that local businesses are helping out the community, and deserve recognition for their contributions. Critics argue that the school board should not form such partnerships, because schools will become tainted with "corporate advertising" throughout the school. Should schools allow corporate partners to help provide funding and materials? If so, should there be any restrictions on what can and cannot be donated?

Support your opinion with specific reasons.

Topic 2

What is the best class you have taken? Did you enjoy the class because of the teacher or because of the subject matter? What did you like about the class? What has this classroom experience taught you that you will be able to use when you become a teacher?

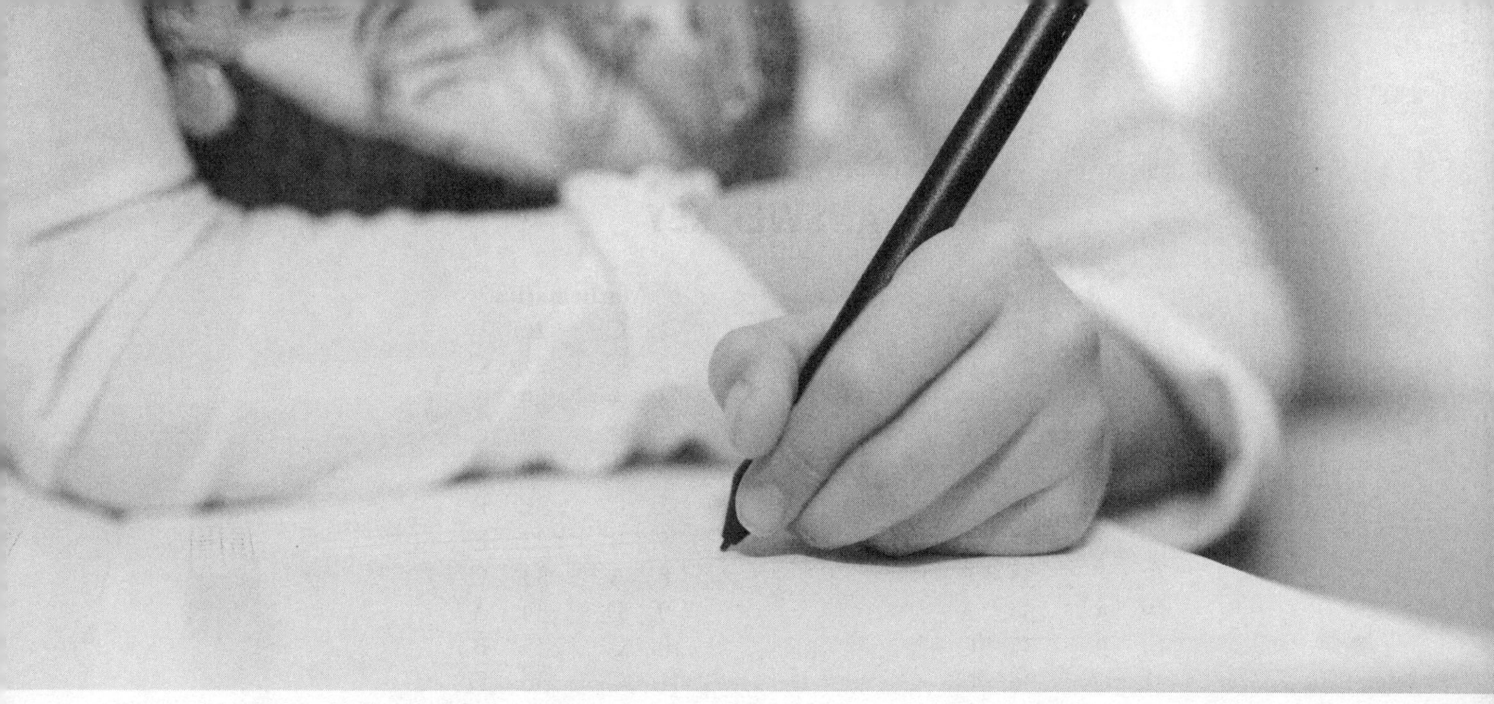

Chapter 13
Practice Test 2: Answers and Explanations

ANSWER KEY

Reading		Mathematics	
1. B	26. D	1. C	26. B
2. C	27. C	2. C	27. C
3. D	28. D	3. A	28. C
4. D	29. A	4. B	29. C
5. B	30. B	5. A	30. E
6. E	31. C	6. C	31. B
7. B	32. D	7. B	32. E
8. C	33. E	8. A	33. C
9. A	34. A	9. D	34. A
10. B	35. C	10. C	35. B
11. C	36. C	11. C	36. D
12. E	37. E	12. A	37. A
13. A	38. D	13. C	38. E
14. E	39. A	14. A	39. D
15. C	40. A	15. C	40. D
16. B	41. B	16. A	41. A
17. A	42. E	17. E	42. D
18. B	43. C	18. C	43. E
19. D	44. C	19. E	44. D
20. A	45. C	20. C	45. C
21. B	46. B	21. D	46. C
22. B	47. A	22. A	47. A
23. D	48. E	23. C	48. A
24. C	49. D	24. C	49. A
25. A	50. E	25. C	50. A

SECTION I: TEST OF READING

1. **B** The information is contained in the last sentence of the first paragraph in the passage.

2. **C** Often an author will use a word in quotations to imply a meaning similar to the literal meaning of the word. Choice (B) is out of scope. Choice (D) contradicts the information in the passage, and (A) and (E) are not stated anywhere in the passage.

3. **D** The use of the automobile example is designed to show the impressive features of the DS1 system.

4. **D** Although the number $30,000 is contained in the passage, we cannot tell exactly how much money someone in debt will save. All we know is that they may be eligible for extended payment options.

5. **B** If you are unfamiliar with the phrase, information in the passage implies that he is not an experienced tennis player. The first sentence of the passage ("I'm not much of a tennis player") helps to eliminate (A) and (D).

6. **E** The author takes a lighthearted tone in this passage, and is the first to acknowledge that he does not need the new racquets. However, he enjoys learning about and using the top of the line racquets.

7. **B** Choices (D) and (A) are out of scope. Choice (C) is too specific. Choice (E) does not provide an appropriate title because the passage concerns tennis equipment, not the author's "tennis journey" in general.

8. **C** The chain of events is described in the second paragraph. The primary reason the otter population is declining is due to killer whales' need for additional food, since sea lions and seals have been losing weight.

9. **A** The information is neither very complex nor very scientific, so (B), (D), and (E) can be eliminated. Very little opinion, if any, is stated in the passage, so eliminate (C). Since the information is described as recent, it would most likely appear in a newspaper article.

10. **B** The passage starts with the conclusion that the otter population is in great danger. That conclusion is then supported by a detailed explanation of how this phenomenon is supposedly occurring.

11. **C** While (A) is the most popular definition, the author uses the word here to indicate a tragic series of events. This series of events is then described in the next paragraph.

12. **E** An assumption is an unstated assertion that the author believes is true that is necessary for the line of reasoning to hold up. If you negate an assumption, there will be a logical hole in the argument and the reasoning will not work. In this case the author wants to buy her sister a gift that her sister *really likes.* She decides to buy her the blue dress because her sister wears blue more often than she wears red. However, if her sister wears blue because she is required to (for example, in keeping with a dress code for a sorority), then she might actually like the red dress more than the blue one. Negating answer choice (E) destroys the author's line of reasoning, while negating the other answer choices does not.

13. **A** One clue is the first few words of the next sentence—"at least those institutions." We know that the blank sentence must talk about some types of institutions other than big banks.

14. **E** The statement, "adult education has never been better" represents the feelings of the author, and would be difficult to prove. All other statements are facts.

15. **C** The passage starts with the story of Tom. From there, we learn about the growing trends in adult education.

16. **B** In the passage, the author describes the advantages of taking classes while still collecting an income and at the convenient location of the workplace.

17. **A** We could try to speculate why many companies are providing educational assistance to their employees, but we cannot prove any of the explanations. Choices (B), (D), and (E) all seem like good reasons, but we can't prove them. We can infer, however, that companies believe these programs are beneficial. Companies are reimbursing employees and setting up their own programs, both of which indicate a belief that it is in the companies' interests to do so.

18. **B** The category of "experiment basics" is where one could find general information on how to perform experiments. Most of the other categories list specific types of experiments.

19. **D** Most of the subheadings under the category "Experiments" list different types of experiments. Remember that the question stem asks for the *primary* organizational pattern used, so Choice (D) is correct even though "Experiment Basics" is not a type of experiment. We have no way of evaluating answer choices (C) and (E).

20. **A** The farmers claim that their poor crop production was due to the genetically modified seeds. In order to weaken that claim, another reason needs to be provided to explain the poor crop production. Poor weather does provide a reason.

21. **B** The passage starts by describing farmers as upset about "broken promises" and failed results. At some point, farmers must have been told about the benefits of genetically modified seeds.

22. **B** The goal of the farmers is to gain support from as many other farmers as possible to fight against genetically modified seeds. The farmers seek to collaborate with as many other groups as possible.

23. **D** When asked for the main idea or central theme, remember to skim the passage using the 2-T-2 technique.

24. **C** We can eliminate (D) and (E) because the passage does not start with either a question or a quote. Choice (A) can be eliminated because the passage does not end with a quotation.

25. **A** The scientists have found a new method that has yet to be discovered by anyone else. This key piece of insight is the focus of the article.

26. **D** The main point of the paragraph is that there are ethical considerations with this new technology. It would be out of place for the author to suddenly state his or her own views, as in (C) and (E), or end the issue immediately, as in (A) and (B).

27. **C** The author is concerned about Top-100 lists being viewed as factual truths, instead of just promotional items designed to spark debate.

28. **D** The author uses sarcasm to make a point. The best example of this is the third sentence of the second paragraph. Choices (A) and (C) are wrong in light of the whimsical tone of the passage. Choices (B) and (E) are way too extreme, and the former ignores the author's concerns.

29. **A** Choices (B), (C), and (E) contradict the author's overall message. Choice (A) correctly completes the main idea of the second paragraph.

30. **B** We can add up the total number of applicants for each of the years labeled 1 through 7.

31. **C** The second paragraph transitions from the discussion of the romanticized version of a Victorian picnic (paragraph 1) to a discussion of the unpleasant reality. Accordingly, a word that indicates a change in direction (such as "however") is required for the first blank (choices A, D, and E can be eliminated). The first sentence of paragraph 2 discusses the negative aspects of horses in Victorian life, and the next sentence discusses the negative aspects of Victorian attire. A word or phrase that indicates continuity (such as "in addition") is required for the second blank. Choice (B) is wrong because the word "thus" indicates a logical connection between horse stench and ladies' attire that is not suggested.

32. **D** The author attacks a viewpoint (the romanticized idea of Victorian life as illustrated by the picnic image) by introducing additional information (all the negative facts) that contradict that pleasant view. The author does not attack anyone's motives (choice A) or use statistics (choice B). Nor does the author use an analogy, which involves a comparison between two things (choice C). The author uses facts, not theory, to refute a single viewpoint (choice E is wrong as well).

33. **E** If rich Victorians could ensure that their food was unadulterated, that would contradict the author's statements that the genteel picnickers at issue were probably eating unsafe food. All the other answer choices are consistent with the author's reasoning.

34. **A** The passage is very vague and general, so we can eliminate choices (B), (C), and (E). The passage does not state any strong opinions, making a book review the most likely publication.

35. **C** Choice (A) is wrong because it reflects the main point of Harris' book, not the main point of the passage.

36. **C** The study found no harm to mothers or their children who consumed saltwater fish during pregnancy. Choice (A) is too broad and the study provides no information to assess whether choices (B), (D), and (E) are true.

37. **E** The focus of the passage is the misrepresentation of names and advertisements of groups against Prop. 200.

38. **D** The author has not stated any opinion about Prop. 200 or its underlying issues, only that certain practices of those who oppose it are objectionable.

39. **A** To gain a better understanding of the vocabulary in context, read the remainder of the sentence, which uses the word "misleading" to help define "sap."

40. **A** The passage describes how toys are becoming new status symbols for parents, and what toy companies are doing to profit from this trend. Choice (B) does not summarize the idea that parents and toy companies are determining which toys are desirable, which is a critical point.

41. **B** The passage mentions how toy sales took off after exposure on a network show. Toy executives are using these product release events with this effect in mind.

42. **E** The final paragraph describes how national exposure can lead to large sales. Speculation on the economy is not relevant to the overall meaning of the paragraph.

43. **C** The passage describes the impact new toys have on parents. Choice (B) is wrong because we don't know how the author thinks parents should address the toy issue with their children.

44. **C** Information on how to travel by taxi can be found on page 72.

45. **C** The goal of the final sentence in the first paragraph is to link the idea of playing catch with the role of being a parent. Choices (B) and (D) mention both topics, but (C) provides a better connection between the two.

46. **B** The game of catch is a metaphor for her relationship with her son.

47. **A** The author reflects on what it feels like to play a game of catch, and what it feels like to raise her son.

48. **E** The word "fortunately" in sentence 5 indicates that the author *approves* of the fact that many states are now moving to streamline their firing procedures. Unlike sentences 1-4, which simply state facts, the inclusion of that one word makes the statement an opinion.

49. **D** The passage describes the lengthy procedures used to terminate a teacher who is not in good standing.

50. **E** Choices (A) and (B) go against the general point of the passage. Choice (D) is out of scope. Choice (E) best fits the desire to speed up termination procedures that currently take a very long time.

SECTION II: TEST OF MATHEMATICS

1. **C** When subtracting decimals, be sure to align the decimals vertically, as shown below:

$$\begin{array}{r} 2.500 \\ -\ .167 \\ \hline = 2.333 \end{array}$$

2. **C** To find the answer, divide 63 ÷ 89, which equals approximately 0.71, or 71%.

Remember to ballpark. 63 ÷ 89 can be approximated as 60 ÷ 90, or $\frac{2}{3}$. We can eliminate each of the other answers, because they are too far from the estimate. Note that (E) is a trap answer—it's the result of 89 ÷ 63 instead of 63 ÷ 89.

3. **A** To find the median, first put the list in numerical order.

23, 30, 36, 42, 59, 61, 75

The middle number is 42. This is the median. The question asks, which number can be added in order to make the median the same as the mode. Currently, there is no mode, since each number is unique. However, if we add another 42 to this list, then the mode would be 42, and the median would also be 42.

4. **B** To solve this problem, add the two values together, and don't forget to Ballpark. Starting with the integer parts, add 27 + 8 = 35. Eliminate (E), since it is too small. The two fractional parts $\left(\frac{3}{4}\right)$ and $\left(\frac{5}{6}\right)$ are each close to 1, so their sum is close to 2. That brings the total close to 37, which means that (A) is too large, and you can probably feel comfortable choosing (B) from the remaining choices. To add the fractions, use the Bowtie method:

$$\left(\frac{3}{4}\right)+\left(\frac{5}{6}\right)=\left(\frac{18}{24}\right)+\left(\frac{20}{24}\right)=\left(\frac{38}{24}\right).$$

This is equal to $1\ \frac{14}{24}$ or $1\ \frac{7}{12}$ That means the total is $35 + 1 + \frac{7}{12}$, or $36\ \frac{7}{12}$.

5. **A** Start by filling in the information given into the average circle. The number of things is three (3 tests), and the average is 81. Multiply to find the total of 243. 243 is the sum of the three tests. If we subtract the first two exams (78 and 90) from 243, we are left with 75, his score on the third test. Choice (E) is a partial answer. It gives us the total for all three tests. Note that we can also use Backsolving. When we plug in (A), we get an average of 81, like so: $(78 + 90 + 75) \div 3 = 81$.

6. **C** 4 sandwiches equal $13.00. There are 6 condiments that cost a total of $1.50, and two orders of cheese, which cost $1.00 total. The total sum of Frank's order is therefore $15.50.

7. **B** Rather than take the time to add each individual value, estimate, and use Ballparking. There are eleven numbers. If all eleven were equal to 50, the sum would be 550. Eliminate (A). If all eleven were equal to 40, the sum would be 440. Eliminate (D) and (E). The middle value is around 45. 45×11 is approximately 500, which is the correct answer.

8. **A** The average of a set of numbers must always be between the lowest and highest numbers, so (A) must be true. One way to check our answer is to test different values for the unknown mileage during the week.

   If the lowest daily mileage was 36, then it's possible for each of the unknown days to equal 36 miles. That means that we would have $(6 \times 36) + 102 = 318$ miles. Therefore, the lowest possible average is $318 \div 7 = 45.4$ miles.

   If the highest daily mileage was 102, then it's possible for each of the unknown days to equal 102 miles. That means that we would have a total of 648 miles, and the highest possible average is 92.6 miles.

9. **D** Division is the opposite, or the reciprocal of multiplication. The reciprocal of $\frac{3}{4}$ is $\frac{4}{3}$. You could also select a number to see how this works. $12 \times \frac{3}{4}$ is 9. 12 divided by $\frac{4}{3}$ also gives us 9.

10. **C** The total number of employees is 282. Subtract $282 - (64 + 123 + 56)$.

    $282 - 243 = 39$.

11. **C** This is a percent decrease question. Use the formula for percent change = difference ÷ original. The difference between the two amounts is $14.00, and the original amount is $70.00. That reduces to $\frac{1}{5}$, which is 20%.

12. **A** Estimate to find the correct answer. First, if there were more pizza votes than sandwich votes, the number of sandwich votes needs to be less than half the total number of votes. Only (A) is less than half of the total number of votes. Note that we can also use Backsolving. When we plug in (A), we find that there were 55 votes for pizza (21 + 34), for a total of 76 votes (21 + 55). This matches the information in the problem.

13. **C** First, you should be able to eliminate some answer choices. If the dress is on sale, the new price will be lower than the original price of $120.00. Thus, (E) cannot be correct. Choice (A) is extremely small—the price has only been discounted by 15%. To find 15% of $120.00, multiply $.15 \times 120.00$. The result is $18.00. Subtract $18.00 from the original price to get the new total of $102.00.

14. **A** In rounding to the nearest thousand, look at the hundreds place. In this case, since the hundreds place has a value less than 5, do not round up. The correct answer is 654,000.

15. **C** Divide the number of pictures by the number of pictures per album. 412 divided by 34 comes out to be more than 12 (it won't divide evenly—there will be a remainder). Thus, we need 13 albums in order to hold all the photographs.

16. **A** We know that they ate a total of 7 hot dogs. Fiona ate one hot dog, and Rich ate more than Chris. While we don't know exactly how many hot dogs Rich ate (he may have had 6, 5, or 4), we know that Rich had the most.

17. **E** If peanuts cost $.50, the total cost of peanuts is $1.50. From the information given above, we know that hot dogs cost $.75 more, or $1.25. The total cost of hot dogs is $\$1.25 \times 7$, or $8.75. Soft drinks must cost more than $1.25. The total of peanuts and hot dogs is $10.25. Four soft drinks must cost more than $5.00 ($\$1.25 \times 4$). So, the total must be more than $15.25. Only (E) works.

18. **C** This is a proportion question. First, identify the relationship we are given: 3 game stamps: 1 large drink. We set this equal to the one we want to know: 60 game stamps: ? large drinks. The equation looks like:

$$\frac{3 \text{ game stamps}}{1 \text{ large drink}} = \frac{60 \text{ game stamps}}{x \text{ large drinks}}$$

If we cross multiply, we get $3x = 60$; $x = 20$.

19. **E** When adding fractions, it's most efficient to find the lowest common denominator. This is the lowest number that can be divided by each of the existing fractions. Look at choices (C), (D), and (E), since they each mention using a common denominator. 10 would not work as a common denominator, since 10 is not divisible by 4 (the denominator for $\frac{3}{4}$). Eliminate (C). 40 would work as a common denominator, since it is divisible by 2, 4, and 5. However, since this is not the lowest possible common denominator, this is not the most efficient way to add these fractions. Eliminate

(D). 20 would work as a common denominator, since it is divisible by 2, 4, and 5. This is the lowest possible common denominator for these fractions. Choose (E). Eliminate (A), since subtracting from one will not result in the sum of the fractions. Eliminate (B), since multiplying the denominators will not result in the sum of the fractions.

20. **C** Rewrite the problem to be:

$$\frac{280 \times 12 \times 9}{3 \times 70 \times 9}$$

You can simplify and reduce this further, to come out to approximately 16.

21. **D** If we add up the number of goods sold by all the other people, we get 105,000. To get to 150,000, we need to have Tom sell 45,000 goods.

22. **A** Simplify the equation to get:

$$15y - 42 = 3$$
$$15y = 45$$
$$y = 3$$

23. **C** Don't forget to Ballpark. $\frac{3}{8}$ is halfway between $\frac{2}{8}$ and $\frac{4}{8}$. $\frac{2}{8}$ is equal to $\frac{1}{4}$, which is 25%. $\frac{4}{8}$ is equal to $\frac{1}{2}$, which is 50%. Eliminate (A) and (E), since they are outside the range of these two values. The value of $\frac{3}{8}$ is 37.5%, which is halfway between 25% and 50%. The answer that has the correct range is (C).

24. **C** Choices (A) and (B) are smaller than –.345 (they are to the left of –.345 on the number line). Choices (D) and (E) are greater than .008.

25. **C** First, we can approximate the number of cards that Marty owns. If he has 70% of the total, then we know he'll have more than half. Choices (A) and (B) are too small, and can be eliminated. To get the exact total, multiply .7 × 3,500.

26. **B** Multiply to find out how much of the fence Oliver has built. 5 × 25 = 125 feet. Subtract this from the total of 170, and we get 45 feet remaining.

27. **C** First, figure out how many days it will take James to write all of the cards. $\frac{300}{12} = 25$, so it will take 25 days. Include February 1, since the problem states that he "begins" on that day. That means that James works on cards on the days 1-25. He should finish on February 25.

28. **C** Start with the percentile scores, since there are three percentiles given. From this information, we know that Debbie scored higher than Kristen, who scored higher than Jen. Ignoring Amy for now, we can eliminate any answers that do not match these percentile ranks. In fact, only (C) matches this ranking.

Note that the CBEST does not require you to convert stanine scores to percentiles. Just remember that stanines are ranked 1–9, lowest to highest. In this case, we know for certain that Amy scored higher than Kristen. We can use the other information given to solve this question.

29. **C** There are three feet in one yard. Multiply 485 by 3 to get the correct total. Don't forget to ballpark!

30. **E** Multiply the number of hours per day times the total number of days. $165 \times 3 = 495$. Don't forget to ballpark!

31. **B** This is a proportion question. We are given the relationship 2 students go to Butterick College: 5 total students. If we set this equal to our unknown relationship, we have the equation:

$$\frac{\text{2 students to Butterick}}{\text{5 total students}} = \frac{x \text{ students to Butterick}}{\text{240 total students}}$$

If we cross multiply, we get $5x = 480$. $x = 96$.

32. **E** To calculate the cost of 2 dozen reams of paper, multiply 24 × \$2.00. The cost of 17 boxes of crayons is 17 × \$3.45. The cost of 33 dry erase markers is 33 × \$.65. The answer that reflects this correctly is choice (E).

33. **C** To correctly translate this question, remember that "what percent" means "$\left(\frac{x}{100}\right)$," "of" means multiply, and "is" means "=."

$$\left(\frac{x}{100}\right) \times 20 = 5$$

Then solve for x.

$$\frac{x}{100} = \frac{5}{20}$$

$$x = \frac{500}{20}$$

$$x = 25$$

34. **A** The amount of the discount is 15%, and the discounted price is \$425. If the original price is 100% of p, then the discounted price is 85% of p (100% – 15% = 85%). In other words, 85% of p gives us the discounted price of \$425.

35. **B** This is a percent increase problem. Use the formula for percent change = difference ÷ original. The difference between the two amounts is 50,000, and the original amount is 250,000. That reduces to $\frac{1}{5}$, which is 20%.

36. **D** First, compare the leftmost decimal places. In the tenths place, only (B) and (D) have a zero—eliminate all others. In the thousandths place, (D) has a 6 while (B) has an 8. (D) is smaller.

37. **A** 5% of 20 is equal to 1. If we add 1 more student to the total of 20, we get the new total of 21.

38. **E** There are 36 squares total. 9 squares are shaded. The fraction of shaded squares is $\frac{9}{36}$, or $\frac{1}{4}$.

39. **D** The question is asking for $\frac{1}{3}$ of $\frac{3}{8}$ of 120. For fractions and percents, remember that "of" means multiply. Calculate $\left(\frac{1}{3}\right) \times \left(\frac{3}{8}\right) \times 120$. It may be easy to start with $\left(\frac{1}{3}\right) \times 120$, which is 40. Then multiply $40 \times \left(\frac{3}{8}\right)$, which equals 15.

40. **D** Cross multiply to get $3x = 36$. Divide by 3 to get $x = 12$.

41. **A** First, we need to find the total number of points Brooke scored on her first six tests. Adding these together gives us a total of 534. If the total of all seven tests is 612, we can subtract to find the score on the seventh test. 612 – 534 is 78.

42. **D** The gray line shows the 10-year average rainfall for the indicated dates. The black line shows the rainfall for the eight dates indicated in April 2012. There are FIVE points on the black line that are higher than the gray line. $\frac{5}{8} = .625$, which is approximately 63%.

43. **E** The question asks for the greatest DECREASE. Compare each answer.

April 5-6 shows an increase. Eliminate (A).

April 6-7 shows a decrease of about 0.2.

April 7-8 shows a decrease of about 0.5.

April 9-10 shows an increase. Eliminate (D).

April 11-12 shows a decrease of about 0.7. Since this is the greatest decrease, select (E).

44. **D** If you divide $\frac{52}{12}$ directly, you'll get $4\frac{1}{3}$. However, the question asks how many boxes are needed. Since we can't have $4\frac{1}{3}$ boxes, we must use 5 boxes.

45. **C** Take each statement step by step, and write down the information you find. First, Steve answered 60% of the questions correct. 60% of 150 questions is 90 ($\frac{60}{100} \times 150$). Next, find the number of questions Stephanie answered correctly. She answered 105 questions correctly ($\frac{70}{100} \times 150$). The difference between Stephanie's total and Steve's total is 15 (105 – 90) questions.

46. **C** Mike has approximately 13,000 marbles. If he adds half of that amount, he adds approximately 6,500 marbles (13,000 × .5). The sum of 13,000 and 6,500 is 19,500 marbles. Choice (C) is the closest answer.

47. **A** There are four types of cards in a deck, each equally likely to occur. There are four possible outcomes, and we want one of them. Thus, the probability is $\frac{1}{4}$.

48. **A** If you plot the points on a number line, only (A) is to the left of –7 on the number line. For negative numbers, the number closer to zero on the number line is the greater number.

49. **A** If the yard is 10 feet wider on each side, then the swimming pool is 30 feet by 20 feet. The perimeter is 30 + 20 + 30 + 20, which equals 100. (It might help to draw a figure.)

50. **A** Statement (A) is a contrapositive of the If-Then statement that is presented in the problem. If we denote the If-Then statement as If A, Then B, the contrapositive is If Not B, then Not A. It is the only logical inference we can make from the information given. If Mitch does not appear in the movie, we know that he did not direct the movie.

SECTION III: TEST OF WRITING

Topic 1

The amount of money available from the state budget for school district X has not increased in the last three years, despite the increasing number of students and rising administrative costs. As a result, members of the school board have formed partnerships with local businesses. Some of these partnerships involve free books, maps, and textbooks from a particular company. Others involve food from local fast-food establishments. Supporters of these partnerships argue that local businesses are helping out the community, and deserve recognition for their contributions. Critics argue that the school board should not form such partnerships, because schools will become tainted with "corporate advertising" throughout the school. Should schools allow corporate partners to help provide funding and materials? If so, should there be any restrictions on what can and cannot be donated? Support your opinion with specific reasons.

Sample Essay #1: Overall Score = 4 (Pass)

The issue of allowing corporate advertising in public schools is a controversial one. Some argue that private money will become a vital part of helping to fund our schools, especially during difficult economic periods. Others believe that corporate partnerships can negatively commercialize a school by bringing corporate logos into the school environment. After careful thought, I believe the school board should allow funding and donations from corporate partners, but with specific regulations that minimize the possibility of a school becoming a corporate billboard.

If the school board is struggling in its effort to provide all of its desired programs and materials to students, it should look for outside help. New textbooks and computers are important to help students learn the most relevant information. Children need exposure to the latest technology in order to be ready for the outside world. Private money can help make those budget dreams a reality. If done well, schools can form powerful alliances with the community. Schools can draw from the knowledge and expertise of various businesses, and learn how to bring that information to their students. Schools can benefit with extra dollars to spend on items that would otherwise be unavailable. Ultimately, the concern of the school board needs to be the quality of education its students are receiving. If the budget does not allow for the board to completely provide for its students, it should look for outside help.

Of course, there are some possible dangers associated with corporate partnerships. If not done properly, corporate products can quickly commercialize a school. Corporate logos could start to appear on everything from textbooks to a student's lunch. As adults, we can recognize when a business is advertising to us. We can make decisions about what products we do and do not want to use. However, children, especially those in elementary school, probably can't recognize subtle advertising. We should not allow corporations an opportunity to form brand loyalties at a very early age with our children.

In order to prevent the commercialization of our schools, the district must set tough guidelines when receiving gifts from corporate sponsors. If private corporations are donating goods instead of money, their logos should be removed from the goods. We don't want our children in an environment that tries to force product loyalty at an early age (imagine the horror of reading "This textbook brought to you buy Slushy, the drink for the next generation," on the cover of a mathematics book). Children already receive enough advertising, mainly through television. To be fair, corporations deserve recognition for their donations. After all, they should expect to "do well by doing good." I would recommend that the school board put together a list of all corporate donors, and send that list to all parents. That way, parents can see which companies are supporting their children, and repay those companies by supporting their businesses. There should be space for corporate advertising in parent newsletters or bulletins. Schools may even want to create plaques recognizing the efforts of private businesses. Corporations deserve exposure for these good deeds, and there are ways to provide that exposure without posting billboards all over campus.

Unfortunately, budget crunches and an increasing number of students have left the school district with less money per student. Sadly, this comes at a time when operating costs are higher, and technology changes are rapid. Corporate donations can help fill in the gap, and so we should allow them, for the good of our children. If done properly, the school board can give proper recognition to its corporate partners without tainting the classroom environment. It is important that we keep the classroom a place for learning, not a place for advertising.

Sample Essay #2: Overall Score = 3 (Marginal Pass)

The school board will be making a big mistake if it allows local businesses to provide money and materials to support the school. There are too many possible dangers associated with using outside private businesses, and monitoring the partnerships would take school board members away from their real jobs—helping the students.

Probably the greatest concern of business sponsorship is the free and unfiltered advertising that would accompany the donation of materials. I've heard of one school that has a lunch every Thursday from the fast-food restaurant "Taco Hut." The employees of the restaurant come down in their uniforms and serve lunch to students all day. The items are exactly the same as those served at their fast-food establishments. I've even heard that the workers will give out mascots of Taco Hut Joe to students. As you can see, it makes a ton of sense for the people at Taco Hut to do this. They lose some money each week by giving out free lunches, but they will receive that back in bunches if they create a new generation of children who like to go to Taco Hut. Parents should have more influence on what they introduce their children to.

While corporate logos and advertisements seem the most obvious, a more subtle concern would be that corporations would donate material that is unobjective or biased, therefore tainting the objectivity of material taught in the classrooms. For example, a local computer company might donate a bunch of materials and manuals on the history of computers. These could be used in a computer class. But what if they portray their company in too favorable a view? What if the information they include is biased so that their company appears to be much better than it actually is? We all know that textbooks, no matter who they are written by, have certain biases. However, a textbook from a private company could be very skewed from the truth.

I'd prefer school board members to figure out how to revise their budget or raise more money within the school than to look to outside companies for assistance. There are too many potential dangers in working with outside corporations. While corporate money may seem to help solve a number of problems, it could unfortunately create a whole new set of problems.

Sample Essay #3: Overall Score = 2 (Marginal Fail)

I disagree that the school board should look too local businesses to provide additional funding for their school. It would be much better if the school board looked to parents and the government for additional funding. These two groups are a more reliable way of getting money.

Local funding by businesses may not last. You could get corporate funding one year, and then all of a sudden it may be gone the next year. For the school board, that would be very difficult to plan for. If a company gave $5,000 one year, and then none the next, it would provide a difficult challenge for the board to decide how to create a budget (not knowing how much money they have is tough). Businesses would probably give when the economy is good, but that's ironic cause when the economy is good the school board would probably have enough money already. So it's when the economy isn't good that schools will need to find additional money.

If the school board wants to make a lasting change on the budget problem, it needs to make its case to the local or statewide government. It should makeup a list of what is missing from its school and request it. It should ask that someone high up in the school administration come visit the school and reevaluate its budget formula for the school. Maybe the way in which money is distributed is bad, and someone can change that. Or maybe someone will see that things aren't getting done and go back and change some rules to help the school.

Finally, parents can help the school to raze money. Bake sales, raffles, etc. are all ways to raze money for the school. Also, if parents donate money directly, they probably won't have any requests for it unlike corporations. Parents are the most concerned about the schools being good for there students, so they are the most likely to give.

Therefore, the school board should look to parents and the state school administration to raise money instead of local businesses, for the reasons I've listed above.

Sample Essay #4: Overall Score = 1 (Fail)

If the school bored needs money, it should get it any way it can. And if local businesses are willing to give back to the community and the school, who are we to stop them?

Money is tight these days at schools. Look at the date on some of the textbooks at a local scholl and u will see that some materials have not been updated in a really long time. More money could change that. I would prefer to have students have all new books and computers then watching a school district struggling on its own.

A little advertising for the businesses seems like a fair exchange for lots of money from the company. As the old saying goes "There's no such thing as a free lunch".

Topic 2

What is the best class you have taken? Did you enjoy the class because of the teacher or because of the subject matter? What did you like about the class? What has this classroom experience taught you that you will be able to use when you become a teacher?

Sample Essay #1: Overall Score = 4 (Pass)

When I reflect on my high school experience, I can vividly remember almost everything that happened during my fourth period Latin class; everything, that is, except the subject material. Mr. Cser turned a difficult and boring topic into an exciting event. My friends and I actually looked forward to his class prior to lunch. Mr. Cser's enthusiasm, concern for his students, and passion toward his profession, have influenced my decision to become a teacher and provide platforms that I aspire to reach.

Mr. Cser possesses a wonderful charm and enthusiasm, which turned a dull language class into an excited classroom. Attending his class was like attending a rock concert. Mr. Cser would lecture while feverishly walking back and forth across the room, raising his voice at the hint of something interesting. He provided humor and support within his class, putting all students in a good mood before the end of the period. When the bell ended the class at around 12:15 P.M., students left with a smile on their face, ready to discuss the previous 45 minutes of class. Discussions of his class would occupy most of the lunchroom talk for most of that year.

Latin was certainly not my favorite subject. In fact, I found it to be the most challenging subject I studied in high school. In general, I excelled in English and History classes, and therefore poured most of my energy into those areas. For two years, I had received mediocre grades in Latin. When I had Mr. Cser for my third year of Latin, though, things began to change. Mr. Cser possessed a rare ability to inspire me to study the language. Once you witnessed the passion that he brought to the subject, it was hard to dislike the material. Sure, it was still difficult, but I began to take an interest in the topic thanks to Mr. Cser. I felt that he had given the class so much of his dedication and energy that I needed to give back the same effort. That year, I spent more time on Latin than any other topic, and my improved grade reflected that effort.

At times, our Latin class would not focus on the language at all. If Mr. Cser could tell that students were too exhausted to study another round of conjugating verbs, he would avoid the topic entirely and have one of his "life chats." Somehow, he was able to turn these discussions into very thoughtful and relevant debates, unlike most teachers, who treated such discussions like a bad public service announcement. These discussions did not occur often—maybe only five or six times that year. But each day, I left the room with a lot to think about. He challenged us to always do the right thing, to take accountability for our actions, and to be fair. In many ways, he had the ability to be a parent and a role model.

I've known for quite some time that my career goal was to become a teacher. Mr. Cser would rank quite highly on my short list of people who have helped influence my decision to pursue teaching. Mr. Cser has taught me that one of my responsibilities as a teacher is to excite students about the subject material. I now know that subject matter alone does not determine a student's interest in a class. The effort and concern shown by a teacher can have a dramatic influence on how students view a class. If I can bring the same passion and energy to my science classes as Mr. Cser brought to his Latin classes, I believe that many seventh graders will have newfound excitement about the world of science. I'm not sure I can recreate the atmosphere of Room 12's "Cser Palace," but I know I can make Science Lab 4 a fun place to learn.

Sample Essay #2: Overall Score = 3 (Marginal Pass)

How do you choose which of your classes is the best? Is it as simple as the one you get the best grade? Or is something that provides you with more meaning and experience long after the class is over? Is it the quality of the teacher, or the quality of the material that is studied? I'm sure that people can come up with reasons to justify a number of ways to rate which class is the best. For me, my "Teamwork and Leadership Seminar" my senior year of college was my best class, not for the material or the instructor, but for the interactions with my classmates.

The teamwork and leadership seminar was a two unit class that several of us took during our senior year of college. It was recommended to students who wanted to gain some experience tackling problems in a group environment. The students that enrolled in the class did so for many different reasons. Some were going into consulting jobs, and wanted some group work experience before entering the business world. Others, like my boyfriend and me, were going to be teachers. And some just took the class because they said it sounded easy! Well, it wasn't. The course was designed to present situations with a number of problems, and the groups were to come up with action plans to resolve the problems. Some of these problems were failing businesses, others were disputes between political parties, and others were environmental problems. Each problem was complex, without easy answers.

Once we received a topic, the group would have approximately one week before it needed to present the case and action plans to the instructor. I learned a lot about teamwork in this class. It was amazing how difficult it was to actually get the group organized and on the "same page". Some of the students were definite leaders—wanting to organize the group, and use their solution to the problem. Others like myself were much more reserved—happy to contribute, but reluctant to organize what everyone else would be doing. This group dynamic was great exposure to the real working environment. I can often compare various people in my leadership class to current people I work and teach with.

It was disappointing though when I once asked our instructor for some help. I received a response that was something like "go figure it out yourself", without any encouragement or guidance. If there is anything I've learned from this classroom experience, it would unfortunately be what <u>not</u> to do in a classroom. I know he had taught the class for many years, and that he wanted students to really work on their own, but he seemed to carry no concern for the students either. I'll be sure not to do that when I get my own classroom.

Sample Essay #3: Overall Score = 2 (Marginal Fail)

All of us have had a class or two that we find very memorable. Mine would have to be Biology with Mrs. Stumpf. I still remember it today, even though I took the class my freshman year of high school. the class was really cool because of the way in which she organized her classes.

We did a different thing in Biology each day. On Monday, we would get a basic lecture from Mrs. Stumpf. The lectures were always pretty lame, but they were only once a week so I managed to survive them. Tuesday's were a discussion day, which was more open to student-teacher interaction. We would discuss a relevant topic to the chapter of material that we were studying. Wednesday was homework and problem sets. We would review the answers to the home work problems that were asigned on Monday. Then, on Thursday we would be in the lab, doing an experiment. We would always have a lab partner to do the experiments with. Finally, the week ended on a down note, cause there were quizzes every Friday. These quizzes and a final test were the only thing that determined your grade, so they were very important.

I'm not sure if I really liked Biology all that much, but at least it was interesting. You knew that you only did the same thing once per week, which was good. The Biology class was the final class of the day, so I was already pretty restless. Luckily, Mrs. Stumpf mixed up the material.

Sample Essay #4: Overall Score = 1 (Fail)

It would definitely have to be Chemistry 6A. And it would definitely not cause of the teacher. That guy was not a good lecturer at all. But I would still choose Chemistry 6A cause I like Chemistry and because I got a good grade in the class.

This was the first class of 3 Chemistry classes that I needed to take in order to pass out of my general education science requirements. I liked the class cause I had most of the material already in high school, so it wasn't all that challenging. But I still had to perform really well on the final. I went in to the final test with a score of around 88, and I had to get the average up to like a 91 in order to get an A. So, I studied a ton for that test, even the stuff I already knew, just in case I forgot some of the details or something. Well, when I got my grades over the internet, I was pleased to see that my work paid off, and I got an A in Chemistry. Unfortunately, that wasn't the case when I later took Chemistry 6B.

Chapter 14
Practice Test 3

SECTION I: TEST OF READING

Directions: Each question in the Reading section of the practice test is a multiple-choice question with five answer choices. Read each question carefully and choose the ONE best answer. Record each answer on the answer sheet provided in the back of this book.

You may work on the multiple-choice questions in any order that you choose. You may wish to monitor how long it takes you to complete the practice test. When taking the actual CBEST, you will have one four-hour test session in which to complete the section(s) for which you registered.

Read the passage below; then answer the four questions that follow.

For centuries royal imposters posed a very real threat to the ruling families of Europe. When the heir to the throne or a close relative died or disappeared under mysterious circumstances, which was not uncommon, inevitably some pretender would emerge years later claiming to be that person. Some imposters managed to gain widespread acceptance and even convince members of the deceased royal's family that they were indeed who they claimed to be. This phenomenon is even more <u>peculiar</u> when the imposter is of a different nationality from the royal. This was the case with Anna Anderson, a polish factory worker who spoke no Russian but was able to successfully impersonate the Grand Duchess Anastasia, who had been murdered as a teenager in the Bolshevik Revolution. Perkin Warbeck, a fifteenth-century Flemish man, was even able to raise an army in support of his claim to the English throne. For years Warbeck managed to pass himself off as Richard, Duke of York, the son of King Edward IV. Richard was presumed to have been murdered as a child in the Tower of London by his uncle, Richard III.

____________________________. In the modern age it can be hard to fathom just how difficult it was in centuries past to prove one's identity. Not only was DNA testing unavailable, but there were no audio or video recordings by which to familiarize oneself with the individual's voice or physical appearance. Prior to the nineteenth century there were no photographs either, so the only likenesses of royalty were portraits, which were scarce and sometimes unreliable. One must also remember that royals were continuously surrounded by servants and other close associates, so "private" information, by which one could presumably weed out false claimants, was limited or nonexistent. Perhaps the most compelling explanation for the success of imposters, however, is simply that the reemergence of the royal in question would be desirable. As in the case of Karl Wilhelm Naundorff, an eighteenth-century German clockmaker who impersonated the murdered son of Marie Antoinette and King Louis XVI of France with some success, people often believe what they want to believe.

1. Which of the following is the best meaning of the word peculiar as it is used in the first paragraph?

   A. uncommon

   B. odd

   C. distinctive

   D. belonging to

   E. harmful

2. Which of the following sentences, if inserted into the blank at the beginning of the second paragraph, would be consistent with the logical flow of ideas presented in the passage?

   A. Twenty-first century technology has not put an end to the phenomenon of royal imposters.

   B. Royal pretenders have emerged in recent times as well.

   C. Why is it that royal imposters were able to gain such credibility?

   D. The case of Karl Wilhelm Naundorff illustrates how an unlikely claimant to a throne can be successful.

   E. Today royal imposters often use technology to their advantage.

3. According to the information presented in the passage, the case of Anna Anderson is strange because:

   A. she spoke no Russian.

   B. her attempt at impersonation was more successful than that of Perkin Warbeck.

   C. there was no DNA evidence to support her claim.

   D. the real Grand Duchess had been murdered as a teenager.

   E. she impersonated the Grand Duchess in the twentieth century.

4. Which of the following statements can be properly inferred from the passage?

   A. Karl Wilhelm Naundorff was a more believable impostor than was Anna Anderson.

   B. There were no royal imposters in non-European countries.

   C. More people would have believed Karl Wilhelm Naundorff's claim if he had been French as opposed to German.

   D. Richard, Duke of York, was often surrounded by servants and close associates.

   E. Royal imposters relied heavily on portraits in order to alter their physical appearances.

Read the passage below; then answer the four questions that follow.

[1]Cryptozoology is the study of creatures whose reported existence has not been established. [2]Often these "cryptids" gain legendary status, such as the giant aquatic Loch Ness Monster or the Chupacabra – a grotesque rat-like predator that supposedly inhabits South America and the southern United States. [3]The most <u>prominent</u> cryptid is undoubtedly the famed ape-like "Sasquatch," more commonly known as "Bigfoot," which reportedly roams the remote forested areas of the Pacific Northwest. [4]There have been innumerable eyewitness accounts of Bigfoot going back hundreds of years. [5] ________ , there have even been shocking allegations of abduction in which people claim to have been held captive by Bigfoot-like creatures for extended periods! [6]To date none of these sightings, however, has been corroborated by irrefutable physical evidence such as a body. [7]_________ , many people believe in Bigfoot, and some local legislatures have even made it a serious criminal offense to kill one of these cryptids without justification. [8]One can only imagine the penalties that these legislators would impose if some depraved criminal were to viciously assault the Tooth Fairy or rob Santa Claus of his Christmas stash.

5. Which of the following sentences expresses a statement of opinion about Bigfoot?

   A. Sentence 3

   B. Sentence 5

   C. Sentence 6

   D. Sentence 7

   E. Sentence 8

6. Which of the following best expresses the meaning of the word <u>prominent</u> as it is used in the passage?

   A. excellent

   B. easily noticeable

   C. flamboyant

   D. well-known

   E. dangerous

7. Which of the following pairs of words, if inserted into the blanks of the passage *in order,* would help the reader understand the author's flow of ideas?

   A. Moreover; For example

   B. However; In addition

   C. Moreover; Nonetheless

   D. For example; In addition

   E. Nonetheless; However

8. Which of the following would be an appropriate title for the passage?

   A. Bigfoot Abductions: Are They real?

   B. A History of Cryptozoology

   C. A Case for the Existence of Sasquatch

   D. An In-Depth Analysis of Reported Bigfoot Sightings

   E. The Dubious Case for Bigfoot

Read the passage below; then answer the four questions that follow.

[1] Movies just aren't as good as they used to be. [2] When I was a kid my friends and I would have the time of our lives at the movies watching that summer's big hit. [3] Nowadays, more often than not, I leave the theater sorely disappointed. [4] The problem is the importance that Hollywood producers place on making movies that will earn tens—and even hundreds—of millions of dollars. [5] Movies now cost so much to make, and the stakes are so high, that filmmakers are unwilling to take the kinds of creative risks that they did in the past. [6] If an expected blockbuster flops at the box office it could very well bankrupt a studio, so few are willing to go out on a limb with a novel idea and a truly original script. [7] The unfortunate result is an endless array of remakes, reboots, sequels, and prequels: a continual recycling of the same worn out old material. [8] With these big-budget projects directors are also less willing to chance casting unknown yet promising actors, so talent is often sacrificed for the security of having an A-list celebrity in the film. [9] Moreover, studios are under such pressure to sell as many tickets as possible for a stellar opening weekend that they sometimes ruin the movie by releasing trailers that spoil the film's plot and feature its best moments. [10] I'm still a movie-lover at heart, but until Hollywood <u>changes its tune</u> I don't expect the majority of its films to be worth the price of admission.

9. Which of the following best summarizes the main idea of the passage?

   A. Hollywood directors should cast more unknown yet talented actors instead of A-list celebrities.

   B. The quality of Hollywood movies would improve if more original ideas were made into films.

   C. The preoccupation of Hollywood movie studios with making large amounts of money from their films has, in general, reduced the overall quality of the viewing experience for those films.

   D. Moviegoers should only pay to see films that were not produced by Hollywood, such as foreign films and those produced by independent film studios on relatively small budgets.

   E. The entertainment industry in the United States has been corrupted by greed.

10. Which of the following best characterizes an assumption made by the author?

   A. Hollywood blockbusters should not have trailers.

   B. Most films that are made outside the major Hollywood studio system are of high quality.

   C. Hollywood producers care nothing about the quality of the films they produce.

   D. Many Hollywood actors care more about money than the quality of their film performances.

   E. Some unknown actors are more talented than some A-list celebrity actors.

11. Which of the following best expresses the meaning of the phrase <u>changes its tune</u> as it is used in Sentence 10?

A. stops making movies

B. values quality above profit

C. casts more talented singers in musicals

D. releases trailers without plot spoilers

E. changes the overall tone of the films it produces

12. Which sentence is LEAST relevant to the author's argument?

A. Sentence 2

B. Sentence 4

C. Sentence 5

D. Sentence 8

E. Sentence 9

Read the passage below; then answer the three questions that follow.

[1]Next week at the city council meeting the police officers' union should demand a 10% annual raise in salary—not a penny less! [2]The service that our brave men and women in blue provide to the residents of this city is invaluable. [3]Mayor Jones stated at last month's meeting that, because the city's budget for next year has been reduced, it would be "fiscally irresponsible" to raise our salaries. [4]We are the ones out there selflessly risking our lives every day apprehending dangerous criminals—not the mayor, so we shouldn't let him sell out our interests. [5]Maybe if Mayor Jones gives up the ridiculously large raise that the council voted to give *him* next year, then there will be adequate funds to compensate our officers for their loyal service.

13. The passage is most likely addressed to which of the following audiences?

    A. Mayor Jones

    B. the city council

    C. city police officers

    D. local criminals

    E. the general public

14. The author uses which one of the following persuasive techniques?

    A. creating an analogy

    B. attacking personal motives

    C. offering a counterexample

    D. appealing to authority

    E. using statistics

15. Which of the following sentences is a statement of fact?

    A. Sentence 1

    B. Sentence 2

    C. Sentence 3

    D. Sentence 4

    E. Sentence 5

Use the excerpt below from an index to answer the two questions that follow.

16. On which page(s) would one look for information about possible defenses to a charge of battery?

A. 368

B. 369–374

C. 374–385

D. 386–399

E. 400–410

17. Which of the following best describes the way in which the index is organized?

A. according to historical chronology

B. according to the seriousness of the crime

C. according to the severity of the punishment

D. according to the type of crime

E. according to importance (in descending order)

Read the passage below; then answer the four questions that follow.

Common sense would suggest that a group of people who come together to make a decision would do a better job than would a single person left to his or her own devices. After all, the reasoning goes—several heads are better than one! Surely the combined critical thinking skills of a whole group of individuals would reduce the likelihood of a serious error in judgment based on carelessness, ignorance, misunderstanding, or the like. Moreover, the negative effects of each group member's personal biases, prejudices, and personality quirks would be minimized. When critical decisions need to be made, certainly there must be safety in numbers.

Psychological research has shown, however, that the opposite is in fact true: group decision-making processes are often seriously flawed. Groupthink is a phenomenon whereby members of a group censor dissenting opinions and potentially divisive information in order to preserve the unity of the group. The members are often unaware that they are engaging in groupthink behaviors as they unknowingly join the consensus and encourage other members to do so. As a result, crucial considerations and alternative options are not adequately explored and the resulting decision may be a bad one. The key to groupthink is cohesiveness: the closer the group members are and the greater the need for intragroup harmony, the greater the risk of groupthink occurring. Analysts have pointed to groupthink as an explanation for several disastrous decisions in American history. Such incidents include the ill-fated Bay of Pigs invasion by the Kennedy administration, the Watergate scandal, and the failure to anticipate the Japanese attack on Pearl Harbor.

18. The author's main purpose is most likely to:

    A. criticize several past presidential administrations for the bad decisions described in the final sentence of the second paragraph.

    B. argue in favor of groupthink decision-making.

    C. inform the reader about groupthink.

    D. attack the research findings of psychologists who deny that groupthink exists.

    E. analyze an apparent case of groupthink in depth.

19. Based on the information in the passage, which one of the following groups would be most vulnerable to a groupthink process?

    A. a jury composed of twelve strangers

    B. a group of students from several different colleges brought together for a psychology experiment about decision-making

    C. a studio audience of three hundred people asked to vote electronically for the best performer

    D. the student body of a large university asked to vote for class president by secret ballot

    E. a close-knit group of six friends deciding whether to expel a seventh member of their group for bad behavior

20. Which of the following best describes the organization of the passage?

A. A position is set forth is paragraph 1, which is then discredited in paragraph 2 by describing a theory and offering real-world examples.

B. A formal psychological theory is explained in paragraph 1 and then elaborated on in paragraph 2.

C. Two competing psychological theories are discussed in paragraph 1, then one is dismissed in favor of the other in paragraph 2.

D. A position is set forth and then rejected in paragraph 1 and two competing theories are explained in paragraph 2.

E. A position is set forth in paragraph 1 and then discredited by means of statistics cited in paragraph 2.

21. Which of the following can reasonably be concluded from the information in the passage?

A. At least some of the members of the Kennedy administration who were responsible for the Bay of Pigs invasion knew one another previously.

B. Groups of strangers care nothing about harmony within their respective groups.

C. Cohesive groups always make poor decisions.

D. Those responsible for orchestrating the Watergate scandal never argued with one another when making pertinent decisions.

E. If not for groupthink, Pearl Harbor would never have been attacked.

Use the chart below to answer the question that follows.

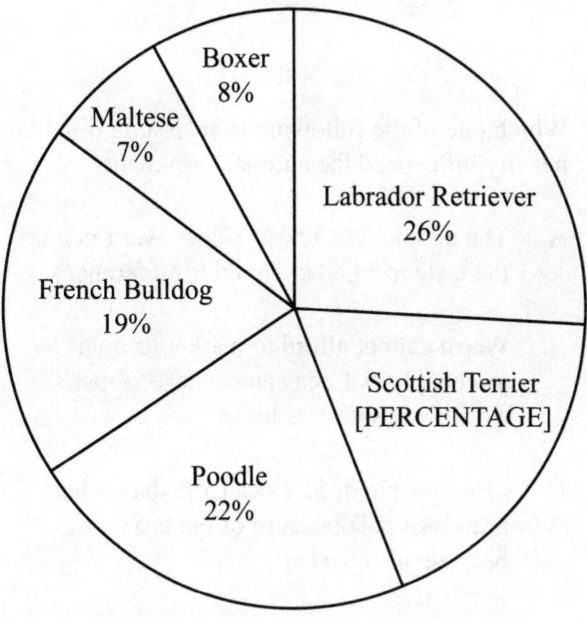

22. Which of the following can be concluded from the information in the chart above?

   A. More Labrador retrievers won dog shows in the U.S. in 2015 than did Malteses and boxers combined.

   B. 19% of dog show winners in the U.S. each year are French bulldogs.

   C. Less than one-fourth of U.S. dog show winners from 2011 to 2015 were poodles.

   D. From 2000 through 2014, more Labrador retrievers won dog shows in the U.S. than did any other breed.

   E. Each year fewer Malteses win dog shows in the U.S. than do Labrador retrievers.

Read the passage below; then answer the two questions that follow.

Loca Cola is the best-testing soft drink in the world! After all, each year millions more people drink Loca Cola worldwide than any other brand of cola, including Wepsi cola, so it's clear that Loca is far superior in taste. In fact, in a recent taste test 4 out of 5 people chose Loca Cola over Wepsi—hands down! Loca is even less expensive than Wepsi and most other colas.

23. Which sentence, if added to the end of the passage, would most accurately reflect the author's primary purpose and target audience?

    A. So independent research should be conducted in order to see if the test taste results can be replicated.

    B. So it would be helpful to know how many subjects participated in the taste test.

    C. So we should expect our annual sales to reach or exceed those of Wepsi Cola.

    D. So consumers who want to choose a brand of cola should perform their own taste tests.

    E. So if you want great taste in a cola at a fabulous low price, drink Loca Cola!

24. Which one of the following is an assumption that heavily influenced the author's argument?

    A. The people who chose Wepsi over Loca in the taste test lied about their preferences.

    B. Wepsi cannot afford to market its cola as cheaply as Loca can because Wepsi's worldwide sales are lower.

    C. More people drink Loca Cola than other brands of cola because of the taste, not because it's cheaper.

    D. If the test taste discussed in the passage were performed again under similar circumstances, all participants would choose Loca over Wepsi.

    E. Most people who buy Wepsi have never tasted Loca.

Read the passage below; then answer the four questions that follow.

It is bitterly ironic that Western civilization has made so many advancements in learning over the last century, yet writing skills have dramatically deteriorated. Young people's ability to express themselves in writing is worse than ever and this lamentable situation shows no signs of improving anytime soon. Electronic communication is largely to blame, with texting (that thorn in the side of every English teacher!) being the worst culprit. The younger generation has developed its own texting "language" with little or no regard for the proprieties of English. One can only wonder what teenagers who write "u" for "you" and "ur" for "your" do with all that extra time they've saved. Sadly, poor writing is not only fast and expedient, it's also often seen as "cool." How rare is it today for a young person to write thoughtful handwritten letters and "thank you" notes (in complete and properly punctuated sentences!) to friends and family. Nowadays one is more likely to receive a one-word text and an emoji.

Teachers need not admit defeat. It is imperative to resist the temptation to grade students' writing according to an abysmal standard of what is considered the modern norm. There is proper English and there is improper English, and the latter must always be corrected. If teachers instill good values in their students and demand competent writing from them, at least some young people will take this message to heart. From the time that elementary school students learn grammar, usage, and diction, every teacher with whom the child has contact should reinforce this basic knowledge. Grade accordingly!

25. Which of the following best summarizes the main point of each paragraph in the above passage?

    A. Paragraph 1: Young people's writing skills are worse than ever, largely because of electronic communication and the culture that surrounds it.

       Paragraph 2: Teachers should not relax their standards of evaluation, but rather grade stringently based on objective criteria.

    B. Paragraph 1: Young people's writing skills would improve if teachers would impose higher standards.

       Paragraph 2: Teachers should resist the temptation to grade writing skills on a curve.

    C. Paragraph 1: Texting and the culture surrounding it are doing more harm than good for young people.

       Paragraph 2: Teachers should encourage their students to write letters and personal notes instead of texting.

    D. Paragraph 1: It is ironic that western civilization has advanced in so many ways, yet writing skills have gotten worse.

       Paragraph 2: Teachers are to blame for young people's poor writing skills.

    E. Paragraph 1: Young people have poor values nowadays.

       Paragraph 2: Teachers should reinforce good values in their students.

26. The author is most likely addressing:

    A. students.

    B. parents.

    C. teachers.

    D. linguists.

    E. the general public.

27. Which of the following is true based on the information in the passage?

A. If young people stopped texting, their writing skills would improve.

B. Teachers' grading standards have deteriorated dramatically in recent years.

C. A student who makes grammatical errors on a writing assignment should fail that class.

D. One hundred years ago most young people wrote handwritten "thank you" notes.

E. Texting "language" includes deviations from proper English.

28. Which of the following best expresses the meaning of the word "lamentable" as it is used in the first paragraph?

A. confusing

B. unfortunate

C. agreeable

D. frightening

E. amusing

Read the passage below; then answer the three questions that follow.

For centuries sailors told seemingly incredible stories about giant "monster" waves they encountered at sea that were as high as 90 or 100 feet (as tall as a modern six-story building). These enormous waves were so steep they were almost vertical and would appear to suddenly come out of nowhere. Such accounts were almost always dismissed as tall tales, even well into the 19th century, and sailors who insisted on being taken seriously were often publicly ridiculed. As science progressed analysts used mathematical linear models to predict how high waves could form. The Gaussian function was the standard model used in the 20th century, which was utilized to calculate wave height. This formula did allow in theory for the formation of one of these "rogue waves"—as they came to be called, but such an occurrence was deemed so unlikely as to be nonexistent from a practical standpoint. According to the Gaussian model, a rogue wave as high as 65 feet could only occur about once every 10,000 years. This belief prevailed until 1995—when the first rogue wave was scientifically recorded.

In early 1995 a laser detector installed on the Draupner oil-drilling platform, located approximately 100 miles off the coast of Norway, recorded a wave that was 85 feet high. The wave was not only enormous but also substantially larger than any other wave in the area at the time. The Draupner wave, as it became known, caused the scientific community to completely reevaluate its beliefs about rogue waves. Even larger waves were recorded very soon afterwards, debunking the idea that the first one was a freak occurrence. Scientists now estimate that as many as ten rogue waves could be forming somewhere in the world's oceans at any given moment. This has serious implications for the safety of sea vessels. No cargo ship—or passenger cruise liner for that matter—is built sturdy enough to withstand the colossal force with which a 90-foot wave could strike. Moreover, the seemingly random nature of rogues makes it nearly impossible to predict them given the current state of scientific knowledge. Analysts now suspect that many cases of vessels that mysteriously sank or disappeared were actually the result of rogue waves. Even the famed tragedy of the Edmund Fitzgerald, which sunk in Lake Superior in 1975 and was immortalized by a popular song, may have been caused by the "Three Sisters"—a phenomenon whereby three rogue waves strike in quick succession.

29. According to the passage, the Gaussian function:

    A. disproves the existence of rogue waves.

    B. predicts that rogue waves occur much more frequently than previously thought.

    C. was the equipment used to record the first documented rogue wave.

    D. was used by ancient sailors to explain rogue waves.

    E. estimated that a rogue wave would occur only once every 10,000 years.

30. Which of the following would be the most appropriate title for the passage?

    A. Rogue Waves: The Menace of the Sea

    B. How to Survive a Rogue Wave

    C. The Enduring Myth of the Monster Wave

    D. The Controversy Continues: Are Rogue Waves Fact or Fiction?

    E. How to Predict Rogue Waves Using the Gaussian Function

31. Which of the following best summarizes the main idea of the first paragraph?

    A. Rogue waves were considered either a myth or an exceedingly rare occurrence up until the late twentieth century.

    B. The sailors who claimed to have experienced rogue waves years ago should have been believed.

    C. Scientists who used the Gaussian function to predict the likelihood of rogue waves were wrong to do so.

    D. Rogue waves occurred in the distant past but were extremely rare.

    E. Prior to 1995 most scientists believed that rogue waves were common, even though no such wave had been scientifically documented.

Use the table of contents below from a book about tea to answer the two questions that follow.

32. To find out how to make strawberry tarts for a tea party, which page should one consult?

A. Page 4

B. Page 17

C. Page 30

D. Page 33

E. Page 49

33. If the information on page 12 regarding herbal teas were inadequate or insufficient, where should one look to attempt to supplement that information?

A. Page 2

B. Page 3

C. Page 40

D. Page 45

E. Page 49

Read the passage below; then answer the three questions that follow.

High-ranking foreign diplomats (and often their staff and family members) are generally afforded blanket immunity from criminal prosecution in the host nation. This concept—known as diplomatic immunity—is generally regarded as necessary to protect diplomats from politically motivated persecution. Individuals shielded by diplomatic immunity in this way cannot be prosecuted or punished for any offenses that they commit while in the host country, irrespective of the nature of the crime. This privilege is commonly abused with respect to minor offenses, such as parking and traffic violations, particularly when the diplomat comes from a country that is hostile to the host nation. Immunity is, however, also occasionally invoked for serious crimes. In such cases the diplomat's home country may choose to waive immunity and allow the accused to be prosecuted just like any other defendant. While this is often done among friendly nations, when relations between the two countries involved are strained there is much less chance that immunity will be waived. Similarly, the home country also has the prerogative of trying the accused itself, but—once again—hostile nations are less likely to do so. Even if the home nation does place the accused on trial, there is no guarantee that the proceedings will be fair or the punishment adequate. If the home nation is unwilling to seek justice, the only remedy the host nation has is to expel the accused individual from its borders. In that case the diplomat or protected person becomes "*persona non grata*"—or officially unwelcome in that country.

For example, a high-level diplomat from a nation traditionally hostile to the United States might be exposed as a serial killer. This individual might have committed heinous crimes that resulted in the deaths of several innocent American citizens. Nonetheless, the accused diplomat could go on television and confess his or her misdeeds to the entire world with impunity—there's absolutely nothing the U.S. government could do to effect punishment. All that would happen is that the individual would have to leave the country. Where is the justice in that? Surely a system that would allow a vicious murderer to simply walk away—with no recourse at all for the victims' families—cannot be a good one. Diplomatic immunity might be justifiable when it comes to parking tickets, or even mid-level offenses, but not for serious felonies. The ends simply fail to justify the means.

34. The author's approach switches from:

A. arguing a position to offering a hypothetical example to providing a counterexample.

B. explaining a situation to offering a hypothetical example to stating an opinion.

C. rejecting an argument to offering a counterexample to stating an opinion.

D. analyzing an argument to rejecting an opinion to providing a counterexample.

E. stating an opinion to analyzing a counterexample to explaining a situation.

35. According to the information in the passage, a diplomat who commits a crime in the host country:

A. cannot be tried anywhere for that offense.

B. will automatically have diplomatic immunity waived by the home country.

C. can be expelled from the host country as *persona non grata.*

D. can be tried by the host country only if the crime is a serious felony.

E. must be permitted to continue in his or her diplomatic capacity in the host country.

36. Which of the following best represents the author's opinion concerning diplomatic immunity?

A. It should not apply to the most serious offenses.

B. It is necessary in order to protect American diplomats accused of murder in other countries.

C. It should be eliminated altogether.

D. It should not apply to diplomats from hostile nations.

E. It routinely results in serious injustices.

Read the passage below; then answer the three questions that follow.

When evaluating the logical correctness of a person's argument, one must consider the argument as an independent entity. In other words, the argument must stand or fall on its own merits, irrespective of whoever is making it. An argument is no worse logically because it is designed or articulated by a person who is evil, dishonest, deceptive, immoral, unintelligent, incompetent—or any other negative trait of which one can conceive. Moreover, no aspect of the speaker's personal circumstances is pertinent to the question of whether the argument is valid. The Latin phrase *tu quoque* (pronounced too kwoh-kwe) means "you also" or "you're another." This error in reasoning involves an attempt to discredit a person's logic because he or she is guilty of some sort of hypocrisy. For example, if your friend tells you that you should stop eating so much junk food because it is bad for your health and your health is very important, you should assess the quality of that argument with no regard for your friend's own junk-food-eating propensities. ________________. If you are in fact eating too much junk food, you should probably heed your friend's advice. To attempt to discredit your friend's words with a retort to the effect that he or she isn't really one to talk would be <u>fallacious</u> reasoning.

37. Which of the following, if inserted into the blank line in the passage, is most consistent with the author's pattern of development?

A. If your friend routinely eats piles of cakes and cookies and is in extremely poor health, this is important information.

B. If your friend routinely eats piles of cakes and cookies and is in extremely poor health, you should advise him or her to start eating better.

C. If your friend routinely eats piles of cakes and cookies and is in extremely poor health, your friend is behaving illogically.

D. If your friend routinely eats piles of cakes and cookies and is in extremely poor health, this is wholly irrelevant from a logical standpoint.

E. If your friend routinely eats piles of cakes and cookies and is in extremely poor health, your friend has made a *tu quoque* error.

38. Which of the following is the best meaning of the word <u>fallacious</u> as it is used in the passage?

A. clever

B. unsound

C. hypocritical

D. dangerous

E. appalling

39. Which of the following best represents the central theme of the passage?

A. Dismissing an argument because of the apparent hypocrisy of the person making that argument is a logical error.

B. One should take a friend's advice if that advice is logical.

C. *Tu quoque* errors occur more frequently than once thought.

D. An argument should be viewed as a separate entity from the person making it.

E. One should not offer advice that is logically flawed.

Read the passage below; then answer the three questions that follow.

[1]Very little is random when you walk into a store. [2]Store owners and managers employ high-priced consultants who use psychological techniques to influence shoppers' behavior. [3]The bakery is strategically placed at the front of a grocery store so that entrants, enticed by the delightful aroma of freshly baked bread, will be more likely to stay. [4]Milk, a staple for most people, is cleverly placed at the back of the store so that one must traverse all the other aisles to get it. [5]Oversized carts are provided to make it seem as though more shopping always needs to be done. [6]Clothing stores often use the buy-one-get-one-free (BOGO) tactic in order to lure the customer into a false sense of frugality, often in conjunction with "while supplies last" language to create the impression of scarcity. [7]Stores that sell expensive items, such as electronics, frequently use "decoy" pricing. [8]A manager might feature a less valuable computer in an advertisement at an inflated price, for example, so that another model (the computer that the store really wants to sell) looks like a steal in comparison. [9]Moreover, stores of all types place their goods on shelves according to a detailed system. [10]It is true that some items are put on lower shelves for reasons of safety, such as heavy or breakable items. [11]However, most of the stock is arranged to maximize sales. [12]Relatively expensive items are placed at eye level, while less expensive items—or items the store considers unimportant or unlikely to sell—are placed on the highest and lowest shelves. [13]Merchandise that is appealing to children, such as candy and toys, are placed at the eye level of a child of the age that would most likely be attracted to that item.

There are, however, some tips that can help you be a savvy shopper. Don't go grocery shipping when you're hungry; this will help you buy less and avoid being baited by savory smells or free samples. Moreover, always bring a detailed list of what you need so that you can focus on necessary items and avoid impulse purchases. When you see a BOGO-type promotion that looks like a great deal, ask yourself whether you truly need or want multiple items. Will you really wear two pairs of those jeans, or will one suffice? Even if you get an excellent price on a particular item or obtain free merchandise, remember that you're only coming out ahead if you will make good use of what you've acquired. Most importantly, shop around and familiarize yourself with prices! If you know how much an item typically sells for you'll be better able to buy what you need at a competitive price.

40. Which of the following best organizes the main topics addressed in the passage?

  A. Paragraph 1: How stores manipulate customers into spending more money

     Paragraph 2: How to be a more discriminating shopper

  B. Paragraph 1: Grocery store schemes to get customers to buy more

     Paragraph 2: How to spend less at the grocery store

  C. Paragraph 1: Methods by which stores cheat customers

     Paragraph 2: Ways to avoid becoming a victim

  D. Paragraph 1: The psychology of store layout

     Paragraph 2: Tips for avoiding impulse purchases

  E. Paragraph 1: Marketing strategies of major product lines

     Paragraph 2: How to buy more for less money

41. According to the information in the passage, an item on the top shelf of a grocery store is most likely:

A. heavy or breakable.

B. an item very appealing to children (such as candy) that the store wants parents to notice.

C. a relatively high-priced item

D. a well-advertised BOGO item

E. a relatively low-priced item

42. Which of the following sentences is LEAST relevant to the central theme and line of reasoning of the first paragraph?

A. Sentence 2

B. Sentence 5

C. Sentence 7

D. Sentence 10

E. Sentence 12

Read the passage below; then answer the three questions that follow.

[1]I had a really bad day yesterday. [2]I told my science teacher that my best friend Bob was home sick with the flu. [3]Bob was actually at the mall playing hooky from school and I knew it, but I certainly wasn't going to get my friend into trouble. [4]Bob got caught and we both got detention—him for cutting school and me for lying. [5]Principal Johnson told me that lying is always wrong. [6]I argued with him and said that isn't true. [7]I asked him what I should do if somebody who meant harm to Bob asked me where he was? [8]Would it be wrong to lie and say that Bob was somewhere other than where he was at the time? [9]Of course it wouldn't—and I told him so. [10]I added that adults in authority aren't always right. [11]Mr. Johnson wasn't too happy with my response. [12]He said that my argument was foolish: if everybody went around lying whenever they felt like it, nobody could trust anyone. [13]I still think I'm right and he was wrong.

43. The author relies on which one of the following persuasive techniques to challenge Mr. Johnson's conclusion that lying is always wrong?

A. He appeals to emotion.

B. He appeals to authority.

C. He attacks Mr. Johnson on a personal level.

D. He provides a counterexample that seems to disprove a general rule.

E. He argues that because lying would be morally correct in one hypothetical instance, it would be correct in most cases.

44. The main point of the passage is that:

A. the author had a bad day yesterday.

B. neither the author nor Bob should have received detention.

C. adults in authority aren't always right.

D. the author correctly argued that lying is not always wrong.

E. Mr. Johnson was disrespectful to the author.

45. The logic Mr. Johnson uses in sentence 12 is questionable because:

A. Mr. Johnson rejects the author's argument simply because the latter is only a student.

B. he misstates the author's position and then attempts to refute it.

C. he speaks in general terms about lying instead of addressing the author's behavior.

D. he is rude to the author.

E. he speaks hypothetically.

Read the passage below; then answer the two questions that follow.

In centuries past the color purple was closely associated with royalty and prestige and only the most eminent persons wore it. Sumptuary laws, which were designed to restrict extravagance and reinforce the social hierarchy, even formally prohibited those of inferior rank from wearing purple. However, <u>there was probably little effort required to enforce such edicts</u>. Tyrian purple (or "royal purple") was made from a chemical precursor located within the hypobranchial glands of certain snails. The snails were smashed and this extremely foul-smelling colorless fluid was extracted. After soaking in water for a few hours, the remains of the snails would undergo a fermentation process lasting about ten days. The putrid liquid was subjected to heat while in a lidded pot, as light would break down the dye and ruin the ultimate color. After fermentation, cloth was placed into the mixture for about a half hour and then exposed to air. If the procedure had been performed correctly, after a few minutes the fabric would turn bright purple. Unfortunately it usually took at least a thousand snails to produce enough of the chemical precursor to make a single cloak or gown, making this unpleasant job extremely tedious and time-consuming. Making Tyrian purple was so difficult and laborious that the process was extraordinarily expensive. No matter how desirable purple garments might be to ordinary people, only the elite few could afford such luxury. Accordingly, purple was the ultimate status symbol.

46. According to the passage, which one of the following is true of Tyrian purple?

A. It is made by extracting purple-colored fluid from the hypobranchial glands of snails.

B. The process by which it is made can be foul-smelling if not performed properly.

C. It can require a thousand or more snails to produce enough dye to make one garment.

D. The process requires bright light during the ten-day period of fermentation.

E. The chemical precursor extracted from the snails must be kept away from heat.

47. Based on the information presented in the passage, the statement <u>there was probably little effort required to enforce such edicts</u> refers to the fact that:

A. only royalty and other prestigious persons wanted to wear purple.

B. the lower classes knew their place in ancient society.

C. the process of purple-making was tedious.

D. garments made with Tyrian dye were prohibitively expensive.

E. snail fluids are extremely foul-smelling.

Read the passage below; then answer the three questions that follow.

Planning a production of Shakespeare's *Macbeth* presents some interesting creative decisions for the director who must interpret the work. First performed in the early seventeenth century, the play is filled with witches casting spells, ghosts seeking vengeance, and other fantastic elements that were taken quite seriously by contemporary audiences. While Shakespeare did include supernatural elements in some of his other works, *Macbeth* is notable for the ambiguity of these characters. If one is predisposed to accept the idea that otherworldly beings directly influence our fates, the play can be interpreted that way. If, however, a modern audience chooses to view the events in terms of psychological phenomena, that would work as well. For instance, the scene in which the murdered Banquo's ghost torments Macbeth could be viewed as a genuine haunting by an accusatory spirit. However, the ghost could just as easily be interpreted as a hallucination generated by Macbeth's guilty conscience as he descends into madness.

Should the director have the ghost of Banquo appear on stage, or should Macbeth be seen to rant and rave at thin air? A thoughtful case can be made for either approach. Moreover, how witchlike should the "weird sisters" who persecute Macbeth be? As one-dimensional as they are, should these "witches" be subtly portrayed to suggest that they are ordinary women who simply understand the human psyche well enough to bring about the protagonist's downfall through clever manipulation? What would Shakespeare have wanted? One must look beyond the stage directions that he included for Banquo's ghost because, despite what these instructions seem to suggest, it is very unlikely that Shakespeare believed in spirits and witches in a literal sense. Shakespeare was nothing if not brilliant, and he knew where his proverbial bread was buttered. James I was king of England at the time, and James was a dedicated believer of witches, ghosts, and other manifestations of the supernatural world.

48. Which of the following details from the passage best supports the author's view that Shakespeare did not believe in ghosts or witches?

    A. Shakespeare was a brilliant writer.

    B. The appearance of Banquo's ghost could easily be interpreted as a hallucination.

    C. King James I strongly believed in the existence of witches and other supernatural beings, and Shakespeare "knew where his proverbial bread was buttered."

    D. Shakespeare included supernatural elements in some of his other notable works.

    E. The witches in *Macbeth* are one-dimensional characters.

49. It can be reasonably inferred from the passage that:

    A. most modern audience members would prefer that Banquo's ghost not be visibly present on stage.

    B. *Macbeth* was a very popular play in the 17th century.

    C. King James 1 greatly enjoyed *Macbeth.*

    D. Shakespeare had contempt for King James I because of the latter's belief in the supernatural.

    E. the original stage directions for *Macbeth* had the ghost of Banquo visibly present.

50. The word fantastic, as it is used in the passage, most strongly suggests that:

    A. the author doubts the existence of ghosts.

    B. the author greatly admires Shakespeare's work.

    C. the author thinks that Macbeth is an extraordinarily well-written play.

    D. the author believes in the existence of supernatural beings.

    E. the author dislikes King James I.

SECTION II: TEST OF MATHEMATICS

Directions: Each question in the Mathematics Section of the practice test is a multiple-choice question with five answer choices. Read each question carefully and choose the ONE best answer. Record each answer on the answer sheet provided in the back of this book.

You may work on the multiple-choice questions in any order that you choose. You may wish to monitor how long it takes you to complete the practice test. When taking the actual CBEST, you will have one four-hour test session in which to complete the section(s) for which you registered.

1. At a publishing company, approximately $\frac{3}{8}$ of all proofreaders are junior-level employees. If there are 600 proofreaders at the company, how many of them are junior-level employees?

   A. 175

   B. 225

   C. 275

   D. 325

   E. 375

2. Simplify the following expression:

   $-58 + 26 \times 2$

   A. 64

   B. 24

   C. 10

   D. –6

   E. –64

3. At Lincoln High School, the football team reported the following numbers of ticket sales for the first five games: 220, 350, 170, 280, and 310. What was the average number of ticket sales for the first five games?

A. 170

B. 266

C. 280

D. 354

E. 1330

4. Courtney's puppy eats 1 cup of kibble every 8 hours. How many cups of kibble does the puppy eat in one week (7 days)?

A. 9 cups

B. 12 cups

C. 15 cups

D. 18 cups

E. 21 cups

5. **Use the table below to answer the question that follows.**

Number of days Taylor met goal	Total number of days in the month	Month
27	28	February
28	31	March
30	30	April
29	31	May

Taylor's goal is to exercise for one hour every day. The chart shows the number of days that Taylor's goal was met. What is the percentage of days, in February through May, in which the goal was met?

A. 82%

B. 84%

C. 90%

D. 95%

E. 98%

6. Nathan has written 879 words for his final project. If Ramona has written 3 times as many words as Nathan, which is the best estimate of the number of words Ramona has written?

A. 1,800

B. 2,100

C. 2,400

D. 2,700

E. 3,200

7. Which of the following units is the most appropriate for measuring the width of a dinner plate?

A. inches

B. feet

C. yards

D. ounces

E. teaspoons

8. A library has a book donation drive for the local schools. It received 97 books in the first week, 52 books in the second week, and 71 books in the third week. If the library wants to divide the books evenly among 11 schools, how many books will each school receive?

A. 12

B. 17

C. 20

D. 24

E. 36

9. A restaurant charges $12.89 for its lunch special. If a customer purchases the lunch special and uses a coupon for 10% off, how much will the meal cost with the discount? Assume no sales tax or other charges.

A. $1.28

B. $6.45

C. $10.31

D. $11.60

E. $14.18

10. **Use the diagram below to answer the question that follows.**

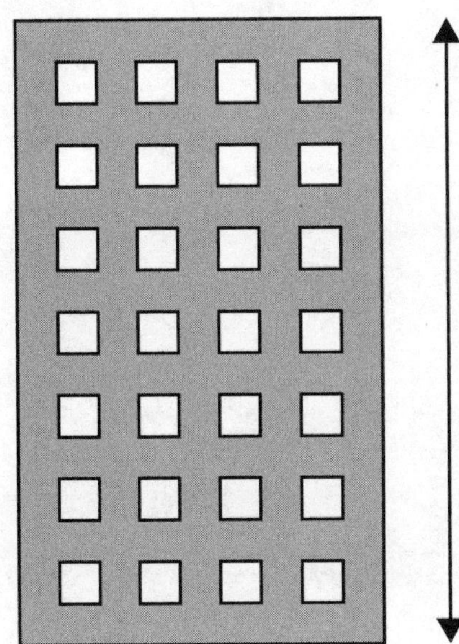

If the scaled height of the building in the diagram measures 6 units, then what is the scale of the diagram (to the nearest tenth)?

A. 1 unit = 52.3 meters

B. 1 unit = 50.2 meters

C. 1 unit = 49.8 meters

D. 1 unit = 49.4 meters

E. 1 unit = 48.7 meters

11. Which of the following is the best estimate for 1,526,423 + 493,497?

A. 2,000,000

B. 2,200,000

C. 2,400,000

D. 2,600,000

E. 2,800,000

12. Ryan takes a standardized test and receives the score report indicated below:

Raw Score	Percentile	Stanine
38	82	7

Ryan's test scores indicate that:

A. She answered 38% of the problems correctly.

B. 82% of test takers scored better than she did.

C. She scored better than 82% of test takers.

D. She is meeting or exceeding the standards for her grade level.

E. She scored better than 7 out of 10 test takers.

13. **Use the diagram below to answer the question that follows.**

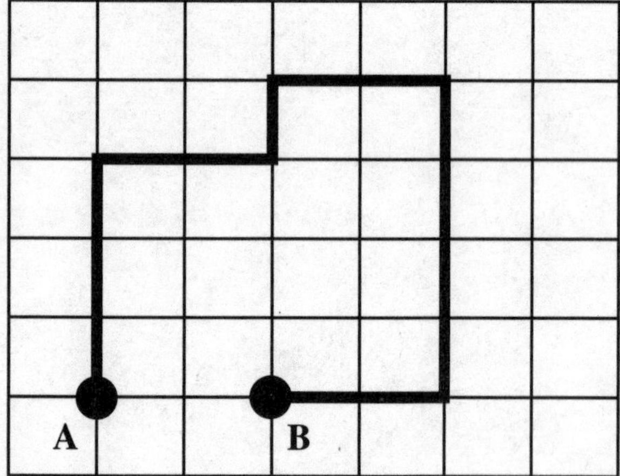

Emanuel participated in a fundraising race. The diagram shows his path, from point A to point B, with each grid unit representing ½ mile of the race. If Emanuel raised $120 for each mile he ran, how much money did he raise in the race?

A. $700

B. $840

C. $980

D. $1220

E. $1680

14. A family photo measures 4 inches by 6 inches. If the owner places the photo in a scrapbook, so that is surrounded by a 2-inch ribbon border on all sides, what are the outer dimensions of the rectangular ribbon border?

A. 2 inches by 3 inches

B. 2 inches by 6 inches

C. 4 inches by 9 inches

D. 6 inches by 8 inches

E. 8 inches by 10 inches

15. In a trivia club, there is a Red Team with 5 members, a Green Team with 6 members, and a Blue Team with 4 members. Last week, Karen from the Red Team was randomly chosen to be Quizmaster. If Karen is not eligible to be Quizmaster again this week, what is the probability that someone from the Red Team will be selected as Quizmaster?

A. $\frac{1}{3}$

B. $\frac{2}{3}$

C. $\frac{5}{14}$

D. $\frac{2}{7}$

E. $\frac{4}{15}$

16. Ethan draws custom cartoon characters for his fans on a social media site. If he can draw one character in 45 minutes, then at this rate, how many characters can he draw in 9 hours?

A. 8

B. 10

C. 12

D. 15

E. 18

17. A new business reported a financial loss of $6,750 in February. In December, the business made a profit of $27,950. Which of the following is the best estimate of the difference between the earnings in February and the earnings in December?

A. $21,000

B. $35,000

C. $42,000

D. $49,000

E. $63,000

18. Kiran is purchasing panels of fencing material for a backyard. If each panel has a length of 65 inches, and Kiran purchases 30 panels, what is the total length of the fencing material purchased?

A. 126 feet, 9 inches

B. 162 feet, 5 inches

C. 162 feet, 6 inches

D. 178 feet, 4 inches

E. 195 feet, 10 inches

19. At a garden store, Abby is planting ferns into clay pots. At 10:00 a.m., she notices that she has 50 ferns that still need to be potted. At 10:45 a.m., she checks her progress again. If Abby has been working continuously at a rate of 20 ferns per hour, how many ferns are remaining at 10:45 a.m.?

A. 10

B. 15

C. 20

D. 25

E. 35

20. A student reads the following problem:

5 is what percent of 30?

The student sets up the following equation to solve the problem:

$$5 = \frac{x}{100} \times 30$$

Which of the following equivalent equations could the student also use to solve the problem?

A. $\frac{5}{x} = 100 \times 30$

B. $30 = \frac{x}{100} \times 5$

C. $0.05 = \frac{x}{30}$

D. $\frac{5 \times 30}{100} = x$

E. $\frac{5}{30} = \frac{\text{x}}{100}$

21. Sidney is planning to ask for a 15% raise in her salary. If Sidney currently earns $60,000 per year, what would be her new salary after her proposed raise?

A. $51,000

B. $69,000

C. $75,000

D. $80,000

E. $82,000

22. Micah is baking lasagna for a company picnic. He has enough pasta for $2\frac{3}{4}$ pans of lasagna, enough cheese for $3\frac{2}{3}$ pans, and enough sauce for $3\frac{1}{2}$ pans. If he doesn't obtain any more ingredients, how many full pans of lasagna can Micah make?

A. 2

B. 3

C. 5

D. 8

E. 9

23. Which of the following number sentences is correct?

A. $5\frac{2}{3} < 6\frac{1}{3} < 5\frac{1}{3}$

B. $6\frac{1}{3} < 5\frac{2}{3} < 5\frac{1}{3}$

C. $5\frac{1}{3} < 6\frac{1}{3} < 5\frac{2}{3}$

D. $5\frac{1}{3} < 5\frac{2}{3} < 6\frac{1}{3}$

E. $5\frac{2}{3} < 5\frac{1}{3} < 6\frac{1}{3}$

24. In order to pass his history class, Phoenix needs to score an average of 80% on his exams. His first four exam scores were 72%, 84%, 93%, and 86%. What is the minimum score that Phoenix must earn on his fifth exam, in order to ensure that his average for all five exams is at least 80%?

A. 0%

B. 55%

C. 65%

D. 80%

E. 92%

25. Which of the following numbers is between 23.984 and 27.135?

A. 22.405

B. 23.374

C. 23.937

D. 24.419

E. 28.248

26. **Use the mathematical statement below to answer the question that follows.**

$$\frac{2}{5} < \square < \frac{5}{8}$$

Which of the following, when substituted for the unknown value, will make the statement true?

A. $\frac{1}{2}$

B. $\frac{2}{5}$

C. $\frac{7}{8}$

D. $\frac{3}{10}$

E. $\frac{3}{4}$

27. **Use the information below to answer the question that follows.**

Week 1	Week 2	Week 3	Week 4
$467	–$165	$323	$575

Reuben keeps track of his earnings for his landscaping business. In Week 2, he had to purchase some new equipment. What was the average weekly earnings for the four weeks shown?

A. $600

B. $560

C. $510

D. $400

E. $300

28. At a paper supply company, 512 cartons of printer paper were sold. 3/4 of the cartons were plain white paper. Half of the remaining cartons were bright-colored paper. All other remaining cartons were specialty premium paper. How many cartons of specialty premium paper were sold?

A. 32

B. 64

C. 128

D. 192

E. 384

29. Connor is purchasing fabric for a project. If he needs 14 yards of fabric, and the fabric costs $2.86 per yard, which of the following is the best estimate of the cost of the fabric he needs?

A. $45

B. $60

C. $75

D. $90

E. $105

30. In the problem below, two numbers are multiplied, with steps shown. What is the missing digit in the first number of the problem?

$$\begin{array}{r} \mathbf{4}\square \\ \times\,\mathbf{27} \\ \hline 301 \\ +\,860 \\ \hline 1161 \end{array} \quad \text{result}$$

A. 8

B. 7

C. 5

D. 4

E. 3

31. Which of the following expressions is equivalent to $(50 + 30 + 20 + 40a)$?

A. $\dfrac{5 + 3 + 2 + 4}{a}$

B. (80)(130)

C. $a(50 + 30 + 20 + 40)$

D. $10\,(5 + 3 + 2 + 4a)$

E. $\dfrac{5 + 3 + 2 + 4}{a}$

32. **Use the information below to answer the question that follows.**

> Players can participate in the E-Sports Tournament only if they pass the Qualifying Round.
>
> Players must win 10 games in the Tournament in order to participate in the Championship.
>
> The player who wins the Championship will win the Grand Prize.

If Stefan won only 8 games in the Tournament, which of the following statements must be true?

A. Stefan will win the Grand Prize.

B. Stefan did not pass the Qualifying Round.

C. Stefan will not participate in the Championship.

D. Stefan did not participate in the Tournament.

E. Stefan lost exactly two games in the Tournament.

33. Solve for x.

$2x - 4 + 3x = 31$

A. 7

B. 6

C. 5

D. 4

E. 3

34. A member of a hotel cleaning crew takes about 15 minutes to clean each room. At this rate, if he cleans 27 rooms, and begins cleaning at 11:00 a.m., at what time will he finish the last room?

A. 5:15 p.m.

B. 5:45 p.m.

C. 6:15 p.m.

D. 6:30 p.m.

E. 6:55 p.m.

35. Emily sells 14 cakes per week and earns $24 per cake. She later increases her prices to $26 per cake. If she still sells 14 cakes per week, what is the total increase in her weekly earnings?

A. $26

B. $28

C. $52

D. $336

E. $364

36. **Read the information below; then answer the question that follows.**

> To paint a house, Jordan purchased 3 gallons of exterior blue paint, 2 gallons of interior white paint, and 4 gallons of interior beige paint. During the first day of painting, Jordan used 2.5 gallons of the paint that was purchased.

Which of the following can be determined from the information above?

A. The total amount of exterior paint used

B. The total amount of paint needed for the project

C. The square footage of the walls to be painted

D. The total cost of paint materials

E. The amount of paint remaining from what was purchased

37. Aaron is calculating his average test score for English class. His scores on four exams are 89%, 82%, 78%, and 94%. He uses the following expression to calculate his average exam score as a decimal:

$$\frac{0.89 + 0.82 + 0.78 + 0.94}{4}$$

Which of the following expressions could Aaron have also used?

A. $(0.89 + 0.82 + 0.78 + 0.94) \div (\frac{1}{4})$

B. $\frac{89 + 82 + 78 + 94}{400}$

C. $100(0.89 + 0.82 + 0.78 + 0.94) \div 4$

D. $\frac{89 + 82 + 78 + 94}{25}$

E. $100(89 + 82 + 78 + 94) \div 4$

38. **Use the information below to answer the question that follows.**

Volunteer Participants for Local School and District

Grade	Hamilton School	Desert School District
9th	18	105
10th	23	129
11th	31	111
12th	26	134

Hamilton School is in the Desert School District. The above chart shows the number of student participants, at each grade level, for the nature conservation project last year. Of all the participants from Desert School District, how many were *not* Hamilton School students?

A. 98

B. 107

C. 283

D. 381

E. 479

39. For a wedding, a decorator decides to style the guests' chairs with white satin ribbon. There are 8 rows of chairs, with each row requiring 12 feet of ribbon. If the ribbon costs $0.49 per yard, which of the following is closest to the total cost of the ribbon?

A. $16

B. $32

C. $48

D. $96

E. $144

40. **Use the information below to answer the question that follows.**

Charley and Oliver are each walking towards the park. Charley's home is 2 miles from the park, and Oliver's home is 3.5 miles from the park.

Based on the information above, which of the following can be determined?

A. Charley's home and Oliver's home are at most 5.5 miles apart.

B. Charley's home and Oliver's home are less than 1.5 miles apart.

C. Charley's home and Oliver's home are exactly 1.5 miles apart.

D. Charley's home and Oliver's home are at least 5.5 miles apart.

E. Charley's home and Oliver's home are exactly 2 miles apart.

41. **Read the problem below; then answer the question that follows.**

Jayda is making chili for a party. The recipe calls for 6 pounds of pinto beans, 5 pounds of diced tomato, 4 pounds of beef, and $\frac{3}{4}$ pound of chili seasoning mix. If Jayda is planning to serve 20 guests, how many pounds of each ingredient does she need?

Which single piece of information is necessary to solve the problem above?

A. The volume of the bowls used for serving

B. The price of the ingredients used

C. The number of servings yielded by the recipe

D. The capacity of the cooking pot Jayda will use

E. The total pounds of ingredients used in the recipe

42. **Use the chart below to answer the question that follows.**

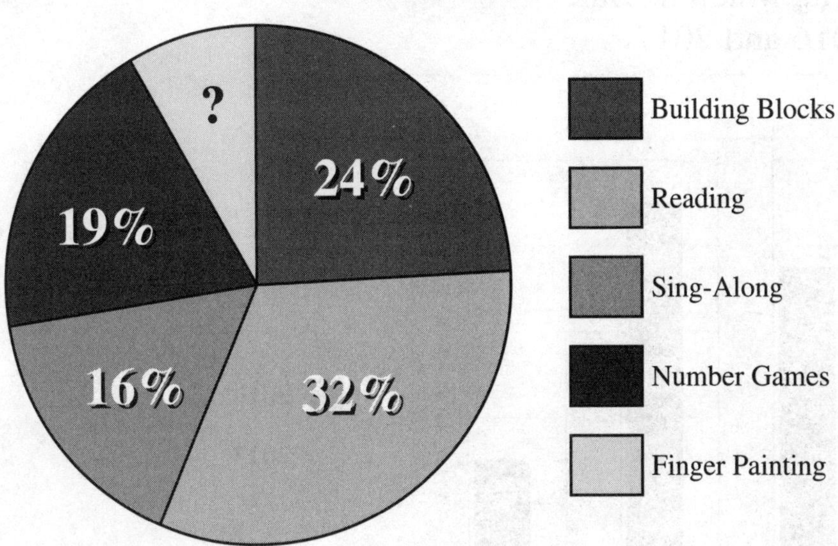

A day care center logs the amount of time spent on various activities during one week, with the results shown in the chart above. What percent of time was spent on finger painting (shown with a question mark)?

A. 9%

B. 13%

C. 15%

D. 19%

E. 21%

43. Logan ran for 36 more minutes on Saturday than he did on Wednesday. If he ran for a total of 160 minutes on these two days, how many minutes did he run on Saturday?

A. 98

B. 72

C. 62

D. 44

E. 36

44. **Use the chart below to answer the question that follows.**

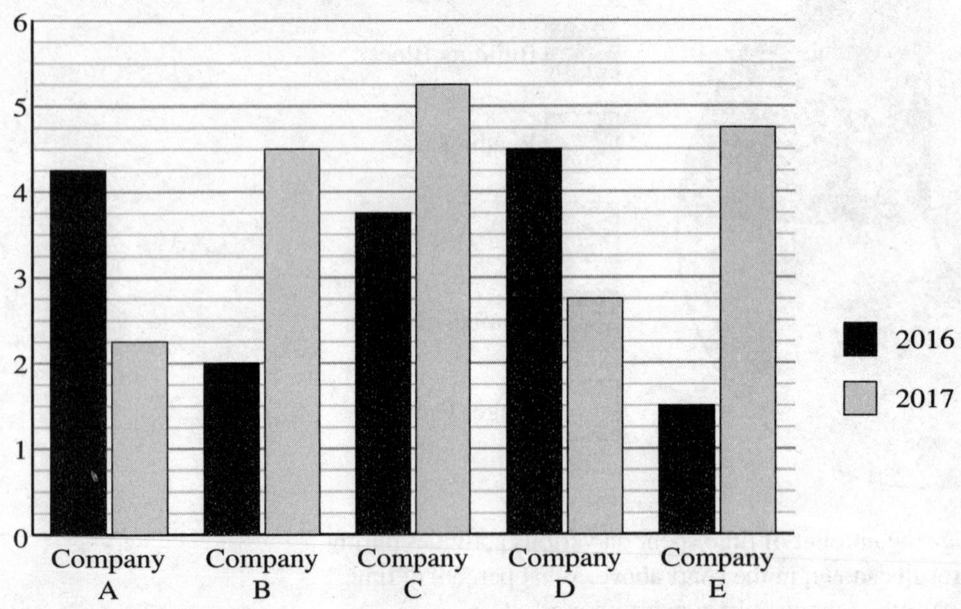

The chart shows the number of sales of dishwashing machines by various companies in 2016 and 2017. Each unit in the vertical axis represents 100,000 sales. Which company had the largest increase in sales from 2016 to 2017?

A. Company A

B. Company B

C. Company C

D. Company D

E. Company E

45. **Use the chart below to answer the question that follows.**

x	y
5	8
7	12
9	
11	20

The values of x and y have a direct relationship, with some of the values shown. What is the value that is missing?

A. 14

B. 16

C. 18

D. 20

E. 22

46. **Read the problem below; then answer the question that follows.**

> Ariana begins work at a factory at 8:00 a.m. She seals 120 packages in the morning, takes a 45-minute break for lunch, and then seals 135 more packages before the end of her shift. What is Ariana's average rate of packages sealed per hour, not counting her lunch break?

Which single piece of information is necessary to solve the problem above?

A. The amount of time that she worked before lunch

B. The size of the packages produced in the factory

C. The total number of boxes produced in the factory

D. The time of day that she finished her shift

E. The average amount of time that she pauses between packages

47. Solve for y.

$5(3y - 4) = 115$

A. 5

B. 6

C. 7

D. 8

E. 9

48. For an event, a caterer pays her staff by the hour. She pays a bartender \$15.85 per hour for 5 hours, servers \$19.65 per hour for 25 combined hours, and cleaning crew \$12.35 per hour for 10 combined hours. If each of the hourly rates is rounded to the nearest dollar, what is the average hourly rate for all the hours worked at the event?

A. \$16.00

B. \$16.50

C. \$17.00

D. \$17.25

E. \$17.50

49. Phoebe plays a carnival game, for which she has a 20% chance of winning. If she plays the game twice, what is the probability that she will win the game at least one of the two tries?

A. 4%

B. 18%

C. 36%

D. 42%

E. 64%

50. Amir drives 36 miles to work each day. His car's average gasoline usage rate is 24 miles per gallon, and gasoline costs $3.80 per gallon. Approximately how much money does Amir spend on gasoline in order to drive to work for 5 days?

A. $12.66

B. $19.54

C. $28.50

D. $65.43

E. $91.20

SECTION III: TEST OF WRITING

Directions: The Writing section of the CBEST assesses basic skills and concepts that are important in performing the job of an educator in California. This section includes two topics that assess your ability to write effectively. One of the topics asks you to analyze a situation or statement; the other asks you to write about a personal experience. You will not be expected to demonstrate any specialized knowledge in your responses.

You should be sure to write only on the topics presented, respond to both topics, address all of the points presented in the topics, and support generalizations with specific examples. Before you begin writing, read each topic and organize your thoughts carefully

Your written response must be your original work, written in your own words, and must not be copied or paraphrased from some other work.

When you take the actual CBEST, scorers will read and evaluate each of your responses using a standard set of criteria, which are outlined in the writing score scale (see Part IV of this book).

The following written performance characteristics, which are incorporated in the CBEST Writing Score Scale, are evaluated during scoring.

I. *Rhetorical Force:* the clarity with which the central idea or point of view is stated and maintained; the coherence of the discussion and the quality of the writer's ideas

II. *Organization:* the clarity of the writing and the logical sequence of the writer's ideas

III. *Support and Development:* the relevance, depth, and specificity of supporting information

IV. *Usage:* the extent to which the writing shows care and precision in word choice

V. *Structure and Conventions:* the extent to which the writing is free of errors in syntax, paragraph structure, sentence structure, and mechanics (e.g., spelling, punctuation, capitalization)

VI. *Appropriateness:* the extent to which the writer addresses the topic and uses language and style appropriate to the given audience and purpose

WRITING TOPICS

TOPIC 1

Eleanor Roosevelt once observed, "In the long run, we shape our lives, and we shape ourselves……and the choices we make are ultimately our own responsibility." In an essay to be read by an audience of educated adults, state whether you agree or disagree with this viewpoint. Support your position with logical arguments and specific examples.

TOPIC 2

While we often seek to avoid disagreements with others, conflict can lead to positive change when we alter our viewpoints, opinions, or behavior for the better. In an essay written for an audience of educated adults, describe an instance wherein having a disagreement with someone caused you to change in a positive way. With whom did you disagree and about what? How did your views, opinions, or behavior change as a result? Why do you consider this change a positive one?

Chapter 15
Practice Test 3: Answers and Explanations

ANSWER KEY

Reading

1.	B	26.	C
2.	C	27.	E
3.	A	28.	B
4.	D	29.	E
5.	E	30.	A
6.	D	31.	A
7.	C	32.	D
8.	E	33.	D
9.	C	34.	B
10.	E	35.	C
11.	B	36.	A
12.	A	37.	D
13.	C	38.	B
14.	B	39.	A
15.	C	40.	A
16.	E	41.	E
17.	D	42.	D
18.	C	43.	D
19.	E	44.	D
20.	A	45.	B
21.	A	46.	C
22.	D	47.	D
23.	E	48.	C
24.	C	49.	E
25.	A	50.	A

Mathematics

1.	B	26.	A
2.	D	27.	E
3.	B	28.	B
4.	E	29.	A
5.	D	30.	E
6.	D	31.	D
7.	A	32.	C
8.	C	33.	A
9.	D	34.	B
10.	A	35.	B
11.	A	36.	E
12.	C	37.	B
13.	B	38.	D
14.	E	39.	A
15.	D	40.	A
16.	C	41.	C
17.	B	42.	A
18.	C	43.	A
19.	E	44.	E
20.	E	45.	B
21.	B	46.	D
22.	A	47.	E
23.	D	48.	E
24.	C	49.	C
25.	D	50.	C

SECTION I: TEST OF READING

1. **B** The author is explaining that the phenomenon of the royal imposter is even more odd when the imposter is of a different nationality; it would presumably be harder to impersonate someone who speaks a different language and was reared in a different culture. Choice (A) is wrong because the author did not state that the royal imposter phenomenon was uncommon, so it would not make sense to describe royal imposters of a different nationality as "even more uncommon." Choices (C) and (D) are legitimate definitions of the word "peculiar" but make no sense in this context. Choice (E) is not a correct meaning of the word.

2. **C** In paragraph 2 the author contrasts modern times, with technology such as video and DNA, with centuries past in order to explain why it would be much easier to impersonate a royal back then. Choices (A), (B), and (E) are wrong because paragraph 2 does not discuss any recent cases of royal imposters. Choice (D) is wrong because Karl Wilhelm Naundorff is only mentioned in the final sentence as an example; his unlikely claim is not the focus of the paragraph.

3. **A** The author states that transnational royal imposters were peculiar (i.e., strange), then states that this was the case with Anna Anderson—a Polish factory worker who spoke no Russian. Nothing in the passage suggests that (B) is true. Choices (C), (D), and (E) are all facts of the Anderson case, but the author does not indicate that any of them make her attempt at impersonation strange. Moreover, paragraph 2 suggests that a lack of DNA evidence, (C), is the norm for these cases (DNA is a modern tool that would likely expose an imposter).

4. **D** An inference must be clearly supported by the information in the passage. Paragraph 1 states that Richard, Duke of York, was the son of King Edward IV and the heir to the English throne. Paragraph 2 states that royalty were continuously surrounded by servants and close associates. The combination of these facts makes (D) undeniably true. In contrast, there is no support anywhere for the remaining choices. While paragraph 1 does broadly characterize transnational imposters as strange, the author never suggests that Naundorff in particular would have had a better claim had he been French instead of German; (C) is wrong.

5. **E** Sentence 8 is clearly sarcastic and ridicules believers, placing Bigfoot into the same category as fictitious characters like Santa Claus and the Tooth Fairy. The remaining sentences are all statements of fact. The author's use of language such as "reportedly" (A) and "claim to have been held captive," (B), while implying doubt, does not render the statements opinion rather than fact. The existence of Bigfoot has not been proved, so the author is appropriately indicating that information about the creature has not been substantiated.

6. **D** The author is conveying that the "famed" Bigfoot is prominent in the sense of being the best-known of the cryptids. Choices (C) and (E) are not correct definitions of the word and (A) makes no sense in this context. Choice (B) is wrong because Bigfoot, irrespective of size, is not easily noticeable. The passage explains that cryptids, by definition, are extremely elusive (if they exist at all) and that no credible evidence of a Bigfoot sighting has been offered.

7. **C** For the first blank, Sentence 4 explains how there have been many sightings of Bigfoot over the years. Sentence 5 then builds on that idea by stating that there have even been reported abductions, so (B) and (E) can be eliminated ("however" and "nonetheless" both indicate a change in direction). Sentence 6 states that no Bigfoot sighting has been corroborated, but then Sentence 7 states that some people believe in Bigfoot. A word signaling a change in direction is therefore required and (C) is the only remaining answer that works.

8. **E** The author emphasizes the lack of irrefutable evidence for the existence of Bigfoot and then mocks the legislators who presumed that the creature is real. Accordingly, (E) is correct and (C) is wrong. Choice (A) is too narrow in scope because the author only briefly mentions alleged abduction cases. Choice (D) is wrong because no reported sightings are analyzed in any depth. Choice (B) is wrong because "cryptozoology" is too broad in scope, as the passage deals primarily with Bigfoot, and no history is presented.

9. **C** Based on the information in the passage the author would agree with (A) and (B), but they are both too narrow in scope; each addresses only one of the author's key points. Choice (D) is wrong because the passage does not mention independent or foreign films. While (E) expresses the idea that the desire for money is the key problem, it is too broad in scope and too extreme in tone. The passage deals with movies, not the entire U.S. entertainment industry. Moreover, the passage does not go so far as to accuse anyone of corruption or greed, only the need to avoid losing money on investments.

10. **E** An assumption is an unstated assertion that the author accepts as true that is necessary for the argument to make logical sense. It is essentially a fact that the author takes for granted, without which the argument has a hole. Sentence 8 explains that the studios sacrifice talent for security when they hire A-list celebrities instead of unknown actors. The author is assuming (i.e., taking for granted) that at least some unknown actors are more talented than the A-listers who are cast instead. If the A-listers are actually the most talented actors, the author's point falls flat. Choices (A) through (D) are not critical to the logic of the argument: if you negate the statements, the author's argument doesn't fall apart. (Moreover, choices B and D weren't even mentioned.)

11. **B** Sentence 10 is a conclusory statement that sums up the author's argument: Hollywood needs to "change its tune" (i.e., change its profit-driven approach to moviemaking) or else the quality of its films will remain poor. Choices (C) and (E) are wrong because neither musicals nor film tone was mentioned in the passage. While spoiler-free trailers, (D), were in fact discussed immediately prior to the statement about changing tune, this is only one aspect of the overall argument. It is not the main point of the entire argument that the author is concluding by means of sentence 10. Choice (A) goes too far. The author wants Hollywood to make better movies, not cease making them altogether.

12. **A** Sentences 4, 5, 8 and 9 are all critical to the author's argument, as they either describe the essence of the problem with Hollywood or develop key points. Sentence 2, in contrast, simply elaborates on the idea that movies aren't as good as they used to be (stated in Sentence 1) by recounting the author's childhood experiences. Sentence 2 could easily be deleted from the passage without leaving any holes in the argument's development.

13. **C** Language such as "*our* salaries" and "*we* shouldn't let him sell out *our* interests" indicates that the author is a police officer addressing other police officers.

14. **B** The author is attacking the mayor on a personal level, implying that he is motivated to deny a raise for police officers because he selfishly wants a generous raise for himself. Choices (A) and (E) are wrong because the author uses neither an analogy (a comparison between two otherwise unlike things), nor any statistics. Choice (C) is wrong because the author does not refute a claim by offering an example that defies that general rule (i.e., a counterexample). Choice (D) is wrong because the author does not attempt to bolster this argument by appealing to an authority.

15. **C** *What the mayor stated* at the previous meeting is a matter of fact, even though what he stated may have been his opinion. The remaining statements all reflect the author's opinion.

16. **E** To find this information you would look under "Crimes of violence," then under the subcategory of "battery," then under "defenses" (pages 400–410).

17. **D** This index is organized according to type of crime (e.g., crimes against property vs. violent crimes). Although the degrees of certain crimes are listed in order of seriousness (e.g., first degree, then second degree, etc.), this organizational pattern only applies to the subcategories (the crimes), not to the overall structure of the index; (B) is wrong. Choice (A) is wrong because there is no chronological aspect, and (C) is wrong because there is no reference anywhere to punishment. Choice (E) is wrong because crimes of violence (the second category listed) are no less important than crimes against property (the first category listed).

18. **C** The author's purpose is to inform the reader about the basic principles of groupthink. While the author might be critical of the historical decisions outlined in paragraph 2, these are only mentioned briefly as supporting examples—(A) is wrong. Choice (B) is wrong because the author would not argue in favor of groupthink, which is a negative phenomenon. While the author does lay out and then dismiss the basic argument that group decision-making is better than individual decision-making, he or she does not attack any specific research findings of psychologists who deny the existence of groupthink; (D) is wrong. Choice (E) is wrong because the author does not examine any particular case in depth.

19. **E** The passage states that the key to groupthink is group cohesiveness: critical thinking is sacrificed to preserve harmony among group members. Choice (E) is the only situation that involves a tight-knit group of people who would want to censor dissenting opinions in order to avoid conflict. Moreover, for (C) and (D), the decisions are being made individually without the knowledge of the other group members.

20. **A** The author sets forth a position in paragraph 1 (group decision-making is superior to individual decision-making). That position is then discredited in paragraph 2 by describing a theory (groupthink) and offering real-world examples (Bay of Pigs, Watergate, and Pearl Harbor). Choice (E) is wrong because no statistics are discussed in the passage.

21. **A** The other choices are all too extreme and involve major leaps of logic. Just because groupthink processes have been documented doesn't mean that strangers care *nothing* about intragroup harmony, (B), or that cohesive groups *always* make bad decisions, (C). Similarly, just because analysts have suggested that groupthink might have been a factor in Watergate doesn't mean that those responsible *never* argued when making pertinent decisions, (D). Nor can it reasonably be concluded that the Pearl Harbor attack would not have occurred if groupthink did not occur, (E).

22. **D** The chart displays the percentages of dogs by breed who won dog shows in the U.S. (2000 to 2014). Since the chart covers a fifteen-year period and the percentages shown are simply averages, one cannot draw any conclusions about percentages for any given *year*; (A), (B) and (E) are wrong. Similarly, (C) is wrong as well because one cannot draw conclusions about which dogs won over the five-year period from 2011 to 2015. For example, 26% of the winners could have been poodles during that period, but only 18% for the previous five years (yielding an average of 22% for that ten-year period). If 22% of the winners from 2000 to 2004 were poodles, then it would work out that more than *one-fourth* of the winners from 2011 through 2015 were in fact poodles (with a fifteen-year average of only 22%).

23. **E** This passage is uniformly and emphatically positive in tone about Loca Cola. This suggests that it's an advertisement of some sort designed to get people to buy the product, so (E) is correct. Choice (B) is wrong because it implicitly questions the results of the taste test by asking how many people took part (if it were only five then the results would be essentially meaningless!). Similarly, (A) calls for a second taste test to see if the results can be replicated and (D) suggests that customers conduct their own taste tests. These types of skeptical statements would not be in an advertisement. The reference in (C) to "our annual sales" and the more restrained tone suggest a Loca Cola inter-office communication of some sort, not an advertisement.

24. **C** Once again, an assumption is a fact that the author takes for granted in order for the argument to flow logically. The passage states that each year millions more people drink Loca than Wepsi (or any other brand of cola) worldwide, then concludes that Loca is superior in taste. The author is assuming that more people drink Loca because of the taste, not simply because it's cheaper. If that's *not* the case, the argument falls apart; (C) is correct. There is nothing to suggest that the author believes that those who chose Wepsi over Loca in the taste test lied, (A), that everybody would choose Loca if the test were conducted again, (D), or that most Wepsi drinkers have never tasted Loca, (E). A small minority may simply prefer Wepsi's taste. Nor does the author assume that Wepsi costs more because its sales are relatively low, (B). Wepsi could simply be more expensive to produce.

25. **A** Keep in mind that *both* paragraph summaries must be correct here! If you can eliminate one of them, the answer choice is incorrect. The paragraph 1 summary for (B) mentions teachers imposing higher standards, which is only discussed in paragraph 2; (B) is therefore wrong. The paragraph 1 summary for (C) states that texting and texting culture are harming young people, with no mention of writing skills—the main focus of the passage. Choice (C) should be eliminated at this point, but, if there's any doubt, the paragraph 2 summary is clearly wrong. Letters and personal notes were only discussed in the first paragraph. The paragraph 1 summary for (D) may be deceptively appealing. However, the main point of the paragraph is not that poor writing skills are ironic in light of other advancements in learning, it's that writing skills are poor and electronic communication and associated values are to blame. The paragraph 2 summary is also wrong in that the author never blames teachers for the problem per se, but merely argues that teachers can effectively remedy it. Both summaries are wrong for (E) because they reference "values" with no mention of writing skills.

26. **C** The second paragraph makes it clear that the author is offering advice to teachers (featuring statements such as "grade accordingly!").

27. **E** You know from the passage that texting language involves deviations from standard English—two ("u" and "ur") are mentioned in the first paragraph. All the other statements are unsubstantiated. You do not know that students' writing skills would improve if they stopped texting (the damage could already be done), so (A) is wrong. Nor can you conclude that teachers' grading standards have deteriorated (the author simply advises teachers *not* to lower their standards); (B) is wrong as well. Choice (C) is wrong because the author never advised teachers to go so far as to *fail* students who make grammatical errors. Choice (D) is wrong because you can't conclude from the information given that *most* young people wrote handwritten notes a hundred years ago (all you know is that they rarely do so today).

28. **B** The author is obviously not happy about the fact that young people's writing skills are poor and views the situation in a very negative light. Any word with a positive meaning should therefore be eliminated, so "agreeable," (C), is wrong. "Amusing," (E), should also be eliminated. Although the author does make some sarcastic comments, he or she seems more upset than amused by this state of affairs. "Confusing," (A), should be eliminated as well, as the author explains why writing skills are poor and doesn't indicate any confusion about the situation. "Frightening," (D), is too extreme. The author seems genuinely concerned, and perhaps slightly alarmed, but not frightened. "Unfortunate," (B), is the best fit.

29. **E** Paragraph 1 explains that the Gaussian function is the mathematical model that scientists used to predict wave height for about a century before the Draupner wave; (C) and (D) are wrong. It allowed for the existence of rogue waves, but only approximately once every ten thousand years; (A) and (B) are wrong.

30. **A** The passage explains that the existence of rogue waves has now been proved conclusively through scientific measurement; (C) and (D) are wrong. Choice (B) is wrong because the passage does not address survival strategies for encountering rogue waves (if indeed there are any!). Choice (E) is wrong because the passage does not deal with any specifics of the Gaussian function (which is no longer used to predict rogue waves anyway). Choice (A) is the best fit.

31. **A** The main point of paragraph 1 is that rogue waves weren't taken seriously until 1995; they were either dismissed as a fanciful tale or considered astronomically unlikely. While the author would probably agree that the sailors who reported rogue waves should have been believed, the sailors' credibility is not the main point. The point is that the existence of rogue waves was denied throughout history; (B) is wrong. Similarly, the author would most likely agree that scientists were incorrect to rely on the Gaussian function, but the scientists' error is not the main point either; (C) is wrong. Choice (D) is not supported by the passage, which suggests that rogue waves have occurred much more frequently than anyone realized. Choice (E) is not supported by the passage either; paragraph 1 indicates that scientists dismissed the rogue wave phenomenon as theoretically possible but extraordinarily rare.

32. **D** Tarts are pastries, so a recipe for them would be found in the section beginning on page 33. "Tart Dish"—page 17, (B)—is listed under "tea equipment," so this would be a plate of some sort used for serving tarts that have already been made. The section entitled "fruit salads"—page 30; (C)—would deal with recipes consisting primarily of fruit, not pastry items.

33. **D** The bibliography would presumably list similar sources about tea that could be used to supplement the information in the book. The foreword—page 2; (A)—is simply a brief introductory statement that is typically written by someone other than the author. Similarly, the introduction—page 3; (B)—would not contain detailed information about herbal teas either; it briefly describes the purpose and goals of the book. The glossary—page 40; (C)—merely defines the terms used in the book, and the index—page 49; (E)—is just an alphabetical listing of topics and page numbers that is more detailed than the table of contents.

34. **B** In the first paragraph the author *explains a situation*: he or she sets forth the rules governing diplomatic immunity and informs the reader about what generally happens in practice. In the second paragraph the author offers a *hypothetical example* (the case of the serial killer) and then *states an opinion* (in order to prevent injustices, diplomatic immunity should not apply to very serious crimes such as murder).

35. **C** Paragraph 1 states that immune persons cannot be tried in the host country (without a waiver) regardless of the seriousness of the crime; (D) is wrong. Further, the home country *can* waive immunity if it chooses to do so—(B) is wrong—or prosecute the accused within its own borders; (A) is wrong. The host country can also expel the accused as *persona non grata*; (E) is wrong as well.

36. **A** In paragraph 2 the author states that diplomatic immunity might be justifiable for minor offenses but not for very serious ones such as murder; (B) and (C) are wrong. While the author does explain how immunity is usually more of a problem when hostile nations are involved, he or she never suggests that only diplomats from friendly nations should be protected; (D) is wrong. In paragraph 1 the author states that immunity is routinely abused for some minor offenses, but only occasionally for *serious* crimes; (E) is wrong as well.

37. **D** The preceding sentence states that you should not consider whether your friend eats junk food when logically evaluating the advice you've been given; (A) is wrong. Telling your friend to eat better would also be focusing on the friend's junk-food-eating behavior, which is not relevant to the logical analysis of the argument; (B) is wrong. Choices (C) and (E) are distractors. Once again, we are not concerned with the friend's *behavior* in terms of whether his or her eating habits are logical; we only care about the logical correctness of the argument at issue; (C) is wrong. The *tu quoque* error is not committed by the (possibly hypocritical) friend in this case, but rather by the reader to whom the author is addressing; (E) is wrong as well.

38. **B** The author makes it clear that *tu quoque* reasoning is incorrect, so any words with positive meanings such as "clever," (A), should be eliminated. Choices (D) and (E) are both too extreme: the author's attitude towards *tu quoque* arguments is not negative enough for "appalling" to make sense here, nor does the passage go so far as to suggest that faulty logic is "dangerous." The distractor choice here is (C). The *tu quoque* fallacy involves hypocrisy in that it wrongly takes another person's hypocrisy into consideration when evaluating his or her argument. However, the reasoning itself is not hypocritical (it is unsound).

39. **A** The author's main point is that *tu quoque* reasoning is flawed. The hypothetical example about a friend's advice is simply a way to illustrate this central theme; (B) and (E) are wrong. The author does not address the frequency with which *tu quoque* errors are made; (C) is wrong. Choice (D) is too broad in scope. This passage deals specifically with the *tu quoque* error; the first sentence is more general information that is used to explain why *tu quoque* reasoning is illogical.

40. **A** Paragraph 1 discusses the various ways that stores manipulate customers into buying and spending more, while paragraph 2 discusses ways to outsmart these strategies and be a discriminating shopper. When choosing the best answer keep in mind that both paragraph summaries need to be correct. The passage deals with more than grocery stores, (B), and store layout, (D), so these are both too narrow in scope. Choice (E) centers on marketing strategies for major product lines, which goes well beyond the scope of this passage about stores. Choice (C) is too strong because stores aren't necessarily cheating or victimizing their customers.

41. **E** The passage explains that relatively high-priced items or items that the store really wants or expects to sell (such as a well-advertised BOGO item) will be placed at eye level; relatively low-priced items or ones of less importance will be placed on the highest and lowest shelves; (C) and (D) are wrong. Items that appeal to children will be placed low-down at children's eye level; (B) is wrong. Choice (A) contradicts the passage; heavy or breakable items will be placed on lower shelves for safety reasons.

42. **D** Choices (A), sentence 2; (B), sentence 5; (C), sentence 7; and (E), sentence 12, discuss tactics used by stores to influence customers to spend more. Choice (D), sentence 10, simply notes an exception to this general practice: some items are placed on shelves for safety reasons. If the author did not mention this fact, the argument would be no less persuasive.

43. **D** A counterexample is an example that is used to disprove an assertion with which it is inconsistent. Mr. Johnson set forth a general rule that lying is always wrong. In response, the author presented a hypothetical case wherein he lies about Bob's whereabouts in order to protect him from harm. It would seem (to the author and probably to many others as well) that lying would not be wrong in that instance. While the hypothetical case did deal with potential harm coming to Bob, the author did not appeal in any obvious way to emotion. Such an appeal would involve something like vividly describing the harm that would come to Bob if he were found and the suffering that he would endure, etc.—(A) is wrong. The author challenged the reasoning of adults in authority, but did not appeal to any authority in support of *his* argument; (B) is wrong. Nowhere did the author attack Mr. Johnson personally in terms of his traits, circumstances, behavior, etc.—(C) is wrong. Choice (E) goes too far in terms of what the author is arguing. He asserts that lying is not always wrong, not that it would be right in *most* cases.

44. **D** The author's main point is that he was correct in his assertion that lying is not always wrong. The fact that the author had a bad day yesterday is only incidental (note that the first sentence of the passage is not always the main point—or even important); (A) is wrong. Choice B is wrong because the author never actually argued that he should not have received detention, or even that he was right to lie in this instance—only that lying is not always wrong! The author certainly never argued that Bob should not have received detention for cutting class; (B) is wrong. While the author did state that adults in authority are not always right, that was merely incidental to his main point—that lying is morally correct under certain circumstances. Lying was the focus of the argument, not the fallibility of authoritative adults; (C) is wrong. The author never suggests that Mr. Johnson treated him disrespectfully, so (E) is wrong as well.

45. **B** The author provided a counterexample of a hypothetical situation in which he lied to save Bob from harm. He concludes that lying is not always wrong because lying would not be wrong under those circumstances. Mr. Johnsons calls it a foolish argument, stating, "If everybody went around lying whenever they felt like it, nobody could trust anyone." However, the author had simply argued that it's right to lie sometimes, not that it's right for everybody to lie whenever they feel like it. Misstating someone's argument in a weaker form and then attacking it is sometimes called a "straw man" fallacy and it constitutes questionable logic. Choice (A) is wrong because Mr. Johnson did not reject the argument on the grounds that the author is a student, and whether or not someone is rude is logically irrelevant; (D) is wrong as well. Since the author made a hypothetical argument, a response that deals with hypothetical instances would be appropriate; (E) is wrong. Similarly, the two were debating whether lying is wrong as a general rule, so arguing in general terms was logically sound; (C) is wrong as well.

46. **C** The fluid extracted from the snails is "colorless," not purple; the purple hue is ultimately produced after a lengthy fermentation process; (A) is wrong. The process by which Tyrian purple is made is foul-smelling, even when performed correctly; (B) is wrong. The fermentation process requires heat, but light will ruin the results; (D) and (E) are wrong as well.

47. **D** The second-to-last line of the passage states that purple was extremely expensive, so ordinary people couldn't afford it even though they desired it; (A) is wrong. The passage doesn't state anything to suggest whether the lower classes knew "their place" in society. Moreover, the author does state that common people *desired* purple items; (B) is wrong. The fact that the process of making Tyrian purple was both tedious and foul-smelling—(C) and (E)—doesn't mean that the lower classes would not wear purple if they could afford it. Again, since the common folk desired purple, they may well have considered it worth all the trouble. What is clear from the passage, however, is that purple was prohibitively expensive for all but an elite few. Little effort would be required to enforce the prohibition against wearing purple because hardly anyone could *afford* to wear it.

48. **C** The author states in paragraph 2 that James 1 believed in witches and ghosts, and that Shakespeare knew where his "bread was buttered." The clear implication is that Shakespeare included supernatural elements in *Macbeth* in order to curry favor with King James. Choice (A) is wrong because the fact that Shakespeare was brilliant does not mean that he didn't believe in the supernatural, especially at a time when such belief was the norm. Choice (B) is wrong because the fact that Banquo's ghost *could* be interpreted as a hallucination does not mean that Shakespeare believed that an alternative supernatural explanation was impossible. Choice (E) is wrong because the mere fact that the witch characters are one-dimensional does not in any way suggest that real witches don't exist (many human characters in plays are one-dimensional). The inclusion by Shakespeare of supernatural beings in his other works would tend to suggest that he did believe in these entities, so (D) is wrong.

49. **E** The passage states that one must "look beyond the stage directions" because "despite what these instructions seem to suggest," Shakespeare did not believe in ghosts or witches. It is reasonable to infer from these statements that the original stage directions had the ghost on stage. Choice (A) is wrong because there is nothing to suggest that modern audiences would prefer the ghost not be present, despite the fact that fewer people today believe in supernatural phenomena. They may simply wish to see a physical representation of a mythical being. Similarly, nothing in the passage suggests how well *Macbeth* was received by contemporary audiences—(B) is wrong—or by King James. The king may have disliked the play for reasons unrelated to its supernatural characters; (C) is also wrong. The passage implies that Shakespeare attempted to ingratiate himself with the king by including witches and ghosts in *Macbeth.* There is nothing to indicate, however, that Shakespeare was contemptuous of the King James because of his views; (D) is wrong as well.

50. **A** The author states that *Macbeth* contains witches, ghosts, and other "fantastic" elements that were taken seriously in the 17th century. The word is clearly being used here in the sense of "fanciful" or "imaginary," which strongly suggests that the author does not believe in these supernatural entities; (D) is wrong. The word is *not* being used in the informal sense of "great" or "wonderful"; choices (B) and (C) are wrong. There is no indication anywhere in the passage that the author dislikes King James 1; (E) is wrong as well.

SECTION II: TEST OF MATHEMATICS

1. **B** To calculate $\frac{3}{8}$ of 600, you can multiply by 3, and then divide by 8.

   $600 \times 3 = 1800$
   $1800 \div 8 = 225$

   Note: Estimate! You should notice that $\frac{3}{8}$ is less than $\frac{1}{2}$ (since $\frac{1}{2}$ is equal to $\frac{4}{8}$, and $\frac{3}{8}$ is less than $\frac{4}{8}$).

   The answer must be less than half of 600 (so, less than 300). Eliminate (D) and (E).

2. **D** Use the correct order of operations to solve this question. Multiply first, so $-58 + (26 \times 2) = -58 + 52$. Then add $-58 + 52 = -6$.

   Note: If you chose (E) −64, you probably did the addition step first, which is incorrect.

3. **B** To find the average, first find the sum: 220 + 350 + 170 + 280 + 310 = 1330. Then, divide the sum by 5 (the number of games):

   $\frac{1{,}300}{5} = 266$

   If you chose (E) 1330, be careful – that is the sum, not the average. Also, choice (C) 280 is the median, not the average.

4. **E** There are 24 hours in a day, and the puppy eats 1 cup every 8 hours. This means the puppy eats 3 cups of kibble per day ($\frac{24}{8} = 3$). In 7 days, the puppy eats 21 cups of kibble ($7 \times 3 = 21$).

5. **D** To find the percentage, first find the total number of days that Taylor's goal was met: 27 + 28 + 30 + 29 = 114.

   Next, find the total number of days in February through May: 28 + 31 + 30 + 31 = 120. Divide the two numbers: $114 \div 120 = 0.95$, or 95%.

6. **D** This is an estimation question, so don't calculate the exact answer. The answers appear to be rounded to the hundreds place; therefore, for the best estimate, round 879 to 900, then multiply by 3.

   $900 \times 3 = 2700$

   Note: If you rounded down to 800 instead, be aware that this violates rounding rules. Since the tens digit is 7, round the hundreds place up, not down.

7. **A** To measure the width of a dinner plate, the most appropriate unit (from the available choices) would be inches. Feet and yards are too large to accurately measure something small such as a plate. Ounces are not a unit for length, but rather weight. Teaspoons are a unit for volume.

8. **C** First, find the sum: $97 + 52 + 71 = 220$. Then, divide $220 \div 11 = 20$. Don't forget to ballpark! In this case, you could estimate the sum as $100 + 50 + 70$, which is also 220 (this is a coincidence). Then, you would know that the answer is close to 20 ($220 \div 11$) or 22 ($220 \div 10$). Eliminate (A) and (E).

9. **D** Note: "10% off" means that you need to *subtract* 10% from the original amount. To calculate 10% off of $12.89, first multiply $12.89 × 0.10 = $1.289. Then, subtract $12.89 – $1.289 = $11.601. Round to the nearest cent, for $11.60 (D).

   Eliminate (A), since this is the result of multiplying $12.89 × 0.10—without subtracting.

   Eliminate (E), since this is the result of *adding* 10% to the original amount. The discounted amount should be lower than the original. (Ballpark!)

10. **A** To find the scale of the diagram, divide the number of actual meters by the number of scaled units. $314 \div 6 \approx 52.333$, or 52.3 meters.

11. **A** This is an estimation question, so don't calculate the exact answer. The answers appear to be rounded to the hundred-thousands place. Therefore, for the best estimate, round 1,526,423 to 1,500,000, and round 493,497 to 500,000. The estimated sum is 2,000,000.

12. **C** *Percentile* is a ranking of students, from 1 to 99. If the percentile rank is 82, it means that she scored better than 82% of test takers. Choice (B) says the opposite—that Ryan scored lower than 82% of test takers. Eliminate (B).

    The *raw score* is the number of questions answered correctly. It is not necessarily a percentage. Eliminate (A).

    Since this is only one test, you cannot be certain that Ryan is meeting or exceeding the standards for her grade level. Eliminate (D).

    Stanine score is a ranking that corresponds to the normal curve. Ryan's score does not mean that she scored better than 7 out of 10 students. Eliminate (E).

13. **B** First, count the total units that Emanuel ran. Starting at point A, you have 3 + 2 + 1 + 2 + 4 + 2 = 14 total units. The question indicates that each unit represents $\frac{1}{2}$ mile, so that means Emanuel ran a total of 7 miles ($14 \times \frac{1}{2}$).

Next, calculate the money raised: 7 miles × \$120 = \$840.

Note: \$1680 (E) is what you might have chosen if you forgot to multiply the units by $\frac{1}{2}$ mile.

14. **E** If you add two inches to all sides of the photo, then the width is increased by 4 inches *and* the length is increased by 4 inches. The new dimensions are 8 inches (4 + 2 + 2) by 10 inches (6 + 2 + 2).

Note: You can eliminate (A) and (B), since they are both smaller than the original photo. (D) increases the length and width by 2 inches, instead of 4 inches.

It might help to sketch a diagram for this question.

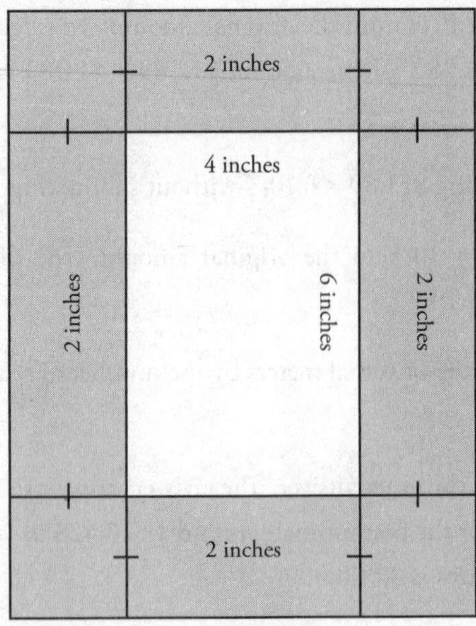

15. **D** Since Karen is ineligible to be selected, you need to remove her from *both* the Red Team and the total. In other words, if you are choosing randomly from a group without Karen, then you have 4 members on the Red Team, and 14 members total (4 + 6 + 4 = 14). Next, reduce the fraction.

$$\frac{4}{14} = \frac{2}{7}$$

Note: If you selected $\frac{1}{3}$ (A), this is equivalent to $\frac{5}{15}$, which means that you forgot to remove Karen from the group. Similarly, if you selected $\frac{5}{14}$ (C), you decreased the total, but not the Red Team. If you selected $\frac{4}{15}$ (E), you decreased the Red Team, but not the total.

16. **C** One way to solve this question is to convert the total hours to minutes. $9 \times 60 = 540$ minutes. Since Ethan can draw one character in 45 minutes, divide $\frac{540}{45} = 12$.

Note: You should eliminate (A), since it is too small. A drawing takes less than 1 hour, so you know Ethan can draw more than 9 characters in 9 hours.

17. **B** A financial loss is negative, and a *profit* is positive. Estimate –$6,750 as –$7,000, and $27,950 as $28,000. To find the difference, subtract the negative number, making it positive:

$28{,}000 - (-7{,}000) = 28{,}000 + 7{,}000$
$28{,}000 + 7{,}000 = 35{,}000$

Note: If you recognized that the difference would be larger than both numbers, then you could eliminate (A). Also, choice (E) is more than double $27,950, and can be eliminated.

18. **C** To find the total length of fencing, first multiply 65 inches × 30 panels = 1950 inches. You're not done yet! The answer choices are in feet, with remainders in inches. To convert the answer to feet, divide 1950 ÷ 12 = 162, remainder 6. The answer is 162 feet, 6 inches.

Note: If you obtained a decimal answer, you would have 162.5 feet, and you might have been tempted to choose (B). However, 0.5 feet is not the same as 5 inches. (5 tenths is not equal to 5 twelfths.) You might have also been tempted to choose (E), since 195 feet might look like 1950 inches.

19. **E** This problem might seem complicated at first, but don't forget to ballpark! Abby checks her progress after 45 minutes, so if her rate was 20 ferns per hour, she will have completed *less than* 20 ferns during this time. Therefore, she must have more than 30 ferns remaining. This only matches choice (E).

You can calculate the answer. However, before you set up a complicated proportion, think about how much time has passed. One hour is 60 minutes, so 45 minutes is simply $\frac{3}{4}$ of an hour. Therefore, she completed $\frac{3}{4}$ of her hourly rate: $20 \times \frac{3}{4} = 15$ ferns. Note that you aren't done yet, and (B) is a trap answer. You need to know how many ferns are remaining. $50 - 15 = 35$ ferns.

20. **E** To find the correct answer, it may be best to solve each equation for x and simplify. The original expression can be solved as follows:

$$5 = \frac{x}{100} \times 30$$

$$\frac{5}{30} = \frac{x}{100}$$

$$\frac{5 \times 100}{30} = x$$

$$\frac{500}{30} = x$$

$$\frac{50}{3} = x$$

The answer choices are solved with steps shown below. Only (E) matches the correct value for x.

(A)	(B)	(C)	(D)	(E)
$\frac{5}{x} = 100 \times 30$	$30 = \frac{x}{100} \times 5$	$0.05 = \frac{x}{30}$	$\frac{5 \times 30}{100} = x$	$\frac{5}{30} = \frac{x}{100}$
$5 = 100 \times 30 \times x$	$\frac{30}{5} = \frac{x}{100}$	$0.05 \times 30 = x$	$\frac{5 \times 3}{10} = x$	$\frac{5 \times 100}{30} = x$
$\frac{5}{100 \times 30} = x$	$\frac{100 \times 30}{5} = x$	$1.5 = x$	$\frac{15}{10} = x$	$\frac{500}{30} = x$
$\frac{5}{3000} = x$	$\frac{3000}{5} = x$	Eliminate (C).	Eliminate (D).	$\frac{50}{3} = x$
$\frac{1}{600} = x$	$600 = x$			Select (E).
Eliminate (A)	Eliminate (B).			

Note: You may be able to eliminate sooner if you compare the steps to the solution of the original equation.

Another method would be to plug in the value you found for x ($\frac{50}{3}$) into each of the answer choices.

21. **B** First, find 15% of \$60,000: $0.15 \times 60{,}000 = 9{,}000$. This is the amount of the increase, which you need to add to the original salary. \$60,000 + \$9,000 = \$69,000.

Note: You should eliminate (A), since it is a decrease, not an increase.

22. **A** Since Micah needs *each* of these ingredients to make pans of lasagna, you don't add them together. The pasta ingredient has the lowest amount—$2\frac{3}{4}$ pans. If he doesn't buy any more ingredients, then he can only make $2\frac{3}{4}$ pans of lasagna, no matter how much cheese and sauce he has.

Further, the question asks how many *full pans* Micah can make. You must eliminate (B)—Micah does not have enough ingredients for 3 full pans of pasta; it is less than this. He can only make 2 full pans.

23. **D** Each answer choice is a compound inequality, which is two inequalities combined. You can view each single inequality on its own, as shown below. Select the answer where both inequalities are true.

(A) $5\frac{2}{3} < 6\frac{1}{3}$ **and** $6\frac{1}{3} < 5\frac{1}{3}$. The first inequality is true, but the second is false.

(B) $6\frac{1}{3} < 5\frac{2}{3}$ **and** $5\frac{2}{3} < 5\frac{1}{3}$. Both inequalities are false.

(C) $5\frac{1}{3} < 6\frac{1}{3}$ **and** $6\frac{1}{3} < 5\frac{2}{3}$. The first inequality is true, but the second is false.

(D) $5\frac{1}{3} < 5\frac{2}{3}$ **and** $5\frac{2}{3} < 6\frac{1}{3}$. Both inequalities are **true**.

(E) $5\frac{2}{3} < 5\frac{1}{3}$ **and** $5\frac{1}{3} < 6\frac{1}{3}$. The first inequality is false, and only the second is true.

24. **C** Try using the Average Circle!

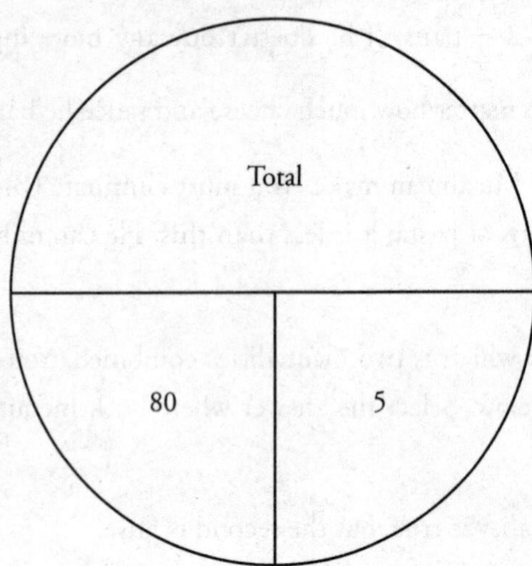

Since you're given the number of tests (5), and the average needed (80), it's a good idea to solve for the total before proceeding. You know that average = $\frac{\text{(total)}}{\text{(number)}}$, so $80 = \frac{\text{(total)}}{5}$. That means the total must equal 80×5, or 400.

You have four known exam scores, and one unknown. You can now use the Total to find the unknown value easily:

$400 = 72 + 84 + 93 + 86 + x$
$400 = 335 + x$
$400 - 335 = 65 = x$

If Phoenix scores 65% on his fifth exam, he will have an average of 80%.

25. **D** The correct answer must be greater than 23.984, and less than 27.135. Compare each answer choice with these two values.

(A) 22.405 is less than 23.984. Eliminate (A).
(B) 23.374 is less than 23.984. Eliminate (B).
(C) 23.937 is less than 23.984. Eliminate (C).
(D) 24.419 is greater than 23.984, and it is less than 27.135. Select (D).
(E) 28.248 is greater than 27.135. Eliminate (E).

Note: if you multiply each value by 1,000, then this clears the decimal points, and you can compare the numbers as integers. If you use this method, just be certain that you multiply each value by the *same* amount.

26. **A** To compare all these fractions, it's best to use a common denominator. The common denominator for $\frac{2}{5}$ and $\frac{5}{8}$ is 40, and this denominator works for the answer choices as well. So, use 40.

The original statement ($\frac{2}{5} < \square < \frac{5}{8}$) is equivalent to $\frac{16}{40} < \square < \frac{25}{40}$. Therefore, the correct answer choice must be between these two values.

(A) $\frac{1}{2} = \frac{20}{40}$. This is between $\frac{16}{40}$ and $\frac{25}{40}$.

(B) $\frac{2}{5} = \frac{16}{40}$. Eliminate (B). (Careful, $\frac{2}{5}$ is not *less than* $\frac{2}{5}$).

(C) $\frac{7}{8} = \frac{35}{40}$. Eliminate (C).

(D) $\frac{3}{10} = \frac{12}{40}$. Eliminate (D).

(E) $\frac{3}{4} = \frac{30}{40}$. Eliminate (E).

You can also use the Bowtie Method to compare these fractions. For example, with the correct answer (A), you have $\frac{2}{5} < \frac{1}{2}$ and $\frac{1}{2} < \frac{5}{8}$. Using the Bowtie Method, you can confirm each of these two inequalities separately.

27. **E** To find the average, first calculate the sum: \$467 + –\$165 + \$323 + \$575 = \$1200.

Divide by the number of weeks (4): \$1200 ÷ 4 = \$300.

Note: An average must always be *somewhere* between the highest and lowest amounts. You should eliminate (A), since it is too large.

28. **B** Read the problem carefully, and solve one step at a time. $\frac{3}{4}$ of the cartons were plain white paper, so calculate $512 \times \frac{3}{4} = 384$ cartons. Eliminate (E), since you aren't done yet.

The problem says that half of the *remaining* cartons were bright-colored paper, so first you need to know how many cartons were *not* plain white paper: 512 – 384 = 128. Eliminate (C).

Half of this number was bright-colored paper: 128 ÷ 2 = 64. Now, subtract 512 – 384 – 64 = 64. This is the number remaining after subtracting the plain white paper and bright-colored paper. Select (B).

Note: you split the 128 in half; that's why the number 64 appears twice.

29. **A** The best estimate would be \$15 × 3, or \$45. Note that the actual value would be a little less than this, since you rounded the numbers up, so you should eliminate all of the larger answers (B), (C), (D), and (E).

30. **E** One way to solve this question is to guess and check the answer choices. However, you can save some time if you think about the steps shown in the problem.

If you try 8 (A), then the original problem would be 48×27, and the first step would be to multiply the *ones* digits: $8 \times 7 = 56$. This tells you that the first step of the solution would end in 6; however, the first step shown has 301. Eliminate (A). Then, if you try (B), (C), and (D), you can eliminate these on the first step as well, for the same reasoning. Choice (E) gets you the steps and result shown.

Another approach is to think about the second step of the solution (showing 860). The zero is a placeholder, and so 86 is the result of multiplying $4\square \times 2$. Divide $86 \div 2 = 43$, so $4\square$ is 43. Check answer (E) to make sure it is correct.

31. **D** Use the Distributive Property. Each term is divisible by 10, so you can factor a 10 from each term, placing 10 outside the parentheses.

$(50 + 30 + 20 + 40a) = (5 \times 10 + 3 \times 10 + 2 \times 10 + 4a \times 10) = 10\,(5 + 3 + 2 + 4a)$

32. **C** Since Stefan did not win 10 games in the Tournament, he will not be able to participate in the championship (see second statement). This matches choice (C).

Since he will not participate in the Championship, eliminate (A). He must win the Championship in order to win the Grand Prize (see third statement).

If he participated in the Tournament, he must have passed the Qualifying Round (see first statement). Eliminate (B).

The question indicates Stefan won 8 games in the Tournament, so eliminate (D).

You aren't told how many games are in the Tournament, so you don't know exactly how many games Stefan lost. Eliminate (E).

33. **A** You can solve algebraically:

$2x - 4 + 3x = 31$

$5x - 4 = 31$ combine like terms

$5x = 35$ add 4 to both sides

$x = 7$

Backsolving is also a great way to solve this question. When you try the correct answer (7), you get:

$2(7) - 4 + 3(7) = 31$

$14 - 4 + 21 = 31$

$10 + 21 = 31$ Correct

34. **B** You might have started this question by calculating the total number of minutes to clean the 27 rooms. However, it's a bit simpler if you realize that he is cleaning 4 rooms per hour. ($15 \times 4 = 60$ minutes). Therefore, you can divide $27 \div 4 = 6.75$, for the total number of hours spent cleaning.

Now, you just need to know what time he finishes. If you notice that 6.75 is the same as $6\frac{3}{4}$, then you might realize that it is 6 hours and 45 minutes ($\frac{3}{4}$ of an hour = 45 minutes). If you weren't sure, you could do a proportion. Use the decimal part alone: $0.75 = \frac{x}{60}$, then $x = 45$. So 0.75 hours is 45 minutes.

Finally, starting at 11 a.m., count up 6 hours (5:00 p.m.) and add 45 minutes (5:45 p.m.)

35. **B** Initially, Emily makes $14 \times \$24 = \$336$ per week. After the price increase, she makes $14 \times \$26 = \$364$ per week. You should eliminate (D) and (E), since these are the two totals, and the problem is asking you to find the amount of the increase.

The increase is the difference between these two values. $\$364 - \$336 = \$28$.

36. **E** In the information provided, you are told how much paint was purchased, and how much of that paint was used on the first day. From this, you can determine how much paint remains after the first day. (You would use subtraction; however, you don't need to actually answer that question here).

The information does not tell you which type(s) of paint Jordan used, so you have to eliminate (A).

You are not told how much paint is actually needed—only what was purchased. Jordan might have purchased too much, or too little. Eliminate (B). Similarly, you do not know the square footage of the house (or even a usage rate that would allow you to calculate it), so eliminate (C). Finally, you have no information about the price of the paint, so you must eliminate (D).

37. **B** To compare the expressions, it may be best to simplify each one. To simplify the original expression, add the numbers in the numerator. This equals $\frac{3.43}{4}$, or $\frac{343}{400}$. The correct answer must match this value.

Choice (A) simplifies to $3.43 \div (\frac{1}{4})$, or 3.43×4. This is not the correct value.

Choice (B) simplifies to $\frac{343}{400}$, so it is the correct value.

Choice (C) simplifies to $100(3.43) \div 4$, or $343 \div 4$. This is not the correct value.

Choice (D) simplifies to $\frac{343}{25}$. This is not the correct value.

Choice (E) simplifies to $100(343) \div 4$, or $34{,}300 \div 4$. This is not the correct value.

38. **D** You'll need to add up the total number of Hamilton participants, and the total number of Desert School District participants. There are 98 participants from Hamilton School (18 + 23 + 31 + 26), and 479 from Desert School District (105 + 129 + 111 + 134).

Now, subtract 479 – 98 = 381.

39. **A** Calculate the total length of ribbon: 8 rows × 12 feet = 96 feet. The ribbon is priced per *yard*, so convert 96 feet to yards. $\frac{96 \text{ feet}}{x \text{ yards}} = \frac{3 \text{ feet}}{1 \text{ yard}}$, so to find the length in yards, you can divide 96 ÷ 3 = 32. Finally, the price is \$0.49 per yard. You can estimate this as \$0.50, or half a dollar.

32 × \$0.50 = \$16. (Notice that the question asks for the *closest* answer).

40. **A** You don't know exactly how the two homes are positioned. However, the maximum distance between the two homes is a straight line, with the park in between them.

This means that the homes are at *most* 5.5 miles (2 + 3.5) apart. This matches choice (A). Eliminate (E), because it says at *least* 5.5 miles.

Also, the minimum distance between the two homes is a straight line, with the park at one end.

This means the homes are at *least* 1.5 miles (3.5 – 2) apart. Eliminate (B), because it says *less* than 1.5 miles, and (C), because it says *exactly* 1.5 miles.

You should also eliminate (E), because although it is in the correct range of possible values, you have no way of knowing the exact distance between the homes.

41. **C** You know the recipe, and you know how many guests Jayda plans to serve. However, you don't know how many servings she can expect to produce from the recipe. This is the information most needed to solve the problem.

Choice (A) doesn't solve the problem, because the size of the "bowls" isn't enough to tell you how much chili to make. Additionally, the recipe is given in pounds, not volume units.

The problem is unrelated to price, so eliminate (B).

The size of a cooking pot is not sufficient to tell you how much chili she needs for a party, so eliminate (D).

You can already determine the total pounds of ingredients used in the recipe, so eliminate (E). (These kinds of problems are about information that is missing). Additionally, the total for the recipe is not enough to tell you how much she needs for a party.

42. **A** In a pie chart, percentages add up to 100%. Add up the known values: 24% + 32% + 16% + 19% = 91%. The remaining amount is 9% (100% – 91%).

Remember to ballpark! The pie slice seems smaller than 16% (the next smallest value shown). Eliminate (D) and (E).

43. **A** Try Backsolving! First, note that Saturday's value will be larger than Wednesday's, since the problem states that Logan ran more on Saturday. Starting with (C): If Logan ran for 62 minutes on Saturday, then he ran for 26 minutes on Wednesday. (Subtract 62 – 36 = 26). The problem indicates that he ran for 160 total minutes, so this answer is too small (62 + 26 = 88).

When you get to answer (A), you'll find that Logan ran for 98 minutes on Saturday and 62 minutes on Wednesday (98 – 36 = 62). Note that Wednesday's value was a trap answer, (C). Add 98 + 62 = 160, which matches the total indicated in the problem.

44. **E** Compare the increases for each company. First, eliminate (A) and (D), since these companies showed a decrease, not an increase. Company E had the largest increase (4.75 – 1.5 = 3.25), followed by Company B (4.5 – 2 = 2.5), then Company C (5.25 – 3.75 = 1.5). Select (E).

45. **B** In the x column, the values are increasing by 2. In the y column, it seems that the numbers are increasing by 4, based on the first two values. Try 16, and see if the pattern makes sense: 8, 12, 16, 20. Each y value increases by 4. Select (B).

Don't forget to ballpark! The values are increasing in both x and y. Therefore, the missing value should be between 12 and 20. Eliminate (D) and (E).

46. **D** The information indicates the number of packages that Ariana sealed, as well as her starting time. However, you do not know how much total time she spent working. If you knew the time that her shift ended, this would be sufficient to solve the problem.

Choice (A) would be sufficient to give her work rate for the time she spent before lunch. However, this might be a different rate than for the rest of the day. Eliminate (A).

Eliminate (B) and (C), because neither is related to Ariana's individual rate of work.

Choice (E) seems a bit relevant to her work rate; however, this does not tell you how long it takes her to seal a package, or how much time she worked for the whole day. Eliminate (E).

47. **E** $5(3y - 4) = 115$
$(3y - 4) = 23$
$3y = 27$
$y = 9$

You can also solve this question by backsolving. Try 7 (C) first.

$5(21 - 4) = 115$
$5(17) = 115$
$85 = 115$ FALSE.

Try a larger number next. Choice (E) results in 115 = 115, so it is the correct answer.

48. **E** To find the average rate for all the hours worked, you must find the *total* number of hours, and the *total* amount paid. Use the Average Circle!

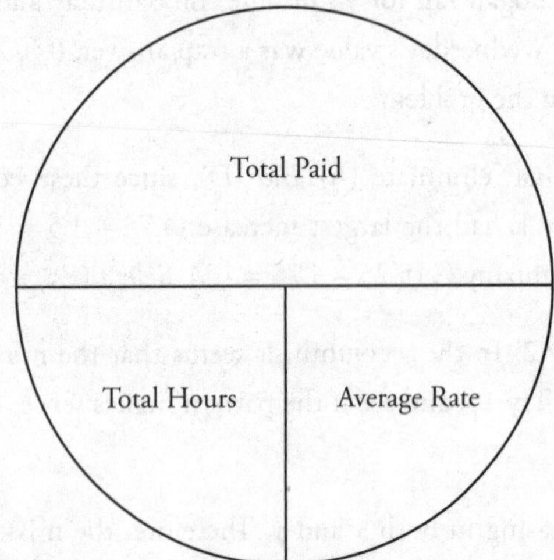

To find the total hours, add the hours for each job: 5 + 25 + 10. To find the total amount paid, you must calculate ($16 × 5) + ($20 × 25) + ($12 × 10). (Remember to round each rate to the nearest dollar). The total amount paid is $80 + $500 + $120, or $700.

The average hourly rate is $\frac{\$700}{40} = \$17.50$.

Note: If you chose (A), this was a trap answer (simply the average of $16, $20, and $12). Since the number of hours was different for each job, you must calculate fully as shown above.

49. **C** You know how to calculate the probability of two events happening in a row: you multiply the probabilities together. This question seems complicated, but think about it this way: what is the probability that Phoebe *loses* two tries in a row? The probability that she loses a game is 80%, or 0.8. (This is 100% – 20%). The probability that she loses both tries is 0.8 × 0.8, or 0.64.

The probability that she wins *at least once* is same as the probability of *not losing both tries.* So, you subtract 1.0 – 0.64 = 0.36, or 36%.

Note: You should eliminate (A) and (B). Since she plays twice, the probability of winning at least once should be higher than 20%.

50. **C** Amir drives 36 miles per day, for 5 days. $36 \times 5 = 180$ total miles. His car uses one gallon of gas for every 24 miles. $180 \div 24 = 7.5$ total gallons of gas.

The gas costs \$3.80 per gallon. $\$3.80 \times 7.5 = \$28.50$.

Remember to ballpark! He uses a little more than 1 gallon of gas per day. (If his trip were 24 miles, he would use 1 gallon of gas, but it's a little longer than that). Estimate $\$4 \times 5$ days, or around \$20. The cost should be a little higher than \$20, so eliminate (A) and (B). Also, (D) and (E) are probably too high.

SECTION III: TEST OF WRITING

Topic 1

Eleanor Roosevelt once observed, "In the long run, we shape our lives, and we shape ourselves……and the choices we make are ultimately our own responsibility." In an essay to be read by an audience of educated adults, state whether you agree or disagree with this viewpoint. Support your position with logical arguments and specific examples.

Sample Essay #1: Overall Score = 4 (Pass)

"In the long run, we shape our lives, and we shape ourselves …. and the choices we make are ultimately our own responsibility." This profound observation by Eleanor Roosevelt is undoubtedly true. Each of us is responsible for the kind of person we become, and, no matter what obstacles or adversity we have to face, we can all choose our individual destinies. It's true that we can't change everything and that some unfortunate circumstances are beyond our control. However, we can choose to do the very best with what we have and, in taking responsibility for our lives, shape ourselves into the kind of people we want to be.

Bethany Hamilton was a promising surfer whose arm was tragically bitten off by a shark. Instead of feeling sorry for herself and adopting a victim mentality, so chose to overcome this huge obstacle and learn to surf with one arm. She couldn't change what happened to her, but she took responsibility for her future and refused to give up her passion. Bethany beat the odds and became a successful professional surfer despite her disability, even winning prestigious competitions! She chose to do her very best with a horrifying circumstance that was thrust upon her by chance—an experience that would have devastated many young athletes. In choosing to fight for what she wanted, she shaped the rest of her life—and she shaped herself into an even greater champion than she was before.

Like Bethany Hamilton, Christopher Reeve (the actor who played Superman in the movies) suffered a life-changing injury: he was thrown from a horse and became a quadriplegic. Unlike Bethany, he couldn't resume his former activities because he was physically incapacitated, and he never realized his dream of regaining sensation. It would have been very easy to view him as a helpless victim of terrible circumstances. Nonetheless, he promoted critical stem cell research and founded centers to help people with spinal cord injuries and other disabilities. Christopher never walked again, but he helped many other injured people to walk through his efforts. He even continued to act (albeit in limited roles) and inspired others never to give up their dreams. Christopher Reeve chose to be the brave "Superman" everyone saw him as, even though he couldn't get out of his wheelchair, and he shaped himself into a real-life American hero.

Even ordinary people, who lack the fame and resources to influence the general public, can overcome major obstacles and aspire to greatness. When I volunteered at the hospital there was a woman named "Sue," a former teacher, who was bedbound from injuries she sustained in a car accident that wasn't her fault. While Sue could have chosen to live her life feeling bitter and being idle, she chose to spend her time supporting and advising the other patients and their families. She told me that "life is what you make it" and that, even though she couldn't teach in a classroom anymore, she would "teach" others to help themselves. Sue may not have chosen her fate as an accident victim, but she never blamed anyone and took responsibility for who she ultimately became. In doing so she shaped herself into a person as remarkable as any celebrity or famous athlete.

In conclusion, we do shape our lives and ourselves: no matter what fate has in store for us, we are ultimately responsible for who we become. We cannot always control what happens to us or "shape" every aspect of our lives, but we can choose to make the best of whatever good we have and become exceptional individuals. Whether famous heroes or champions like Christopher Reeve and Bethany Hamilton, or ordinary people like Sue, we can all overcome misfortune and become the kind of person we want to be.

Sample Essay #2: Overall Score = 3 (Marginal Pass)

I agree with the Eleanor Roosevelt quote. Sometimes we can't control what happens to us, but we can control how we respond to it. No matter what happens to us, we can still make choices and through this process we shape our own lives and our own selves.

Bethany Hamilton was a surfer whose arm was bitten off by a shark. She could have chosen to give up surfing (many people would say its impossible to surf competitively with only one arm), but she chose to work hard to remain a professional surfer. Unlike many people she took responsibility for her future and chose her own destiny, even though the odds were against her. Bethany even won major surfing competitions despite her injury and has become a surfing icon. A similar circumstance involved Christopher Reeve, the actor who played Superman. He was thrown from a horse a became a quadriplegic, but he inspired and helped millions of people with similar injuries. He never acheived his dream of a full recovery, but he never stopped fighting for himself and for others. Unlike Bethany, Christopher couldn't continue to do much of what he used to do (like ride horses or play Superman). However, he refused to give up and did the best he could with what he had. He continued to act in limited roles, worked in films behind the camera, and never stopped trying to walk. He never walked again, but he helped others to walk by promoting research for spinal chord injuries. Christopher Reeve took responsibility for his choices in life and shaped himself into a true real life hero.

Most people arent famous or rich and can't help or inspire millions of people. However, they can still shape their lives and themselves and become the people they want to be. Instead of being bitter and feeling like victims of fate, many sick or disabled people keep a good attitude and inspire others to do that as well. Maybe they can't run a marathon but they can bravely fight for their goals of walking down the hospital hallway. They can be a sunny spot in the lives of others by keeping a cheerful demeanor and being a kind person. They can choose who they want to be despite what has happened beyond their control.

In conclusion the Eleanor Roosevelt quote is very true. We shape our lives and ourselves and the choices we make are ultimately our own responsibility. We can't control everything that happens to us, but we can choose the type of person we want to be and do the very best with what we have. Nobody should consider themselves a victim of fate.

Sample Essay #3: Overall Score = 2 (Marginal Fail)

I totally agree with Eleanor Roosevelts quote about shaping our lives and our choices being our own responsibility! They say life is what you make it. Adversity is no excuse for failure and becoming a bad person. Millions of people overcome hardships and problems much worse than what you or me have to deal with. These people still become awesome people through making good choices. Christopher Reeve, Bethany Hamilton, and just ordinary sick people can be an example to all of us.

Bethany Hamilton was a surfer who tragically got her arm bitten off by a shark. Instead of just laying down and feeling sorry for herself she continued to be a professional surfer and even win competitions! She couldnt shape her life by avoiding her injury but shaped it by making good choices and not giving up. If more people were like Bethany than the world would be a much better place. She is a true role model!

Christopher Reeve was the famous actor who played Superman. He was thrown from a horse and was paralyzed. He swore he would walk again 1 day but he didnt. So he couldnt shape his life in terms of still being Superman or even an actor who got lots of roles, but he shaped it by becoming an activist and helping people with spinal cord injuries. He made good choices and shaped his life instead of just freaking out because he was paralyzed. Some people cant really help millions of other people because their not famous actors like Christopher Reeve. Ive known sick people who really had no hope of getting better but helped others in their lives through being inspirational and just good people in general with a positive attitude. Like Christopher Reeve they made good choices.

In conclusion I agree that we shape our lives and ourselves through our choices. If we make good choices we can overcome the obstacles that are thrown at us. If we could all make good choices the world would be a much better place.

Sample Essay #4: Overall Score = 1 (Fail)

Sometimes people can shape there own life through hard work and guts, like people who were in bad accidents but still manage to accomplish amazing things. Like that surfer girl who got her arm bit off by a shark and Christopher Reeves the actor who played Superman. Christopher Reeves worked hard too become a rich and famous movie star until he fell off of a horse and was in a wheel chair.

He swore he would walk again (TBH that wasnt gonna happen) but at least he tried and inspired a lot of people to do better to. If something bad happens to you like getting your arm bit off or winding up on a respirator you can either lay down and take it or chose to fight back. They chose to fight back and alot of people copied them and chose to fight back against there own hardships to. Life is about choices and you should shape your own life (YOLO!), although sometimes your limited by what happens to you if its bad enough.

You can only go so far in life if your a one armed surfer or an actor in a wheel chair. Christopher Reeve couldnt really get alot of roles but he still tried and thats what matters. Life is what you make it.

Topic 2

> While we often seek to avoid disagreements with others, conflict can lead to positive change when we alter our viewpoints, opinions, or behavior for the better. In an essay written for an audience of educated adults, describe an instance wherein having a disagreement with someone caused you to change in a positive way. With whom did you disagree and about what? How did your views, opinions, or behavior change as a result? Why do you consider this change a positive one?

Sample Essay #1: Overall Score = 4 (Pass)

The worst conflict that I ever had with my parents turned out to be just what I needed to get my life on track. During the summer of my freshman year of college I decided to drop out of school and pursue my dream of becoming a Hollywood actor. My parents were horrified at the idea and did everything they could do to persuade me to change my course. The ensuing conflict was intense, but it definitely changed my life for the better. The disharmony between my parents and me ultimately turned me into the mature young adult that I am today.

Ever since we were in the third grade together my best friend Joe and I would talk about becoming Hollywood stars. We would imagine ourselves on the set of some Hollywood blockbuster or strutting down the red carpet at the Academy Awards ceremony. Joe never went to college because he decided to pursue his acting goals straight out of high school. I admit I was envious. There I was in school having to sit through excruciatingly boring lectures about biology or classic literature—subjects that meant nothing to me and, I truly believed, had no relevance to my life. All I cared about was Hollywood, so I decided to quit school and join Joe in Los Angeles. I thought I was invincible: I never considered what I would do if I didn't find success as an actor. All I could think about was what I wanted for my life right then - at age eighteen.

My parents were horrified when I told them of my plans to leave college. They tried to persuade me not to go by emphasizing how important it was to my future to have a good education. When that approach didn't work, they brought former actors to our house to tell me about their disheartening experiences trying to find work in Hollywood. My parents believed in always making responsible decisions, even if doing so doesn't always get you what you want right at that moment. They didn't want me to ruin my future chasing some Hollywood pipe dream.

Eventually I realized that my parents were right. After many weeks of anger and frustration on both sides, I finally stopped arguing and started listening. I thought about where I would be, with no education and no skills, if my acting career didn't work out. The failed actors that I spoke with were talented artists who just couldn't seem to get a break in Hollywood—and that really concerned me. I came to understand that my parents were so angry with me because they knew I was acting foolishly. I decided to stay in school for another year—and then another year—and then another. Now I just completed my coursework (with honors!) and my college graduation ceremony is next week.

The conflict that I had with my parents over college was a watershed moment that changed my life for the better. After that semester I paid more attention to my schoolwork (and discovered that I actually enjoyed some classic literature after all)! Prior to that time everything seemed boring compared to my future as a Hollywood star—which I came to realize was just a childhood fantasy. I learned that I needed to plan a realistic future for myself, and that involved receiving a well-rounded education. Now I have a college degree and plan to become a teacher. (Unfortunately Joe never found fame or fortune in Hollywood; he's working at a gas station for minimum wage.) When I think about where my life would be now if I had quit school in search of Hollywood glory, I am thankful for the conflict that I had with my parents in the summer of my freshman year.

Sample Essay #2: Overall Score = 3 (Marginal Pass)

I've always dreamed of being a Hollywood star. This dream caused a lot of conflict between my parents and I during my freshman year of college. I wanted to quit school and try to make it in L.A. as an actor. They believed in the importance of a good education and wanted me to stay in school and earn my degree. We had very different views on the subject, but they convinced me to change my opinion and my behavior for the better.

During my freshman year I realized that I didn't like college. All I could think about was going to California to live with my best friend Joe, he was trying to make it in Hollywood. We thought that it would take a little work, but we'd make it eventually and be walking down the red carpet with the A list stars. We believed that we had to become successful while we were still young because otherwise we would be too old to be Hollywood heartthrobs. I didn't care about an education—whats a degree from a local college when I could be making millions of dollars for a single movie? I had packed my things and was ready to join Joe in L.A. the following week.

My parents were extremely upset that I was leaving. They did everything to try to get me to stay. They even introduced me to people who had tried to make it in Hollywood for years and years and failed. These people were good actors who went to hundreds of auditions and never got famous (they never even got any decent roles!) Now those poor actors are stuck in dead end jobs because they never pursued education. My parents and I fought hard about it but eventually I realized they were right and stayed in school.

I realize now that Hollywood was an adolescent fantasy and that education is the most important thing you can do for yourself. All that conflict with my parents was unpleasant, but Im glad they did what they did. I would advise anybody who is thinking of quitting school to become an actor to stop fantasizing and deal with the reality of life. Education and planning for your future is whats important. Dont wind up like all those poor and unemployed people who chased fame and have nothing to show for it but shattered dreams.

Sample Essay #3: Overall Score = 2 (Marginal Fail)

When I was in my freshman year my parents and me had conflict. They wanted one thing for my life and I wanted something else. They thought I should stay in college my first year. I thought me and my friend joe should try to make it big in Hollywood while were still young enough. My view was that being a famous actor was the most important thing and that I needed to take my shot. Their view was that that's not going to happen and I would wind up with no degree and no future. Me and my parents had disagreeing opinions because they wanted one thing and I wanted another thing for my life and they won out. Im glad because it changed my views, opinions, and behavior positively for the better.

Sometimes people have disagreements, its part of life. Sometimes you listen to the other person and you realize that their right. My parents and me fought alot during my freshman year because I wanted to quit school and try to make it in Hollywood with joe. Now I realize seriously that my parents knew what they were talking about. I decided to listen to my parents and stay in college and I'm so glad I did! BTW, Joe never made it in Hollywood and now he has no education and no perspective job. If I hadnt of had conflict with my parents I would probably be pumping gas along side joe right now instead of ordering my cap and gown (lol). I listened to my parents opinion because they never steered me wrong and because of the conflict we had everything turned out ok for me.

This was a positive change for me because I changed my views and opinions about the value of a good education and realized that stardom as an actor is just a pipe dream! Now I am going to graduate college and become a teacher not an actor and have a good job. That is a positive change!

Sample Essay #4: Overall Score = 1 (Fail)

Its hard to resist the lights of Hollywood their pretty brite. Me and my friend Joe took acting class together in high school, we would dream about becoming big Hollywood star's together. I wanted to make it big time as an actor but that meant I couldnt finish college so I stayed. We would talk about walking the red carpet like johnny depp and ryan gosling and winning oscar's. Now joe is still pumping gas after 3 years in LA!!! and he cant even get a job as an extra half the time. The last acting job he got was a tuna fish commersial 3 years ago (lol)! Me on the other hand, I managed to get a pretty decent GPA and Im now in my senior year. I changed my opinion positively and now my future is truly brite.

The Princeton Review®

Completely darken bubbles with a No. 2 pencil. If you make a mistake, be sure to erase mark completely. Erase all stray marks.

1.

YOUR NAME: ______________________________ (Print) Last First M.I.

SIGNATURE: ______________________________ DATE: ___/___/___

HOME ADDRESS: ______________________________ (Print) Number and Street

______________________________ City State Zip Code

PHONE NO.: ______________________________ (Print)

IMPORTANT: Please fill in these boxes exactly as shown on the back cover of your test book.

2. TEST FORM

3. TEST CODE

0	A	J	0	0
1	B	K	1	1
2	C	L	2	2
3	D	M	3	3
4	E	N	4	4
5	F	O	5	5
6	G	P	6	6
7	H	Q	7	7
8	I	R	8	8
9			9	9

4. REGISTRATION NUMBER

0	0	0	0	0	0
1	1	1	1	1	1
2	2	2	2	2	2
3	3	3	3	3	3
4	4	4	4	4	4
5	5	5	5	5	5
6	6	6	6	6	6
7	7	7	7	7	7
8	8	8	8	8	8
9	9	9	9	9	9

5. YOUR NAME

First 4 letters of last name				FIRST INIT	MID INIT
A	A	A	A	A	A
B	B	B	B	B	B
C	C	C	C	C	C
D	D	D	D	D	D
E	E	E	E	E	E
F	F	F	F	F	F
G	G	G	G	G	G
H	H	H	H	H	H
I	I	I	I	I	I
J	J	J	J	J	J
K	K	K	K	K	K
L	L	L	L	L	L
M	M	M	M	M	M
N	N	N	N	N	N
O	O	O	O	O	O
P	P	P	P	P	P
Q	Q	Q	Q	Q	Q
R	R	R	R	R	R
S	S	S	S	S	S
T	T	T	T	T	T
U	U	U	U	U	U
V	V	V	V	V	V
W	W	W	W	W	W
X	X	X	X	X	X
Y	Y	Y	Y	Y	Y
Z	Z	Z	Z	Z	Z

6. DATE OF BIRTH

Month	Day		Year	
JAN				
FEB	0	0	0	0
MAR	1	1	1	1
APR	2	2	2	2
MAY	3	3	3	3
JUN		4	4	4
JUL		5	5	5
AUG		6	6	6
SEP		7	7	7
OCT		8	8	8
NOV		9	9	9
DEC				

7. SEX

MALE

FEMALE

The Princeton Review®

Test 1 Start with number 1 for each new section.
If a section has fewer questions than answer spaces, leave the extra answer spaces blank.

Section I—Reading

1. A B C D E
2. A B C D E
3. A B C D E
4. A B C D E
5. A B C D E
6. A B C D E
7. A B C D E
8. A B C D E
9. A B C D E
10. A B C D E
11. A B C D E
12. A B C D E
13. A B C D E
14. A B C D E
15. A B C D E
16. A B C D E
17. A B C D E
18. A B C D E
19. A B C D E
20. A B C D E
21. A B C D E
22. A B C D E
23. A B C D E
24. A B C D E
25. A B C D E
26. A B C D E
27. A B C D E
28. A B C D E
29. A B C D E
30. A B C D E
31. A B C D E
32. A B C D E
33. A B C D E
34. A B C D E
35. A B C D E
36. A B C D E
37. A B C D E
38. A B C D E
39. A B C D E
40. A B C D E
41. A B C D E
42. A B C D E
43. A B C D E
44. A B C D E
45. A B C D E
46. A B C D E
47. A B C D E
48. A B C D E
49. A B C D E
50. A B C D E

Section II—Mathematics

1. A B C D E
2. A B C D E
3. A B C D E
4. A B C D E
5. A B C D E
6. A B C D E
7. A B C D E
8. A B C D E
9. A B C D E
10. A B C D E
11. A B C D E
12. A B C D E
13. A B C D E
14. A B C D E
15. A B C D E
16. A B C D E
17. A B C D E
18. A B C D E
19. A B C D E
20. A B C D E
21. A B C D E
22. A B C D E
23. A B C D E
24. A B C D E
25. A B C D E
26. A B C D E
27. A B C D E
28. A B C D E
29. A B C D E
30. A B C D E
31. A B C D E
32. A B C D E
33. A B C D E
34. A B C D E
35. A B C D E
36. A B C D E
37. A B C D E
38. A B C D E
39. A B C D E
40. A B C D E
41. A B C D E
42. A B C D E
43. A B C D E
44. A B C D E
45. A B C D E
46. A B C D E
47. A B C D E
48. A B C D E
49. A B C D E
50. A B C D E

The Princeton Review®

Completely darken bubbles with a No. 2 pencil. If you make a mistake, be sure to erase mark completely. Erase all stray marks.

1.

YOUR NAME: ______________________ (Print) Last / First / M.I.

SIGNATURE: ______________________ DATE: ___/___/___

HOME ADDRESS: ______________________ (Print) Number and Street

______________________ City / State / Zip Code

PHONE NO.: ______________________ (Print)

IMPORTANT: Please fill in these boxes exactly as shown on the back cover of your test book.

2. TEST FORM

3. TEST CODE

0	A	J	0	0
1	B	K	1	1
2	C	L	2	2
3	D	M	3	3
4	E	N	4	4
5	F	O	5	5
6	G	P	6	6
7	H	Q	7	7
8	I	R	8	8
9			9	9

4. REGISTRATION NUMBER

0	0	0	0	0	0
1	1	1	1	1	1
2	2	2	2	2	2
3	3	3	3	3	3
4	4	4	4	4	4
5	5	5	5	5	5
6	6	6	6	6	6
7	7	7	7	7	7
8	8	8	8	8	8
9	9	9	9	9	9

5. YOUR NAME

First 4 letters of last name | FIRST INIT | MID INIT

A B C D E F G H I J K L M N O P Q R S T U V W X Y Z (in each column)

6. DATE OF BIRTH

Month	Day		Year	
JAN				
FEB	0	0	0	0
MAR	1	1	1	1
APR	2	2	2	2
MAY	3	3	3	3
JUN		4	4	4
JUL		5	5	5
AUG		6	6	6
SEP		7	7	7
OCT		8	8	8
NOV		9	9	9
DEC				

7. SEX

MALE

FEMALE

The Princeton Review®

Test 2 Start with number 1 for each new section.
If a section has fewer questions than answer spaces, leave the extra answer spaces blank.

Section I—Reading

1.	A	B	C	D	E	26.	A	B	C	D	E
2.	A	B	C	D	E	27.	A	B	C	D	E
3.	A	B	C	D	E	28.	A	B	C	D	E
4.	A	B	C	D	E	29.	A	B	C	D	E
5.	A	B	C	D	E	30.	A	B	C	D	E
6.	A	B	C	D	E	31.	A	B	C	D	E
7.	A	B	C	D	E	32.	A	B	C	D	E
8.	A	B	C	D	E	33.	A	B	C	D	E
9.	A	B	C	D	E	34.	A	B	C	D	E
10.	A	B	C	D	E	35.	A	B	C	D	E
11.	A	B	C	D	E	36.	A	B	C	D	E
12.	A	B	C	D	E	37.	A	B	C	D	E
13.	A	B	C	D	E	38.	A	B	C	D	E
14.	A	B	C	D	E	39.	A	B	C	D	E
15.	A	B	C	D	E	40.	A	B	C	D	E
16.	A	B	C	D	E	41.	A	B	C	D	E
17.	A	B	C	D	E	42.	A	B	C	D	E
18.	A	B	C	D	E	43.	A	B	C	D	E
19.	A	B	C	D	E	44.	A	B	C	D	E
20.	A	B	C	D	E	45.	A	B	C	D	E
21.	A	B	C	D	E	46.	A	B	C	D	E
22.	A	B	C	D	E	47.	A	B	C	D	E
23.	A	B	C	D	E	48.	A	B	C	D	E
24.	A	B	C	D	E	49.	A	B	C	D	E
25.	A	B	C	D	E	50.	A	B	C	D	E

Section II—Mathematics

1.	A	B	C	D	E	26.	A	B	C	D	E
2.	A	B	C	D	E	27.	A	B	C	D	E
3.	A	B	C	D	E	28.	A	B	C	D	E
4.	A	B	C	D	E	29.	A	B	C	D	E
5.	A	B	C	D	E	30.	A	B	C	D	E
6.	A	B	C	D	E	31.	A	B	C	D	E
7.	A	B	C	D	E	32.	A	B	C	D	E
8.	A	B	C	D	E	33.	A	B	C	D	E
9.	A	B	C	D	E	34.	A	B	C	D	E
10.	A	B	C	D	E	35.	A	B	C	D	E
11.	A	B	C	D	E	36.	A	B	C	D	E
12.	A	B	C	D	E	37.	A	B	C	D	E
13.	A	B	C	D	E	38.	A	B	C	D	E
14.	A	B	C	D	E	39.	A	B	C	D	E
15.	A	B	C	D	E	40.	A	B	C	D	E
16.	A	B	C	D	E	41.	A	B	C	D	E
17.	A	B	C	D	E	42.	A	B	C	D	E
18.	A	B	C	D	E	43.	A	B	C	D	E
19.	A	B	C	D	E	44.	A	B	C	D	E
20.	A	B	C	D	E	45.	A	B	C	D	E
21.	A	B	C	D	E	46.	A	B	C	D	E
22.	A	B	C	D	E	47.	A	B	C	D	E
23.	A	B	C	D	E	48.	A	B	C	D	E
24.	A	B	C	D	E	49.	A	B	C	D	E
25.	A	B	C	D	E	50.	A	B	C	D	E

Completely darken bubbles with a No. 2 pencil. If you make a mistake, be sure to erase mark completely. Erase all stray marks.

1.

YOUR NAME: ______________________________ (Print) Last / First / M.I.

SIGNATURE: ______________________________ DATE: ___/___/___

HOME ADDRESS: ______________________________ (Print) Number and Street

______________________________ City / State / Zip Code

PHONE NO.: ______________________________ (Print)

IMPORTANT: Please fill in these boxes exactly as shown on the back cover of your test book.

2. TEST FORM

3. TEST CODE

0	A	J	0	0
1	B	K	1	1
2	C	L	2	2
3	D	M	3	3
4	E	N	4	4
5	F	O	5	5
6	G	P	6	6
7	H	Q	7	7
8	I	R	8	8
9			9	9

4. REGISTRATION NUMBER

0	0	0	0	0	0
1	1	1	1	1	1
2	2	2	2	2	2
3	3	3	3	3	3
4	4	4	4	4	4
5	5	5	5	5	5
6	6	6	6	6	6
7	7	7	7	7	7
8	8	8	8	8	8
9	9	9	9	9	9

5. YOUR NAME

First 4 letters of last name					FIRST INIT	MID INIT
A	A	A	A		A	A
B	B	B	B		B	B
C	C	C	C		C	C
D	D	D	D		D	D
E	E	E	E		E	E
F	F	F	F		F	F
G	G	G	G		G	G
H	H	H	H		H	H
I	I	I	I		I	I
J	J	J	J		J	J
K	K	K	K		K	K
L	L	L	L		L	L
M	M	M	M		M	M
N	N	N	N		N	N
O	O	O	O		O	O
P	P	P	P		P	P
Q	Q	Q	Q		Q	Q
R	R	R	R		R	R
S	S	S	S		S	S
T	T	T	T		T	T
U	U	U	U		U	U
V	V	V	V		V	V
W	W	W	W		W	W
X	X	X	X		X	X
Y	Y	Y	Y		Y	Y
Z	Z	Z	Z		Z	Z

6. DATE OF BIRTH

Month	Day		Year	
JAN				
FEB	0	0	0	0
MAR	1	1	1	1
APR	2	2	2	2
MAY	3	3	3	3
JUN		4	4	4
JUL		5	5	5
AUG		6	6	6
SEP		7	7	7
OCT		8	8	8
NOV		9	9	9
DEC				

7. SEX

MALE

FEMALE

The Princeton Review®

Test 3

Start with number 1 for each new section.
If a section has fewer questions than answer spaces, leave the extra answer spaces blank.

Section I—Reading

1. A B C D E
2. A B C D E
3. A B C D E
4. A B C D E
5. A B C D E
6. A B C D E
7. A B C D E
8. A B C D E
9. A B C D E
10. A B C D E
11. A B C D E
12. A B C D E
13. A B C D E
14. A B C D E
15. A B C D E
16. A B C D E
17. A B C D E
18. A B C D E
19. A B C D E
20. A B C D E
21. A B C D E
22. A B C D E
23. A B C D E
24. A B C D E
25. A B C D E
26. A B C D E
27. A B C D E
28. A B C D E
29. A B C D E
30. A B C D E
31. A B C D E
32. A B C D E
33. A B C D E
34. A B C D E
35. A B C D E
36. A B C D E
37. A B C D E
38. A B C D E
39. A B C D E
40. A B C D E
41. A B C D E
42. A B C D E
43. A B C D E
44. A B C D E
45. A B C D E
46. A B C D E
47. A B C D E
48. A B C D E
49. A B C D E
50. A B C D E

Section II—Mathematics

1. A B C D E
2. A B C D E
3. A B C D E
4. A B C D E
5. A B C D E
6. A B C D E
7. A B C D E
8. A B C D E
9. A B C D E
10. A B C D E
11. A B C D E
12. A B C D E
13. A B C D E
14. A B C D E
15. A B C D E
16. A B C D E
17. A B C D E
18. A B C D E
19. A B C D E
20. A B C D E
21. A B C D E
22. A B C D E
23. A B C D E
24. A B C D E
25. A B C D E
26. A B C D E
27. A B C D E
28. A B C D E
29. A B C D E
30. A B C D E
31. A B C D E
32. A B C D E
33. A B C D E
34. A B C D E
35. A B C D E
36. A B C D E
37. A B C D E
38. A B C D E
39. A B C D E
40. A B C D E
41. A B C D E
42. A B C D E
43. A B C D E
44. A B C D E
45. A B C D E
46. A B C D E
47. A B C D E
48. A B C D E
49. A B C D E
50. A B C D E

NOTES

NOTES

NOTES

NOTES

NOTES

NOTES

NOTES